MODERN LITERATURE

AND

LITERARY MEN

BEING A

Second Gallery of Literary Portraits.

BY

GEORGE GILFILLAN.

FOURTH AMERICAN EDITION.

NEW-YORK:
D. APPLETON & COMPANY,
443 & 445 BROADWAY.
M.DCCC.LX.

ADVERTISEMENT.

The Author in again appearing before the public, cannot do so without acknowledging the kindness with which his former work was received, both in this and in other lands. It has made him a vast multitude of friends among those whose faces he never hopes to see "in the flesh." He thanks also the Press for the very general indulgence with which it treated the first production of one then unknown. In the succeeding sketches he has aimed at a tone somewhat more subdued, and a style of criticism more discriminating than in the former. *This* is not so much a gallery of "heroes" as of notable individuals whom he is sometimes obliged rather sternly to analyze. There is "a time to embrace, and a time to refrain from embracing"—a "time to pull down, as well as a time to build up." Notwithstanding what the cold, the stupid, or the fastidious may say of the acknowledgment, he confesses to a much deeper satisfaction in the practice of praise than of blame, although in both he is sincere. He may add, that he has given "second sittings" in this series, more lengthy than formerly, to several individuals who were somewhat cursorily treated in his first "Gallery."

He might well have husbanded his enthusiasm, having committed himself to one of the greatest of critical tasks, a review of the "Bards of the Bible,"—a subject, to use the language of Dr. Croly, "where you cannot think too profoundly, or eulogize too warmly." This task, he may announce, is more than two-thirds achieved, and, if God spare him, he hopes to issue the entire work in spring.

In answer to many inquiries, the author may also intimate his intention of issuing soon a revised edition of his first "Gallery," the other having been long out of print.

Dundee, 1*st December*, 1849.

CONTENTS.

SECOND GALLERY

OF

LITERARY PORTRAITS.

JOHN MILTON.

PERHAPS some may be astonished at the subject selected—John Milton. Can any thing new, that is true—or true that is new, be said on such a theme? Have not the ages been gazing upon this "mighty orb of song" as at the sun? and have not almost all its gifted admirers uttered each his glowing panegyric, till now they seem to be ranged like planetary bodies round his central blaze? What more can be said or sung? Is it not impossible to add to, however easy to diminish, our sense of his greatness? Is not the ambition rash and presumptuous which seeks to approach the subject anew? Surely the language of apology, at least, is the fit preface to such a deed of daring.

No apology, however, do we intend to make. We hold that every one who has been delighted, benefited, or elevated by a great author, may claim the privilege of gratitude, to tell the world that, and how, he has. We hold, too, that the proof of the true greatness of a man lies in this, that every new encomiast, if in any measure qualified for the task, is sure to find in him some new proof that the praises of all time have not been wasted or exaggerated. Who that reads or thinks at all, has not frequent occasions to pass by the cairn which a thankful word has reared to Milton's memory? and who can, at one time or other, resist the impulse to cast on it another stone, however rough and small that stone may be? Such is all we at present propose.

Every man is in some degree the mirror of his times. A man's times stand over him, as the sun above the earth, compelling an image from the dewdrop, as well as from the great deep. The difference is, that while the small man is a small, the great man is a broad and full, reflection of his day. But the effect of the times may be seen in the baby's bauble and cart, as well as in the style of the painter's pencil and the poet's song. The converse is equally true. A man's times are reflective of the man, as well as a man of the times. Every man acts on, as well as is acted on by, every other man. The cry of the child who falls in yonder gutter, as really affects the progress of society as the roar of the French Revolution. There is a perpetual process going on of action and reaction, between each on the one side, and all on the other. The characteristic of the great man is, that his reaction on his age is more than equal to its action upon him. No man is wholly a creator, nor wholly a creature of his age. The Milton or the Shakspeare is more the creator than he is the creature.

Some men pass through the atmosphere of their time as meteors through the air, or comets through the heavens—leaving as little impression, and having with it a connection equally slight; while others interpenetrate it so entirely that the age becomes almost identified with them. Milton was intensely the man of his time; and, although he shot far before it, it was simply because he more fully felt and understood what its tendencies really were; he spread his sails in its breath, as in a favorable gale, which propelled him far beyond the point where the impulse was at first given.

A glance at the times of Milton would require to be a profound and comprehensive one; for the times that bore such a product must have been extraordinary. One feature, perhaps the chief, in them was this: Milton's age was an age attempting, with sincere, strong, though baffled endeavor, to be earnest, holy, and heroic. The church had, in the previous age, been partially and nominally reformed; but it had failed in accomplishing its own full deliverance, or the full deliverance of the world. It had shaken off the nightmare of popery, but had settled itself down into a sleep, more composed, less disturbed, but as deadly. Is the Reformation, thought the high hearts which then gave forth their thunder throbs in England, to turn out a mere sham? Has all that bloody seed of martyrdom been sown in vain? Whether is worse, after all, the incubus of superstition, or the sleep of death? We have got rid of the Pope, indeed, but not of the world, or of the devil, or the flesh; we must, therefore, repair our repairs—amend our amendments—reform our Reformation—and try, in this way, to get religion to come down, as a practical living power, into the hearts and lives of Englishmen. We must squeeze our old folios into new facts—we must see the dead blood of the martyrs turned into living trees of righteousness—we must have character as well as controversies—life, life at all hazards, we must have, even though it be through the destruction of ceremonies, the damage of surplices, the dismissal of bishops—aye, or the death of kings. Such was the spirit of that age. We speak of its real onward tendency—the direction of the main stream. We stay not to count the numerous little obstinate opposing eddies that were taking chips and straws—Lauds and Clarendons—backwards; thus and no otherwise, ran the master current of the brain, the heart, and the hand of that magnificent era.

Are we not standing near the brink of another period, in some points very similar to that of English Puritanism? Is not our age getting tired of names, words, pretensions; and anxious for things, deeds, realities? It cares nothing now for such terms as Christendom—Reformed Churches—Glorious Constitution of 1688. It wants a Christendom where the character of Christ—like that of Hamlet—is not omitted by special desire; it wants re-reformed churches, and a glorious constitution, that will do a little more to feed, clothe, and educate those who sit under its shadow, and have long talked of, without tasting, its blessed fruits. It wants, in short, those big, beautiful words—Liberty, Religion, Free Government, Church and State, taken down from our flags, transparencies, and triumphal arches, and introduced into our homes, hearths, and hearts. And, although we have now no Cromwell and no Milton, yet, thank God, we have thousands of gallant hearts, and gifted spirits, and eloquent tongues, who have vowed loud and deep, in all the languages of Europe, that falsehoods and deceptions, of all sorts and sizes, of all ages, statures, and complexions, shall come to a close.

To Milton's time we may apply the words of inspiration —" The children are brought to the birth, but there is not strength to bring forth." The great purpose of the age was formed, begun, but left unfinished—nay, drowned in slavery and blood. How mortifying to a spirit such as his! It was as if Moses had been taken up to Pisgah, but had been struck dead before he saw the land of milk and honey. So Milton had labored, and climbed to the steep summit, whence he expected a new world of liberty and truth to expand before him, but found instead a wilder chaos and a fouler hell than before. But dare we pity him, and need we pity ourselves? But for Milton's disappointment, and disgust with the evil days and evil tongues on which he latterly fell, he would not have retired into the solitude of his own soul; and had he not so retired, the world would have wanted its greatest poem—the "Paradise Lost." That was the real fruit of the Puritanic contest—of all its tears, and all its blood; and let those who are still enjoying a result so rich, in gratitude declare "how that red rain did make the harvest grow." No life of Milton, worthy of the name, has hitherto been written. Fenton's sketch is an elegant trifle. Johnson's is, in parts, a heavy invective —in parts, a noble panegyric; but in nowise a satisfactory life. Sir Egerton Brydges has written rather an ardent apology for his memory than a life. St. John's is a piece of clever book-making. There is but, perhaps, one man in Britain, since Coleridge died, fully qualified for supplying this desideratum—we mean Thomas de Quincey. We have repeatedly urged it on his attention, and are not without hopes that he may yet address himself to a work which shall task even his learning, genius, and eloquence. We propose to refresh ourselves and others, by simply jotting down a few particulars of the poet's career, without professing to give, on this head, any thing new.

John Milton was born in Bread-street, London—a street lying in what is called, technically, the City, under the shadow of St. Paul's—on the 9th of December, 1608. His father was a scrivener, and was distinguished for his classical attainments. John received his early education under a clergyman of the name of Young; was afterwards placed at St. Paul's School, whence he was removed, in his seventeenth year, to Christ's Church, Cambridge, where he distinguished himself for the facility and beauty of his Latin versification. We are not aware, although placed at such a mathematical university, that he ever excelled in geometry; it is uncertain whether he ever crossed the *Pons asinorum*, although it is certain that he was whipped for a juvenile contumacy, and that he never expresses any gratitude to his *Alma Mater*. Universities, in fact, have often proved rather stepmothers, than mothers, to men of genius, as the cases of Gibbon, Shelley, Coleridge, Pollok, and many others, demonstrate. And why? Because their own souls are to them universities; and they cannot fully attend to both, any more than they can be in two places at the same time. He originally intended to have entered the Church, but early formed a dislike to subscriptions and oaths, as requiring, what he terms, an "accommodating conscience"—a dislike which he retained to the last. He could not stoop his giant stature beneath the low lintel of a test. He was too religious to be the mere partisan of any sect. From college he carried nothing with him but a whole conscience and the ordinary degree of A. M., for he never afterwards received another: indeed the idea of Dr. Milton is ludicrous. As well almost speak of Dr. Isaiah, Professor Melchisedec, or —— Ezekiel, Esq.

His father, meanwhile, had retired from business, to Horton, Buckinghamshire, where the young Milton spent five years in solitary study. Of these years, little comparatively is known; but, to us, they seem among the most interesting of his life. Then the "dark foundations of his mind were laid;" then, stored up those profound stores of learning, which were commensurate with his genius, and on which that genius fed, free and unbounded, as a fire feeds on a mighty forest. There, probably, much time was spent in the contemplation of natural scenery, and in the exercises of devotion; and there he composed those exquisite minor poems, which, alone, would have made his name immortal—"L'Allegro," "Il Penseroso," "Comus," and "Lycidas." At the age of thirty, having obtained leave from his father to travel, he visited Paris, Florence, Rome, and Naples. His name had gone before him, and his progress was a triumph. Public dinners and pieces of plate did not abound in those days; but the nobility of the country entertained him at their mansions, and the literati wrote poems in his praise.

We may conceive with what delight he found his dreams of the continent realized—with what kindling rapture his eye met the Alps, gazed on the golden plains of Italy, or perused the masterpieces of Italian art in the halls of Florence, or the palaces of Rome. Milton in the Coliseum, or standing at midnight upon Mount Palatine, with the ruins of Rome dim-discovered around him—it were a subject for a painting or a poem. At this time a little incident of romance occurred. In his youth he was extremely handsome, so much so, that he was called the lady of his college. When in Italy, he had lain down to repose during the heat of the day in the fields. A young lady of high rank was passing with her servant; she was greatly struck with the appearance of the slumberer, who seemed to her eye as one of the angels whom he afterwards described reposing in the vales of heaven. She wrote a few extempore lines in his praise with a pencil, laid them down at his side, and went on her way. When Milton awoke, he found the lines lying, but the fair writer gone. One account says that he spent some time in searching for her, but in vain. Another (on which Bulwer has founded a poem) relates that she, still stung by the recollection of his beauty, followed him to England; and was so mortified at finding him by this time married that she died of a broken heart. Milton had intended to extend his tour to Sicily and Greece, but the state of affairs in England drew him home. "I deemed it dishonorable," he said, "to be lingering abroad, even for the improvement of my mind, while my fellow-citizens were contending for their liberty at home." There spoke the veritable man and hero, John Milton, one who measured every thing by its relation not to delight, but to duty; and felt himself "ever in his great Taskmaster's eye." The civil war had by this time broken out in flames which were not to be slaked for twenty years, and into which even a king's blood was to fall like oil. Milton, though an admirable fencer, and as brave as his own

Michael, thought he might serve the popular cause better by the pen than by the sword. He calmly sat down, therefore, to write down royalty, prelacy, and every species of arbitrary power. At the same time, he opened a school for the education of the young. This has actually formed a count of indictment against him. Milton has been thought by some to have demeaned himself by teaching children the first element of knowledge, although it be, in truth, one of the noblest avocations—although the fact of the contempt in which it is held, ought to be a count of indictment against an age foolish enough to entertain it—although it be an avocation rendered illustrious by other names besides that of Milton, the names of Socrates, Plato, Aristotle, Buchanan, Parr, Johnson, and Arnold—and although the day is coming when the titles of captain, or colonel, or knight-at-arms—yea, and those of a king, kaiser, and emperor, will look mean and contemptible compared to that of a village-schoolmaster who is worthy of his trade. Louis Philippe, if we are not mistaken, once taught a school; and it is, perhaps, a pity that he ever did any thing else. The ingenious Mr. Punch lately proposed an asylum for discrowned continental monarchs; we think a better idea would be, if they would set up a joint-stock academy in the neighborhood of London—Louis Philippe teaching French and fortification—the Emperor of Austria German and Italian—the King of Prussia metaphysics—and the King of Bavaria, assisted by Lola Montes, the elements of morality and religion; Nicholas might, by and by, be appointed president of the academy—Metternich would make a capital head usher; and the whole might be called the *New* Royal Institution.

Schoolmaster as he was, and afterwards Latin secretary to Cromwell, Milton found time to do and to write much in the course of the eighteen or twenty years which elapsed between his return to England and the Restoration. He found time for writing several treatises on divorce, for publishing his celebrated tractate on education, and his still more celebrated discourse on the liberty of unlicensed printing, for collecting his minor poems in Latin and English, and for defending, in various treatises, the execution of Charles I., and the Government of Cromwell, besides commencing an English History, an English Grammar, and a Latin Dictionary. Meanwhile, his first wife, who had borne him three daughters, died in child-bed. Meanwhile, too, a disease of the eyes, contracted by intense study, began gradually to eclipse the most intellectual orbs then glowing upon earth. Milton has uttered more than one noble complaint over his completed blindness. We could conceive him to have penned an expostulation to the advancing shadow, equally sublime and equally vain, for it was God's pleasure that this great spirit should, like himself, dwell for a season in the thick darkness. And scarcely had the last glimmer of light been extinguished, than, as if the coming calamities had been stayed and spell-bound hitherto by the calm look of the magician, in one torrent they came upon his head; but although it was a Niagara that fell, it fell like Niagara upon a rock. In an evil hour, as it seemed at the time at least, for Britain, for Milton, for the progress of the human race, the restored Charles arrived. The consequences were disastrous to Milton. His name was proscribed, his books burned, himself obliged to abscond, and it was what some would call a miracle that this blinded Samson was not led forth to give his enemies sport, at the place of common execution, and that the most godlike head in the world did not roll off from the bloody block. But "man is immortal till his work be done." *We* speak of accidents and possibilities; but, in reality, and looking at the matter upon the God-side of it, Milton could no more have perished then than he could a century before. His future works were as certain, and inevitable, and due at their day, as "summer and winter, as seed-time and harvest."

Even after the heat of persecution had abated, and his life was, by sufferance, secure—it was never more—the prospects of Milton were aught but cheering. He was poor, he was blind, he was solitary—his second wife dead; his daughters, it would appear, were not the most congenial of companions; his country was enslaved; the hopes of the Church and of the world seemed blasted;—one might have expected that disappointment, regret, and vexation would have completed their work. Probably his enemies expected so too. Probably they said, "We'll neglect him, and see if that does not break his heart—we'll bring down on his head the silence of a world, which was wont to ring with his name."

—They did not know their man. They knew not that here was one of the immortal coursers, who fed on no vulgar or earthly food. He "had meat to eat that the world knew not of."

It was the greatest crisis in the history of the individual man. Napoleon survived the loss of his empire; and men call him great, because he survived it. Sir Walter Scott not only survived the loss of his fortune, but he struggled manfully amid the sympathy of the civilized species to repair it. But Milton, amidst the loss of friends, fortune, fame, sight, safety, domestic comfort, long cherished hopes, not only survived, but stood firm as a god above the ruins of a world; and not only stood firm, but built, alone and unaided, to himself an everlasting monument. Whole centuries of every-day life seem condensed in those few years in which he was constructing his work; and it is too daring a conception—that of the Great Spirit watching from on high its progress, and saying of it, as he did of his own creation, when finished, "It is very good?"

But, indeed, *his own* work it was. For, strong as this hero felt himself in his matured learning—in his genius, so highly cultured, yet still so fresh and young, in his old experience, he did not venture to put his hand to the task till, with strong crying and tears, he had asked the inspiration and guidance of a higher power. Nor were these denied him. As Noah into the ark of old, the Lord "shut" Milton in within the darkened tabernacle of his own spirit, and that tabernacle being filled with light from heaven, "Paradise Lost" arose, the joint work of human genius and of divine illumination.

We have seen the first edition of this marvellous poem —a small, humble duodecimo, in ten books, which was the original number; but to us it seemed rich all over, as a summer's sunset with glory. Every one has heard, probably, of the price, the goodly price, at which it was prized and bought—five pounds, with a contingency of fifteen more in case of sale. For two years before it seems to have slumbered in manuscript, and very likely was the while carried round the trade, seeking for one hardy enough to be its literary accoucheur. But let us not imagine that in our day it would have met with a different reception. We can well fancy Adam Black, or John Murray, saying to Milton, "Splendid poem, sir—great genius in it; but it won't sell, we fear—far too long—too many learned words in it—odd episode that on sin and death. If you could rub it down into a tragedy, and secure Macready for Satan, and Helen Faucit for Eve, it might take; or, if you could write a few songs on the third French Revolution, or something in the style of 'Dombey and Son.' Good morning, Mr. Milton." It appeared in 1667, but was a long time of rising to its just place in public estimation. The public preferred Waller's insipid commonplaces, and Dryden's ranting plays, to the divine blank verse of Milton. Waller himself spoke of it as a long, dull poem in blank verse; if its length could not be considered a merit, it had no other. The case is not singular. Two of the greatest poems in English of this century are, in our judgment, Wordsworth's "Excursion" and Bailey's "Festus." Both were for years treated with neglect, although we are certain that both will survive the "Course of Time" and the "Pickwick Papers." Between his masterpiece and his death, little occurred except the publication of some minor, but noble productions, including "Paradise Regained," "Samson Agonistes," "A system of Logic," "A Treatise of True Religion," and a collection of his familiar epistles in Latin. At last, in November, 1647, at the age of sixty-six, under an exhaustion of the vital powers, Milton expired, and that spirit, which was "only a little lower than the angels," went away to mingle with his starry kindred. It is with a certain severe satisfaction that we contemplate the death of a man like Milton. We feel that tears and lamentations are here unbecoming, and would mar the solemn sweetness of the scene. With serenity, nay, joy, we witness this majestic man-child caught up to God and his throne, soaring away from the many shadows which surrounded him on earth, into that bright element of eternity, in which he seemed already naturalized. Who seeks to weep, as he sees the river, rich with the spoils of its long wandering, and become a broad mirror for the heavens, at length sinking in the bosom of the deep? Were we permitted to behold a star re-absorbed into its source, melted down in God, would it not generate a delight, graver, indeed, but as real, as had we stood by its creation; and although there were no shouting, as on its natal morn, might there not be silence—the silence of joyous wonder among the sons of God? Thus died Milton, the prince of modern men, accepting death as gently and silently as the sky receives into its arms the waning moon. We are reminded of a description in "Hyperion," of the death of Goethe: "His majestic eyes looked for the last time on the light of a pleasant spring morning. Calm like a god, the old man sat, and, with a smile, seemed to bid farewell to the light of day, on which he had gazed for more than eighty years. Books were near him, and the pen which had just dropped from his dying fingers. 'Open the shutters, and let in more light,' were his last words. Slowly stretching forth his hand, he seemed to write in the air, and, as it sank down again and was motionless, the spirit of the old man was gone."

The next portion of our task is, to speak of the constituents of Milton's mind. Many critics have spoken of him as one who possessed only two or three faculties in a supreme and almost supernatural degree. They speak of his imagination and intellect as if they were his all. Now, in fact, Milton, as well as Goethe or Shakspeare, seems to us a many-sided man. He was complete in all powers and accomplishments, almost as his own Adam. He had every faculty, both of body and of mind, well developed and finely harmonized. He had philosophic sagacity, and could, upon occasion, reason as acutely as Thomas Aquinas. He had broad grasp as well as subtle discrimination, and some of his treatises nearly exhaust the topics of which they treat. He had, in vast measure, understanding, the power which comprehends; memory, the power which retains; imagination, the power which combines and reproduces; will, the power which moves; and eloquence, the power which communicates. He had, besides, the subordinate talents of wit, sarcasm, invective, rhetoric, and logic; even the characters of the sophist and the buffoon he could adopt at pleasure. In what species of literature did he not shine? In the epic, in the drama, in the pastoral, in the ode, in the elegy, in the masque, in the sonnet, in the epistle, in the song, in the satire, in the argument, in the essay, in the religious discussion, in the history, and in the etymological treatise, he was equally a master. He added more than the versatility of Voltaire to more than the sublimity of Homer.

While Voltaire skips from topic to topic with the agility of an elated monkey, Milton's versatility reminds you of the great Scripture image, "The *mountains* leaping like rams, and the hills like lambs." And if it be asked, what was it that gave him that august air of unity, which has made many overlook his multiform nature? We answer, it was the subordination of all his varied powers to a religious purpose, such as we find in no other uninspired man; and it was again, that glare of awful grandeur which shone around him in all his motions, and made even his least efforts, even his failures, and almost his blunders, great. As St. Peter's in Rome seems one, because it unites, condenses, and rounds in all the minutiæ and details of its fabric into a dome, so lofty and proud that it seems a copy of the sky to which it points—to imitate as well as to adore—so Milton gathers in all the spoils of time, and all the faculties of man, and offers them as in one sacrifice, and on one vast altar to heaven.

In attempting a climactic arrangement of his poetical works, we may trace his whole life over again, as in a calm under-current; not that, in point of chronological order, his works form a complete history of the man, inasmuch as "Paradise Lost," in which his genius culminated, preceded "Samson Agonistes"—still some of the epochs of his life are distinctly marked by the advancing stages of his writings. Lowest in the scale, then, are usually ranked his Latin poems, which, with many beauties, are rather imitations and echoes of the classical poets than the native utterances of his mind; it is in them, as in many modern Latin and Greek poems, where the strange dress, the graceful veil, the coy half-perceived meaning, as with the beauty of female coquettes, give a factitious interest to very ordinary and commonplace thoughts. Half the merit of the classics themselves springs from the difficulty we have in understanding them, and if we wish effectually to disguise nonsense, let us roll it up in Greek or Latin verse, and it may lie there unsuspected for centuries together. Milton could not write nonsense, to be sure, even in Latin, but his usual power and majesty here well nigh forsake him; and in hexameters and pentameters he walks like a Titan in irons, and in irons too narrow for his limbs. We may rank next, as next lowest in popular estimation, his sonnets. We are not sure, however, but that popular estimation has underrated those productions. Dr. Johnson certainly did. When asked once his opinion of Milton's sonnets, he said, "Milton could hew out a Colossus from a rock, but he could not carve heads upon cherry-stones." Literally, of course, he could not do either the one or the other; but had he been a sculptor, we believe that the slightest stroke of his chisel would, as well as his most elaborate work, have evinced the master. Hogarth's genius appeared as really in those sketches which he used to draw on his thumb-nail, as in his "Rake's Progress," or "Marriage a la Mode." So Milton's sonnets are sonnets which Milton, and none but Milton, could have written. We see, in the compass of a crown-piece, his most peculiar qualities: his gravity, his severe and simple grandeur, his chaste and chary expression, his holy purpose, and the lofty and solitary character of his soul. His mind might be compared to a mountain river, which having first torn its way through high rocks, then polishes the pebbles over which it rolls at their base.

> "'Tis the same wind unbinds the Alpine snow,
> And comforts violets on their lowly beds."

We confess, however, that we are not much in love with the structure of the sonnet. Its principle, which is to include into fourteen lines one thought or sentiment, seems too artificial, and savors too much of the style of taste from which have sprung anagrams and acrostics, and the like ingenious follies. When a large thought is successfully squeezed into it, it reminds us irresistibly of a big head which has worked and wriggled its way into a narrow night-cap; and when a small thought is infused into it, it becomes almost invisible in the dilution.

We come next to that delightful class of Milton's poems, which we call pastorals, namely, "Arcades," "L'Allegro," and "Il Penseroso." They breathe the sweetest spirit of English landscape. They are composed of every-day life, but of every-day life shown under a certain soft ideal strangeness, like a picture or a prospect, through which you look by inverting your head. Your wonder is, how he can thus elevate the tame beauties of English scenery, which are so tiny that they might be fitly tenanted by Lilliputians, and through which men stalk like monstrous giants. L'Allegro is an enumeration of agreeable images and objects, pictured each by a single touch, and set to a light easy measure, which might accompany the blithe song of the milkmaid, and the sharp whetting of the mower's scythe. "Il Penseroso" is essentially the same scenery, shown as if in soft and pensive moonlight. Both, need we say, are exquisitely beautiful; but we think the object would have been better gained, could two poets, of different temperaments, have, in the manner of Virgil's shepherds, exchanged their strains of joy and pensiveness in alternate verses, or if Milton had personated both in this way. As the poems are, it is too obviously one mind describing its own peculiar sources of gratification in different moods. A modern poet might now, if he had genius enough, effect what we mean, by describing a contest between Horace and Dante, or Moore and Byron—the one singing the pleasures of pleasure, the other the darker delights which mingle even with misery, like strange, scattered, bewildered flowers, growing on the haggard rocks of hell!

An acute critic, in an Edinburgh periodical, has undertaken the defence of "The Town" *versus* "The Country" as the source of poetry—has called us, among others, to account for preferring the latter to the former—and has ventured to assert that, *cæteris paribus*, a poet residing in the town will describe rural scenery better than one living constantly in the country, and adduces Milton in proof. We admit, indeed, that there will be more freshness in the feeling of the Cockney, let loose upon the country in spring, be he poet or porter, just as there will be more freshness in the feeling of the countryman entering London for the first time, and gaping with unbounded wonder at every sign, and shop, and shopkeeper he sees. But we maintain, that those always write best on any subject who are best acquainted with it, who know it in all is shades and phases; and that such minute and personal knowlege can only be obtained by long residence in, or by frequent visits to, the country. We cannot conceive, with this writer, that the country is best seen in the town, any more than that the town is best seen in the country. Bennevis is not visible from Edinburgh any more than Edinburgh from Bennevis.

We can never compare the beggarly bit of blue sky seen from a corner of Goosedubs, Glasgow, with the "dread magnificence of heaven" broadly bending over Benlomond; nor the puddles running down the Wellgate of Dundee, after a night of rain, with the red roaring torrents from the hills, which meet at the sweet village of Comrie. And even the rainbow, when you see it at the end of a dirty street, loses caste, though not color, and can hardly pass for a relation to that arch of God, which seems erected by the hands of angels, for the passage of the Divine footsteps between the ridges which confine the valley of Glencoe. And among our greatest descriptive poets, how many have resided in the country, either all their lives, or at least in their youth! Think of Virgil and Mantua, of Thomson and Ednam, of Burns and Mossgiel, of Shelley and Marlowe, of Byron and Lochnagar, of Coleridge and Nether Stowey, of Wilson and Elleray, of Scott and Abbotsford, of Wordsworth and Rydal Mount, and of Milton and Horton, where, assuredly, his finest rural pieces were composed: and say with Cowper, the Cowper of Olney, as we have said with him already—"God made the country, and man made the town."

We pass to two pieces, which, though belonging to different styles of poetry, class themselves together by two circumstances—their similar length, and their surpassing excellence—the one being an elegy, and the other a hymn. The elegy is "Lycidas"—the hymn is on the "Nativity of Christ." To say that "Lycidas" is beautiful, is to say that a star or rose is beautiful. Conceive the finest and purest graces of the Pagan mythology culled and mingled, with modest yet daring hand, among the roses of Sharon and the lilies of the valley—conceive the waters of Castalia sprinkled on the flowers which grow in the garden of God—and you have a faint conception of what "Lycidas" means to do. Stern but short-sighted critics have objected to this as an unhallowed junction. Milton knew better than his judges. He felt that, in the millennial field of poetry, the wolf and the lamb might lie down together; that every thing at least that was beautiful might enter here. The Pagan mythology possessed this pass-word, and was admitted; and here truth and beauty accordingly met, and embraced each other. A *museum* he felt, had not the severe laws of a *temple*. There, whatever was curious, interesting, or rare, might be admitted. Pan's pipe might lean upon the foot of the true cross—Apollo's flute and David's lyre stand side by side—and the thunderbolts of Jove rest peacefully near the fiery chariot of Elijah.

But what shall we say of his hymn? Out of the Hebrew Scriptures, it is (besides his own "Hymn of our First Parents," and Coleridge's "Hymn to Mont Blanc") the only one we remember worthy of the name. When you compare the ordinary swarm of church hymns to this, you begin to doubt whether the piety which prompted the one, and the piety which prompted the other, were of the same quality—whether they agreed in any thing but the name. We have here no trash, as profane as it is fulsome, about "sweet Jesus! dear Jesus!" no effusions of pious sentimentalism, like certain herbs, too sweet to be wholesome; but a strain which might have been sung by the angelic host on the plains of Bethlehem, and rehearsed by the shepherds in the ears of the Infant God. Like a belated member of that deputation of Sages who came from the East to the manger at Bethlehem, does he spread out his treasures, and they are richer than frankincense, sweeter than myrrh, and more precious than gold. With awful reverence and joy, he turns aside to behold this great sight—the Eternal God dwelling in an infant! Here the fault (if fault it be) with which "Lycidas" has been charged is sternly avoided. From *the Stable* he repulses the heathen deities, feeling that the ground is holy. And yet, methinks, Apollo would have desired to stay—would have lingered to the last moment—to hear execrations so sublime:—

"The oracles are dumb,
No voice or hideous hum
Runs through the arch'd roof in words, deceiving
Apollo from his shrine,
Can no more divine,
With hollow shriek the steep of Delphos leaving.
No nightly trance or breathed spell
Inspires the pale-eyed priest from the prophetic cell.
He feels from Judah's land
The dreadful Infant's hand:
The rays of Bethlehem blind his dusky eyne.
Nor all the gods beside
Dare longer now abide,
Nor Typhon huge, ending in snaky twine:

> Our Babe, to show his Godhead true,
> Can, in his swaddling bands, control the damned crew."

"Samson Agonistes" is perhaps the least poetical, but certainly by no means the least characteristic of his works. In style and imagery, it is bare as a skeleton, but you see it to be the skeleton of a Samson. It is the purest piece of *literary sculpture* in any language. It stands before you, like a statue, bloodless and blind. There can be no doubt that Milton chose Samson as a subject, from the resemblance in their destinies. Samson, like himself, was made blind in the cause of his country; and through him, as through a new channel, does Milton pour out his old complaint, but more here in anger than in sorrow. It had required—as the Nile had seven mouths—so many vents to a grief so great and absolute as his. Consolation Samson has little, save in the prospect of vengeance, for the prospect of the resurrection-body had not fully dawned on his soul. He is, in short, a hard and Hebrew shape of Milton. Indeed, the poem might have been written by one who had been born blind, from its sparing natural imagery. He seems to spurn that bright and flowery world which has been shut against him, and to create, within his darkened tabernacle, a scenery and a companionship of his own, distinct as the scenery and the companionship of dreams. It is, consequently, a naked and gloomy poem; and as its hero triumphs in death, so it seems to fall upon and crush its reader into prostrate wonder rather than to create warm and willing admiration. You believe it to be a powerful poem, and you tremble as you believe.

What a contrast in "Comus," the growth and bloom rather than the work of his youth! It bears the relation to the other works of Milton, that "Romeo and Juliet" does to the other works of Shakspeare. We can conceive it the effluence of his first love. He here lets his genius run riot with him—"in the colors of the rainbow live, and play i' the plighted clouds." It is rather a dream than a drama—such a dream as might have been passing across the fine features of the young Milton, as he lay asleep in Italy. It is an exercise of fancy, more than of imagination. And if our readers wish us, ere going farther, to distinguish fancy from imagination, we would do so briefly, as follows:—They

2

are not, we maintain, essentially different, but the same power under different aspects, attitudes, and circumstances. Have they ever contemplated the fire at even-tide? then must they have noticed how the flame, after warming and completely impregnating the fuel, breaks out above it into various fantastic freaks, motions, and figures, as if, having performed its work, it were disposed to play and luxuriate a little, if not for its own delectation, for the amusement of the spectator. Behold in the evening experiences of the fire the entire history of the mind of genius. There is first the germ, or spark, or living principle, called thought, or intuition, or inspiration. That fiery particle, coming into contact with a theme, a story, with the facts of history, or the abstractions of intellect, begins to assimilate them to itself, to influence them with its own heat, or to brighten them into its own light. That is the imaginative, or shall we call it the transfiguring process by which dead matter is changed into quick flame—by which an old fabulous chronicle becomes the tragedy of "Macbeth"—or by which some lascivious tale in an Italian novel is changed into the world-famous, and terribly-true story of "Othello, the Moor of Venice." But after this is done, does the imaginative power always stop here? No; in the mere exuberance of its strength—in the wantonness of its triumph—it will often, like the fire on the hearth, throw out gushes of superfluous but beautiful flame; in other words, images, "quips, cranks, and wreathed smiles"—and thus and here we find that glorious excrescence or luxury, which we call fancy. Fancy is that crown of rays round the sun which is seen in the valley of Chamouni, but not on the summit of Mont Blanc, where a stern and stripped stillness proclaims collected and severe power. It is the dancing spray of the waterfall, not the calm, uncrested, voluminous might of the river; or it may be compared to those blossoms on the apple-tree, which that tree pours forth in the exuberance of its spring vigor, but which never produce fruit. Imagination is the war-horse pawing for the battle—fancy, the war-horse curvetting and neighing on the mead. From such notions of imagination and fancy, there follow, we think, the following conclusions:—First, that true fancy is rather an excess of a power than a power itself. Secondly, that it is generally youthful, and ready to vanish away with the energy and excitement of youth. Thirdly, that it is incident to, though not inseparable from, the highest genius—abounding in Milton, Shakspeare, and Shelley—not to be found, however, in Homer, Dante, or Wordsworth. Fourthly, that the want of it generally arises from severity of purpose, comparative coldness of temperament, or the acquired prevalence of self-control; and, fifthly, that a counterfeit of it exists, chiefly to be known by this, that its images are not representative of great or true thoughts; that they are not original; and that, therefore, their profusion rather augurs a mechanical power of memory than a native excess of imagination. In "Comus" we find imagination, and imagination with a high purpose; but more than in any of Milton's works do we find this imagination at play, reminding us of a man whose day's work is done, and who spends his remaining strength in some light and lawful game. Our highest praise of "Comus" is, that when remembering and repeating its lines, we have sometimes paused to consider whether they were or were not Shakspeare's. They have all his mingled sweetness and strength, his careless grace or grandeur, his beauty as unconscious of itself as we could conceive a fair woman in some world where there was not even a river, or lake, or drop of water to mirror her charms. In this poem, to apply his own language, we have the "stripling cherub," all bloom, and grace, and liveliness; in the "Paradise Lost" we have the "giant angel," the emblem of power and valor, and whose very beauty is grave and terrible like his strength.

"Paradise Regained" stands next in the catalogue. No poem has suffered more from comparison than this. Milton's preference of it to "Paradise Lost" has generally been quoted as an instance of the adage, that authors are the worst judges of their own works; that, like some mothers, they prefer their deformed and sickly offspring. We should think, however, that even were the work much worse than it is, Milton's liking for it might have been accounted for on the principle that authors are often fondest of their last production; like the immortal Archbishop of Granada, whom Gil Blas so mortally offended by hinting that his sermons were beginning to smell of his apoplectic fit, instead of, as a wise flatterer would have done, stretching out his praises till they threatened to crack against the horizon. But, in truth, Milton was not so much mistaken as people suppose. There are men who at all times, and there are moods in which all men prefer the 23d Psalm to the 18th, the first Epistle of John to the Apocalypse; so there are moods in which we like the "Paradise Regained," with its profound quiet—with its Scriptural simplicity—with its insulated passages of unsurpassed power and grandeur—with its total want of effort —and with its modest avoidance of the mysterious agonies of the crucifixion, which Milton felt was a subject too sublime even for his lyre—to the more labored and crowded splendors of the "Paradise Lost." The one is a giant tossing mountains to heaven in trial of strength, and with manifest toil; the other is a giant gently putting his foot on a rock, and leaving a mark inimitable, indelible, visible to all after time. If the one remind you of the tumultuous glories and organ-tempests in the Revelation, the other reminds you of that silence which was in heaven for the space of half an hour.

The principal defect of this poem is the new and contemptible light in which it discovers the Devil. The Satan of the "Paradise Lost" had many of the elements of the heroic, and even when starting from his toad-shape, he recovers his grandeur instantly by his stature reaching the sky. But the Satan of the "Paradise Regained" is a mean, low, crawling worm—a little and limping fiend. He never looks the Saviour full in the face, but keeps nibbling at his heels. And although in this Milton has expressed the actual history of intellect and courage, when separated from virtue, happiness and hope, and degraded into the servile vassals of an infernal will, yet it is not so pleasing for us to contemplate the completed as it is the begun ruin. Around the former some rays of beauty continue to linger; the latter is desolation turned into despicable use. The Satan of the "Paradise Lost," the high, the haughty, the consciously second only to the Most High, becomes, in the "Paradise Regained," at best, a clever conjurer, whose tricks are constantly baffled, and might, as they are here described, we think, be baffled by an inferior wisdom to that of incarnate Omnipotence.

We pass to the greatest work of Milton's genius; and

here we feel as if, in using the word art or genius, we were guilty of profanation; for so long have we been accustomed to think and speak of the "Paradise Lost," that it seems to us to rank with the great works of nature themselves. We think of it as of Enoch or Elijah, when just rising out of the sphere of earth's attraction, and catching a brighter radiance than any that earth owns upon their ascending forms. And there are works of genius which seem standing and stretching up towards the measure and the stature of the works of God, and to which *these* seem to nod in responsive sympathy. For, as the poet says—

"Earth proudly wears the Parthenon
As the best gem upon her zone;
And morning opes with haste her lids
To gaze upon the Pyramids;
O'er England's abbeys bends the sky
As on its friends with kindred eye;
For out of thought's interior sphere
These wonders rose to upper air,
And nature gladly gave them place,
Adapted them into her race,
And granted them an equal date
With Andes and with Ararat."

Such a work is that of "Paradise Lost," where earth and heaven appear contending for the mastery—where, as over the morning star, the night and the dawning seem engaged in contest as to the possession of a thing so magnificent, because in it, and in fine proportions, gloom and glory—the gloom of hell and the glory of heaven—have met and embraced each other.

"Paradise Lost" has sometimes been called the most perfect of human productions—it ought to be called the most ambitious. It is the Tower of Babel, the top of which did not, indeed, reach unto heaven, but did certainly surpass all the other structures then upon earth. It stands alone, unequalled—*Man's Mountain.* It is a Samson throw, to reach which, in our degenerate days, no one need aspire. Even to higher intelligences it may appear wonderful, and strange as to us those likenesses of the stars and of man which are to be found in flowers and animals. In the language of Pope, they may

"Admire such wisdom in an earthly shape,
And show a *Milton* as men show an ape.'

But in proportion, perhaps, as this work rises above the works of man, and hangs aloft like a half-born celestial product, it loses a portion of its interest with "human mortals." It is not, on the one hand, a book like the Bible, commanding all belief as well as all admiration; it is not, on the other hand, a popular and poetical manual, like the "Pilgrim's Progress," commending itself to the hearts of all who have hearts to feel its meaning; nor is it a work valuable to a party, as having inshrined and transfigured some party notion, which, like a Gipsy in the wild, had been wandering undistinguished, till a sudden slip of sunshine had bathed him in transient glory. It is the written-out, illuminated creed of a solitary, independent, daring, yet devout man, which all ages have agreed to admire in Milton's poem. And hence the admiration awarded has been rather general than particular—rather that of the whole than of the part, —rather that of stupefied and silent amazement than of keen, warm, and anxious enthusiasm—rather the feeling of those who look hopelessly upon a cloud or a star, or a glowing west, than of those who look on some great, yet imitable perfection, in the arts of painting, statuary, or poesy.

We must be permitted a word about the hero of this poem, about its picture of hell, about its pictures of paradise and heaven, about the representation of Adam and Eve, about its subordinate machinery of angels and devils, and about its place and comparative merits when put beside the other masterpieces of the human mind. Its hero is undoubtedly, as Dryden long ago asserted, Satan, if the most interesting character in the book deserves the name of hero —if, for example, Fergus MacIvor, and not Waverley, is the hero of that tale—if of Ivanhoe not that insipid personage himself, but Richard, the lion-hearted, be the real hero. Wherever Satan appears, he becomes the centre of the scene. Round him as he lies on the fiery gulf, floating many a rood, the flames seem to do obeisance, even as their red billows break upon his sides. When he rises up into his proper stature, the surrounding hosts of hell cling to him, like leaves to a tree. When he disturbs the old deep of Chaos, its Anarchs, Orcus, Hades, Demogorgon, own a superior.

When he stands on Niphates, and bespeaks that sun which was once his footstool, Creation becomes silent to listen to the dread soliloquy. When he enters Eden, a shiver of horror shakes all its roses, and makes the waters of the four rivers to tremble. Even in heaven, the Mountain of the Congregation on the sides of the north, where he sits, almost mates with the throne of the Eternal. Mounted on the night as on a black charger, carrying all hell in his breast, and the trail of heaven's glory on his brow—his eyes eclipsed suns—his cheeks furrowed not by the traces of tears but of thunder—his wings two black forests—his heart a mount of millstone—armed to the teeth—doubly armed by pride, fury, and despair—lonely as death—hungry as the grave—intrenched in immortality—defiant against every difficulty and danger, does he pass before us, the most tremendous conception in the compass of poetry—the sublimest creation of the mind of man. There is but one other, which approaches it at a distance—that of Lucifer, in Dante, who appears with three faces:—

> "Under each shot forth
> Two mighty wings, enormous, as became
> A bird so vast. Sails never such I saw
> Outstretched on the wide sea. No plumes had they,
> But were in texture like a bat, and these
> He flapped i' the air, that from them issued still
> Three winds, wherewith Cocytus to its depth
> Was frozen. At six eyes he wept; the tears
> Adown three chins distill'd with bloody foam!
> At every mouth his teeth a sinner champ'd,
> Bruised as with ponderous engine.
> Judas is he that hath his head within,
> And plies the feet without; of the other two,
> The one is Brutus: lo! how he doth writhe,
> And speaks not. The other Cassius, that appears
> So large of limb."

Nothing can be more frightfully picturesque than this description, but it is, perhaps, too grotesque to be sublime; and the thought of the Devil being a vast windmill, and creating ice by the action of his wings, is ludicrous. One is reminded of Don Quixotte's famous mistake of the windmills for giants.

Burns, in one of his letters, expresses a resolve to buy a pocket-copy of Milton, and study that noble character, Satan

We cannot join in this opinion entirely, although very characteristic of the author of the "Address to the De'il;" but we would advise our readers, if they wish to see the loftiest genius passing into the highest art—if they wish to see combined in one stupendous figure every species of beauty, deformity, terror, darkness, light, calm, convulsion—the essence of man, devil, and angel, collected into a something distinct from each, and absolutely unique—all the elements in nature ransacked, and all the characters in history analyzed, in order to deck that brow with terror—to fill that eye with fire—to clothe that neck with thunder—to harden that heart into stone—to give to that port its pride, and to that wing its swiftness—and that glory so terrible to those nostrils, snorting with hatred to God, and scorn to man—to buy, beg, or borrow a copy of Milton, and study the character of Satan, not like Burns, for its worth, but for the very grandeur of its worthlessness. An Italian painter drew a representation of Lucifer so vivid and glowing, that it left the canvas, and came into the painter's soul; in other words, haunted his mind by night and day—became palpable to his eye, even when he was absent from the picture—produced at last a frenzy, which ended in death. We might wonder that a similar effect was not produced upon Milton's mind, from the long presence of his own terrific creation (to be thinking of the Devil for six or ten years together looks like a Satanic possession), were it not that we remember his mind was more than equal to confront its own workmanship. Satan was not a spasm, but a calm, deliberate production of Milton's mind: he was greater, therefore, than Satan, and was enabled, besides, through his habitual religion, to subdue and master his tone of feeling in reference to him.

Milton's Hell is the most fantastic piece of fancy, based on the broadest superstructure of imagination. It presents such a scene, as though Switzerland were set on fire. Such an uneven colossal region, full of bogs, caves, hollow valleys, broad lakes, and towering Alps, has Milton's genius cut out from chaos, and wrapped in devouring flames, leaving, indeed, here and there a snowy mountain, or a frozen lake, for a variety in the horror. This wilderness of death is the platform which imagination raises and peoples with the fallen thrones, dominations, princedoms, virtues, and powers. On it the same power, in its playful, fanciful mood, piles up the pandemonian palace, suggests the trick by which the giant fiends reduce their stature, shrinking into imps, and seats at the gates of hell the monstrous forms of sin and death. These have often been objected to, as if they were unsuccessful and abortional efforts of imagination; whereas they are the curvettings and magnificent nonsense of that power after its proper work—the creation of hell—has been performed. The great merit of Milton's hell, especially as compared to Dante's, is the union of a general sublime indistinctness, with a clear statuesque marking out from, or painting on, the gloom, of individual forms. From a sublime idea of hell, he descends to severely-selected particular forms and features. Dante, on the contrary (although *literally* descending), in reality ascends, on endless lost spirits, as on steps, to that dreadful whole which he calls the Inferno; and in the strange inverted climax lies much of the power of the poem. Milton is the synthetist, Dante the analyst of hell—the one here practises the transcendental, the other the ascendental method. The one describes hell like an angel, passing through it in haste, and with time only to behold its leading outlines and figures—the other, like a pilgrim, compelled with slow and painful steps to thread all its highways and byways of pain and punishment. Milton has pictured to us the young flames, and unpeopled wastes of hell as well as of earth. By Dante's time, it is overflowing with inhabitants, and teeming with sad incidents. The hell of each has its root as much in the heart as in the imagination—it is to each a red reservoir, into which he pours his ire and disappointment; but as Milton's sadness was of a milder type than Dante's, so his hell is less savage and more sublime. He gazes reverently, and from a distance, on the awful scene—whereas the fierce Florentine enters into its heart, goes down on his knees to watch more narrowly the degradations of the down-trodden damned—nay, applies a microscope to their quivering flesh and fire-shrivelled skin; nor did Ugolino, over the skull, go to his task with a more terrible and tingling gusto.

In Milton's Paradise, no less than in his Pandemonium, we find the giant character of his genius. It is no snug garden-plot,—it is no tame, though wide, landscape; no

English hall, with garden and park—it is a large undulating country as bold as beautiful; and as in hell he made Switzerland run fire, in Paradise he makes Britain flow with milk and honey. As the one was a wilderness of death, this is a wilderness of sweets. There are roses in it, but there are also forests. There are soft vales, but there are also mountains. There are rippling, dancing streams; but there is also a large, grave river, running south. There are birds singing on the branches; but there is also Behemoth reposing below. There is the lamb; but there is the lion too, even in his innocence awful. There is a bower in the midst; but there is a wall vast and high around. There are our happy parents within; but there are hosts of angels without. There is perfect happiness; but there is also, walking in the garden, and running amid the trees, a low whisper, prophesying of change, and casting a nameless gloom over all the region.

Such is the Paradise of Milton. It is not that of Macaulay, whose description of it in "Byron," vivid as it is, gives us the idea rather of a beautiful, holy and guarded *spot*, than of a great *space*, forming a broad nuptial crown to the young world.

In his Heaven, Milton finds still fuller field for the serious as well as sportive exercise of his unbounded imagination. He gives us the conception of a region immeasurably large. Many earths are massed together to form one continent surrounding the throne of God—a continent, not of cloud, or airy light, but of fixed solid land, with steadfast towering mountains, and soft slumbrous vales; to which Pollok, in his copy of it, has added, finely, wastes and wildernesses—retreats, even there, for solitary meditation; and it is a beautiful thought, that of there being hermits even in heaven. Afar, like a cloud, rises, the centre and pinnacle of the region, the throne of Jehovah, now bathed in intolerable light, and now shaded by profound darkness. Thus far imagination, sternly and soberly, accomplishes her work. But then she describes the cave, whence, by turns, light and darkness issue—the artillery employed by the rebel angels—their punning speeches to each other—their tearing up mountains—the opening and closing of their wounds—she runs wild; nor is her wildness beautiful; it is the play rather of false than of true fancy—rather a recollection of the "Arabian Nights," than the carol and spring of a Titanic original faculty. The councils of the Godhead are proverbial for feebleness and prolixity. Milton's hand trembles as it takes down the syllables from the Divine lips; and he returns, with eager haste, to the consult, on the midnight Mount of the Congregation. But the coming forth of the Messiah to destroy his foes is the most sublime passage in the poem. It is a "torrent rapture" of fire. Its words do not run, but rush, as if hurrying from the chariot of the Son. They seem driven, even as the fiends are driven, before him. Suggested partly by Hesiod's "War of the Giants," and partly by Achilles coming forth upon the Trojans, it is superior to both—indeed, to any thing in the compass of poetry. As the Messiah, in his progress, snatched up his fallen foes, and drove them before him like leaves on the blast, Milton, in the whirlwind of his inspiration, snatches up words, allusions, images, from Homer, Hesiod, and the Book of God, and bears them, in terror and in triumph, on. As soon call a tornado the plagiarist of the boughs, rafters, houses, and woods which it tears up, and carries forward in the fury of its power, as Milton, in a mood like this. To quote any part of it, were as wise as to preserve a little of the air of a hurricane. We must read it at a sitting—nay we cannot; for though sitting as we commence it, we will be standing up—feet, hair, and soul—ere we are done. And would, we cry aloud, that the same pen of living fire had described for us that second and sublimer rising of the Son of man, when he shall be revealed from heaven with his mighty angels; which must now remain undescribed, till every eye shall see it, and all kindreds of the earth shall wail because of it. Even so. Amen.

The difficulty which met Milton in his portrait of our first parents was, obviously, to make them perfect, without being unnatural—to make them sinless, and yet distinguish them from angels—to show them human, yet unfallen; to make, in short, a new thing on the earth, a man and a woman, beautiful beyond desire, simple beyond disguise, graceful without consciousness, naked without shame, innocent but not insipid, lofty but not proud; uniting, in themselves, the qualities of childhood, manhood, and womanhood, as if, in one season, spring, summer, and autumn could be imagined. This was the task Milton had to accomplish; and, at his bidding, there arose the loveliest creatures of the human imagination, such as poet's eye never, before or since, imaged, in the rainbow or the moonshine, or saw in the light of dreams; than fairies more graceful, than the cherubim and the seraphim themselves more beautiful. It is the very image of God set in clay; and, in proportion to the baseness of the material, is the costliness and the masterdom of the work. "Oh, man! over all," we exclaim, "be thou blessed for ever. And thou, his sister and spouse, his softer self, man's moon and miniature, may every flower be thy lover, every bird thy morning and evening songstress; may the day be but thy sunny mantle, and the stars of night seem but gems in thy flowing hair!"

Milton's Adam is, himself, as he was in his young manhood, ere yet the cares of life had ploughed his forehead or quenched his serene eyes. Eve, again, is Milton's life-long dream of what woman was, and yet may be—a dream, from which he again and again awoke, weeping, because the bright vision had passed away, and a cold reality alone remained. You see, in her every lineament, that he was one who, from the loftiness of his ideal, had been disappointed in woman. In the words, frequently repeated as a specimen of a *bull*—

> "Adam, the goodliest man of men, since born
> His sons—the fairest of her daughters Eve"—

he has unwittingly described the process by which his mind created them. Adam is the goodliest of his sons, because he is formed from them, by combining their better qualities; and thus are the children the parents of their father. Eve is the fairest of her daughters; for it would require the collected essence of all their excellences to form such another Eve. How beautiful the following words of Thomas Aird! "Lo! now the general father and mother! What a broad, ripe, serene, and gracious composure of love about them! O! could but that mother of us all be permitted to make a pilgrimage over the earth, to see her many sons and daughters! How kindly would the kings and queens of the world entreat her in their palaces! How affectionately would her outcast children of the wilderness give her honey and milk, and wash her feet! No thought of the many woes she brought upon us! No reproaches! Nothing but love! So generous is the great soul of this world!"

Let the world, however, take comfort. If Eve has not accomplished such a pleasant peregrination (not so pleasant, by the way, for her to pass through such infernal nurseries as the "high viced" cities and reeking battle-fields of the earth), her picture and her lord's have visited some millions of her children, who have shown their affection for her by admiring two of the most monstrous of that progeny which French affectation and self-conceit, mistaking the pressure of nightmare for the stoop of the god, have ever produced. Approach, ye admirers of Milton's matchless pair, and see them translated into French, and tell us whether you think Monsieur Adam—himself a proof (were he a portrait) that the species did not need two progenitors, being as much a black as a white; or Madame Eve, smacking more of the Palais Royal than of Paradise—the *first* man and woman or the *last* man and woman—the first noble beginning, or the last meretricious and degraded end of their species? Such artificial beings, you feel, are quite secure. They cannot fall: they are fallen already, and too far ever to arise. One is reminded of the words of Shakspeare:—"If Adam fell in his innocency, no wonder though John Falstaff fall in his sin." We cease to wonder at their fall, and humbly think that that of Sir John, in the gutter before the Boar's Head, Eastcheap, might as soon have provoked the fantastic and forced symptoms of nature's sympathy with which the "Expulsion" abounds.

Milton's management of his angels and devils proves as much as any thing in the poem the versatility of his genius, the delicacy of his discrimination of character, that Shakspearean quality in him which has been so much overlooked. To break up the general angel or devil element into so many finely-individualized forms—to fit the language to the character of each—to do this, in spite of the dignified and somewhat unwieldy character of his style—to avoid insipidity of excellence in his seraphs, and insipidity of horror in his fiends—to keep them erect and undwindled, whether in the presence of Satan on the one side, or of Messiah on the other—was a problem requiring skill as well as daring, dramatic as well as epic powers. No mere mannerist could have succeeded in it. Yet, what vivid portraits has he drawn of Michael, Raphael, (how like, in their difference from each other, as well as in their names, to the two great Italian painters!) Abdiel, Uriel, Beelzebub, Moloch, Belial, Mammon—all perfectly distinct—all speaking a leviathan language, which, in all, however, is modified by the character of each, and in none sinks into mannerism. If Milton had not been the greatest of epic poets, he might have been the second of dramatists. Macaulay has admirably shown *how*, or rather *that* Shakspeare has preserved the distinction between similar characters, such as Hotspur and Falconbridge; and conceded even to Madame d'Arblay a portion of the same power, in depicting several individuals, all young, all clever, all clergymen, all in love, and yet all unlike each other. But Milton has performed a much more difficult achievement. He has represented five devils, all fallen, all eloquent, all in torment, hate, and hell, and yet all so distinct that you could with difficulty interchange a line of the utterances of each. None but Satan, the incarnation of egotism, could have said—

"What matter where, if I be still the same?"

None but Moloch—the rash and desperate—could thus abruptly have broken silence—

"My sentence is for open war."

None but Belial—the subtle, far-revolving fiend, could have spoken of

"Those thoughts that wander through eternity."

None but Mammon, the down-looking demon, would ever, alluding to the subterranean riches of hell, have asked the question—

"*What can heaven show more?*"

Or, who but Beelzebub, the Metternich of Pandemonium, would have commenced his oration with such grave, terrific irony as—

"Thrones, and imperial powers, offspring of heaven,
Ethereal virtues, or these titles now

> Must we renounce, and changing style, be called
> Princes of hell?"

Shakspeare could have done a similar feat, by creating five men, all husbands, all black, and all jealous of their white wives; or else, five human fiends, all white, all Italian, and all eager to throw salt and gunpowder on the rising flame of jealousy, and yet each distinct from our present Othello and Iago; and this Shakspeare might have done, and done with ease, though he did it not.

Perhaps, to settle the place, and comparative merit, of the "Paradise Lost," is an attempt which appears more difficult than it really is. Milton himself may have, and has a considerable number of competitors, and, in our judgment, two superiors: Shakspeare and Dante. His work can be compared properly to but two others; the "Iliad" and the "Divina Comedia." These are the first three among the productions of imaginative genius. Like Bennevis, Benmacdhui, and Cairntoul, still contesting, it is said, the sovereignty of Scotland's hills, (now rising above, and now sinking below each other, like three waves of the sea,) seem those surpassing masterpieces. We cannot, in our limits, even enter into a field so wide as the discussion of all the grounds on which we prefer the English poem. It is not because it is of later date than both, and yet as original as either. Time should never be taken into account when we speak of an immortal work; what matters it whether it was written in the morning, in the evening, or at noon? It is not that it was written amid danger and darkness—who knows how Homer fared as he rhapsodized the "Iliad?" or who knows not that Dante found in his poem the escape of immeasurable sorrow? It is not (Warton notwithstanding) that it has borrowed so much from Scripture: such glorious spangles we are ready to shear off, and deduct, in our estimate of the poem's greatness. It is not that it bears unequivocal traces of a higher path of genius, or that it is more highly or equally finished. But it is that, begun with a nobler purpose, and all but equal powers, it has called down, therefore, a mightier inspiration. Homer's spur to write or rhapsodize was that which sends the war-horse upon the spears; and the glory of the "Iliad" is that of a garment rolled in blood. In Dante, the sting is that of personal anguish, and the acmé of his poem is in the depth of hell—a hell which he has replenished with his foes. Milton, in fact, as well as in figure, wrote his work to vindicate the "ways of God to men;" and this purpose never relinquished—penetrating the whole poem straight as a ray passing through an unrefracting medium, gathering around it every severe magnificence and beauty, attracting from on high, from the very altar of celestial incense, burning coals of inspiration—becomes at last the poem's inaccessible and immortal crown.

Let us glance for a moment, ere we close, at what was even finer than Milton's transcendent genius—his character. His life was a great epic itself; Byron's life was a tragi-comedy; Sheridan's was a brilliant farce; Shelley's was a wild, mad, stormy tragedy, like one of Nat Lee's; Keats' life was a sad, brief, beautiful lyric; Moore's has been a love-song; Coleridge's was a "Midsummer Night's Dream;" Schiller's was a harsh, difficult, wailing, but ultimately victorious war ode, like one of Pindar's; Goethe's was a brilliant, somewhat melodramatic, but finished novel; Tasso's was an elegy; but Milton, and Milton alone, acted as well as wrote an epic complete in all its parts—high, grave, sustained, majestic. His life was a self-denied life. "Susceptible," says one, "as Burke, to the attractions of historical prescription, of royalty, of chivalry, of an ancient church, installed in cathedrals, and illustrated by old martyrdoms—he threw himself, the flower of elegance, on the side of the reeking conventicle—the side of humanity, unlearned and unadorned." It was a life of labor and toil; labor and toil unrewarded, save by the secret sunshine of his own breast, filled with the consciousness of divine approbation, and hearing from afar the voice of universal future fame. It was a life of purity. Even in his youth, and in the countries of the south, he seems to have remained entirely unsullied. Although no anchorite, he was temperate to a degree, saying with John Elliot, "Wine is a noble, generous liquor, and we should be thankful for it, but water was made before it." Rapid in his meals, he was never weary of the refreshment of music; his favorite instrument, as might have been expected, being the organ. It was a life not perfect: there were spots on his fame, acerbities of temper, harshness of language, peculiarities of opinion, which proved him human, and grappled him with difficulty to earth, like a vast balloon ere it takes its bound upwards. It was in some measure a complete life, not a tantalizing fragment, nor separated segment; but it evolved as gradually and certainly as a piece of solemn music. It was the life of a patriot, faithful found among the faithless, faithful only he; and Abdiel, that dreadless angel, is just Milton transferred to the skies. It was, above all, the life of a Christian—yes, the life of a Christian, although the Evangelical Alliance would now shut its door in his face. It was a life of prayer, of faith, of meek dependence, of perpetual communing with heaven. Milton's piety was not a hollow form, not a traditional cant, not a bigotry, not the remains merely of youthful impression, as of a *scald* received in childhood; it was founded on personal inquiry; it was at once sincere and enlightened, strict and liberal; it was practical, and pressed on his every action and word, like the shadow of an unseen presence. Hence was his soul cheered in sorrow and blindness, the more he lived in daily, hourly expectation of Him whom he called "the shortly-expected King," who, rending the heavens, was to, and shall yet, give him a house from heaven, where they that look out at the windows are not darkened.

Thus faintly have we pictured John Milton. Forgive us, mighty shade! wherever thou art, mingling in whatever choir of adoring spirits, or engaged in whatever exalted ministerial service above, or whether present now among those "millions of spiritual creatures which walk the earth;" forgive us the feebleness, for the sake of the sincerity of the offering; and reject it not from that cloud of incense which, with enlarging volume, and deepening fragrance, is ascending to thy name, from every country and in every language!

We say with enlarging volume, for the fame of Milton must not only continue but extend. And perhaps the day may come, when, after the sun of British empire is set, and Great Britain has become as Babylon, and as Tyre, and even after its language has ceased to be a living tongue, the works of Milton and Shakspeare shall alone preserve it—for these belong to no country, and to no age, but to all countries, and all ages, to all ages of time—to all cycles of eternity. Some books may survive the last burning, and be preserved in celestial archives, as specimens and memorials of extinguished worlds; and if such there be, surely one of them must be the "Paradise Lost."

In fine, we tell not our readers to imitate Milton's genius—that may be too high a thing for them; but to imitate his life, the patriotism, the sincerity, the manliness, the purity, and the piety of his character. When considering him, and the other men of his day, we are tempted to say, "There were giants in those days," while we have fallen on the days of little men—nay, to cry out with her of old, "I saw gods ascending from the earth, and one of them is like to an *old man whose face is covered with a mantle.*" In these days of rapid and universal change, what need for a spirit so pure, so wise, so sincere, and so gifted, as his! and who will not join in the language of Wordsworth?—

> "Milton! thou shouldst be living at this hour.
> England hath need of thee. She is a fen
> Of stagnant waters. We are selfish men.
> . . . .
> Thy soul was like a star; and dwelt apart;
> Pure as the naked heavens, majestic, free.
> So didst thou travel on life's common way,
> In cheerful godliness; and yet thy heart
> The lowliest duties on itself did lay."

LORD BYRON.

An objection may meet us on the threshold of this, as well as on that of our previous paper. It may seem that to attempt a new estimate of a character so thoroughly scrutinized, and so widely appreciated as Byron's, is an attempt alike hopeless and presumptuous. And if we did approach it with the desire of finding or saying any thing absolutely new, we should feel the full force of the objection. But this is far from being our ambition. We have decided to sketch Lord Byron's genius for the following reasons. In the first place, a very minute is never a very wide, a very particular is seldom a very just, scrutiny or estimate. In the second place, the criticism of single works pouring from the press, however acute and admirable, is not equivalent to a review of those works taken as a whole. A judgment pronounced upon the first, second, or third stories of a building, as they successively arise, does not forestall the opinion of one who can overlook the completed structure. Of Byron's several writings we have every variety of separate critiques, good, bad, and indifferent—of his genius, as animating his whole works, we have little criticism, either indifferent, bad, or good. In the third place, the tumult which all Byron's productions instantly excited, the space they cleared and burnt out for themselves, falling like bombshells among the crowd, the strong passions they awakened in their readers, through that intense personality which marked them all, rendered cool appreciation at the time impossible. They came upon the public like powerful sermons on an excited audience, sweeping criticism away before them, blotting out principles of art from the memory of the severest judges, whose hearts they stormed, whose passions they inflamed—at the same time that they sometimes revolted their tastes, and sometimes insulted their understandings. At night there was intoxication—in the morning calm reflection came. But, in the meantime, the poet was away, his song had become immortal, and the threatened arrows were quietly returned to the quiver again. In the next place, Byron's life and story formed a running commentary upon his works, which tended at once to excite and to bewilder his readers. His works have now illustrated editions: they did not require this while he lived. Then, his romantic history, partially disclosed, and, therefore, more effective in its interest—his early, hapless love—his first unfortunate publication—his Grecian travels—his resistless rush into fame—his miserable marriage—his amours—the glorious backgrounds which he chose for his tragic attitudes, Switzerland and Italy—his personal beauty—his very lameness—the odd and yet unludicrous compound which he formed of Vulcan and Venus, of Apollo and Satyr, of favorite and football of destiny—the mysterious spectacle he presented of a most miserable man, composed of all the materials which make others happy—the quaint mixture of all opposites in his character, irreconcilable till in the ruin of death—the cloak of mystery which he now carefully threw over, and now pettishly withdrew from, his own character—the impossibility of either thoroughly hating, or loving, or laughing at him—the unique and many-sided puzzle which he thus made, had the effect of maddening the public, and of mystifying his critics. Hal is charged by Falstaff with giving him medicines to make him love him. Byron gave men medicines to educe toward himself a mixture of all possible feelings—anger, envy, admiration, love, pity, blame, horror, and, above all, wonder as to what could be the conceivable issue of a life so high and so low—so earthly and so unearthly—so spiritual and so sensual—so melancholy and so mirthful, as he was notoriously leading. This was the perpetual stimulus to the readers of his works—this the face and figure, filling the margins of all his pages. This now is over. That strange life is lived—that knot, too hard and twisted for man, is away elsewhere to be solved—that heart, so differently reported of by different operators, has undergone the stern analysis of death. His works have now emerged from that fluctuating and lurid shadow of himself, which seemed to haunt and guard them all; and we can now judge of them, though not apart from his personal history, yet undistracted by its perpetual protrusion. In the next place, Byron was the victim of two opposite currents in the public feeling—one unduly exalting, and the other unduly depressing his name—both of which have now so far subsided, that we can judge of him out of the immediate and overbearing influence of either. And in the last place, as intimated already, no attempt has been made since his death, either to collect the scattered flowers of former fugitive criticism, to be bound in one chaplet round his pale and noble brow, or to wreath for it fresh and independent laurels. Moore's life is a long apology for his memory, such as a partial friend might be expected to make to a public then partial, and unwilling to be convicted of misplaced idolatry. Macaulay's critique is an elegant *fasciculus* of all the fine things which, it had occurred to him, might be said on such a theme—exhibits, besides, the coarse current of Byron's life caught in crystal and tinged with *couleur de rose*, like a foul winter stream shining in ice and evening sunshine—and has many beautiful remarks about his poems; but neither abounds in original views, nor gives, what its author could so admirably have given, a collection of common opinions on his entire genius and works, forming a full-length portrait, ideally like, vigorously distinct, and set, in his own brilliant imagery and language, as in a frame of gold.

Our endeavor at present is to make some small contribution towards a future likeness of Byron. And whatever may be the effect of our remarks upon the public, and however they may or may not fail in starting from slumber the "coming man" who shall criticise Byron as Thomas Carlyle has criticised Jean Paul, and Wilson, Burns: this, at least, shall be ours—we shall have expressed our honest convictions—uttered an idea that has long lain upon our minds—and repaid, in part, a debt of gratitude which we owe to Byron, as men owe to some terrible teacher, who has at once roused and tortured their minds; as men owe to the thunder-peal which has awakened them, sweltering, at the hour when it behoved them to start on some journey of life and death.

We propose to methodise our paper under the following outlines: We would, in the first place, inquire into Byron's purpose. Secondly, into the relation in which he has stood to his age, and the influence he has exerted over it. Thirdly, into the leading features of his artistic execution. Fourthly, speak of the materials on which his genius fed. Fifthly, glance at the more characteristic of his works. And, sixthly, try to settle his rank as a poet. We would first ask at Byron the simple question, "What do you mean?" A simple question truly, but significant as well, and not always very easy to answer. It is always, however, our duty to ask it; and we have, in general, a right, surely, to expect a reply. If a man come and make us a speech, we are entitled to understand his language as well as to see his object. If a man administer to us a reproof, or salute us with a sudden blow, we have a double right to turn round and ask, "Why?" Nay, if a man come professing to utter an oracular deliverance, even in this case we expect some glimmer of definite meaning and object; and if glimmer there be none, we are justified in concluding that neither has there been any oracle. "Oracles speak;" oracles should also shine. Now, in Byron's case, we have a man coming forward to utter speeches, to administer reproofs, to smite the public on both cheeks—in the attitude of an accuser, impeaching man—of a blasphemer, attacking God—of a prophet expressing himself, moreover, with the clearness and the certainty of profound and dogmatic conviction; and we have thus more than a threefold right to inquire, what is your drift, what would you have us to believe, or what to do? Now here, precisely, we think, is Byron's fatal defect. He has no such clear, distinct, and overpowering object, as were worthy of securing, or as has secured, the complete concentration of his splendid powers. His object! What is it? Not to preach the duty of universal despair; or to inculcate the propriety of an "act of universal, simultaneous suicide;" else, why did he not, in the first place, set the example himself, and from "Leucadia's rock," or Etna's crater, precipitate himself, as a signal for the species to follow? and why, in the second place, did he profess such trust in schemes of political amelioration, and die in the act of leading on a revolutionary war? Not to teach, nor yet to impugn any system of religion: for if one thing be more certain about him than another, it is, that he had no settled convictions on such subjects at all, and was only beginning to entertain a desire toward forming them when the "great teacher," death, arrived. Nor was his purpose merely to display his own powers and passions in imposing aspects. Much of this desire indeed mingled with his ambition, but he was not altogether a vain attitudinizer. There is sterling truth in his taste and style of writing—there is sincerity in his anguish—and his little pieces, particularly, are the mere wringings of his heart. Who can doubt that his brow, the index of the soul, darkened as he wrote that fearful curse, the burden of which is "Forgiveness?" The paper on which was written his farewell to Lady Byron, is still extant, and it is all blurred and blotted with his tears. His poem entitled "The Dream," is as sincere as if it had been penned in blood. And was he not sincere in sleep, when he ground his teeth to pieces in gnashing them? But his sincerity was not of that profound, constant, and consistent kind which deserves the stronger name of earnestness. It did not answer to the best description in poetry of the progress of such a spirit, which goes on—

> "Like to the Pontic sea
> Whose icy current and compulsive course
> Ne'er feels retiring ebb, but keeps right on
> To the Propontic and the Hellespont."

It was a sincerity such as the falsest and the most hollow of men must express when stung to the quick; for hath not he, as well as a Jew, "eyes, hands, organs, dimensions, senses, affections, passions. Is he not fed with the same food, and hurt by the same weapons? If you prick him, does he not bleed? If you tickle him, does he not laugh? If you poison him, does he not die? And if you wrong him, does he not revenge?" Purpose, therefore, in its genuine simplicity, and quiet deep sincerity, was awanting in Byron's character. And this greatly accounts for the wreck which he became; and for that misery—a misery which was wonderful, passing the wo of man—which sat down upon his spirit. Many accounts have been given of his grief. Macaulay says that he was a spoiled child. Shelley declares—

> "The thought that he was greater than his kind
> Had struck, methought, his eagle spirit blind
> By gazing at its own exceeding light."

But the plain prose and English of it lay in his union of intensity of power with the want of intensity of purpose. He was neither one thing nor yet another. Life with him was neither, on the one hand, an earnest single-eyed effort, nor was it, could it be, a mere display. He believed, and trembled as he believed, that it was a serious thing to die, but did not sufficiently, if at all, feel that it was as serious a thing to live. He would not struggle: he must shine; but could not be *content* with mere shining without struggle. And hence, ill at ease with himself, aimless and hopeless, "like the Cyclops—mad with blindness," he turned to bay against society—man—and his Maker. And hence, amid all that he has *said* to the world—and said so eloquently, and said so mournfully, and said amid such wide, and silent, and profound attention—he has *told* it little save his own sad story.

We pass, secondly, to speak of the relation in which he stood to his age. The relations in which a man stands to his age are perhaps threefold. He is either before it or behind it, or exactly on a level with it. He is either its forerunner; or he is dragged as a captive at its chariot wheels; or he walks calmly, and step for step, along with it. We behold in Milton the man before his age—not, indeed, in point of moral grandeur or mental power; for remember, his age was the age of the Puritans, the age of Hampden, Selden, Howe, Vane, and of Cromwell, who was a greater writer than Milton himself—only, it was with the sword that he wrote —and whose deeds were quite commensurate with Milton's words. But in point of liberality of sentiment and width of view, the poet strode across entire centuries. We see in Southey the man behind his age, who, indeed, in his youth, took a rash and rapid race in advance, but returned like a beaten dog, cowed, abashed, with downcast head, and tail between his legs, and remained, for the rest of his life, aloof from the great movements of society. We behold in Brougham one whom once the age was proud to claim as its child and champion, the express image of its bustling, restless, versatile, and onward character, and of whom we still at least say, with a sigh, he *might* have been the man of his time. In which of these relations, is it asked, did Byron stand to his age? We are forced to answer, in none of them. He was not before his age in any thing—in opinion, or in feeling. He was not, in all or many things, disgracefully behind it; nor did he move with equal and measured step in its procession. He stood to the age in a most awkward and uncertain attitude. He sneered at its advancement, and he lent money, and ultimately lost his life, in attempting to promote it. He spoke with uniform contempt, and imitated with as uniform emulation, the masterpieces of its literature. He abused Wordsworth in public, and in private "rolled him as a sweet morsel under his tongue;" or rather, if you believe himself, took him as a drastic dose, to purify his bilious and unhappy nature, by the strongest contrasted element that he could find. He often reviled and ridiculed revealed religion, and yet read the Bible more faithfully and statedly than most professed Christians—made up in superstition what he wanted in faith —had a devout horror at beginning his poems, undertaking his journeys, or paring his nails on a Friday—and had he lived, would probably have ended, like his own Giaour, as "brother Byron," with hair shirt, and iron-spiked girdle, in some Achaian or Armenian convent. He habitually trampled on, and seems sometimes to have really despised, the opinion of the public; and yet, in some points, felt it so keenly, that, says Ebenezer Elliot, "he would have gone into hysterics had a tailor laughed at him." And although, when the "Edinburgh Review" sought to crush him like a worm, he rose from the heel, a fiery, flying dragon; yet, to the assaults of the meaner creatures of the press, he was pervious all over, and allowed minikin arrows, which were beneath his laughter, to rouse his rage. Absurd and ludicrous the spectacle of this Laocoon, covered from head to foot with the snakes of supernal vengeance, yet bearing their burden with deep agonized silence, starting and shrieking upon the application of a thorn, which the hand of some puny passing malignant had thrust into his foot. In one respect we grant that Byron was the spirit of the age; he was the representative of its wants, its weakness, its discontents, its dark unrest—but not of its aspirations, its widening charity, and its hopeful tendencies. His voice was the deep vague moan of the world's dream—his writhing anguish, the last struggle of its troubled slumber: it has since awakened, or is awakening, and, "as a dream when one awakeneth," it is despising, too much despising, his image. He stood high yet helpless between the old and the new, and all the helpless and the hopeless rallied round to constitute him first magistrate over a city in flames—supreme ruler in a blasted and ruined realm. In one thing he was certainly a prophet; namely, a prophet of evil. As misery was the secret sting of all his inspiration, it became the invariable matter of all his song. In some of his poems, you have misery contemplating; in others, misery weeping aloud; in others, misery revolving and reproducing the past; in others, misery bursting the confines of the world, as if in search of a wider hell than that in which it felt itself environed; in others, misery stopping to turn and rend its real or imaginary foes; and in others, misery breaking out into hollow, hopeless, and heartless laughter. (What a terrible thing is the *laugh* of the unhappy! It is the very "echo to the seat where sorrow is throned.") But in all, you have misery; and whether he returns the old thunder in a voice of kindred power and majesty, or sings an evening song with the grasshopper at his feet—smiles the smile of bitterness, or sheds the burning tears of anger—his voice still speaks of desolation, mourning, and woe; the vocabulary of grief labors under the demands of his melancholy genius; and never, never more, till the scene of tears and sighs be ended, shall we meet with a more authentic and profound expounder of the wretchedness of man. And as such we have deemed him to have done good service; first, because he who approaches toward the bottom of human woe, proves that it is not altogether bottomless, however deep; because, if human grief spring from human greatness, in unveiling the grief he is illustrating the grandeur of man; and, because, the writings of Byron have saved us, in this country, what in France has been so pernicious, "the literature of desperation:" they are a literature of desperation in themselves; they condense into one volume what in France has been diluted throughout many, and, consequently, our country has drained off at one gulp, and survived the experiment, the poison which our neighbors have been sipping for years to their deadly harm.

Thus, on the whole, we regard Byron neither as, in any sense, a creator, nor wholly, as a creature of his period; but rather as a stranger entangled in the passing stream of its crowd, imperfectly adjusted to its customs, indifferently reconciled to its laws—among men, but not of them—a man of the *world*, but not a man of the age; and who has rather fallen furiously through it—spurning its heights, and seeking its depths—than left on it any deep or definite impression. Some men are buried, and straightway forgotten—shovelled out of memory as soon as shovelled into the tomb. Others are buried, and from their graves, through the hands of ministering love, arise fragrant flowers and verdant branches, and thus are they in a subordinate sense, "raised in glory." Others, again, lie down in the dust, and though no blossom or bough marks the spot, and though the timid shun it at evening-tides as a spot unblessed—yet, forgotten it can never be, for there lies the record of a great guilty life extinct, and the crown of crime sits silent and shadowy on the tombstone. This is Byron's memorial in the age. But, as even on Nero's tomb "some hand unseen strewed flowers," and as "nothing dies but something mourns," let us lay a frail garland upon the sepulchre of a ruin—itself a desolation—and say *Requiescat in pace*, as we hurry on.

We come, thirdly, to speak of the leading features of his artistic execution, and the materials which his genius used. And here there are less mingled feelings to embarrass the critical contemplator. Strong, direct intellect, descriptive force, and personal passion, seem the main elements of Byron's poetical power. He sees clearly, he selects judiciously for effect from among the points he does see, and he paints them with a pencil dipped in his own fiery heart. He was the last representative of the English character of mind. His lordly independence and high-spiritedness; his fearless avowal of his prejudices, however narrow, and passions, however coarse; his constant clearness and decision of tone and of style; his manly vigor and directness; his strong unreasoning instinctive sense; his abhorrence of mysticism; and his frequent caprices—all savored of that literature which had reared Dryden, Pope, and Johnson; and every peculiarity of the English school seems to have clustered in and around him, as its last splendid specimen. Since then our higher literature is rapidly charging with the German element. Byron was *ultimus Romanorum*—the last, and with the exception of Shakspeare and Milton, the greatest *purely English* poet. His manner had generally all the clearness and precision of sculpture; indeed his clearness serves often to disguise his depth. As obscurity sometimes gives an air of mystic profundity and solemn grandeur to a shallow puddle, so, on the other hand, we have seen pools among the mountains, whose pellucidity made them appear less profound, and where every small shining pebble was a bright liar as to the real depth of the waters; such pools are many of the poems of Byron, and, we may add, of Campbell.

His dominion over the darker passions is one of the most obvious features in his poetic character. He rode in a chariot drawn, if we may use the figure, by those horses described in the visions of the Apocalypse, "whose heads were as the heads of lions, and out of their mouths issued fire, and smoke, and brimstone." And supreme is his management of these dreadful coursers. Wherever human nature is fiercest and gloomiest—wherever furnace-bosoms have been heated seven times hotter by the unrestrained passions and the torrid suns of the east and the south—wherever man verges toward the animal or the fiend—wherever misanthropes have folded their arms, and taken their desperate attitude—wherever stands "the bed of sin, delirious with its dread"—wherever devours "the worm that cannot sleep, and never dies"—there the melancholy muse of Byron finds its subjects and its haunts. Driven from a home in his country, he seeks it in the mansions of all unhappy hearts, which open gloomily and admit him as their tenant and their bard. To escape from one's self is the desire of many, of all the miserable—the desire of the drunkard, of the opium-eater, of those who plunge into the vortex of any dissipation, who indulge in any delicious dream; but it is the singularity of Byron that he uniformly escapes from himself into something worse and more miserable. His being transmigrates into a darker and more demoniac shape; he becomes an epicure even in wretchedness; he has supped full of common miseries, and must create and exhaust imaginary horrors. What infinite pity that a being so gifted, and that might have been so noble, should find it necessary perpetually to evade himself! Hence his writings abound, more than those of other authors, with lines and phrases which seem to concentrate all misery within them—with texts for misanthropes, and mottoes for the mouths of suicides. "Years all winters"—what a gasp is that, and how characteristic of him to whose soul summer had not come, and spring had for ever faded! The charge of affectation has often been brought against Byron's proclamations of personal woe. But no one, we believe, was ever a constant and consistent hypocrite in such a matter as misery; and we think we can argue his sincerity, not merely from his personal declarations, but from this fact, that all the characters into whom he shoots his soul are unhappy. Tasso writhing in the dungeon. Dante prophesying evil, not to speak of imaginary heroes, such as Conrad, Alp, the Giaour, and Childe Harold, betray in what direction ran the master current of his soul; and as the bells and bubbles upon the dark pool form an accurate measurement of its depth, so his mirth, in its wildness, recklessness, and utter want of genuine gayety, tells saddest tales about the state of a heart which neither on earth nor in heaven could find aught to cheer or comfort it.

Besides those intensely English qualities which we have enumerated as Byron's, there sprung out from him, and mainly through the spur of woe, a higher power than appeared originally to belong to his nature. After all his faculties seemed fully developed, and after critics and craniologists had formed their unalterable estimate of them, he began, as if miraculously, to grow into a loftier shape and stature, and compelled these same sapient judges, slowly and reluctantly, to amend their conclusions.—In his "Cain" his "Heaven and Earth," and his "Vision of Judgment," he exhibited the highest form of the faculty divine—the true afflatus of the bard. He seemed to rise consciously into his own region; and, certainly, for gloomy grandeur, and deep, desolate beauty, these productions surpass all the writings of the period. Now, for the first time, men saw the Pandemonian palace of his soul fully lit, and they trembled at its ghastly splendor; yet, curious it is to remark that those were precisely the poems which the public at first received most coldly. Those who shouted applause when he issued the two first elegant, but comparatively shallow, cantos of "Childe Harold," which were the reflection of other minds, shrank from him when he displayed the terrible riches of his own.

We need only mention the materials on which Byron's genius fed—and, indeed, we must substitute the singular term—for his material was not manifold, but one; it was the history of his own heart that his genius reproduced in all his poems. His poetry was the mirror of himself.

In considering, fourthly, the more characteristic of his works, we may divide them into his juvenile productions, his popular, and his proscribed works. His juvenile productions testified to nothing but the power of his passions, the strength of his ambition, and the uncertainty of his aims. His "Hours of Idleness" was, in one respect, the happiest hit he ever made: it was fortunate enough to attract abuse from the highest critical authority in the empire, and thereby stirred his pride, and effectually roused his faculties. It required a scorching heat to hatch a Byron! In his "English Bards" he proved himself rather a pugilist than a poet. It is the work of a man of Belial, "flown with insolence and *wine.*" His popular productions were principally written when he was still a favorite son of society, the idol of drawing-rooms, and the admired, as well as observed, of all observers. "Childe Harold" is a transcription of the serious and *publishable* part of his journal, as he travelled in Greece, Spain, and Italy. "The Giaour" is a powerful half-length picture of himself. "The Bride of Abydos" is a tender and somewhat maudlin memory of Greece. "The Corsair" was the work of one fierce fortnight, and seems to have brought one period of his life, as well as of his popularity, to a glittering point. In all this class of his poems we see him rather revolving the memory of past, than encountering the reality of present, misery. You have pensive sentiment rather than quick and fresh anguish. But his war with society was now about to begin in right earnest; and in prophetic anticipation of this, he wrote his "Parisina" and his "Siege of Corinth." These were the first great drops of the thunder-storm he was soon to pour down upon the world; and the second of them, in its heat and frenzied haste, proclaims a troubled and distracted state of mind. In referring his medical advisers to it as a proof of his mental insanity, he rather blundered; for although it wants the incoherence, it has the fury of madness. It is the most rapid and furious race he ever ran to escape from himself. Then came his open breach with English society, his separation from his lady, and his growling retreat to his Italian den. But ere yet he plunged into that pool, where the degradation of his genius, and where its power was perfect, he must turn round, and close in wilder, loftier measures the sad song of "Childe Harold," which in life's summer he had begun; and strange it was to mark, in those two last cantos, not only their deepened power and earnestness, but their multiplied sorrow. He seemed to have gone away to Addison's "Mountain of Miseries," and exchanged one burden for a worse—sorrow for despair. He had fallen so low, that suicide had lost its charms; and when one falls beneath the suicide point, his misery is perfect; for his quarrel then is not with *life* but with *being.* Yet how horribly beautiful his conversation with the dust of empires

—with the gigantic skeleton of Rome—with the ocean, which meets him like that simulacrum of the sea which haunted the madness of Caligula—with all the mighty miserable in the past—with those spirits which he summons from the "vasty deep"—or with those ill-favored ones "who walk the shadow of the vale of death." He speaks to them as their equal and kindred spirit. "Hell from beneath is moved to meet him at his coming: they speak, and say unto him, Art thou become like unto us?" As another potentate, do those "Anarchs old"—Orcus, Hades, and the "dreaded name of Demogorgon"—admit him into their chaotic company, and make him free of the privileges of their dreary realm.

Having thus taken a last proud farewell of society, with all its forms and conventionalities, he turned him to the task of pouring out his envenomed and disappointed spirit in works which society was as certain to proscribe as it was to peruse; and there followed that marvellous series of poems to which we have already referred as his most peculiar and powerful productions—most powerful, because most sincere. And yet the public proved how false and worthless its former estimate of Byron's genius had been, by denouncing those, his best doings, not merely for their wickedness, but for their artistic execution. It is humiliating to revert to the reviews and newspapers of that period, and to read the language in which they speak of "Cain," "Sardanapalus," and the "Vision of Judgment," uniformly treating them as miserable fallings-off from his former self—beneath even the standard of his "English Bards and Scotch Reviewers." "Cain" we regard not only as Byron's noblest production, but as one of the finest poems in this or any language. It is such a work as Milton, had he been miserable, would have written. There is nothing in "Paradise Lost" superior to Cain's flight with Lucifer through the stars, and nothing in Shakspeare superior to his conversations with his wife Adah. We speak simply of its merits as a work of art—its object is worthy of all condemnation: that is, to paint a more soured and savage Manfred, engaged in a controversy, not merely with himself, but with the system of which he is one diseased and desperate member; in the unequal strife overwhelmed, and, as if the crush of Omnipotence were not enough, bringing down after him, in his fall, the weight of a brother's blood; and the object of the fable is not, as it ought to have been, to show the madness of all selfish struggle against the laws of the universe, but to more than intimate the poet's belief, that the laws which occasion such a struggle are cruel and unjust. There is an unfair distribution of misery and guilt in the story. The misery principally accrues to Cain; but a large proportion of the guilt is caught, as by a whirlwind, and flies up in the face of his Maker. The great crime of the poem is not that its hero utters blasphemies, but that you shut it with a doubt whether these blasphemies be not true. Milton wrote his great poem to "justify the ways of God to man;" Byron's object seems to be, to justify the ways of man to God—even his wildest and most desperate doings. The pleading is eloquent, but hopeless. It is the bubble on the ridge of the cataract praying not to be carried over and hurried on. Equally vain it is to struggle against those austere and awful laws by which moments of sin expand into centuries of punishment. Yet this was Byron's own life-long struggle, and one which, like men who fight their battles o'er again in sleep, he renewed again and again in every dream of his imagination.

"The Vision of Judgment," unquestionably the best abused, is also one of the best, and by no means the most profane, of his productions. It sprung from the savage disgust produced in his mind by Southey's "double-distilled" cant, in that poem of his on the death of George III. —which, reversing the usual case, now lives suspended by a tow-line from its caricature. All other hatred—that of Johnson—that of Burke—that of Juvenal—that of all, save Junius—is tame and maudlin compared to the wrath of Byron expressed in this poem. Scorn often has the effect of cooling and carrying off rage—but here "the ground burns frore, and cold performs the effect of fire." His very contempt is molten; his tears of laughter, as well as of misery, fall in *burning* showers. In what single lines has he concentrated the mingled essence of the coolest contempt, and the hottest indignation!

"A better farmer ne'er brushed dew from lawn.
A worse king never left a realm undone."

"When the gorgeous coffin was laid low,
It seem'd the mockery of hell to fold
The rottenness of eighty years in gold."

"'Passion!' replied the phantom dim,
'I loved my country and I hated him.'"

There spoke the authentic shade of Junius, or at least a spirit worthy of contending with him for the honor of being the "Best Hater" upon record.

And yet, mixed with the strokes of ribaldry, are touches of a grandeur which he has rarely elsewhere approached. His poetry always rises above itself, when painting the faded splendor wan—the steadfast gloom—the hapless magnanimity of the prince of darkness. With perfect ease he seems to enter into the soul, and fill up the measure and stature of the awful personage.

It were unpardonable, even in a rapid review, to omit all notice of "Don Juan," which, if it bring our notion of the man to its lowest point, exalts our idea of the poet. Its great charm is its conversational ease. How coolly and calmly he bestrides his Pegasus even when he is at the gallop. With what exquisitely quiet and quick transitions does he pass from humor to pathos, and make you laugh and cry at once as you do in dreams. It is less a man writing, than a man *resigning* his soul to his reader. To use Scott's beautiful figure—"the stanzas fall off as easily as the leaves from the autumnal tree." You stand under a shower of withered gold. And in spite of the endless touches of wit, the general impression is most melancholy; and not Rasselas, nor Timon, casts so deep a shadow on the thoughtful reader as the "very tragical mirth" of Don Juan.

In settling, lastly, his rank as a poet, we may simply say, that he must be placed, on the whole, beneath and apart from the first class of poets, such as Homer, Dante, Milton, Shakspeare, and Goethe. Often, indeed, he seems to rush into their company, and to stand among them, like a daring boy amid his seniors, measuring himself proudly with their superior stature. And, possibly, had he lived, he might have ultimately taken his place amongst them, for it was in his, power to have done this. But life was denied him. The wild steed of his passions—like his own "Mazeppa"—carried him furiously into the wilderness, and dashed him into premature death. And he now must take his place as one at the very head of the second rank of poets, and arrested when he was towering up towards the first.

His name has been frequently but injudiciously coupled with that of Shelly. This has arisen principally from their accidental position. They found themselves together one stormy night in the streets, having both been thrust out by the strong arm from their homes. One had been kicking up a row and kissing the servant-maids; the other had been trying to rouse the family, but in so awkward a fashion, that in his haste he had put out all the lustres, and nearly blown up the establishment. In that cold, desolate, moonless night, they chanced to meet—they entered into conversation—they even tried, by drawing near each other, to administer a little kindly warmth and encouragement. Men seeing them imperfectly in the lamp-light, classed them together as two dissolute and disorderly blackguards. And, alas, when the morning came that might have accurately discriminated them, both were found lying dead in the streets. In point of purpose—temperament—tendency of intellect—political creed—feeling—sentiments—habits—and character, no two men could be more dissimilar.

We remember a pilgrimage we made some years ago to Lochnagar. As we ascended, a mist came down over the hill, like a veil dropped by some jealous beauty over her own fair face. At length the summit was reached, though the prospect was denied us. It was a proud and thrilling moment. What though darkness was all around? It was the *very* atmosphere that suited the scene. It was "dark Lochnagar." And only think how fine it was to climb up and clasp its cairn—to lift a stone from it, to be in aftertime a memorial of our journey—to sing the song which made it glorious and dear, in its own proud drawing-room, with those great fog-curtains floating around—to pass along the brink of its precipices—to snatch a fearful joy, as we leant over, and hung down, and saw from beneath the gleam of eternal snow shining up from its hollows, and columns, or rather perpendicular seas of mist, streaming up upon the wind

"Like foam from the roused ocean of deep hell,
Where every wave breaks on a living shore,
Heaped with the damn'd, like pebbles—"

tinged, too, here and there, on their tops, by gleams of sunshine, the farewell beams of the dying day. It was the grandest moment in our lives. We had stood upon many hills—in sunshine and in shade, in mist and in thunder—but never had before, nor hope to have again, such a feeling of the grandeur of this lower universe—such a sense of horrible sublimity. Nay, we question if there be a mountain in the empire, which, though seen in similar circumstances, could awaken the same emotions in our minds. It is not its loftiness, though that be great—nor its bold outline, nor its savage loneliness, nor its mist-loving precipices, but the associations which crown its crags with a "peculiar diadem"—its identification with the image of a poet, who, amid all his fearful errors, had perhaps more than any of the age's bards, the power of investing all his career—yea, to every corner which his fierce foot ever touched, or which his genius ever sung—with profound and melancholy interest. We saw the name of Byron written in the cloud-characters above us. We saw his genius sadly smiling in those gleams of stray sunshine which gilded the darkness they could not dispel. We found an emblem of his passions in that flying rack, and of his character in those lowering precipices. We seemed to hear the wail of his restless spirit in the wild sob of the wind, fainting and struggling up under its burden of darkness. Nay, we could fancy that this hill was designed as an eternal monument to his name, and to image all those peculiarities which make that name for ever illustrious. Not the loftiest of his country's poets, he is the most sharply and terribly defined. In magnitude and round completeness, he yields to many; in jagged, abrupt, and passionate projection of his own shadow, over the world of literature, to none. The Genius of convulsion, a dire attraction, dwells around him, which leads many to hang over, and some to leap down, his precipices. Volcanic as he is, the coldness of wintry selfishness too often collects in the hollows of his verse. He loves, too, the cloud and the thick darkness, and comes "veiling all the lightnings of his song in sorrow." So, like Byron beside Scott and Wordsworth, does Lochnagar stand in the presence of his neighbor giants, Ben-mac-Dhui, and Ben-y-boord, less lofty, but more fiercely eloquent in its jagged outline, reminding us of the *via* of the forked lightning, which it seems dumbly to mimic, projecting its cliffs like quenched batteries against earth and heaven, with the cold of snow in its heart, and with a coronet of mist round its gloomy brow.

No poet, since Homer and Ida, has thus, everlastingly, shot his genius into the heart of one great mountain, identifying himself and his song with it. Nor Horace with Socrate—not Wordsworth with Helvellyn—not Coleridge with Mont Blanc—not Wilson with the Black Mount—not even Scott with the Eildons—all these are still common property, but Lochnagar is Byron's own—no poet will ever venture to sing it again. In its dread circle none durst walk but he. His allusions to it are not numerous, but its peaks stood often before his eye: a recollection of its grandeur served more to color his line than the glaciers of the Alps, the cliffs of Jura, or the "thunder hills of fear," which he heard in Chimari; even from the mountains of Greece he was carried back to Morven, and "Lochnagar, with Ida, looked o'er Troy." Hence the severe Dante-like monumental, mountainous cast of his better poetry; for we firmly believe that the scenery of one's youth gives a permanent bias and coloring to the genius, the taste, and the style, *i. e.*, if there be an intellect to receive an impulse, or a taste to catch a tone. Many, it is true, bred in cities, or amid common scenery, make up for the lack by early travel; so did Milton, Coleridge, and Wilson. But who may not gather, from the tame tone of Cowper's landscapes, that he had never enjoyed such opportunities? And who, in Pollok's powerful but gloomy poem, may not detect the raven hue which a sterile moorland scenery had left upon his mind? Has not, again, the glad landscape of the Howe of the Mearns, and the prospect from the surmounting Hill of Garvock, left a pleasing trace upon the mild pages of Beattie's "Minstrel?" Did not Coila color the genial soul of its poet? Has not the scenery of his "own romantic town" made much of the prose and poetry of Sir Walter Scott what it is? So, is it mere fancy which traces the stream of Byron's poetry in its light and its darkness, its bitterness and its brilliance, to this smitten rock in the wilderness—to the cliffs of Locknagar?

GEORGE CRABBE.

To be the poet of the waste places of Creation—to adopt the orphans of the mighty mother—to wed her dowerless daughters—to find out the beauty which has been spilt in tiny drops in her more unlovely regions—to echo the low music which arises from even her stillest and most sterile spots—was the mission of Crabbe, as a descriptive poet. He preferred the Leahs to the Rachels of nature: and this he did not merely that his lot had cast him amid such scenes, and that early associations had taught him a profound interest in them, but apparently from native taste. He actually loved that beauty which stands shivering on the brink of barrenness—loved it for its timidity and its loneliness. Nay, he seems to love barrenness itself; brooding over its dull page till there arose from it a strange lustre, which his eye distinctly sees, and which in part he makes visible to his readers. It was even as the darkness of cells has been sometimes peopled to the view of the solitary prisoner, and spiders seemed angels in the depths of his dungeon. We can fancy, too, in Crabbe's mind, a feeling of pity for those unloved spots, and those neglected glories. We can fancy him saying, "Let the gay and the aspiring mate with nature in her towering altitudes, and flatter her more favored scenes; I will go after her into her secret retirements, bring out her bashful beauties, praise what none are willing to praise, and love what there are few to love." From his early circumstances, besides, there had stolen over his soul a shade of settled though subdued gloom. And for sympathy with this, he betook himself to the sterner and sadder aspects of nature, where he saw, or seemed to see, his own feelings reflected, as in a sea of melancholy faces, in dull skies, waste moorlands, the low beach, and the moaning of the waves upon it, as if weary of their eternal wanderings. Such, too, at moments, was the feeling of Burns, when he strode on the scaur of the Nith, and saw the waters red and turbid below; or walked in a windy day by the side of a plantation, and heard the "sound of a going" upon the tops of the trees; or when he exclaimed, with a calm simplicity of bitterness which is most affecting—

> "The leafless trees my fancy please,
> Their fate resembles mine."

Oh! where, indeed, can the unhappy repair, to escape from their own sorrows, or worse, from the unthinking glee or constitutional cheerfulness of others, more fitly than into the wastes and naked places of nature? She will not then and there seem to insult them with her laughing luxuriance—her foliage fluttering, as if in vain display, with the glossy gilding of her flowers, or the sunny sparkle and song of her streamlets. But she will uplift a mightier and older voice. She will soothe them by a sterner ministry. She will teach them "old truths, abysmal truths, awful truths." She will answer their sighs by the groans of the creation travailing in pain; suck up their tears in the sweat of her great agonies; reflect their tiny wrinkles in those deep stabs and scars on her forehead, which speak of struggle and contest; give back the gloom of their brows in the frowns of her forests, her mountain solitudes, and her waste midnight darkness; infuse something, too, of her own sublime expectancy into her spirits; and dismiss them from her society, it may be sadder, but certainly wiser men. How admirably is nature suited to all moods of all men! In spring, she is gay with the light-hearted; in summer, gorgeous as its sun to those fiery spirits who seem made for a warmer day; in autumn, she spreads over all hearts a mellow and unearthly joy; and even in winter—when her temple is deserted of the frivolous and the timid, who quit it along with the smile of the sun—she attracts her own few but faithful votaries, who love her in her naked sculpture, as well as in her glowing pictorial hues, and who enjoy her solemn communion none the less that they enjoy it by themselves. To use the words of a forgotten poet, addressing spring—

> "Thou op'st a storehouse for all hues of men.
> To hardihood thou, blustering from the north,

Roll'st dark—hast sighs for them that would complain;
Sharp winds to clear the head of wit and worth;
And melody for those that follow mirth;
Clouds for the gloomy; tears for those that weep;
Flowers blighted in the bud for those that birth
Untimely sorrow o'er; and skies where sweep
Fleets of a thousand sail for them that plough the deep."

Crabbe, as a descriptive poet, differs from other modern masters of the art, alike in his selection of subjects, and in his mode of treating the subjects he does select. Byron moves over nature with a fastidious and aristocratic step—touching only upon objects already interesting or ennobled upon battle fields, castellated ruins, Italian palaces, or Alpine peaks. This, at least, is true of his "Childe Harold," and his earlier pieces. In the later productions of his pen, he goes to the opposite extreme, and alights, with a daring yet dainty foot, upon all shunned and forbidden things—reminds us of the raven in the Deluge, which found rest for the sole of her foot upon carcasses, where the dove durst not stand—rushes in where modesty and reserve alike have forbidden entrance—and ventures, though still not like a lost archangel, to tread the burning marl of hell, the dim gulf of Hades, the shadowy ruins of the pre-Adamitic world, and the crystal pavement of heaven. Moore practises a principle of more delicate selection, resembling some nice fly which should alight only upon flowers, whether natural or artificial, if so that flowers they seem to be; thus, from sunny bowers, and moonlit roses, and gardens, and blushing skies, and ladies' dresses, does the Bard of Erin extract his finest poetry. Shelley and Coleridge attach themselves almost exclusively to the great—understanding this term in a wide sense, as including much that is grotesque and much that is homely, which the magic of their genius sublimates to a proper pitch of keeping with the rest. Their usual walk is swelling and buskined: their common talk is of great rivers, great forests, great seas, great continents: or else of comets, suns, constellations, and firmaments—as that of all half-mad, wholly miserable, and opium-fed genius is apt to be. Sir Walter Scott, who seldom grappled with the gloomier and grander features of his country's scenery (did he ever describe Glencoe or Foyers, or the wildernesses around Ben-mac-Dhui?), had (need we say?) the most exquisite eye for all picturesque and romantic aspects, in sea, shore, or sky; and in the quick perception of this element of the picturesque lay his principal, if not only descriptive power. Wordsworth, again, seems always to be standing above, though not stooping over, the objects he describes. He seldom looks up in wrapt admiration of what is above him; the bending furze-bush and the lowly broom—the nest lying in the level clover-field—the tarn sinking away seemingly before his eye into darker depths—the prospect from the mountain summit cast far beneath him: at highest, the star burning low upon the mountain's ridge, like an "untended watchfire:" these are the objects which he loves to describe, and these may stand as emblems of his lowly yet aspiring genius—Crabbe, on the other hand, "stoops to conquer"—nay, goes down on his knees, that he may more accurately describe such objects as the marsh given over to desolation from immemorial time—the slush left by the sea, and revealing the dead body of the suicide—the bare crag and the stunted tree, diversifying the scenery of the saline wilderness—the house on the heath, creaking in the storm, and telling strange stories of misery and crime—the pine in some wintry wood, which had acted as the gallows of some miserable man—the gorse surrounding with yellow light the encampment of the Gipsies—the few timid flowers, or "weeds of glorious feature," which adorn the brink of ocean—the snow putting out the fire of the pauper, or lying unmelted on his pillow of death—the web of the spider blinding the cottager's window—the wheel turned by the meagre hand of contented or cursing penury—the cards trembling in the grasp of the desperate debauchee—the day stocking forming the cap by night, and the *garter at midnight*—the dunghill becoming the accidental grave of the drunkard—the poor-house of forty years ago, with its patched windows, its dirty environs, its moist and miserable walls, its inmates all snuff, and selfishness, and sin—the receptacle of the outlawed members of English society (how different from "Poosie Nancy's!"), with its gin-gendered quarrels, its appalling blasphemies, its deep debauches, its ferocity without fun, its huddled murders, and its shrieks of disease dumb in the uproar around—the Bedlam of forty years ago, with its straw on end under the restlessness of the insane; its music of groans, and shrieks and mutterings of still more melancholy meaning; its keepers cold and stern, as the snow-covered cliffs above the wintry cataract; its songs dying away in despairing gurgles down the miserable throat; its cells how devoid of monastic silence; its "confusion worse confounded," of gibbering idiocy, monomania absorbed and absent from itself as well as from the world, and howling frenzy; its daylight saddened as it shines into the dim, vacant, or glaring eyes of those wretched men: and its moonbeams shedding a more congenial ray upon the solitude, or the sick-bed, or the death-bed of derangement—such familiar faces of want, guilt, and woe—of nakedness, sterility, and shame, does Crabbe delight in showing us; and is, in very truth, "nature's sternest painter, yet the best." In his mode of managing his descriptions, Crabbe is equally peculiar. Objects, in themselves counted commonplace or disgusting, frequently become impressive, and even sublime, when surrounded by interesting circumstances—when shown in the moonlight of memory—when linked to strong passion—or when touched by the ray of imagination. Then, in Emerson's words, even the corpse is found to have added a solemn ornament to the house where it lay. But it is the peculiarity and the daring of this poet, that he often, not always, tries us with truth and nothing but truth, as if to bring the question to an issue—whether, in nature, absolute truth be not essential though severe poetry. On this question, certainly, issue was never so fully joined before. In even Wordsworth's eye there is a misty glimmer of imagination, through which all objects, low as well as high, are seen. Even his "five blue eggs" *gleam* upon him through a light which comes not from themselves—which comes, it may be, from the Great Bear, or Arcturus and his sons. And when he does—as in some of his feebler verses—strive to see out of this medium, he drops his mantle, loses his vision, and describes little better than would his own "Old Cumberland Beggar." Shakspeare in his witches' caldron, and Burns in "haly table," are shockingly circumstantial; but the element of imagination creeps in amid all the disgusting details, and the light that never was on sea or shore disdains not to rest on "eye of newt," "toe of frog," "baboon's blood," the garter that strangled the babe, the gray hairs sticking to the haft of the parricidal knife, and all the rest of the fell ingredients; Crabbe, on the other hand, would have described the five blue eggs, and besides, the materials of the nest, and the kind of hedge where it was built, like a bird-nesting schoolboy; but he would never have given the "gleam." He would as accurately as Hecate, Canidia, or Cuttysark, have given an inventory of the ingredients of the hell-broth, or of the curiosities on the "haly table," had they been presented to his eye: but could not have conceived them, nor would have slipped in that one flashing word, that single cross ray of imagination, which it required to elevate and startle them into high ideal life. And yet in reading his pictures of poor-houses, &c., we are compelled to say, "Well, that is poetry after all, for it is truth; but it is poetry of comparatively a low order—it is the last gasp of the poetic spirit: and, moreover, perfect and matchless as it is in its kind, it is not worthy of the powers of its author, who can, and has, at other times risen into much loftier ground."

We may illustrate still farther what we mean by comparing the different ways in which Crabbe and Foster (certainly a *prose* poet) deal with a library. Crabbe describes minutely and successfully the outer features of the volumes, their colors, clasps, the stubborn ridges of their bindings, the illustrations which adorn them, &c., so well that you feel yourself among them, and they become sensible to touch almost as to sight. But there he stops, and sadly fails, we think, in bringing out the living and moral interest which gathers around a multitude of books, or even around a single volume. This Foster has amply done. The speaking silence of a number of books, where, though it were the wide Bodleian or Vatican, not one whisper could be heard, and yet, where, as in an antechamber, so many great spirits are waiting to deliver their messages—their churchyard stillness continuing even when their readers are moving to their pages, in joy or agony, as to the sound of martial instruments—their awaking, as from deep slumber, to speak with miraculous organ, like the shell which has only to be lifted, and "pleased it remembers its august abodes, and murmurs as the ocean murmurs there"—their power of drawing tears, kindling blushes, awakening laughter, calming or quickening the motions of the life's blood, lulling to repose, or rousing to restlessness, often giving life to the soul, and sometimes giving death to the body—the meaning which radiates from their quiet countenances—the tale of shame or glory which their title-pages tell—the memories suggested by the character of their authors, and of the readers who have throughout successive centuries perused them—the thrilling thoughts excited by the sight of names and notes inscribed on their margins or blank pages by hands long since mouldered in the dust, or by those dear to us as our life's blood, who had been snatched from our sides—the aspects of gayety or of gloom connected with the bindings and the age of volumes—the effects of sunshine playing as if on a congregation of happy faces, making the duskiest shine, and the gloomiest be glad—or of shadow suffusing a sombre air over all—the joy of the proprietor of a large library who feels that Nebuchadnezzar watching great Babylon, or Napoleon reviewing his legions, will not stand comparison with himself seated amid the broad maps, and rich prints, and numerous volumes which his wealth has enabled him to collect and his wisdom entitled him to enjoy—all such hieroglyphics of interest and meaning has Foster included and interpreted in one gloomy but noble meditation, and his introduction to Doddridge is the true "Poem on the Library."

In Crabbe's descriptions the great want is of selection. He writes inventories. He describes all that his eye sees with cold, stern, lingering accuracy—he marks down all the items of wretchedness, poverty, and vulgar sin—counts the rags of the mendicant—and, as Hazlitt has it, describes a cottage like one who has entered it to distrain for rent. His copies, consequently, would be as displeasing as their originals, were it not that imagination is so much less vivid than eyesight, that we can endure in picture what we cannot in reality, and that our own minds, while reading, can cast that softening and ideal veil over disgusting objects which the poet himself has not sought, or has failed to do. Just as, in viewing even the actual scene, we might have seen it through the medium of imaginative illusion, so the same medium will more probably invest, and beautify its transcript in the pages of the poet.

As a moral poet and sketcher of men, Crabbe is charac terized by a similar choice of subject and the same stern fidelity. The mingled yarn of man's every-day life—the plain homely virtues, or the robust and burly vices of Englishmen—the quiet tears which fall on humble beds—the passions which flame up in lowly bosoms—the *amari aliquid*, the deep and permanent bitterness which lies at the heart of the down-trodden English poor—the comedies and tragedies of the fireside—the lovers' quarrels—the unhappy marriages—the vicissitudes of common fortunes—the early deaths—the odd characters—the lingering superstitions—all the elements, in short, which make up the simple annals of lowly or middling society, are the materials of this poet's song. Had he been a Scottish clergyman we should have said that he had versified his Session-book; and certainly many curious chapters of human life might be derived from such a document, and much light cast upon the devious windings and desperate wickedness of the heart, as well as upon that inextinguishable instinct of good which resides in it. Crabbe, perhaps, has confined himself too exclusively to this circle of common things which he found lying around him. He has seldom burst its confines, and touched the loftier themes, and snatched the higher laurels which were also within his reach. He has contented himself with being a Lillo (with occasional touches of Shakspeare) instead of something far greater. He has, however, in spite of this self-injustice, effected much. He has proved that a poet, who looks resolutely around him—who stays at home—who draws the realities which are near him, instead of the phantoms that are afar—who feels and records the passion and poetry of his daily life—may found a firm and enduring reputation. With the dubious exception of Cowper, no one has made out this point so effectually as Crabbe.

And in his mode of treating such themes, what strikes us first is his perfect coolness. Few poets have reached that calm of his which reminds us of Nature's own great quiet eye, looking down upon her monstrous births, her strange anomalies, and her more ungainly forms. Thus Crabbe sees the loathsome, and does not loathe—handles the horrible, and shudders not—feels with firm finger the palpitating pulse of the infanticide or the murderer—and snuffs a certain sweet odor in the evil savors of putrefying misery and crime. This delight, however, is not an inhuman, but entirely an artistic delight—perhaps, indeed, springing from the very strength and width of his sympathies. We admire as well as wonder at that almost *asbestos* quality of his mind, through which he retains his composure and critical circumspection so cool amid the conflagrations of passionate subjects, which might have burned others to ashes. Few, indeed, can walk through such fiery furnaces unscathed. But Crabbe—what an admirable physician had he made to a lunatic asylum! How severely would he have sifted out every grain of poetry from those tumultuous exposures of the human mind! What clean breasts had he forced the patients to make! What tales had he wrung out from them, to which Lewis's tales of terror were feeble and trite! How he would have commanded them, by his mild, steady, and piercing eye! And yet how calm would his brain have remained, when others, even of a more prosaic mould, were reeling in sympathy with the surrounding delirium! It were, indeed, worth while inquiring how much of this coolness resulted from Crabbe's early practice as a surgeon. That combination of warm inward sympathy and outward phlegm—of impulsive benevolence and mechanical activity—of heart all fire and manner all ice—which distinguishes his poetry, is very characteristic of the medical profession.

In correspondence with this, Crabbe generally leans to the darker side of things. This, perhaps, accounts for his favor in the sight of Byron, who saw his own eagle-eyed fury at man corroborated by Crabbe's stern and near-sighted vision. And it was accounted for partly by Crabbe's early profession, partly by his early circumstances, and partly by the clerical office he assumed. Nothing so tends to sour us with mankind as a general refusal on their part to give us bread. How can a man love a race which seems combined to starve him? This misanthropical influence Crabbe did not entirely escape. As a medical man, too, he had to come in contact with little else than human miseries and diseases; and as a clergyman, he had occasion to see much sin and sorrow: and these, combining with the melancholy incidental to the poetic temperament, materially discolored his view of life. He became a searcher of dark—of the darkest bosoms; and we see him sitting in the gloom of the hearts of thieves, murderers, and maniacs, and watching the remorse, rancor, fury, dull disgust, ungratified appetite, and ferocious or stupefied despair, which are their inmates. And even when he pictures livelier scenes and happier characters, there steals over them a shade of sadness, reflected from his favorite subjects, as a dark, sinister countenance in a room will throw a gloom over many happy and beautiful faces beside it.

In his pictures of life, we find an unfrequent but true pathos. This is not often, however, of the profoundest or most heart-rending kind. The grief he paints is not that which refuses to be comforted—whose expressions, like Agamemnon's face, must be veiled—which dilates almost to despair, and complains almost to blasphemy—and which when it looks to heaven, it is

> "With that frantic air,
> Which seems to ask if a God be there."

Crabbe's, as exhibited in "Phœbe Dawson," and other of his tales, is gentle, submissive; and its pathetic effects are produced by the simple recital of circumstances which might and often have occurred. It reminds us of the pathos of "Rosamund Gray," that beautiful story of Lamb's, of which we once, we regret to say, presumptuously pronounced an unfavorable opinion, but which has since commended itself to our heart of hearts, and compelled that tribute in tears which we had denied it in words. Hazlitt is totally wrong when he says that Crabbe carves a tear to the life in marble, as if his pathos were hard and cold. Be it the statuary of woe—has it, consequently, no truth or power? Have the chiselled tears of the Niobe never awakened other tears, fresh and burning, from their fountain? Horace's *vis me flere*, &c., is not always a true principle. As the wit, who laughs not himself, often excites most laughter in others, so the calm recital of an affecting narrative acts as the meek rod of Moses applied to the rock, and is answered in gushing torrents. You close Crabbe's tale of grief, almost ashamed that you have left so quiet a thing pointed and starred with tears. His pages, while sometimes wet with pathos, are never moist with humor. His satire is often pointed with wit, and sometimes irritates into invective; but of that glad, genial, and bright-eyed thing we call humor (how well *named*, in its oily softness and gentle glitter!) he has little or none. Compare, in order to see this, his "Borough" with the "Annals of the Parish." How dry, though powerful, the one; how sappy the other! How profound the one; how pawky the other! Crabbe goes through his Borough, like a scavenger with a rough, stark, and stiff besom, sweeping up all the filth: Galt, like a knowing watchman of the old school—a *canny Charlie*—keeping a sharp look-out, but not averse to a sly joke, and having an eye to the humors as well as misdemeanors of the streets. Even his wit is not of the finest grain. It deals too much in verbal quibbles, puns, and antitheses with their points broken off. His puns are neither good nor bad—the most fatal and anti-ideal description of a pun that can be given. His quibbles are good enough to have excited the laugh of his curate, or gardener; but he forgets that the public is not so indulgent. And though often treading in Pope's track, he wants entirely those touches of satire, at once the lightest and the most withering, as if dropped from the fingers of a malignant fairy—those faint whispers of poetic perdition—those drops of concentrated bitterness—those fatal bodkin-stabs—and those invectives, glittering all over with the polish of profound malignity—which are Pope's glory as a writer, and his shame as a man.

We have repeatedly expressed our opinion, that in Crabbe there lay a higher power than he often exerted. We find evidence of this in his "Hall of Justice" and his "Eustace Grey." In these he is fairly in earnest. No longer dozing by his parlor fire over the "Newspaper," or napping in a corner of his "Library," or peeping in through the windows of the "Workhouse," or recording the select scandal of the "Borough," he is away out into the wide and open fields of highest passion and imagination. What a tale that "Hall of Justice" hears—to be paralleled only in the "Thousand and One Nights of the Halls of Eblis!"—a tale of misery, rape, murder, and furious despair; told, too, in language of such lurid fire as has been seen to shine o'er the graves of the dead! But, in "Eustace Grey," our author's genius reaches its climax. Never was madness—in its misery—its remorse—the dark companions, "the ill-favored ones," who cling to it in its wild way and will not let it go, although it curse them with the eloquence of hell—the visions it sees—the scenery it creates and carries about with it in dreadful keeping—and the language it uses, high, aspiring, but broken, as the wing of a struck eagle—so strongly and meltingly revealed. And, yet, around the dismal tale there hangs the breath of beauty, and, like poor Lear, Sir Eustace goes about crowned with flowers—the flowers of earthly poetry—and of a hope which is not of the earth. And, at the close, we feel to the author all that strange gratitude which our souls are constituted to entertain to those who have most powerfully wrung and tortured them.

Would that Crabbe had given us a century of such things. We would have preferred to the "Tales of the Hall," "Tales of Greyling Hall," or more tidings from the "Hall of Justice." It had been a darker Decameron, and brought out more effectually—what the "Village Poorhouse," and the sketches of Elliott have since done—the passions, miseries, crushed aspirations, and latent poetry, which dwell in the hearts of the plundered poor; as well as the wretchedness which, more punctually than their veriest menial, waits often behind the chairs, and hands the silver dishes of the great.

We will not dilate on his other works individually. In glancing back upon them as a whole, we will endeavor to answer the following questions: 1st, What was Crabbe's object as a moral poet? 2dly, How far is he original as an artist? 3dly, What is his relative position to his great contemporaries? And, 4thly, what is likely to be his fate with posterity? 1st, His object.—The great distinction between man and man, and author and author, is purpose. It is the edge and point of character; it is the stamp on the subscription of genius; it is the direction on the letter of talent. Character without it is blunt and torpid. Talent without it is a letter, which, undirected, goes no whither. Genius without it is bullion, sluggish, splendid, uncirculating. Purpose yearns after and secures artistic culture. It gathers, as by a strong suction, all things which it needs into itself. Crabbe's artistic object is tolerably clear, and has been already indicated. His moral purpose is not quite so apparent. Is it to satirize, or is it to reform vice? Is it pity, or is it contempt, that actuates his song? What are his plans for elevating the lower classes in the scale of society? Has he any, or does he believe in the possibility of their permanent elevation? Such questions are more easily asked than answered. We must say that we have failed to find in him any one overmastering and earnest object, subjugating every thing to itself, and producing that unity in all his works which the trunk of a tree gives to its smallest, its remotest, to even its withered leaves. And yet, without apparent intention, Crabbe has done good moral service. He has shed much light upon the condition of the poor. He has spoken in the name and stead of the poor dumb mouths that could not tell their own sorrows or sufferings to the world. He has opened the mine, which Ebenezer Elliot and others, going to work with a firmer and more resolute purpose, have dug to its depths.

2dly, His originality.—This has been questioned by some critics. He has been called a version, in coarser paper and print, of Goldsmith, Pope, and Cowper. His pathos comes from Goldsmith—his wit and satire from Pope—and his minute and literal description from Cowper. If this were true, it were as complimentary to him as his warmest admirer could wish. To combine the characteristic excellences of three true poets is no easy matter. But Crabbe has not combined them. His pathos wants altogether the naiveté of sentiment and *curiosa felicitas* of expression which distinguish Goldsmith's "Deserted Village." He has something of Pope's terseness, but little of his subtlety, finish, or brilliant malice. And the motion of Cowper's mind and style in description differs as much from Crabbe's as the playful leaps and gambols of a kitten from the measured, downright, and indomitable pace of a hound—the one is the easiest, the other the severest, of describers. Resemblances, indeed, of a minor kind are to be found; but still Crabbe is as distinct from Goldsmith, Cowper, and Pope, as Byron from Scott, Wordsworth, and Coleridge.

Originality consists of two kinds—one, the power of inventing new materials; and the other, of dealing with old materials in a new way. We do not decide whether the first of these implies an act of absolute creation; it implies all we can conceive in an act of creative power; from elements bearing to the result the relation which the Alphabet does to the "Iliad"—genius brings forth its bright progeny, and we feel it to be new. In this case you can no more anticipate the effect from the elements than you can, from the knowledge of the letters, anticipate the words which are to be compounded out of them. In the other kind of originality, the materials bear a larger proportion to the result—they form an appreciable quantity in our calculations of what it is to be. They are found for the poet, and all he has to do is, with skill and energy, to construct them. Take, for instance, Shakspeare's "Tempest," and Coleridge's "Anciente Marinere"—of what more creative act can we conceive than is exemplified in these? Of course, we have all had beforehand ideas similar to a storm, a desert island, a witch, a magician, a mariner, a hermit, a wedding-guest; but these are only the Alphabet to the spirits of Shakspeare and Coleridge. As the sun, from the invisible air, draws up in an instant all pomps of cloudy forms—paradises brighter than Eden, mirrored in waters, which blush and tremble as their reflection falls wooingly upon them—mountains which seem to bury their snowy or rosy summits in the very heaven of heavens—throne-shaped splendors, worthy of angels to sit on them, flushing and fading in the west—seas of aerial blood and fire—momentary cloud-crowns and golden avenues, stretching away into the azure infinite beyond them;—so from such stuff as dreams are made of, from the mere empty air, do those wondrous magicians build up their new worlds, where the laws of nature are repealed—where all things are changed without any being confused—where sound becomes dumb and silence eloquent—where the earth is empty, and the sky is peopled—where material beings are invisible, and where spiritual beings become gross and palpable to sense—where the skies are opening to show riches—where the isle is full of noises—where beings proper to this sphere of dream are met so often that you cease to fear them, however odd or monstrous—where magic has power to shut now the eyes of kings and now the great bright eye of ocean—where, at the bidding of the poet, new, complete, beautiful mythologies at one time sweep across the sea, and anon dance down from the purple and mystic sky—where all things have a charmed life, the listening ground, the populous air, the still or the vexed sea, the human or the imaginary beings—and where, as in deep dreams, the most marvellous incidents are most easily credited, slide on most softly, and seem most native to the place, the circumstances, and the time. "This is creation," we exclaim; nor did Ferdinand seem to Miranda a fresher and braver creature than does to us each strange settler, whom genius has planted upon its own favorite isle. Critics may, indeed, take these imaginary beings—such as Caliban and Ariel—and analyze them into their constituent parts; but there will be some one element which escapes them—laughing, as it leaps away, at their baffled sagacity, and proclaiming the original power of its Creator: as in the chemical analysis of an *aerolite*, amid the mere earthy constituents, there is something which declares its unearthly origin. Take creation as meaning, not so much Deity bringing something out of nothing, as *filling the void with his Spirit*, and genius will seem a lower form of the same power.

The other kind of originality is, we think, that of Crabbe. It is magic at second-hand. He takes, not makes, his materials. He finds a good foundation—wood and stone in plenty—and he begins laboriously, successfully, and after a plan of his own, to build. If in any of his works he approaches to the higher property, it is in "Eustace Grey," who moves here and there, on his wild wanderings, as if to the rubbing of Aladdin's lamp.

This prepares us for coming to the third question, What is Crabbe's relative position to his great contemporary poets? He belongs to the second class. He is not a philosophic poet, like Wordsworth. He is not, like Shelley, a Vates, moving upon the uncertain but perpetual and furious wind of his inspiration. He is not, like Byron, a demoniac exceeding fierce, and dwelling among the tombs. He is not, like Keats, a sweet and melancholy voice, a tune bodiless, bloodless—dying away upon the waste air, but for ever to be remembered as men remember a melody they have heard in youth. He is not, like Coleridge, all these almost by turns, and besides, a psalmist, singing at times strains so sublime and holy, that they might seem snatches of the song of Eden's cherubim, or caught in trance from the song of Moses and the Lamb. To this mystic brotherhood Crabbe must not be added. He ranks with a lower but still lofty band—with Scott (as a poet), and Moore, and Hunt, and Campbell, and

Rogers, and Bowles, and James Montgomery, and Southey; and surely they nor he need be ashamed of each other, as they shine in one soft and peaceful cluster.

We are often tempted to pity poor posterity on this score. How is it to manage with the immense number of excellent works which this age has bequeathed, and is bequeathing it? How is it to economize its time so as to read a tithe of them? And should it in mere self-defence proceed to decimate, with what principle shall the process be carried on, and who shall be appointed to preside over it? Critics of the twenty-second century, be merciful as well as just. Pity the *disjecta membra* of those we thought mighty poets. Respect and fulfil our prophecies of immortality. If ye must carp and cavil, do not, at least, in mercy, abridge. Spare us the prospect of this last insult, an abridged copy of the "Pleasures of Hope," or "Don Juan," a *new* abridgment. If ye must operate in this way, be it on "Madoc," or the "Course of Time." Generously leave room for "O'Connor's Child" in the poet's corner of a journal, or for "Eustace Grey" in the space of a crown piece. Surely, living in the Millennium, and resting under your vines and fig-trees, you will have more time to read than we, in this bustling age, who move, live, eat, drink, *sleep, and die*, at railway speed. If not, we fear the case of many of our poets is hopeless, and that others, besides the author of "Silent Love," would be wise to enjoy their present laurels, for verily there are none else for them.

Seriously, we hope that much of Crabbe's writing will every year become less and less readable, and less and less easily understood; till, in the milder day, men shall have difficulty in believing that such physical, mental, and moral degradation, as he describes, ever existed in Britain; and till, in future Encyclopædias, his name may be found recorded as a powerful but barbarous writer, writing in a barbarous age. The like may be the case with many who have busied themselves more in recalling the past or picturing the present, than in anticipating the future. But there are, or have been among us, a few who have plunged beyond their own period, nay, beyond "all ages"—who have seen and shown us the coming eras:

> "As in a cradled Hercules you trace
> The lines of empire in his infant face"—

and whose voice must go down, in tones becoming more authoritative as they last, and in volume becoming vaster as they roll, like mighty thunderings and many waters, through the minster of all future time; in lower key, concerting with those more awful voices from within the veil which have already shaken earth, and which, uttered "once more," shall shake not earth only, but also heaven. High destiny! but not his whose portrait we have now drawn.

We have tried to draw his mental, but not his physical likeness. And yet it has all along been blended with our thoughts, like the figure of one known from childhood, like the figure of our own beloved and long-lost father. We see the venerable old man, newly returned from a botanical excursion, laden with flowers and weeds (for no one knew better than he that every weed is a flower—it is the secret of his poetry), with his high narrow forehead, his gray locks, his glancing shoe-buckles, his clean dress somewhat ruffled in the woods, his mild countenance, his simple abstracted air. We, too, become abstracted as we gaze, following in thought the outline of his history—his early struggles—his love—his adventures in London—his journal, where, on the brink of starvation, he wrote the affecting words, "*O Sally, for you*"—his rescue by Burke—his taking orders—his return to his native place—his mounting the pulpit stairs, not caring what his old enemies thought of him or his sermon—his marriage—the entry, more melancholy by far than the other, made years after in reference to it, "*yet happiness was denied*"—the publication of his different works—the various charges he occupied—his child-like surprise at getting so much money for the "Tales of the Hall"—his visit to Scotland—his mistaking the Highland chiefs for foreigners, and bespeaking them in bad French—his figure as he went. dogged by the *caddie* through the lanes of the auld town of Edinburgh, which he preferred infinitely to the new—the "aul' fule" he made of himself in pursuit of a second wife, &c., &c.; so absent do we become in thinking over all this, that it disturbs his abstraction; he starts, stares, asks us into his parsonage, and we are about to accept the offer, when we awake, and, lo! it is a dream.

JOHN FOSTER.

THERE are two classes of character of whom the biography is likely to be peculiarly interesting. One includes those whose lives have been passed in the glare of publicity—who have bulked largely in public estimation, and who have mingled much with the leading characters of the age. The life of such includes in it, in fact, a multitude of lives, and turns out to be, not a solitary picture, but an entire gallery of interesting portraits. The other class comprises those of whom the world knows little, but is eager to know much—who, passing their lives in severe seclusion, have, nevertheless, given such assurance of their manhood as to excite in the public mind an intense curiosity to know more of their habits, feelings, and history. Such a one was John Foster. While his works were widely circulated, and produced a profound impression upon the thinking minds of the country, himself was to the majority only a name. Few could tell what he was, or where he lived—what were the particulars of his outward history, or what had been the course of his mental training. He published little, he seldom appeared at public meetings, his name was never in the newspapers—when he wrote, it was generally in periodicals of limited circulation and sectarian character, and when he preached, it was to small audiences and in obscure villages. There thus hung about him a certain shade of mystery, shaping itself to the colossal estimate of his genius, which prevailed. He appeared a great man under hiding; and while some of his ardent admirers found or forced their way into his grisly den, and ascertained the prominent features of his character and facts in his life, more were left in the darkness of mystification and conjecture. For twenty years, for instance, we ourselves have been enthusiasts in reference to this writer's genius, and yet, till recently, we never so much as saw his portrait.

The veil has at length been removed. In the interesting volumes before us we find, and principally in his own words, a full and faithful register of the leading events in his life, and of the more interesting movements in his spiritual history. The book is arranged on a plan somewhat similar to that adopted in Carlyle's work on Cromwell. The biography constitutes an intermitting chain between the numerous letters, and is executed in a modest and intelligent manner. Besides his correspondence, there are large and valuable excerpts from his journals, and to the whole are appended interesting though slight notices of his character, from the pen of Mr. Sheppard.

Throughout the whole of these volumes we have been impressed with the idea of a mind imperfectly reconciled and indifferently adjusted to the state of society of which it was a part—to the creed to which it had declared its adherence—to the very system of things which surrounded it. This is true of many independent and powerful spirits; but in Foster's mind the antagonism has this peculiarity—it is united to deep reverence and to sincere belief. It is not the fruit of any captious or malignant disposition—it does not spring from any sinister motive. The guilty wish is never, with him, the parent of the gloomy thought. The tremendous doubts which oppress him have forced themselves into the sphere of his soul, and hang there as if sustained by the power of some dark enchantment. You see his mind laboring under an eclipse which will not pass away. In contemplation of the mysteries of earth and time, he stands helpless. Indeed, such gloomy cogitations formed so large a part of his mental scenery, and had so long riveted his gaze, that you can almost conceive him disappointed had they suddenly disappeared. Like the prisoner of Chillon, who, habituated to the gloom of his dungeon, and having made friends with his dismal companions, at last "regained his freedom with a sigh," Foster would have stared strangely, and almost unhappily, though it had been at the apparition of the "new heavens and the new earth" arising in room of the present, which his melancholy fancy had so dreadfully discolored. The causes of this habitual gloom seem to have been complex. In the first place, he was naturally a man of a morbid disposition. His mind fastened and clung to the dark side of every question —to the more rugged horn of each great dilemma—to the shadows, and not to the lights, of every picture. To do this was with him an instinct, which instead of repressing, he nursed into a savage luxury. Secondly, he was for a large portion of his life a solitary, struggling, and disappointed man—preaching to people who did not understand him, struggling with straitened circumstances, and unsustained, till middle-age, by the sympathy of any female friend. Had a man of his temperament met sooner with the breeze of general and generous appreciation; and, above all, had he found in youth such a kindred and congenial spirit as afterwards, in his accomplished and gifted wife, he had lived a much happier and more useful existence, and taken a kindlier, and, we trust, a truer view of the world and of mankind. Thirdly, as an eloquent writer elsewhere observes, Foster never gave himself a real scientific education, and although possessed of keenest sagacity, never rose into the sphere of a great and a trained philosopher. He was to this what a brave bandit is to a regular soldier. Scientific culture is sure to beget scientific calm. The philosopher is taught to take a wide, comprehensive, dispassionate, and rounded view of things, which never frets his heart, if it often fails to satisfy his intellect. Foster's glimpses of truth, on the contrary, are intense and vivid, but comparatively narrow, and are tantalizing in exact proportion to their vividness and intensity. He sees his points in a light so brilliant that it deepens the surrounding darkness. His minute mode of insight. too, contributed to his melancholy. He looks at objects so narrowly that, as to a microscope, they present nothing but naked and enlarged ugliness. His eye strips away all those fine illusions of distance which are after all, as real as the nearer and narrower view. This is the curse which blasts him—to see too clearly, and the lens through which he looks becomes truly a "terrible crystal." Like Cassandra, he might well wail for his fatal gift. It is a dowry she got in wrath, and has faithfully transmitted to many besides Foster, who may with her exclaim—

> "O ill to me the lot awarded,
> Thou evil Pythian god."

From man, thus too utterly bare before him, he turns away, with a deep pensive joy, to Nature, feeling that she is true, were all else untrue—that she is beautiful, were all else deformed—that she stands innocent and erect, though her tenant has fallen—and, like a child in her mother's arms, does he repose, regaining old illusions, and recalling long-departed dreams of joy. There is something to us peculiarly tender and pathetic in Foster's love of nature. It is not so much an admiration as it is a passionate and perpetual longing. It is not a worship, but a love. He throws his being into nature. It is as if he felt his heart budding in the spring trees, his pulse beating high in the midnight tempest and in the ocean billow, his soul shooting up, like living fire, into Snowdon, as he gazes upon it; or we might almost imagine him the divorced spirit of some lovely scene, yearning and panting after renewed communion, "gazing himself away" into the bosom of nature again, while the murmuring of streams, and the song of breezes, and the waving of pines, were singing of these strange nuptials, the soft epithalamium. He engages in mystic converse with the creation. He seeks for meanings in her mighty countenance, which are not always revealed to him. He asks her awful and unanswered questions. He seems to cry out to the river "What meanest thou, thou eloquent babbler; wilt thou never speak plain, wilt thou nerer shape me any distinct utterance, from the vague and soft tumults of thine everlasting song?"—to the rocks and mountains, "Will ye never reveal those secrets of an elder day, which are piled up in your massive walls; to your solemn hieroglyphics shall there never arrive the key?" but to add, in stern resignation, "Be it so, then; retain your tremendous silence, or utter on your inarticulate sounds; better these than the jargon, the laughter, and the blasphemies of the reptile and miscreant race of man; to you, my dumb kindred, I am nearer and dearer than to those that so speak."

In forming, however, such a view of man and of life, Foster has committed, we think, an enormous error—the great mistake of his history. He has failed to see the beauty of life, its hopeful tendencies, the dignity of that discipline which is ripening man for a nobler destiny, the sou of goodness which underlies even the evils, the abuses, and the mistakes of the world, and the glory which springs from human suffering, and shines through human tears. In all this, he sees little else than unmitigated and unredeemed misery and guilt, and flies to the prospect of death for relief, as the opium-eater to his drug, or the drunkard to his dram-bottle. "I have yet," he says, toward the close of his life, "one luminary, the visage of death." And in the rising of that pale luminary, that ghostly sun, he expects a reply to all his questionings, and a rest to all the wanderings of his spirit. Surely he expected far too much from such a source. For, in the first place, since the tale of the universe is infinite, can it be told all at once to a finite being? It is beyond even the might of Death to give to a mind infinite illumination, to which it has failed to give infinite capacity. It may, it must, greatly extend the view, and brighten the medium; but to suppose that it instantly makes all mysteries plain, were to leave little to do for the vast eternity beyond it. Besides, may not mystery continue to be an atmosphere fit for rearing certain future, as it is for rearing certain present, conditions of spiritual being. The caterpillar and the butterfly respire the same air. Certain plants, and those of a strong and hardy kind, grow best in the shade. To suppose that Death should explain every enigma is, in fact, to enthrone it in the room of Omnipotence. Thirdly, unless first we be reconciled to life, unless we learn to interpret its sublime hieroglyphics, to feel its divine beauty, to read its "open secret," to adore while we wonder at its darkest dispensations, what can death do for us? The man who, loathing, despising, reviling life, finding only desolation and barrenness in all its borders, turns away from under the vine and the fig-tree, sits with lonely Jonah under his withered gourd, saying, "I do well to be angry, even unto death," is guilty of cowardice, if not of essential suicide: he may be a gifted, but is hardly a heroic man. "It is," says Schiller, "a serious thing to die—it is a more serious thing to live." So it is a great and glorious thing to die; it is a thing greater, more glorious, god-like, to live a resigned, active, and "blessed," if not happy life. To use the language of

Sartor Resartus, Foster has been in the everlasting no; he has been in the centre of indifference, but he has not reached the everlasting yea; he has not heard, or not received, its sweet and solemn evangel—he has tarried too long in the valley of the shadow of death, and spent many needless hours in the dungeon of the giant Despair; and worse, has dreamed, that to come forth from its threshold was to reach the Celestial City by a single step!

Before proceeding to speak of Foster's merits, we have, in corroboration of these remarks, to advance against him one or two serious charges, made more in sorrow than in anger. We charge him, in the first place, with a sort of moral cowardice, which it is painful to observe in a man of such gigantic proportions. In his views of moral evil there is more of the fascinated fear of the planet-struck than of the strong courage of the combatant. He looks at it rather than seeks to strike it down. Knowing that Omnipotence alone can prostrate it in its entireness—that Omniscience alone can explain its existence—he is not sufficiently alive to the facts that it is reducible, that every one may, in some degree, reduce it, that each smallest reduction proves that it is not infinite, and that the farther you reduce evil, the nearer you reach the solution of the great problems—why it is, and whence it rose. He seems sometimes to regard the efforts of men to remove or mitigate, moral, or even physical, evil, with as much contempt as he would the efforts of barbarians, with their cries and kettle-drums, to drive away an eclipse from off the face of the sun. His *own* attempts to abate evil are thus paralyzed. He keeps, indeed, his post—he maintains the contest—but it is languidly, and with frequent looks cast behind, toward a great reserve of force which he expects to be brought, but which is slow to come, into action. It is the old story of the wagoner and Hercules. The road is miry, the rain is heavy, he is weary, how easy it were for the god to come down and perform the task! And because he will not yet, Foster becomes sullen, disappointed, and all but desperate. Let no one say that we are not fair judges of a mind so peculiar as his, that we know not what doubts and difficulties oppressed him, or how they affected his spirit. Every thinking mind is haunted, more or less, by precisely those questions which Foster felt himself unable to solve. Luther felt them in the Warteburg, but bated on account of them not one jot of heart or hope. Evil there was in the world; he was sent to make it less; that was all he knew, and that was quite sufficient for his resolute and robust spirit. Howard felt them in his "Circumnavigation of Charity," but instead of speculating as to why prisons were needed at all, he went on and made them better. Every missionary to the heathen feels such difficulties meeting them in their very darkest shape, and yet perseveres in his holy work, and if he can smite away but a finger from the black colossal statue of evil which stands up before him, is content. Should any deem that we misrepresent Foster's feelings and sentiments on this subject, we refer them to his journals and letters, and particularly to that most withering and unhappy letter addressed to the Rev. John Harris, author of the "Great Teacher," &c.

We find not less distinct evidence of the same disease in his contributions to the "Eclectic," particularly in his review of "Chalmer's Astronomical Discourses"—in our opinion a very forced, clumsy, and unsatisfactory critique. There, at the supposition of snow existing in some of the other planets, he startles in terror, seeing in it a sign that evil has found its way there as well as here. He is so frightened at this little speck, as almost to back out from the discoveries of modern astronomy altogether. Now, we think this a cowardice unworthy, yet characteristic, of Foster; for, in the first place, what is there so terrific in snow the pure, innocent, beautiful meteor, falling from heaven like the shed feathers of the celestial dove, or lying, a many millioned mirror to the moonbeams? Should not, on the contrary, that far gleam be welcomed as a proof of unity among the heavenly bodies, as attesting the omnipresence of certain general laws, shall we say?—as a white signal from that stranger land, to tell us that a race of beings, not altogether unallied to us, are there, it may be, engaged in similar struggles, and destined to similar triumphs with ourselves? But, secondly, is snow necessarily the sign of a curse, or a certain indication of the existence of sin? This, we think, springs from a theory universally held at one time by a certain school of theologians, which the researches of geology have exploded, and which Foster's powerful intellect ought, apart from these, to have taught him to reject, that every species of physical evil is the product of moral, that every slight inconvenience, as well as formidable mischief, may be traced to the same root. Such an absurd theory teaches its votaries to cower under the falling snow as under the curse of the Eternal—to find a new testimony to the existence of evil in the icicles—glorious ear-rings!—which each morning hang under the eaves; and in every sound, from the earthquake to the sneeze, to overhear the voice of Sin. No; this will never do. Step forth, John Foster, like a brave man, into that strange snow of Mars, and peradventure thou mayest find a braver Evan Dhu, kicking away a luxurious snowball from under the head of his retainer, or a gallant footman offering himself up to the wolves in his master's stead, or a noble little band of explorers cutting their perilous passage to the summit of some wilder Wetterhorn—finer spectacles, be sure, than wert thou to see ever so many perfect, and perfectly insipid ladies and gentlemen, reclining in some lazy lubberland of perpetual sunshine. Step forth, bathe in the bracing cold of the clime, confront its stern winds, consider its laws of austere and awful progress, and come back a healthier, happier, and better man.

Had this speculation on snow been only a passing reverie, it had been unworthy any serious notice. But, like the snow on the dusky and dark-red brow of Mars, it lies significant —a still settled index of much behind and beyond it. It involves in it all the elements of Foster's quarrel with the system of things; for, as assuredly as in Byron's case, it was a quarrel; nor were their grounds so dissimilar as might have been at first supposed. Neither knew the real meaning of that grand old fable of Prometheus, as shadowing forth the history of man, nay, forming a dim but colossal type of that higher mystery—the mystery of godliness—bearing to it such a resemblance as does a battlement of evening clouds to the mountains over which it stands, and whose shapes it mutely mimics—the glory of suffering, the beauty of sorrow, as teachers, friends, guides, were to them in a great measure veiled. Unphilosophically confounding physical and moral evil, of which the one seemed to them the monstrous body, the other the malignant soul, of some portentous and unearthly shape, they both bow before it—to the one it becomes a god, his only god, detested and adored; to the other an object of melancholy wonder and powerless hatred. Indeed, so similar are the feelings of Foster to those entertained and expressed by the Byron school of skeptics, that, as a profound thinker recently remarked to us, the change of a single word will serve to identify them. The Byronling says, *since* so and so is the case, the Deity must be this and that; Foster, and his *foster-bairns* say, *if it* were this and that, the Deity were so and so.

But, secondly, we charge Foster with taking up an attitude of view and observation which rendered any just conception of the universe or its Author impossible, and which *a priori* throws discredit upon any theory of explanation propounded by himself. His attitude is that of one who confounds the shade over his own mind with the universe which it discolors, in whose eye (as in the well-known fable) the monster-fly swallows up the sun, and who, because he is capable of asking the infinite question, imagines that, therefore, he is able, or entitled to receive, the infinite reply. Nothing but such an infinite answer could appease such inquiries as Foster asks at the earth and the heavens. And because the earth spins round, and the skies shine on in silence, and no such reply as he craves will ascend from their deepest caverns, or come down from their loftiest summits, Foster is disappointed, the more in proportion to his love, just as the more you love any individual, the more you are chagrined if he will not answer you some curious question, but remains obstinately dumb. And though, as we have said, he is fond of questioning nature, and loves her old and solemn harmonies, he is no "Fine ear" to catch that subtler speech, that fairy music, that "language within language," that angelic strain, which some few purged and prepared spirits, who can the "bird language fully tell, and that which roses say so well," hear, or seem to hear, in the rustle of the leaves awakened at midnight from their dreams of God—in the great psalm of the autumn blasts—in the blue sweet self-talk of the love-sick summer waves—in the blue smile of the sky—nay, in the hush of evening, and the stammering sparkle of the stars. To these low and silvery whispers, piercing the clash of all common and terrific sounds, like the calm "No" of Shadrach, Meshach, and Abednego, heard amidst the idolatrous symphonies and cymbals on the plain of Dura, Foster's ear is deaf as Byron's. He is aware of their existence, indeed; he listens to hear them, but they will not speak to him their profoundest tidings; he hears only a great tumult, but knows not what it is—a tumult of grandeur, terror—sweet, and despairing tones, endlessly intermingled—and dies, believing that God is love, but not feeling, with Tennyson, that

> "Every cloud that spreads above
> And veileth love itself is Love."

What Foster demands is precisely that which cannot here, perhaps never, be granted: it is a logical demonstration of the goodness and wisdom of God: such a demonstration seems impossible: it supposes the possibility of a just doubt on such a subject; and yet if this doubt do once enter the mind, no mere argument can ever expel it. It represents the question as to the character of Deity in the light of a dreadful game, which may possibly go against him. It proves, after all, no more than this—that there is a very high probability that God is not a demon. On such bladders do some men try to swim on the ocean of the infinite mind. Far better to plunge into it at once, trusting implicitly and fearlessly to those voices within the soul—to those whispers in nature—to those smiles on earth below and heaven above—to those indefinite but profound impressions, not to speak of those distinct declarations of God's Word, which do not demonstrate, but intuitively and irresistibly communicate, the tidings that "All is well!"

"After all, we are in good hands," was the simple conclusive reply of a well-conditioned gentleman of our acquaintance to one who had, in a strain of morbid eloquence, taken the darker side conclusive, because it expressed what is the natural feeling of all untainted and unsophisticated minds, as well as the mature and ultimate result of the highest order of philosophic thinkers. But it is altogether impossible to reach this conclusion, through that faithless process which John Foster employs; as impossible, as by digging down through the darkness of earth to reach the sun and stars of the antipodes. It is otherwise that Sartor comes out at last, into his clear, stern azure. It is otherwise that Goethe meant, it is understood, to lead Faust up into his Mount of Vision and temple of worship.

Our final charge, again, is that he takes too dark, morbid, and monkish a view of man and of society. From this indeed, seem to spring his other errors. He who doubts of man can hardly fail to doubt of God. To believe in man is an indispensable requisite to a proper conception of Deity. Of course we do not mean to deny the doctrine of human depravity; but we do think that Foster's views of man's nature, whether as exhibited in individual character or in collective society, are far too stern and harsh. We would as soon judge of an assembly of living men and women from a book of anatomical sketches, as of the true character of the world from Foster's pictures. Earth is not the combination of hell and chaos which he represents it to be. Men are not the pigmy fiends, Lilliputians in intellect, Brobdignagians in crime, from whose society he shrinks in loathing, and the tie connecting himself with whom he would cut in sunder if he could. The past history of society is not that dance of death, that hideous procession of misery and guilt toward destruction, which paints itself on the gloomy retina of his eye. We protest, in the name of our fallen but human perishing, but princely family, against such libels as Gulliver's Travels and Foster's entire works. Were such statements true, we see no help for it but an act of universal, simultaneous suicide, and a giving up of God's creation, on the part of Adam's sons, as a bad job. What a fierce, impotent scowl, he continually casts upon even the innocent amusements of the race—such as children's balls, social parties—begrudging, it would seem, even to doomed and predestinated criminals, such consolations as their case would admit of. More cruel than the ancient crucifiers, he would grant no stupefying nor cheering draught to the expiring malefactor. How reluctant, too, he is to admit any moral merit (intellectual merit he is always ready to concede) to those who differ from him in creed, not, perhaps, more widely than he is found, after all, to differ from the rest of the Christian world! How he prowls, like a hyena, round the bedsides of dying skeptics, though repeatedly owning himself so far a skeptic, to drink in their last groans, and insult whether the calm or the horror of their closing hours; staking thus in a measure, the holy cause of religion upon a wretched computation of dying beds, upon the *pros* and *cons* of the expressions of disease, delirium, and despair—a task fit enough for a contributor to the "Methodist Magazine," but unworthy of a spirit like Foster's. And how slow to admit any degree of interest, or of poetry, or of grandeur, in those colossal faiths which have ruled for ages the great majority of mankind!—an absurdity as great as though one were to go about to deny the lustre of the serpent's eyes, because his breath was poison, or the beauty of the tiger's skin, because his drink was blood. And, then, by what a safety-valve he does escape from the consequences of his fatalism, by supposing a general jail-delivery of criminals, who, by his own showing, are no more guilty than the avalanche which destroys the Alpine traveller, or the sandy column which whelms the wanderer in the desert!

After all this, it may seem paradoxical to assert that we think Foster an amiable man. He was so, undoubtedly, if universal testimony can be credited; but he was a slave, in the first place, to unsettled doubts, and, ultimately, to a partial and inconsistent system, as well as, throughout all his life, to a gloomy temperament which clouded his native disposition. His genius reminds us of the moon, but of the moon turned into blood, forced, against her nature, into a lowering, portentous aspect—no longer the still, calm mistress of the night, but a meteor of wrath and fear, emitting at best a gloomy smile, and furnishing a light, fit only to guide the footsteps of murderers, and preside at the assignation of ghosts. We turn, now, gladly from these objections to remark some interesting peculiarities in Foster's character and intellect, as evinced in his "Memoirs," "Correspondence," and articles in the "Eclectic Review." We notice, first, his generosity and width as a critic. Narrow as a moral judge, he is, as a critic of authors and books, entirely the reverse. He sympathizes with all genuine excellence. This alone proves, we think, his superiority to Hall. Hall, we fear, had little admiration for other writers beyond a very few, either inferior to, or cognate with himself. His treatment of Coleridge, for instance, would be insufferably insolent, were it not ludicrously absurd. Having never taken the trouble to master so much as the *language* in which Coleridge *thought*, his verdict on him is as worthless as a plain English scholar's were upon the metres of Pindar. To modern poetry, too, and all its miracles, he was notoriously indifferent. Byron he never read, an omission as contemptible as though he had not gone forth to see a comet which had made itself visible at noonday. Wordsworth and Southey he habitually maligned. Now all this may seem very great to such fawning parasites as the late Dr. Balmer, who has carefully recorded it in a bit of Boswellism he contributed to his remains, but seems superlatively unworthy of such a man as Hall. Foster, on the other hand, is a genial and a generous praiser, of much beneath, much on a level, and much above his own mark. He has a kind word to say for poor Cottle and his Fall of Cambria. He is enthusiastic in his admiration of Hall, Chalmers, Fox, Grattan, Curran, Tooke, &c. Coleridge is the god of his idolatry, and bitterly does he deplore his miserable habits. Of a transcendent dramatic work (could it be Cain or the Cenci?) he says, "I was never so fiercely carried off by Pegasus before—the fellow *neighed* as he ascended." All works he seems to have judged, not by an arbitrary canon of his own or of others' establishment, but by the impulse given to his own mind, the stir of respondent strength, whether in contradiction or consent, awakened within him, and the joy which they had the power to spread over his melancholy spirit, like sunshine surprising a sullen tarn into smiles.

We notice in these volumes numerous evidences of Foster's romantic tendencies. He was a lover of solitary and moonlight walks. "In Chichester there is still a chapel, where the well-worn bricks of the aisles exhibit the traces of his solitary pacings to and fro by moonlight." In all beautiful and majestic scenes he invariably lost himself, as men do in the mazes of a wood. Reverie was his principal luxury, and became his darling sin. In combating the romantic tendency in one of his essays, he is, in reality, fighting with himself; just as, strange to tell, the objections he confutes in his famous sermon on missions re-appear, from his own pen, in a letter to Harris, written years afterwards. Formerly we said, "Foster fighting with a fatalist, reminds us of the whole ocean into tempest tossed, to waft a feather, or to drown a fly." Alas, we now find that Foster and the fatalist were forms of the same mind, and that the fatalist remains last upon the field. So, having shrived himself of his original romance by writing an essay against it, the old nature returned with double force than formerly, and was in him to his dying day. In connection with this, we notice the abundance and beauty of his natural imagery. No one has turned to more account, in his writings, the charms of nature, and particularly the evanescent and ghostly glories of the night, the tints of moonlit flowers, the colors of midnight fields, the shadows of woods, the shapes of mountains resting against the stars, all the fine gradations of the coming on of evening, all the wandering voices of the darkness, speaking what in the day they seem to dare not do, and all those "solemn meditations," as peculiar to night as its celestial fires, were well known and inexpressibly dear to the soul of this lonely man. In his use of such images we observe this peculiarity. Some men surround their minds with them *unconsciously*, they go out to the fields without one thought of collecting images or illustrations, and yet come home laden with them, as with burs or other herbage, which we unwittingly gather in the woods. Foster goes out on express purpose to find them, as if he were a-nutting; looks at every object with this question, How can I employ you in the expression of truth? and returns triumphant with a thousand analogies. This, we think, has somewhat affected the naturalness and freedom of his imagery. We should prefer had he allowed the beauties of nature to slide into his soul, and to blend with his thoughts—

> "Like some sweet beguiling melody;
> So sweet, we know not we are listening to it."

Another phase of this romantic tendency was his extreme attachment to the society of cultivated females, and the conception he formed of the married life as the panacea of his ills. In such company he laid aside the monk, and became all gentleness and good humor. It acted like a spell upon him, to soothe his most unquiet feelings, and to lay for a season his darkest doubts. It roused, too, the faculties of his mind, and he never was half so eloquent, neither in his writing, nor in the pulpit, nor in the company of his co-mates in intellect, Anderson and Hall, as when, the evening shadows, or the first moonbeams, stealing into the room, he discoursed to "fascinating females," who could understand as well as listen, and feel as well as understand, of the "feelings and value of genius," or of topics dearer and nobler still, while it seemed, in his own beautiful words, "as if the soul of Eloisa pervaded all the air." Such moments he relished with the intensest gratification; they seemed to him foretastes of Paradise, and of the society of angels, and he might well say that they should never be "forgotten." Out of those "fascinating females" he selected one almost a duplicate of himself—equally intellectual, equally well-informed, equally pious, and equally oppressed with the tremendous darkness of this dark economy. It was like the marriage of two moonlit clouds in the silent sky! To this lady (Miss Maria Snooke—Phœbus, what a name!) he addressed his first celebrated essays. From her society he expected much happiness. On the eve of the marriage, he met, he tells us, "the snow-drops and other signs and approaches of the spring, with a degree of interest which has never accompanied any former vernal equinox." And his expectations seem to have been abundantly fulfilled. After many happy years of intercourse, and latterly, on her part, much severe suffering, she died, leaving him less to regret her loss than to grieve that their spirits had not entered together within that mighty veil which had so long tantalized and saddened both.

"The living are not envied of the dead." But how often are the dead envied by the living! And no one ever felt this solemn envy more than Foster. We can conceive him kneeling in charnel-houses, and praying their ashes to break silence and speak out. We can conceive him crying aloud amid the midnight hills for some wandering spirit of the departed to render up the secret; and as friend after friend dropped away into the silent land, this impatient eargerness strengthened, and almost amounted to a feeling that those he loved were bound to come back and relieve his harrowing anxieties. And it shook him with the very agony of desire when the wife of his bosom and of his soul—his shadow in the other sex, whose doubts, and fears, and desires on this subject were the counterpart of his own—departed first within the veil. We can image him on his widowed pillow praying for and straining his eyes for her re-appearance—less to see her beloved face once more than to hear some authentic tidings of the shadowy world. But she, too, was silent. She, too, had taken the dread oath of secrecy which all the dead must take; and he had to recur, in his disappointed loneliness, to the prospect of speedily joining her in that strange company, and of becoming, in his turn, as intelligent and as uncommunicative as she.

This supposition is the less extravagant, as we find from these memoirs that Foster was a firm believer in apparitions, and in all the other departments of what this enlightened age—which has discovered that the soul of man is a secretion of the brain, and that the snail is growing up by slow stages to the Shakspeare (and we suppose the Shakspeare to the Supreme God!)—calls exploded superstitions. He grasped at every line, however frail, which linked him to the spiritual world. If he saw not visions, he dreamed dreams, felt presentiments, shuddered as he almost called up to his imagination the form of a ghost. This "folly of the wise," if a folly it be, he shared with many of the greatest minds of the age—with Napoleon, Byron, Coleridge, and Shelley, who all felt that there were some things in heaven and earth more than are dreamt of in our philosophies. In Foster these feelings did not amount to fears. They were rather strong yet shuddering desires to know the best or the worst which spiritual beings could tell, or intimate about that future state of existence of which he felt that Revelation had told him little, and Nature nothing at all. From the company of real solid sorrows, and of men whom he deemed "earthly, sensual, devilish," he turned eagerly, yet pensively, to seek communion with the spirits of the departed; but even these sad companions were shy to him—they met him not in his solitary walks, and in all his wanderings he was "alone with the night."

And yet, in spite of all these melancholy musings and romantic tendencies, Foster was a keen, stern, and sarcastic observer of men and manners—of society and political progress. In politics he was a "Radical and something more" —an independent thinker, despising all ties of party, and standing on every question like a fourth estate—one who could sit upon the ground and tell strange stories of the deaths of kings, and who never in one instance sacrificed an atom of the right to an acre of the expedient. It is worth while reading in this work his musings, as of a separate spirit, upon the public transactions of his day. In society, too, he sat an insulated being, whose silence was often more formidable than his words. His face, even when he spoke not, shone a quiet mirror to the "thoughts and intents of the hearts" of those around him, and he came away with their past as well as present history silently inscribed upon his mind. His conversational sarcasm was tremendous. "Was not the Emperor Alexander a very pious man?" "Very pious," he answered; "I believe he said grace ere he swallowed Poland." We could quote, if we durst, unpublished specimens still racier. Hall himself is said to have felt somewhat nervous in his presence when in this mood; and there is a floating rumor of a meeting between him and Lord Brougham on some educational question, in which his lordship came off, and shabbily, second best.

Foster's indolence has been often, but, we think, unjustly, condemned. It ought rather to be deplored. Unfurnished with a regular training, yet furnished with an exquisitely sensitive taste, early "damned to the mines" of hopeless professional toil, transferred thence to the drudgery of writing for bread—never gifted with a fluent language nor a rapid pen—what wonder that he found composition an ungracious task, or that he shrank from it with a growing and deepening disgust? Our surprise is that he wrote so much, and not that he wrote so little. Latterly, but for an overwhelming sense of duty, he would not have written at all. If we saw a giant, whose arms had been cut off, moving in impotent strength his bleeding fragments, who would not weep at the spectacle? In such mutilated might sat Foster at his desk.

His "Journal and Correspondence" contain much attractive and interesting matter. His letters, without ease, have great sincerity, calm discernment, disturbed by bursts of misanthropical power, as when he calls for a tempest of fire and brimstone upon the Russians, on their invasion of Poland, and a perpetual stream of sarcasm, adds a tart tinge to the whole. His "Journal," on the other hand, is rich in those thoughts which procreate thought in others—in descriptions of natural objects which he encountered—in quiet sidelong glances into human character—in the expression of gloomy and desolate feelings, and in sudden, momentary, and timorous glimpses into the deeper abysses of thought than those where his spirit usually dwells. How grand this, for instance:—"Argument from miracles for the truth of the Christian doctrines. Surely it is fair to believe that those who received from heaven superhuman power received likewise superhuman wisdom. Having rung the great bell of the universe, the sermon to follow must be extraordinary." Hear, again, this criticism on Burke:—"Burke's sentences are pointed at the end—instinct with pungent sense to the last syllable; they are like a charioteer's whip, which not only has a long and effective lash, but cracks and inflicts a still smarter sensation at the end. They are like some serpents, whose life is said to be fiercest in the tail." The whole "Journal," indeed, is a repository of such things.

How much of Foster's originality lay in his thoughts, or how much in his images, or how much of it resulted from his early isolation from suitable books and kindred minds, we stay not to inquire. As it is, we have in his works the collected thoughts of a powerful mind that has lived "collaterally or aside" to the world—that never flattered a popular prejudice—that never bent to a popular idol—that never deserted in the darkest hour the cause of liberty—that never swore to the Shibboleth of a party, or, at least, never kept its vow—and that now stands up before us alone, massive and conspicuous, a mighty and mysterious fragment, the Stonehenge of modern moralists. Shall we inscribe *immortality* upon the shapeless yet sublime structure? He who reared it seems, from the elevation he has now reached, to answer, No; what is the thing you call immortality to me, who have cleft that deep shadow and entered on this greater and brighter state of being?

We dare not say, with a writer formerly quoted, that to "Foster the cloud has now become the sun." But certainly we may say that to him, "behold the darkness is past, and the true light now shineth," if not in its noonday effulgence, yet at least in its mild and twilight softness.

In the night he dwelt, and although the visage of death may not have been to him the glorious luminary he expected, yet is it not much that the night is gone, and gone for ever? We take our leave of him in his own words—"'Paid the debt of nature.' No; it is not paying a debt, it is rather like bringing a note to a bank to obtain solid gold in exchange for it. In this case you bring this cumbrous body, which is nothing worth, and which you could not wish to retain long; you lay it down and receive for it, from the eternal treasures, liberty, victory, knowledge, rapture."

THOMAS HOOD.

It is the lot of some men of genius to be born as if in the blank space between Milton's L'Allegro and Penseroso—their proximity to both originally equal, and their adhesion to the one or the other depending upon casual circumstances. While some pendulate perpetually between the grave and the gay, others are carried off bodily, as it happens, by the comic or the tragic muse. A few there are, who seem to say, of their own deliberate option, "Mirth, with thee we mean to live;" deeming it better to go to the house of feasting than to that of mourning—while the storm of adversity drives others to pursue sad and dreary paths, not at first congenial to their natures. Such men as Shakspeare, Burns, and Byron, continue, all their lives long, to pass, in rapid and perpetual change, from the one province to the other; and this, indeed, is the main source of their boundless ascendency over the general mind. In Young, of the "Night Thoughts," the laughter never very joyous, is converted, through the effect of gloomy casualties, into the ghostly grin of the skeleton Death—the pointed satire is exchanged for the solemn sermon. In Cowper, the fine schoolboy glee which inspirits his humor goes down at last, and is quenched like a spark in the wild abyss of his madness—"John Gilpin" merges in the "Castaway." Hood, on the other hand, with his strongest tendencies originally to the pathetic and the fantastic-serious, shrinks in timidity from the face of the inner sun of his nature—shies the stoop of the descending Pythonic power—and, feeling that if he wept at all it were floods of burning and terrible tears, laughs, and does little else but laugh instead.

We look upon this writer as a quaint masker—as wearing above a manly and profound nature, a fantastic and deliberate disguise of folly. He reminds us of Brutus, cloaking under pretended idiocy, a stern and serious design, which burns his breast, but which he chooses in this way only to disclose. Or, he is like Hamlet—able to form a magnificent purpose, but, from constitutional weakness, not able to incarnate it in effective action. A deep message has come to him from the heights of his nature, but, like the ancient prophet, he is forced to cry out, "I cannot speak—I am a child!"

Certainly there was, at the foundation of Hood's soul, a seriousness, which all his puns and mummeries could but indifferently conceal. Jacques, in the forest of Arden, mused not with a profounder pathos, or in quainter language, upon the sad pageant of humanity, than does he; and yet, like him, his "lungs" are ever ready to "crow like chanticleer" at the sight of its grotesquer absurdities. Verily, the goddess of melancholy owes a deep grudge to the mirthful magician, who carried off such a promising votary. It is not every day that one who might have been a great serious poet will condescend to sink into a punster and editor of comic annuals. And, were it not that his original tendencies continued to be manifested to the last, and that he turned his drollery to important account, we would be tempted to be angry, as well as to regret, that he chose to play the fool rather than King Lear in the play.

As a poet, Hood belongs to the school of John Keats and Leigh Hunt, with qualities of his own, and an all but entire freedom from their peculiarities of manner and style. What strikes us, in the first place, about him, is his great variety of subject and mode of treatment. His works are in two small duodecimo volumes; and yet we find in them five or six distinct styles attempted—and attempted with success. There is the classical—there is the fanciful, or, as we might almost call it, the "Midsummer Night"—there is the homely tragic narrative—there is the wildly grotesque—there is the light—and there is the grave and pathetic—lyric. And, besides, there is a style, which we despair of describing by any one single or compound epithet, of which his "Elm Tree" and "Haunted House" are specimens—resembling Tennyson's "Talking Oak"—and the secret and power of which, perhaps, lie in the feeling of mystic correspondence between man and inanimate nature—in the start of momentary consciousness, with which we sometimes feel that in nature's company we are not alone, that nature's silence is not that of death; and are aware, in the highest and grandest sense, that we are "made of dust," and that the dust from which we were once taken is still divine. We know few volumes of poetry where we find, in the same compass, so little mannerism, so little self-repetition, such a varied concert, along with such unique harmony of sound.

Through these varied numerous styles, we find two or three main elements distinctly traceable in all Hood's poems. One is a singular subtlety in the perception of minute analogies. The weakness, as well as the strength of his poetry, is derived from this source. His serious verse, as well as his witty prose, is laden and encumbered with thick coming fancies. Hence, some of his finest pieces are tedious, without being long. Little more than ballads in size, they are books in the reader's feeling. Every one knows how resistance adds to the idea of extension, and how roughness impedes progress. Some of Hood's poems, such as "Lycus," are rough as the Centaur's hide; and, having difficulty in passing along, you are tempted to pass them by altogether. And though a few, feeling that there is around them the power and spell of genius, generously cry, there's true metal here, when we have leisure, we must return to this—yet they never do. In fact, Hood has not been able to infuse human interest into his fairy or mythological creations. He has conceived them in a happy hour; surely on one of those days when the soul and nature are one—when one calm bond of peace seems to unite all things—when the "very cattle in the fields appear to have great and tranquil thoughts"—when the sun seems to slumber, and the sky to smile—when the air becomes a wide balm, and the low wind, as it wanders over flowers, seems telling some happy tidings in each gorgeous ear, till the rose blushes a deep crimson, and the tulip lifts up a more towering head, and the violet shrinks more modestly away as at lovers' whispers; in such a favored hour—when the first strain of music might have arisen, or the first stroke of painting been drawn, or the chisel of the first sculptor been heard, or the first verse of poetry been chanted, or man himself, a nobler harmony than lute ever sounded, a finer line than painter ever drew, a statelier structure and a diviner song, arisen from the dust—did the beautiful *idea* of the "Plea of the Midsummer Fairies" dawn upon this poet's mind: he has conceived his fairies in a happy hour, he has framed them with exquisite skill and a fine eye to poetic proportion, but he has not made them alive, he has not made them objects of love; and you care less for his centaurs and his fairies than you do for the moonbeams or the shed leaves of the forest. How different with the Oberon and the Titania of Shakspeare! They are true to the fairy ideal, and yet they are human—their hearts warm with human passions, as fond of gossip, flattery, intrigue, and quarrel, as men or women can be—and you sigh with or smile at them, precisely as you do at Theseus and Hippolyta. Indeed, we cannot but admire how Shakspeare, like the arc of humanity, always bends in all his characters into the one centre of man—how his villains, ghosts, demons, witches, fairies, fools, harlots, heroes, clowns, saints, sensualists, women, and *even his kings*, are all human, disguises, or half-lengths, or miniatures, never caricatures nor apologies for mankind. How full the cup of manhood out of which he could baptize—now an Iago, and now an Ague-cheek—now a Bottom, and now a Macbeth—now a Dogberry, and now a Caliban—now an Ariel, and now a Timon—into the one communion of the one family—nay, have a drop or two to spare for Messrs. Cobweb and Mustard-seed, who are allowed to creep in too among the number, and who attract a share of the tenderness of their benign father. As in Swift, his misanthropy sees the hated object in every thing, blown out in the Brobdignagian, shrunk up in the Lilliputian, flapping in the Laputan, and yelling with the Yahoo—nay, throws it out into those loathsome reflections, that he may intensify and multiply his hatred; so in the same way operates the opposite feeling in Shakspeare. His love to the race is so great that he would colonize with man, all space, fairy-land, the grave, hell, and heaven. And not only does he give to superhuman beings a human interest and nature, but he accomplishes what Hood has not attempted, and what few else have attempted with success; he adjusts the human to the superhuman actors—they never jostle, you never wonder at finding them on the same stage, they meet without a start, they part without a shiver, they obey one magic; and you feel that not only does one touch of nature make the whole world kin, but that it can link the *universe* in one brotherhood, for the secret of this adjustment lies entirely in the humanity which is diffused through every part of the drama. In it, as in one soft ether, float, or swim, or play, or dive, or fly, all his characters.

In connection with the foregoing defect, we find in Hood's more elaborate poetical pieces no effective story, none that can bear the weight of his subtle and beautiful imagery. The rich blossoms and pods of the peaflower-tree are there, but the strong distinct stick of support is wanting. This defect is fatal not only to long poems but to all save the shortest; it reduces them instantly to the rank of rhymed essays; and a rhymed essay, with most people, is the same thing with a rhapsody. Even dreams require a nexus, a nisus, a nodus, a point, a purpose. Death is but a tame shadow without the scythe. The want of a purpose in any clear, definite, impressive form has neutralized the effect of many poems beside Hood's—some of Tennyson's, and one entire class of Shelley's—whose "Triumph of Life" and "Witch of Atlas" rank with "Lycus" and the "Midnight Fairies"—being, like them, beautiful, diffuse, vague, and, like them, perpetually promising to bring forth solid fruit, but yielding at length leaves and blossoms only.

Subtle fancy, lively wit, copious language, and mellow versification, are the undoubted qualities of Hood as a poet. But, besides, there are two or three moral peculiarities about him as delightful as his intellectual; and they are visible in his serious as well as lighter productions. One is his constant lightsomeness of spirit and tone. His verse is not a chant but a carol. Deep as may be his internal melancholy, it expresses itself in, and yields to, song. The heavy thunder-cloud of woe comes down in the shape of sparkling, sounding, sunny drops, and thus dissolves. He casts his melancholy into shapes so fantastic, that they lure first himself, and then his readers, to laughter. If he cannot get rid of the grim gigantic shadow of himself, which walks ever before him, as before all men, he can, at least, make mouths and cut antics behind its back. This conduct is, in one sense, wise as well as witty; but will, we fear, be imitated by few. Some will continue to follow the unbaptized terror, in tame and helpless submission; others will pay it vain homage; others will make to it resistance equally vain; and many will seek to drown in pleasure, or forget in business, their impression, that it walks on before them—silent, perpetual, pausing with their rest, running with their speed, growing with their growth, strengthening with their strength, forming itself a ghastly rainbow on the fumes of their bowl of festival, lying down with them at night, starting up with every start that disturbs their slumbers, rising with them in the morning, rushing before them like a rival dealer into the market-place, and appearing to beckon them on behind it, from the death-bed into the land of shadows, as into its own domain. If from this dreadful forerunner we cannot escape, is it not well done in Hood, and would it not be well done in others, to laugh at, as we pursued its inevitable steps? It is, after all, perhaps only the future greatness of man that throws back this gloom upon his infant being, casting upon him confusion and despair, instead of exciting him to gladness and to hope.* In escaping from this shadow, we should be pawning the prospects of our immortality.

How cheerily rings Hood's lark-like note of poetry among the various voices of the age's song—its eagle screams, its raven croakings, its plaintive nightingale strains! And yet that lark, too, in her lowly nest, had her sorrows, and, perhaps, her heart had bled in secret all night long. But now the "morn is up again, the dewy morn," and the sky is clear, and the wind is still, and the sunshine is bright, and the blue depths seem to sigh for her coming; and up rises she to heaven's

* This thought we copy from Carlyle, who has copied it from the Germans, or our own John Howe.

gate, as aforetime; and as she soars and sings she remembers her misery no more; nay, hers seems the chosen voice by which Nature would convey the full gladness of her own heart, in that favorite and festal hour.

No one stops to question the songstress in the sky as tc her theory of the universe—"Under which creed, Bezonian! speak or die!" So, it were idle to inquire of Hood's poetry, any more than of Keats's, what in confidence was its opinion of the origin of evil, or the pedobaptist controversy. His poetry is fuller of humanity and of real piety that it does not protrude any peculiarities of personal belief; and that no more than the sun or the book of Esther has it the name of God written on it, although it has the essence and the image. There are writers who, like secret, impassioned lovers, speak most seldom of those objects which they most frequently think of and most fervently admire. And there are others whose ascriptions of praise to God, whose encomiums on religion, and whose introduction of sacred names, sound like affidavits, or self-signed certificates of Christianity—they are so frequent, and so forced. It is upon this principle that we would defend Wordsworth from those who deny him the name of a sacred poet. True, all his poems are not hymns; but his life has been a long hymn, rising, like incense, from a mountain altar to God. Surely, since Milton, no purer, severer, *living* melody has mounted on high. Yet who can deny that the religion of the "Ode to Sound," and of the "Excursion," is that of the "Paradise Lost," the "Task," and the "Night Thoughts?" And without classing Hood in this or any respect with Wordsworth, we dare as little rank him with things common and unclean. Hear himself on this point:—

"Thrice blessed is the man with whom
The gracious prodigality of nature—
The balm, the bliss, the beauty, and the bloom,
The bounteous providence in every feature—
Recall the good Creator to his creature;
Making all earth a fane, all heaven its dome!

. . . .

Each cloud-capped mountain is a holy altar;
An organ breathes in every grove;
And the full heart's a psalter,
Rich in deep hymns of gratitude and love."

And amid all the mirthful details of the long warfare which he waged with Cant (from his "Progress of Cant," downwards), we are not aware of any real despite done to that spirit of Christianity, to which Cant, in fact, is the most formidable foe. To the *mask* of religion his motto is, spare no arrows; but when the real, radiant, sorrowful, yet happy *face* appears, he too has a knee to kneel and heart to worship.

But best of all in Hood is that warm humanity which beats in all his writings. His is no ostentatious or systematic philanthropy; it is a mild, cheerful, irrepressible feeling, as innocent and tender as the embrace of a child. It cannot found soup-kitchens; it can only slide in a few rhymes and sonnets to make its species a little happier. Hospitals it is unable to erect, or subscriptions to give, silver and gold it has none; but in the orisons of its genius it never fails to remember the cause of the poor; and if it cannot, any more than the kindred spirit of Burns, make for its country "some usefu' plan or book," it can "sing a sang at least." Hood's poetry is often a pleading for those who cannot plead for themselves, or who plead only like the beggar, who, reproached for his silence, showed his sores, and replied, "Isn't it begging I am with a hundred tongues?" This advocacy of his has not been thrown utterly away; it has been heard on earth, and it has been heard in heaven.

The genial kind-heartedness which distinguished Thomas Hood did not stop with himself. He silently and insensibly drew around him a little cluster of kindred spirits, who, without the name, have obtained the character and influence of a school, which may be called the Latter Cockney School. Who the parent of this school, properly speaking, was, whether Leigh Hunt or Hood, we will not stop to inquire. Perhaps we may rather compare its members to a cluster of bees settling and singing together, without thought of precedence or feeling of inferiority, upon one flower. Leigh Hunt and Hood, indeed, have far higher qualities of imagination than the others, but they possess some properties in common with them. All this school have warm sympathies, both with man as an individual, and with the ongoings of society at large. All have a quiet but burning sense of the evil, the cant, the injustice, the inconsistency, the oppression, and the falsehood, that are in the world. All are aware that fierce invective, furious recalcitration, and howling despair, can never heal nor mitigate these calamities. All are believers in their future and permanent mitigation; and are convinced that literature—prosecuted in a proper spirit, and combined with political and moral progress—will marvellously tend to this result. All have had, or have, too much real or solid sorrow to make of it a matter of parade, or to find or seek in it a frequent source of inspiration. All, finally, would rather laugh than weep men out of their follies, and ministries out of their mistakes; and in an age which has seen the steam of a tea-kettle applied to change the physical aspect of the earth, all have unbounded faith in the mightier miracles of moral and political revolution which the *mirth of an English fireside* is yet to effect when properly condensed and pointed. We rather honor the motives than share in the anticipations of this witty and brilliant band. Much good they have done and are doing; but the full case, we fear, is beyond them. It is in mechanism after all, not in magic, that they trust. We, on the other hand, think that our help lies in the double-divine *charm* which Genius and Religion, fully wedded together, are yet to wield; when, in a high sense, the words of the poet shall be accomplished—

> "Love and song, song and love, entertwined evermore,
> Weary earth to the suns of its youth shall restore."

Mirth like that of "Punch" and Hood can relieve many a fog upon individual minds, but is powerless to remove the great clouds which hang over the general history of humanity; and around even political abuses it often plays harmless as the summer evening's lightning, or, at most, only loosens without smiting them down. Voltaire's smile showed the Bastile in a ludicrous light, as it fantastically fell upon it; but Rousseau's earnestness struck its pinnacle and Mirabeau's eloquence overturned it from its base. There is a call in our case for a holier earnestness, and for a purer, nobler oratory. From the variety of styles which Hood has attempted in his poems, we select the two in which we think him most successful—the homely tragic narrative, and the grave pathetic lyric. We find a specimen of the former in his "Eugene Aram's Dream." This may be called a tale of the Confessional; but how much new interest does it acquire from the circumstances, the scene, and the person to whom the confession is made. Eugene Aram tells his story under the similitude of a dream, in the interval of the school toil, in a shady nook of the play-ground, and to a little boy. What a ghastly contrast do all these peaceful images present to the tale he tells, in its mixture of homely horror and shadowy dread! What an ear this in which to inject the fell revelation! In what a plain yet powerful setting is the awful picture thus inserted! And how perfect at once the keeping and the contrast between youthful innocence and guilt, gray-haired before its time!—between the eager, unsuspecting curiosity of the listener, and the slow and difficult throes, by which the narrator relieves himself of his burden of years!—between the sympathetic, half-pleasant, half-painful shudder of the boy, and the strong convulsion of the man! The Giaour, emptying his polluted soul in the gloom of the convent aisle, and to the father trembling instead of his penitent, as the broken and frightful tale gasps on, is not equal in interest nor awe to Eugene Aram recounting his dream to the child; till you as well as he wish, and are tempted to shriek out, that he may awake, and find it indeed a dream. Eugene Aram is not like Bulwer's hero—a sublime demon in love; he is a mere man in misery, and the poet seeks you to think, and you can think, of nothing about him, no more than himself can, except the one fatal stain which has made him what he is, and which he long has identified with himself. Hood, with the instinct and art of a great painter, seizes on that moment in Aram's history which formed the hinge of its interest—not the moment of the murder—not the long, silent, devouring remorse that followed—not the hour of the defence, nor of the execution—but that when the dark secret leapt into light and punishment; this thrilling, curdling instant, predicted from the past, and pregnant with the future, is here seized, and startlingly shown. All that went before was merely horrible, all that followed is horrible and vulgar: the poetic moment in the story is intense. And how inferior the labored power and pathos of the last volume of Bulwer's novel to these lines!—

> "That very night, while gentle sleep
> The urchin eyelids kiss'd,
> Two stern-faced men set out from Lynn
> Through the cold and heavy mist;
> And Eugene Aram walk'd between
> With gyves upon his wrist."

And here, how much of the horror is breathed upon us from the calm bed of the sleeping boy!

The two best of his grave, pathetic lyrics are the "Song of the Shirt" and the "Bridge of Sighs." The first was certainly Hood's great hit, although we were as much ashamed as rejoiced at its success. We blushed when we thought that at that stage of his life he needed such an introduction to the public, and that thousands and tens of thousands were now, for the first time, induced to ask, "Who's Thomas Hood?" The majority of even the readers of the age had never heard of his name till they saw it in "Punch," and connected with a song—first-rate, certainly, but not better than many of his former poems! It cast, to us, a strange light upon the chance medleys of fame, and on the lines of Shakspeare—

> "There is a tide in the affairs of men
> Which, taken at the flood, leads on to fortune."

Alas! in Hood's instance, to fortune it did not lead, and the fame was brief lightning before darkness.

And what is the song which made Hood awake one morning and find himself famous? Its great merit is its truth. Hood sits down beside the poor seamstress as beside a sister, counts her tears, her stitches, her bones—too transparent by far through the sallow skin—sees that though degraded she is a woman still; and rising up, swears by Him that liveth for ever and ever, that he will make her wrongs and wretchedness known to the limits of the country and of the race. And hark! how, to that cracked, tuneless voice, trembling under its burden of sorrow, now shrunk down into the whispers of weakness, and now shuddering up into the laughter of despair, all Britain listens for a moment—and for no longer—listens, meets, talks, and does little or nothing. It was much that one shrill shriek should rise and reverberate above that world of wild confused wailings, which are the true "cries of London;" but, alas! that it has gone down again into the abyss, and that we are now employed in criticising its artistic quality instead of recording its moral effect. Not altogether in vain, indeed, has it sounded, if it have comforted one lonely heart, if it have bedewed with tears one arid eye, and saved to even one sufferer a pang of a kind which Shakspeare only saw in part, when he spoke of the "proud *man's* contumely"—the contumely of a proud, imperious, fashionable, hard-hearted *woman*—"one that was a woman, but, rest her soul, she's dead."

Not the least striking or impressive thing in this "Song of the Shirt" is its half-jesting tone, and light, easy gallop. What sound in the streets so lamentable as the laughter of a lost female! It is more melancholy than even the death-cough shrieking up through her shattered frame, for *it* speaks of rest, death, the grave, forgetfulness, perhaps forgiveness. So Hood into the centre of this true tragedy has, with a skilful and sparing hand, dropt a pun or two, a conceit or two; and these quibbles are precisely what make you quake. "Every tear hinders needle and thread," remind us distantly of these words, occurring in the very centre of the Lear agony, "Nuncle, it is a naughty night to swim in." Hood, as well as Shakspeare, knew that, to deepen the deepest woe of humanity, it is the best way to show it in the lurid light of mirth; that there is a sorrow too deep for tears, too deep for sighs, but none too deep for smiles; and that the *aside* and the laughter of an idiot might accompany and serve to aggravate the anguish of a god. And what tragedy in that swallow's back which "twits with the spring" this captive without crime, this suicide without intention, this martyr without the prospect of a fiery chariot!

The "Bridge of Sighs" breathes a deeper breath of the same spirit. The poet is arrested by a crowd in the street: he pauses, and finds that it is a female suicide whom they have plucked dead from the waters. His heart holds its own coroner's inquest upon her, and the poem is the verdict. Such verdicts are not common in the courts of clay. It sounds like a voice from a loftier climate, like the cry which closes the Faust, "She is pardoned." He knows not—what the jury will know in an hour—the cause of her crime. He wishes not to know it. He cannot determine what proportions of guilt, misery, and madness have mingled with her "mutiny." He knows only she was miserable, and she is dead—dead, and therefore away to a higher tribunal. He knows only that, whate'er her guilt, he never ceased to be a woman, to be a sister, and that death, for him hushing all questions, hiding all faults, has left on her "only the beautiful." What can he do? He forgives her in the name of humanity; every heart says amen, and his verdict, thus repeated and confirmed, may go down to eternity.

Here, too, as in the "Song of the Shirt," the effect is trebled by the outward levity of the strain. Light and gay the masquerade his grieved heart puts on; but its every flower, feather, and fringe shakes in the internal anguish as in a tempest. This one stanza (coldly praised by a recent writer in the "Edinburgh Review," whose heart and intellect seem to be dead, but to us how unspeakably dear!) might perpetuate the name of Hood:

"The bleak wind of March
 Made her tremble and shiver,
But not the dark arch,
 Nor the black flowing river;
Mad from life's history—
Glad to death's mystery
Swift to be hurl'd,
Anywhere, anywhere
Out of the world!"

After all this, we have not the heart, as Lord Jeffrey would say, to turn to his "Whims and Oddities," &c. at large. "Here lies one who spat more blood and made more puns than any man living," was his self-proposed epitaph. Whether punning was natural to him or not, we cannot tell. We fear that with him, as with most people, it was a bad habit, cherished into a necessity and a disease. Nothing could be more easily acquired than the power of punning, if, as Dr. Johnson was wont to say, one's mind were but to *abandon* itself to it. What poor creatures you meet continually, from whom puns come as easily as perspiration. If this was a disease in Hood, he turned it into a "commodity." His innumerable puns, like the minikin multitudes of Lilliput, supplying the wants of the Man Mountain, fed, clothed, and paid his rent. This was more than Aram

Dreams or Shirt Songs could have done, had he written them in scores. Some, we know, will, on the other hand, contend that his facility in punning was the outer form of his inner faculty of minute analogical perception—that it was the same power at play—that the eye which, when earnestly and piercingly directed, can perceive delicate resemblances in things, has only to be opened to see like words dancing into each other's embrace; and that this, and not the perverted taste of the age, accounts for Shakspeare's puns; punning being but the game of football, by which he brought a great day's labor to a close. Be this as it may, Hood punned to live, and made many suspect that he lived to pun. This, however, was a mistake. For, apart from his serious pretensions as a poet, his puns swam in a sea of humor, farce, drollery, fun of every kind. Parody, caricature, quiz, innocent *double entendre*, mad exaggeration, laughter holding both his sides, sense turned awry, and downright, staring, slavering nonsense, were all to be found in his writings. Indeed, every species of wit and humor abounded, with, perhaps, two exceptions;—the quiet, deep, ironical smile of Addison, and the misanthropic grin of Swift (forming a stronger antithesis to a laugh than the blackest of frowns) were not in Hood. Each was peculiar to the single man whose face bore it, and shall probably re-appear no more. For Addison's matchless smile we may look and long in vain; and forbid that such a horrible distortion of the "human face divine" as Swift's grin (disowned for ever by the fine, chubby, kindly family of mirth!) should be witnessed again on earth!

"Alas! poor Yorick. Where now thy squibs?—thy quiddities?—thy flashes that wont to set the table in a roar? Quite chopfallen?" The death of a man of mirth has to us a drearier significance than that of a more sombre spirit. *He* passes into the other world as into a region where his heart had been translated long before. To death, as to a nobler birth, had he looked forward; and when it comes, his spirit readily and cheerfully yields to it, as one great thought in the soul submits to be displaced and darkened by a greater. To him death had lost his terrors, at the same time that life had lost its charms. But "can a ghost laugh or shake his gaunt sides"—is there wit any more than wisdom in the grave?—do puns there crackle?—or do Comic Annuals there mark the still procession of the years? The death of a humorist, as the first serious epoch in his history, is a very sad event. In Hood's case, however, we have this consolation: a mere humorist he was not, but a sincere lover of his race—a hearty friend to their freedom and welfare—a deep sympathizer with their sufferings and sorrows; and if he did not to the full consecrate his high faculties to their service, surely his circumstances as much as himself were to blame. Writing, as we are, in Dundee, where he spent some of his early days, and which never ceased to possess associations of interest to his mind; and owing, as we do to him, a debt of much pleasure, and of some feelings higher still, we cannot but take leave of his writings with every sentiment of good-humor and gratitude.

THOMAS MACAULAY.

To attempt a new appraisement of the intellectual character of Thomas Macaulay, we are impelled by various motives. Our former notice of him* was short, hurried, and imperfect. Since it was written, too, we have had an opportunity of seeing and hearing the man, which, as often happens in such cases, has given a more distinct and tangible shape to our views, as well as considerably modified them. Above all, the public attention has of late, owing to circumstances, been so strongly turned upon him, that we are tolerably sure of carrying it along with us in our present discussion.

The two most popular British authors are, at present, Charles Dickens and Thomas Macaulay. The supremacy of the former is verily one of the signs of the times. He has no massive or profound intellect—no lore superior to a schoolboy's—no vast or creative imagination—little philosophic insight, little power of serious writing, and little sympathy with either the subtler or profounder parts of

* In our first "Gallery of Portraits."

man, or with the grander features of nature; (witness his description of Niagara—he would have painted the next pump better!) and yet, through his simplicity and sincerity, his boundless *bon hommie*, his fantastic humor, his sympathy with every-day life, and his absolute and unique dominion over every region of the Odd, he has obtained a popularity which Shakspeare nor hardly Scott in their lifetime enjoyed. He is ruling over us like a Fairy King or Prince Prettyman—strong men as well as weak yielding to the glamour of his tiny rod. Louis XIV. walked so erect, and was so perfect in the management of his person, that people mistook his very size, and it was not discovered till after his death that he was a little and not a large man. So many of the admirers of Dickens have been so dazzled by the elegance of his proportions, the fairy beauty of his features, the minute grace of his motions, and the small sweet smile which plays about his mouth, that they have imagined him to be a Scott, or even a Shakspeare. To do him justice, he himself has seldom fallen into such an egregious mistake. He has seldom, if ever, sought to alter by one octave, the note Nature gave him, and which is not that of an eagle nor of a nightingale, nor of a lark, but of a happy, homely, gleesome "Cricket on the Hearth." Small almost as his own Tiny Tim, dressed in as dandyfied a style as his own Lord Frederick Verisoft, he is as full of the milk of human kindness as his own Brother Cheeryble; and we cannot but love the man who has first loved all human beings, who can own Newman Noggs as a brother, and can find something to respect in Bob Sawyers, and something to pity in a Ralph Nickleby. Never was a monarch of popular literature less envied or more loved; and while rather wondering at the length of his reign over such a capricious domain as that of letters, and while fearlessly expressing our doubts as to his greatness or permanent dominion, we own that his sway has been that of gentleness—of a wide-minded and kindly man; and take this opportunity of wishing long life and prosperity to "Bonnie Prince Charlie."

In a different region, and on a higher and haughtier seat, is Thomas Macaulay exalted. In general literature, as Dickens in fiction, is he held to be *facile princeps*. He is, besides, esteemed a rhetorician of a high class—a states man of no ordinary calibre—a lyrical poet of much mark and likelihood—a scholar ripe and good—and, mounted on this high pedestal, he "has purposed in his heart to take another step," and to snatch from the hand of the Historic Muse one of her richest laurels. To one so gifted in the prodigality of Heaven, can we approach in any other attitude than that of prostration? or dare we hope for sympathy, while we proceed to make him the subject of free and fearless criticism?

Before proceeding to consider his separate claims upon public admiration, we will sum up, in a few sentences, our impressions of his general character. He is a gifted but not a great man. He is a rhetorician without being an orator. He is endowed with great powers of perception and acquisition, but with no power of origination. He has deep sympathies with genius, without possessing genius of the highest order itself. He is strong and broad, but not subtle or profound. He is not more destitute of original genius than he is of high principle and purpose. He has all common faculties developed in a large measure, and cultivated to an intense degree. What he wants is the gift that cannot be given—the power that cannot be counter feited—the wind that bloweth where it listeth—the vision; the joy and the sorrow, with which no stranger intermeddleth—the "the light which never was on sea or shore the consecration and the poet's dream."

To such gifts, indeed, he does not pretend, and never has pretended. To roll the raptures of poetry, without emulating its *speciosa miracula*—to write worthily of heroes, without aspiring to the heroic—to write history without enacting it—to furnish to the utmost degree his own mind, without leading the minds of others one point farther than to the admiration of himself and of his idols, seems, after all, to have been the main object of his ambition, and has already been nearly satisfied. He has played the finite game of talent, and not the infinite game of genius. His goal has been the top of the mountain, and not the blue profound beyond; and on the point he has sought he may speedily be seen, relieved against the heights which he cannot reach—a marble fixture, exalted and motionless. Talent stretching itself out to attain the attitudes and exaltation of genius is a pitiable and painful position, but it is not that of Macaulay. With piercing sagacity he has, from the first, discerned his proper intellectual powers, and sought, with his whole heart, and soul, and mind, and strength, to cultivate them. "Macaulay the Lucky" he has been called; he ought rather to have been called Macaulay the Wise.

With a rare combination of the arts of age and the fire of youth, the sagacity of the worldling and the enthusiasm of the scholar, he has sought self-development as his principal, if not only end.

He is a gifted but not a great man. He possesses all those ornaments, accomplishments, and even natural endowments, which the great man requires for the full emphasis and effect of his power (and which the *greatest* alone can entirely dispense with), but the power does not fill, possess, and shake the drapery. The lamps are lit in gorgeous effulgence; the shrine is modestly, yet magnificently, adorned; there is every thing to tempt a god to descend; but the god descends not—or if he does, it is only Maia's son, the Eloquent, and not Jupiter, the Thunderer. The distinction between the merely gifted and the great is, we think, this—the gifted adore greatness and the great; the great worship the infinite, the eternal, and the godlike. The gifted gaze at the moon-like reflections of the Divine—the great, with open face, look at its naked sun, and each look is the principle and prophecy of an action.

He has profound sympathies with genius, without possessing genius of the highest order itself. Genius, indeed, is his intellectual god. It is (contrary to a common opinion) not genius that Thomas Carlyle worships. The word genius he seldom uses, in writing or in conversation, except in derision. We can conceive a savage cachinnation at the question, if he thought Cromwell or Danton a great genius. It is energy that he so much admires. With genius, as existing almost undiluted in the person of such men as Keats, he cannot away. It seems to him only a long swoon or St. Vitus's dance. It is otherwise with Macaulay. If we trace him throughout all his writings, we will find him watching for genius with as much care and fondness as a lover uses in following the footsteps of his mistress. This, like a golden ray, has conducted him across all the wastes and wildernesses of history. It has brightened to his eye each musty page and worm-eaten volume. Each morning has he risen exulting to renew the search: and he is never half so eloquent as when dwelling on the achievements of genius, as sincerely and rapturously as if he were reciting his own. His sympathies as are as wide as they are keen. Genius, whether thundering with Chatham in the House of Lords, or mending kettles and dreaming dreams with Bunyan in Elstowe—whether reclining in the saloons of Holland House with De Stael and Byron, or driven from men as on a new Nebuchadnezzar whirlwind, in the person of poor wandering Shelley—whether in Coleridge,

> " With soul as strong as a mountain river,
> Pouring out praise to the Almighty giver ;"

or in Voltaire shedding its withering smile across the universe, like the grin of death—whether singing in Milton's verse, or glittering upon Cromwell's sword—is the only magnet which can draw forth all the riches of his mind, and the presence of inspiration alone makes him inspired.

But this sympathy with genius does not amount to genius itself; it is too catholic and too prostrate. The man of the highest order of genius, after the enthusiasm of youth is spent, is rarely its worshipper, even as it exists in himself. He worships rather the object which genius contemplates, and the ideal at which it aims. He is rapt up to a higher region, and hears a mightier voice. Listening to the melodies of Nature, to the march of the eternal hours, to the severe music of continuous thought, to the rush of his own advancing soul, he cannot so complacently bend an ear to the minstrelsies, however sweet, of men, however gifted. He passes, like the true painter, from the admiration of copies, which he may admire to error and extravagance, to that great original which, without blame, excites an infinite and endless devotion. He becomes a personification of art, standing on tip-toe in contemplation of mightier Nature, and drawing from her features with trembling pencil and a joyful awe. Macaulay has not this direct and personal communication with the truth and the glory of things He sees the universe not in its own rich and divine radiance, but in the reflected light which poets have shed upon it. There are in his writings no oracular deliverances, no pregnant hints, no bits of intense meaning—broken, but broken off from some supernal circle of thought—no momentary splendors, like flashes of midnight lightning, revealing how much—no thoughts beckoning us away with silent finger, like ghosts, into dim and viewless regions—and he never even nears that divine darkness which ever edges the widest and loftiest excursions of imagination and of reason. His style and manner may be compared to crystal, but not to the "terrible crystal" of the prophets and apostles of literature. There is the sea of glass, but it is not mingled with fire, or at least the fire has not been heated seven times, nor has it descended from the seventh heaven.

Consequently, he has no power of origination. We despise the charge of plagiarism, in its low and base sense, which has sometimes been advanced against him. He never commits conscious theft, though sometimes he gives all a father's welcome to thoughts to which he has not a father's claim. But the rose which he appropriates is seldom more than worthy of the breast which it is to adorn; thus, in borrowing from Hall the antithesis applied by the one to the men of the French Revolution, and by the other to the restored royalists in the time of Charles II., "dwarfish virtues and gigantic crimes," he has taken what he might have lent, and, in its application, has changed it from a party calumny into a striking truth. The men of the Revolution were not men of dwarfish virtues and gigantic vices; both were stupendous when either were possessed: it was otherwise with the minions of Charles. When our hero lights his torch it is not at the chariot of the sun; he ascends seldom higher than Hazlitt or Hall—Coleridge, Schiller, and Goethe are untouched. But without re-arguing the question of originality, that quality is manifestly not his. It were as true that he originated Milton, Dryden, Bacon, or Byron, as that he originated the views which his articles develop of their lives or genius. A search after originality is never successful. Novelty is even shyer than truth, for if you search after the true, you will often, if not always, find the new; but if you search after the new, you will, in all probability, find neither the new nor the true. In seeking for paradoxes, Macaulay sometimes stumbles on, but more fre quently stumbles over, truth. His essays are masterly treatises, written learnedly, carefully conned, and pronounced in a tone of perfect assurance; the Pythian pantings, the abrupt and stammering utterances of the seer, are a wanting.

In connection with this defect, we find in him little metaphysical gift or tendency. There is no "speculation in his eye." If the mysterious regions of thought, which are at present attracting so many thinkers, have ever possessed any charm for him, that charm has long since passed away. If the "weight, the burden, and the mystery of all this unintelligible world" have ever pressed him to anguish, that anguish seems now forgotten as a nightmare of his youth. The serpents which strangle other Laocoons, or else keep them battling all their life before high heaven, have long ago left, if indeed they had ever approached him. His joys and sorrows, sympathies and inquiries, are entirely of the "earth, earthy," though it is an earth beautified by the smile of genius, and by the midnight sun of the past. It may appear presumptuous to criticise his creed, where not an article has been by himself indicated, except perhaps the poetical first principle that, "Beauty is truth and truth beauty;" but we see about him neither the firm grasp of one who holds a dogmatic certainty, nor the vast and vacant stretch of one who has failed after much effort to find the object, and who says, "I clasp—what is it that I clasp?" Toward the silent and twilight lands of thought, where reside, half in glimmer and half in gloom, the dread questions of the origin of evil, the destiny of man, our relation to the lower animals and to the spirit world, he never seems to have been powerfully or for any length of time impelled. We might ask with much more propriety at him the question which a reviewer asked at Carlyle, "Can you tell us, quite in confidence, your private opinion as to the place where wicked people go?" And, besides, what think you of God? or of that most profound and awful mystery of godliness? Have you ever thought deeply on such subjects at all? Or if so, why does the language of a cold conventionalism, or of an unmeaning fervor, distinguish all your allusions to them? It was not, indeed, your business to write on such themes, but it requires no more a wizard to determine from your writings whether you have adequately *thought* on them, than to tell from a man's eye whether he is or is not looking at the sun.

We charge Macaulay, as well as Dickens, with a systematic shrinking from meeting in a manful style those dread topics and relations at which we have hinted; and this, whether it springs, as Humboldt says in his own case, from a want of subjective understanding, or whether it springs from a regard for, or fear of, popular opinion, or whether it springs from moral indifference, argues, on the first supposition, a deep mental deficiency, on the second, a cowardice unworthy of their position, or, on the third, a state of spirit which the age, in its professed teachers, will not much longer endure. An earnest period, bent on basing its future progress upon fixed principles, fairly and irrevocably set down, to solve the problem of its happiness and destiny, will not long refrain from bestowing the name of brilliant trifler on the man, however gifted and favored, who so slenderly sympathizes with it in this high though late and difficult calling.

It follows almost as a necessity from these remarks, that Macaulay exhibits no high purpose. Seldom have so much energy and eloquence been more entirely divorced from a great uniting and consecrating object; and in his forthcoming history we fear that this deficiency will be glaringly manifest. History, without the presence of high purpose, is but a series of dissolving views—as brilliant it may be, but as disconnected, and not so impressive. It is this, on the contrary, that gives so profound an interest to the writings of Arnold, and invests his very fragments with a certain air of greatness; each sentence seems given in on oath. It is this which glorifies even D'Aubigne's Romance of the Reformation, for he *seeks* at least to show God in history, like a golden thread, pervading, uniting, explaining, and purifying it all. No such passion for truth as Arnold's, no such steady vision of those great outshining laws of justice, mercy, and retribution, which pervade all human story, as D'Aubigne's, and in a far higher degree, as Carlyle's, do we expect realized in Macaulay. His history, in all likelihood, will be the splendid cenotaph of his party. It will be brilliant in parts, tedious as a whole—curiously and minutely learned—written now with elaborate pomp, and now with elaborate negligence—heated by party spirit whenever the fires of enthusiasm begin to pale—it will abound in striking literary and personal sketches, and will easily rise to and above the level of the scenes it describes, just because few of those scenes, from the character of the period, are of the highest moral interest or grandeur. But a history forming a transcript, as if in the short-hand of a superior being, of the leading events of the age, solemn in spirit, subdued in tone, grave and testamentary in language, profound in insight, judicial in impartiality, and final as a Median law in effect, we might have perhaps expected from Mackintosh, but not from Macaulay.*

"Broader and deeper," says Emerson, "must we write our annals." The true idea of history is only as yet dawning on the world; the old almanack form of history has been generally renounced, but much of the old almanack spirit remains. The avowed partisan still presumes to write his special pleading, and to call it a history. The romance writer still decorates his fancy-piece, and, for fear of mistake, writes under it, "This is a history." The bald retailer of the dry bones of history is not yet entirely banished from our literature—nor is the hardy, but one-sided iconoclast, who has a quarrel with all established reputation, and would spring a mine against the sun if he could—nor is the sagacious philosophiste, who has access to the inner thoughts and motives of men who have been dead for centuries, and often imputes to deep deliberate purpose what was the result of momentary impulse, fresh and sudden as the breeze, who accurately sums up and ably reasons on all calculable principles, but omits the incalculable, such as inspiration and frenzy. We are waiting for the full avatar of the ideal historian, who, to the intellectual qualities of clear sight, sagacity, picturesque power, and learning, shall add the far rarer qualities of a love for truth only equalled by a love for man—a belief in and sympathy with progress, thorough independence and impartiality, and an all-embracing charity—and after "Macaulay's History of England" has seen the light, may still be found waiting.

* This work has since appeared. How far it justifies our prophecy, its candid readers will judge.

The real purpose of a writer is perhaps best concluded from the effect he produces on the minds of his readers. And what is the boon which Macaulay's writings do actually confer upon their millions of readers? Much information, doubtless—many ingenious views are given and developed, but the main effect is pleasure—either a lulling, soothing opiatic, or a rousing and stimulating gratification. But what is their mental or moral influence? What new and great truths do they throw like bomb-shells into nascent spirits, disturbing for ever their repose? What sense of the moral sublime have they ever infused into the imagination, or what thrilling and strange joy "beyond the name of pleasure" have they ever circulated through the heart? What long, deep trains of thought have his thoughts ever started, and to what melodies in other minds have his words struck the key-note? Some authors mentally "beget children—they travail in birth with children;" thus from Coleridge sprang Hazlitt; but who is Macaulay's eldest born? Who dates any great era in his history from the reading of his works, or has received from him even the bright edge of any Apocalyptic revelation? Pleasure, we repeat, is the principal boon he has conferred on the age; and without under-estimating this (which, indeed, were ungrateful, for none have derived more pleasure from him than ourselves), we must say that it is comparatively a trivial gift—a fruiterer's or a confectioner's office—and, moreover, that the pleasure he gives, like that arising from the use of wine, or from the practice of novel-reading, requires to be imbibed in great moderation, and needs a robust constitution to bear it. Reading his papers is employment but too delicious—the mind is too seldom irritated and provoked—the higher faculties are too seldom appealed to—the sense of the infinite is never given—there is perpetual excitement, but it is that of a game of tennis-ball, and not the Titanic play of rocks and mountains—there is constant exercise, but it is rather the swing of an easy chair than the grasp and tug of a strong rower striving to keep time with one stronger than himself. Ought, we ask, a grave and solid reputation, as extensive as that of Shakspeare or Milton, to be entirely founded on what is essentially a course of light reading?

We do not venture on his merits as a politician or statesman; but, as a speaker, we humbly think he has been overrated. He is not a sublime orator, who fulminates, and fiercely, and almost contemptuously, sways his audience; he is not a subtle declaimer, who winds around and within the sympathies of his hearers, till, like the damsel in the "Castle of Indolence," they weaken as they warm, and are at last sighingly but luxuriously lost; he is not a being piercing a lonely way for his own mind through the thick of his audience—wondered at, looked after, but not followed—dwelling apart from them even while riveting them to his lips; still less is he an incarnation of moral dignity, whose slightest sentence is true to the inmost soul of honor, and whose plain blunt speech is as much better than oratory as oratory is better than rhetoric. He is the primed mouth-piece of an elaborate discharge, who presents, applies the linstock, and fires off. He speaks rather before than to his audience. We felt this strongly when hearing him at the opening of the New Philosophical Institution in Edinburgh; that appearance had on us the effect of disenchantment; our lofty idea of Macaulay the orator—an idea founded on the perusal of all sorts of fulsome penegyrics—sank like a dream. Macaulay the orator! Why had they not raved as well of Macaulay the beauty? He, is, indeed, a master of rhetorical display; he aspires to be a philosopher; he is a brilliant *litterateur;* but, besides not speaking oratorically, he does not speak at all, if speaking means free communication with the souls and hearts of his hearers. If Demosthenes, Fox, and O'Connell were orators, he is none. It was not merely that we were disappointed with his personal appearance—that is sturdy and manlike, if not graceful—it is, besides, hereditary, and cannot be helped; but the speech was an elaborate and ungraceful accommodation to the presumed prejudices and tastes of the hearers—a piece of literary electioneering—and the manner, in its fluent monotony, showed a heart untouched amid all the palaver. Here is one, we thought, whose very tones prove that his success has been far too easy and exulting, and who has never known by experience the meaning of the grand old words, "perfect through suffering." Here is one in public sight selling his birthright for a mess of pottage and worthless praise, and who may live bitterly to rue the senseless bargain, for that applause is as certainly insincere as that birthright is high. Here is one who, ingloriously sinking with compulsion and laborious flight, consciously confounds culture with mere knowledge—speaking as if a boarding-school Miss, who had read Ewing's "Geography," were therein superior to Strabo. There, Thomas Macaulay, we thought, thou art contradicting thy former and better self, for we well remember thee speaking in an article with withering contempt of those who prefer to that "fine old geography of Strabo" the pompous inanities of Pinkerton. And dost thou deem thyself, all accomplished as thou art, nearer to the infinite mind than Pythagoras or Plato, because thou knowest more? And when he spoke again extempore, he sounded a still lower deep, and we began almost to fancy that there must be some natural deficiency in a mind so intensely cultivated, which could not shake as good, or better speeches, than even his first, "out of his sleeve." But the other proceedings and haranguings of that evening were not certainly fitted to eclipse his brightness, though they *were* calculated, in the opinion of many, to drive the truly eloquent to the woods, to find in the old trees a more congenial audience.

The House of Commons, we are told, hushes to hear him, but this may arise from other reasons than the mere power of his eloquence. He has a name, and there is far too much even in Parliament of that base parasitical element, which, while denying ordinary courtesy to the untried, has its knee delicately hinged to bend in supple homage to the acknowledged. He avoids, again, the utterance of all extreme opinions—never startles or offends—never shoots abroad forked flashes of truth; and, besides, his speaking is, in its way, a very peculiar treat. Like his articles, it generally gives pleasure; and who can deny themselves an opportunity of being pleased? Therefore the House was silent—its perpetual undersong subsided—even Roebuck's bristles were wont to lower, and Joseph Hume's careful front to relax—when the right honorable member for Edinburgh was on his legs. But *he* is, in our idea, the orator who fronts the storm and crushes it into silence—who snatches the prejudices from three hundred frowning foreheads, and binds it as a crown unto him—and who, not on some other and less difficult arena, but on that very field, wins the laurels which he is to wear. Those are the eloquent sentences which, though hardly heard above the tempest of opposition, yet are heard, and felt as well as heard, and obeyed as well as felt, which bespeak the surges at their loudest, and immediately there is a great calm.

We are compelled, therefore, as our last general remark on Macaulay, to call him rather a large and broad, than a subtle, sincere, or profound spirit. A simple child of Nature, trembling before the air played by some invisible musician behind him—what picture could be more exactly his antithesis? But neither has he, in any high degree, either the gift of philosophic analysis, or the subtle idealizing power of the poet. Clear, direct, uncircumspective thought—vivid vision of the characters he describes—an eye to see, rather than an imagination to combine—strong, but subdued enthusiasm—learning of a wide range, and information still more wonderful in its minuteness and accuracy—a style limited and circumscribed by mannerism, but having all power and richness possible within its own range, full of force, though void of freedom—and a tone of conscious mastery, in his treatment of every subject, are some of the qualities which build him up—a strong and thoroughly furnished man, fit surely for more massive deeds than either a series of sparkling essays, or what shall probably be a one-sided history.

In passing from his general characteristics to his particular works, there is one circumstance in favor of the critic. While many authors are much, their writings are little known: but if ever any writings were published, it is Macaulay's. A glare of publicity, as wide almost as the sunshine of the globe, rests upon them; and it is always easier to speak to men of what they know perfectly, than of what they know in part. To this there is perhaps an exception in his contributions to "Knight's Quarterly Magazine." That periodical, some of our readers may be aware, was of limited circulation and limited life. "It sparkled, was exhaled, and went to ——;" yet Professor Wilson has been known to say, that its four or five volumes are equal in talent to any four or five in the compass of periodical literature. To this opinion we must respectfully demur; at least we found the reading of two or three of them rather a hard task, the sole relief being in the papers of Macaulay, and would be disposed to prefer an equal number of "Blackwood," "Tait," or the old "London Magazine."

Macaulay's best contributions to this are a series of poems, entitled "Lays of the Roundheads." These, though less known than his "Lays of the League," which also appeared in "Knight," are, we think, superior. They are fine anticipations of the "Lays of Ancient Rome." Like Scott, vaulting between Claverhouse and Burley, and entering with equal gusto into the souls of both, Macaulay sings with equal spirit the song of the enthusiastic Cavalier and that of the stern Roundhead. He could have acted as poet-laureate to Hannibal as well as to the Republic, and his "Lays of Carthage" would have been as sweet, as strong, and more pathetic than his "Lays of Rome." "How happy could he be with either, were t'other dear charmer away." Not thus could Carlyle pass from his "Life of Cromwell" to a panegyric on the "Man of Blood," whose eyes "*could bear to look on torture, but durst not look on war.*" But Macaulay is the artist, sympathizing more with the poetry than with the principles of the great Puritanic contest.

"His "Roman Lays," though of a later date, fall naturally under the same category of consideration. These, when published, took the majority of the public by surprise, who were nearly as astonished at this late flowering of poetry in the celebrated critic, as were the Edinburgh people, more recently, at the portentous tidings that Patrick Robertson, also, was among the poets. The initiated, however, acquainted with his previous effusions, hailed the phenomenon (not as in Patrick's case, with shouts of spurting laughter) but with bursts of applause, which the general voice more than confirmed. The day when the "Lays" appeared, though deep in autumn, seemed a belated dog-day, so frantic did their admirers become. Homer, Scott, Wordsworth, and Byron, were now to hide their diminished heads, for an old friend under a new face had arisen to eclipse them all; and, for martial spirit, we are free to confess the "Lays" have never been surpassed, save by Homer, Scott, and by Burns, whose one epithet, "red wat shod," whose one description of the dying Scotch soldier in the "Earnest Cry," and whose one song, "Go fetch for me a pint of wine," are enough to stamp him among the foremost of martial poets Macaulay's ballads sound in parts like the thongs of Bellona. Written, it is said, in the War-office, the Genius of Battle might be figured bending over the author, sternly smiling on her *last* poet, and shedding from her wings a ruddy light upon its rapidly and furiously-filling page. But the poetry of war is not of the highest order. Seldom, except when the war is ennobled by some great cause, as when Deborah uttered her unequalled thanksgiving, can the touch of the sword extract the richest life's blood of poetry. Selfish is the exultation over victory, selfish the wailing under defeat. The song of the sword must soon give place to the song of the bell; and the pastoral ditty pronounced over the reaping-hook shall surpass all lyrical baptisms of the spear. As it is, the gulf between the "Lays"—amazingly spirited though they be—and intellectual, or moral poetry, is nearly as wide as between "Chevy Chase" and "Laodamia." Besides, the "Lays" are in a great measure centos; the images are no more original than the facts, and the poetic effect is produced through the singular rapidity, energy and felicity of the narration, and the breathless rush of the verse, "which rings to boot and saddle." One of the finest touches, for example, is imitated from Scott.

> "The kites know well the long stern swell
> That bids the Romans close"—

Macaulay has it. In the "Lady of the Lake" it is:—

> "The exulting eagle scream'd afar,
> She knew the voice of Alpine's war."

Indeed, no part of the "Lays" rises higher than the better passages of Scott. As a whole they are more imitative and less rich in figure and language than his poetry; and we have been unable to discover any powers revealed in them which his prose works had not previously and amply disclosed. In fact, their excessive popularity arose in a great measure from the new attitude in which they presented their writer. Long accustomed to speak to the public, he suddenly volunteered to sing, and his song was harmonious, and between gratitude and surprise was vehemently encored. It was as if Ellen Faucit were to commence to lecture, and should lecture well; or as though Douglas Jerrold were to announce a volume of sermons, and the sermons turn out to be excellent. This, after all, would only prove versatility of talent; it would not enlarge our conception of the real calibre of their powers. Nay, we hesitate not to assert that certain passages of Macaulay's prose rise higher than the finest raptures of his poetry, and that the term eloquence will measure the loftiest reaches of either.

This brings us to say a few words on his contributions to the "Edinburgh Review." We confess, that had we been called on while new from reading those productions, our verdict on them would have been much more enthusiastic. Their immediate effect is absolutely intoxicating. Each reads like a new Waverley tale. "More—give us more—it is divine!" we cry, like the Cyclops when he tasted of the wine of Outis. As Pitt adjourned the court after Sheridan's Begum speech, so, in order to judge fairly, we are compelled to adjourn the criticism. Days even have to elapse ere the stern question begins slowly, through the golden mist, to lift up its head—"What have you gained? Have you only risen from a more refined 'Noctes Ambrosianæ?' Have you only been conversing with an elegant artist? or has a prophet been detaining you in his terrible grasp? or has Apollo been touching your trembling ears?" As we answer we almost blush, remembering our tame and sweet subjection; and yet the moment that the enchantment again assails us, it again is certain to prevail.

But what is the explanation of this power? Is it altogether magical, or does it admit of analysis? Macaulay's writings have one very peculiar and very popular quality. They are eminently clear. They can by no possibility, at any time, be nebulous. You can read them as you run. Schoolboys devour them with as much zest as bearded men. *This* clearness is, we think, connected with deficiency in his speculative and imaginative faculties; but it does not so appear to the majority of readers. Walking in an even and distinct pathway, not one stumbling-stone or alley of gloom in its whole course, no Hill of Difficulty rising, nor Path of Danger diverging, greeted, too, by endless vistas of interest and beauty, all are but too glad, and too grateful, to get so trippingly along. Vanity, also, whispers to the more ambitious: "What we can so easily understand we could easily equal;" and thus are the readers kept on happy terms both with the author and themselves. His writings have all the stimulus of oracular decision, without one particle of oracular darkness. His papers, too, are thickly studded with facts. This itself, in an age like ours, is enough to recommend them, especially when these facts are so carefully selected—when told now with emphasis so striking, and now with negligence so graceful; and when suspended around a theory at once dazzling and slight—at once paradoxical and pleasing. The reader, beguiled, believes himself reading something more agreeable than history, and more veracious than fiction. It is a very waltz of facts that he witnesses; and yet how consoling to reflect that they are facts after all! Again, Macaulay, as we have repeatedly hinted, is given to paradoxes. But then these paradoxes are so harmless, so respectable, so well-behaved—his originalities are so orthodox—and his mode of expressing them is at once so strong and so measured—that people feel both the tickling sensation of novelty and a perfect sense of safety, and are slow to admit that the author, instead of being a bold, is a timorous thinker, one of the literary as well as political *juste-milieu*. Again, his manner and style are thoroughly English. As his sympathies are, to a great degree, with English modes of thought and habits of action, so his language is a stream of English undefiled. All the territories which it has traversed have enriched, without coloring, its waters. Even the most valuable of German refinements—such as that common one of subjective and objective—are sternly shyed. That philosophic diction which has been from Germany so generally transplanted, is denied admittance into Macaulay's grounds, exciting a shrewd suspicion that he does not often require it for philosophical purposes. Scarcely a phrase or word is introduced which Swift would not have sanctioned. In anxiety to avoid a barbarous and Mosaic diction, he goes to the other extreme, and practises purism and elaborate simplicity. Perhaps under a weightier burden, like Charon's skiff, such a style might break down; but, as it is, it floats on, and carries the reader with it, in all safety, rapidity, and ease. Again, this writer has—apart from his clearness, his bridled paradox, and his

English style—a power of interesting his readers, which we may call, for want of a more definite term, tact. This art he has taught himself gradually; for in his earlier articles, such as that on "Milton," and the "Present Administration," there were a prodigality and a recklessness—a prodigality of image, and a recklessness of statement—which argued an impulsive nature, not likely so soon to subside into a tactician. Long ago, however, has he *changé tout cela.* Now he can set his elaborate passages at proper distances from each other; he peppers his page more sparingly with the condiments of metaphor and image; he interposes anecdotes to break the blaze of his splendor; he consciously stands at ease, nay, condescends to nod, the better to prepare his reader, and breathe himself for a grand gallop; and although he has not the art to conceal his art, yet he has the skill always to fix his reader—always to write, as he himself says of Horace Walpole, "what every body will like to read." Still further, and finally, he has a quality different from and superior to all these—he has genuine literary enthusiasm, which public life has not yet been able to chill. He is not an inspired child, but he is still an ardent schoolboy; and what many count and call his vice we count his salvation. It is this unfeigned love of letters and genius which (dexterously managed, indeed) is the animating and inspiring element of Macaulay's better criticisms, and the redeeming point in his worse. It is a love which many waters have been unable to destroy, and which shall burn till death. When he retires from public life, like Lord Grenville, he may say, "I return to Plato and the 'Iliad.'"

We must be permitted, ere we close, a few remarks on some of his leading papers. "Milton" was his "Reuben—his first-born—the beginning of his strength," and thought by many "the excellency of dignity, and the excellency of power." It was gorgeous as an eastern tale. He threw such a glare about Milton that at times you could not see him. The article came clashing down on the floor of our literature like a gauntlet of defiance, and all wondered what young Titan could have launched it. Many inquired, "Starting at such a rate, whither is he likely to go?" Meanwhile the wiser, while admiring, quietly smiled, and whis pered in reply, "At such a rate no man can or ought to ad vance." Meanwhile, too, a tribute to Milton from across the waters, less brilliant, but springing from a more complete and mellow sympathy with him, though at first overpowered, began steadily and slowly to gain the superior suffrage of the age, and from that pride of place has not yet receded. On the contrary, Macaulay's paper he himself now treats as the brilliant bastard of his mind. Of such *splendida vitia* he need not be ashamed. We linger as we remember the wild delight with which we first read his picture of the Puritans, ere it was hackneyed by quotation, and ere we thought it a rhetorical bravura. How burning his print of Dante! The best frontispiece, to this paper on "Milton" would be the figure of Robert Hall, at the age of sixty, lying on his back, and learning Italian, in order to verify Macaulay's description of the "man that had been in hell."

In what a different light does the review of Croker's "Boswell" exhibit our author! He sets out, like Shenstone, by saying, "I will, I will be witty;" and, like him, the will and the power are equal. Macaulay's wit is always sarcasm —sarcasm embittered by indignation, and yet performing its minute dissections with judicial gravity. *Here* he catches *his* Rhadamanthus of the Shades, in the upper air of literature, and his vengeance is more ferocious than his wont. He first flays, then kills, then tramples, and then hangs his victim in chains. It is the onset of one whose time is short, and who expects reprisals in another region. Nor will his sarcastic vein, once awakened against Croker, sleep till it has scorched poor Bozzy to ashes, and even singed the awful wig of Johnson. We cannot comprehend Macaulay's fury at Boswell, whom he crushes with a most disproportionate expenditure of power and anger. Nor can we coincide with his eloquent enforcement of the opinion, first propounded by Burke, then seconded by Mackintosh, and which seems to have become general, that Johnson is greater in Boswell's book than in his own works. To this we demur. Boswell's book gives little idea of Johnson's eloquence or power of grappling with the highest subjects—"Rasselas" and the Lives of the Poets" do. Boswell's book does justice to Johnson's wit, readiness, and fertility; but if we could see the full force of his fancy, the full energy of his invective, and his full sensibility to, and command over, the moral sublime, we must consult such papers in the "Idler" as that wonderful one on the Vultures, or in the "Rambler," as Anningate and Ajut, his London, and his Vanity of Human Wishes. Boswell, we venture to asert, has not saved one *great* sentence of his idol—such as we may find profusely scattered in his own writings—nor has recorded fully any of those conversations, in which, pitted against Parr or Burke, he talked his best. If Macaulay merely means that Boswell, through what he has preserved, and through his own unceasing admiration, gives us a higher conception of Johnson's every-day powers of mind than his writings supply, he is right; but in expressly claiming the immortality for the "careless table-talk," which he denies to the works, and forgetting that the works discover higher faculties in special display, we deem him mistaken.

In attacking Johnson's style, Macaulay is, unconsciously, a suicide; not that his style is modelled upon Johnson's, or that he abounds in *sesquipedalia verba*—he has never needed large or new words, either to cloak up mere commonplace, or to express absolute originality—but many of the faults he charges against Johnson belong to himself. Uniformity of march—want of flexibility and ease—con sequent difficulty in adopting itself to common subjects—perpetual and artfully balanced antithesis—were, at any rate, once peculiarities of Macaulay's writing, as well as of Johnson's, nor are they yet entirely relinquished. After all, such faults are only the awkward steps of the elephant, which only the monkey can deride; or we may compare them to the unwieldly but sublime movements of a giant telescope, which turns slowly and solemnly, as if in time and tune with the stately steps of majesty with which the great objects it contemplates are revolving.

The article on Byron, for light and sparkling brilliance, is Macaulay's finest paper. Perhaps it is not sufficiently grave or profound for the subject. There are, we think, but two modes of properly writing about Byron—the one is the Monody, the other the Impeachment; this paper is neither Mere criticism over such dread dust is impertinent; mere panegyric impossible. Either with condemnation melting down in irrepressible tears, or with tears drying up in strong censure, should we approach the memory of Byron, if, indeed eternal silence were not better still.

Over one little paper we are apt to pause with a peculiar fondness—the paper on "Bunyan." As no one has greater sympathy with the spirit of the Puritans, without having much with their peculiar sentiments, than Carlyle, so no one sympathizes more with the literature of that period, without much else in common (unless we except Southey), than Macaulay. The "Pilgrim's Progress" is to him, as to many, almost a craze. He cannot speak calmly about it. It continues to shine in the purple light of youth; and, amid, all the paths he has traversed, he has never forgotten that immortal path which Bunyan's genius has so boldly mapped out, so variously peopled, and so richly adorned. How can it be forgotten, since it is at once the miniature of the entire world, and a type of the progress of every earnest soul. The City of Destruction, the Slough of Despond, the Delectable Mountains, the Valley of the Shadow of Death, Beulah, and the Black River, are still extant, unchangeable realities, as long as man continues to be tried and to triumph. But it is less in this typical aspect than as an interesting tale that Macaulay seems to admire it. Were we to look at it in this light alone we should vastly prefer "Turpin's Ride to York," or "Tam O'shanter's Progress to Alloway Kirk." But as an unconscious mythic history of man's moral and spiritual advance, its immortality is secure, though its merits are as yet in this point little appreciated. Bunyan, indeed, knew not what he did; but then he spake inspired; his deep heart prompted him to say that to which all deep hearts in all ages should respond; and we may confidently predict that never shall that road be shut up or deserted. As soon stop the current or change the course of the black and bridgeless river.

We might have dwelt, partly in praise and partly in blame, on some of his other articles—might, for instance, have combated his slump and summary condemnation, in "Dryden," of Ossian's poems—poems which, striking, as they did, all Europe to the soul, must have had some merit, and which, laid for years to the burning heart of Napoleon, must have had some corresponding fire. That, said Coleridge, of Thomson's "Seasons," lying on the cottage window-sill, is true fame; but was there no true fame in the fact that Napoleon, as he bridged the Alps, and made at Lodi impossibility itself the slave of his genius, had these poems in his travelling carriage? Could the chosen companion of such a soul, in such moments, be altogether false and worthless? Ossian's Poems we regard as a ruder "Robbers"—a real though clouded voice of poetry, rising in a low age, prophesying and preparing the way for the miracles which followed; and we doubt if Macaulay himself has ever equalled some of the nobler flights of Macpherson. We may search his writings long ere we find any thing so sublime, though we may find many passages equally ambitious, as the "Address to the Sun."

He closes his collected articles with his "Warren Hastings," as with a grand finale. This we read with the more interest. as we fancy it a chapter extracted from his forthcoming history. As such it justifies our criticism by anticipation. Its personal and literary sketches are unequalled, garnished as they are with select scandal, and surrounded with all the accompaniments of dramatic art. Hasting's trial, is a picture to which that of Lord Erskine, highly wrought though it be, is vague and forced, and which, in its thick and crowded magnificence, reminds you of the descriptions of Tacitus, or (singular connection!) of the paintings of Hogarth. As in Hogarth, the variety of figures and circumstances is prodigious, and each and all bear upon the main object, to which they point like fingers; so from every face, figure, aspect, and attitude, in the crowded Hall of Westminster, light rushes on the brow of Hastings, who seems a fallen god in the centre of the godlike radiance. Even Fox's "sword" becomes significant, and seems to thirst for the proconsul's destruction. But Macaulay, though equal to descriptions of men in all difficult and even sublime postures, never describes scenery well. His landscapes are too artificial and elaborate. When, for example, he paints "Paradise" in Byron, or "Pandemonium" in Dryden, it is by parts and parcels, and you see him pausing and rubbing his brows between each lovely or each terrible item. The scene reluctantly comes, or rather is pulled into view, in slow and painful series. It does not rush over his eye, and require to be detained in its giddy passage. Hence his picture of India in "Hastings" is an admirable picture of an Indian village but not of India, the country. You have the "old oaks"—the graceful maiden with the pitcher on her head—the courier shaking his bunch of iron rings to scare away the hyenas—but where the eternal bloom, the immemorial temples, the vast blood-spangled mists of superstition, idolatry, and caste, which brood over the sweltering land—the Scotlands of jungle, lighted up by the eyes of tigers as with infernal stars—the Ganges, the lazy deity of the land, creeping down reluctantly to the sea—the heat, encompassing the country like a sullen, sleepy hell—the swift steps of tropical death, heard amid the sulphury silence—the ancient monumental look proclaiming that all things here continue as they were from the foundation of the world, or seen in the hazy distance as the girdle of the land—the highest peaks of earth soaring up toward the sun, Sirius, the throne of God. Macaulay too much separates the material from the moral aspects of the scene, instead of blending them together as exponents of the one great fact, India.

But we must stop. Ere closing, however, we are tempted to add, as preachers do, a solid inference or two from our previous remarks. First, we think we can indicate the field on which Mr. Macaulay is likely yet to gain his truest and permanent fame. It is in writing the *literary* history of his country. Such a work is still a desideratum; and no living writer is so well qualified by his learning and peculiar gifts—by his powers and prejudices—by his strength and his weakness, to supply it. In this he is far more assured of success than in any political or philosophical history. With what confidence and delight would the public follow his guidance, from the times of Chaucer to those of Cowper, when our literature ceased to be entirely national, and even a stage or two farther! Of such a "progress" we proclaim him worthy to be the Great-heart! Secondly, we infer from a retrospect of his whole career, the evils of a too easy and a too early success. It is by an early Achillean baptism alone that men can secure Achillean invulnerability, or confirm Achillean strength. This was the redeeming point in Byron's history. Though a lord, he had to undergo a stern training, which indurated and strengthened him to a pitch, which all the after blandishments of society could not weaken.

Society did not—in spite of our author—spoil him by its favor, though it infuriated him by its resentment. But *he* has been the favored and petted child of good fortune. There has been no "crook," till of late, either in his political or literary "lot." If he has not altogether inherited, he has approached the verge of the curse, "Woe to you, when all men shall speak well of you." No storms have unbared his mind to its depths. It has been his uniformly to—"Pursue the triumph and partake the gale." Better all this for his own peace than for his power, or for the permanent effect of his writings.

Let us congratulate him, finally, on his temporary defeat in Edinburgh. A few more such victories as he had formerly gained, and he had been undone. A few more such defeats, and if he be, as we believe, essentially a man, he may yet, in the "strength of the lonely," in the consciousness and terrible self-satisfaction of those who deem themselves injuriously assailed, perform such deeds of derring-do as shall abash his adversaries and astonish even himself.

DR. GEORGE CROLY.

Not only is the literary divine not a disgrace to his profession, he is a positive honor. His pulpit becomes an eminence, commanding a view of both worlds. He is a witness at the nuptials of truth and beauty, and the general cause of Christianity is subserved by him in more ways than one; for, first, the names of great men devoted at once to letters and religion neutralize, and more than neutralize, those which are often produced and paraded on the other side; again, they show that the theory of science sanctified, and literature laid down before the Lord, has been proved and incarnated by living examples, and does not therefore remain in the baseless regions of mere hypothesis; and, thirdly, they evince that even if religion be an imposture and a delusion, it is one so plausible and powerful as to have subjugated very strong intellects, and that it will not therefore do for every sciolist in the school of infidelity to pretend contempt for those who confess that it has commanded and convinced them.

Literary divines, next to religious laymen, are the chosen champions of Christianity. We say next to laymen, for when they come forth from their desks, their laboratories, or observatories, and bear spontaneous testimony in behalf of religion, it is as though the earth again should help the woman; and the thunder of a Bossuet, a Massillon, a Hall, or a Chalmers breaking from the pulpit does not speak so loud in behalf of our faith as the 'still, small voice" issuing from the studious chamber of an Addison, a Boyle, a Bowdler, an Isaac Taylor, and a Cowper. But men who might have taken foremost places in the walks of letters and science, and yet have voluntarily devoted themselves to the Christian cause, and yet continue amid all this devotion tremblingly alive to all the graces, beauties, and powers of literature, are surely standing evidences at least of the sincerity of their own convictions, if not of the truth of that faith on which these convictions centre. And when they openly give testimony to their belief, we listen as if we heard science and literature themselves pronouncing the creed or swearing the sacramental oath of Christianity.

Such an one is Dr. George Croly. He might have risen to distinction in any path he chose to pursue; he has attained wide eminence as a literary man; he has never lost sight of the higher aims of his own profession; and he is now in the ripe autumn of his powers, with redoubled energy and hope, about to dive down in search of *new* pearls in that old deep which communicates with the onmiscience of God. He is projecting at present, and has in part begun, to elaborate three treatises on the patriarchs, the prophets, and the apostles, from which great issues may be expected. Meanwhile we propose rapidly running over the general outline of his merits and works.

Dr. Croly is almost the last survivor of that school of Irish eloquence which included the names of Burke, Sheridan, Grattan, Curran, and Flood. He has most of the merits, and some of the faults of that school. A singular school it has been, when we consider the circumstances and character of the country where it flourished. The most miserable has been the most eloquent of countries. The worst cultivated country has borne the richest crop of flowers—of speech. The barrenness of its bogs has been compensated by the rank fertility of its brains. Its groans have been set to a wild and wondrous music—its oratory has been a safety-valve to its otherwise intolerable wrongs. Yet, over all Irish eloquence, and even Irish humor, there hovers a certain shade of sadness. In vain they struggle to smile or to assume an air of cheerfulness. A sense of their country's wretchedness—their Pariah position—the dark doom that seems suspended over every thing connected with the Irish name, lowers over and behind them as they speak or write. Amidst the loftiest flights of Burke's speculation, the gayest bravuras of Sheridan's rhetoric, the fieriest bursts of Grattan's or Curran's eloquence, this stamp of the branding-iron—this downward drag of degradation—is never lost sight of or forgotten.

Ireland! art thou a living string of God's great lyre, the earth; or art thou an instrument, thrown aside like a neglected harp, and only valuable for the chance notes of joy or sorrow, mad mirth or despair, which the hands of passengers can discourse upon thee? Art thou only a wayward child of the mighty mother, or art thou altogether a monstrous and incurable birth? Has nature taught thee thy notes of riant mirth, or yet richer pathos, or have torture and tyranny, like cruel arts of hell, awoke within thee those slumbering energies which it were well for thee had slept for ever? Well for thee it may be, but not for the world; for thy loss has been our gain, and from thy long and living death has flowed forth that long, swelling, sinking, always dying, yet never dead music, which now sounds thy requiem, and may peradventure herald thy future resurrection.

Dr. Croly has not altogether escaped the pervasive gloom of his country's literature. This speaks in the choice of his subjects, and in the lofty, ambitious tone of his manner. He would spring up above the sphere of Ireland's dire attraction! "Farthest from her is best." Irish subjects, therefore, are avoided, although from no want of sympathy with Ireland. Regions either enjoying a profounder calm or torn by nobler agonies than those of Erin, are the chosen fields for his muse. Of his country's wild, reckless humor, always reminding us of the mirth of despairing criminals, singing and dancing out the last dregs of their life, Croly is nearly destitute. For this his genius is too stern and lofty. He does not deal in sheet lightning, but in the forked flashes of a withering and blasting invective. But in richness of figure, in strength of language, in vehemence of passion, and in freedom and force of movement, he is eminently Irish. Stripped, however, he is—partly by native taste, and partly by the friction of long residence in this country—of the more glaring faults of his country's style, its turbulence, exaggeration, fanfaronade, florid diffusion, and that ludicrous pathos which so often, in lieu of tears of grief, elicits tear-torrents of laughter. To use the well-known witticism of Curran, he has so often wagged his tongue in England, that he has at last caught its accent, and his brogue is the faintest in the world. The heat of the Irish blood and its wild poetical afflatus he has not sought, nor, if he had, would have been able to relinquish.

Dr. Croly's principal power is that of gorgeous and eloquent description. There are five different species of the describer. The first describes a scene or character as it appears to him, but as it really is not, he having, through weakness of sight, or inaccuracy of observation, missed the reality and substituted a vague something, more cognate to himself than to his object. The second is the literal describer—the bare, bald truth before him is barely and baldly caught—a certain spirit that hovered over it, as if on wing to fly, having amid the bustling details of the execution been disturbed and scared away. The third is the ideal describer, who catches and arrests that volatile film, expressing the life of life, the gloss of joy, the light of darkness, and the wild sheen of death; in short, the fine or terrible something which is really about the object, but which the eye of the gifted alone can see, even as in certain atmospheres only the rays of the sun are visible. The fourth is the historical describer, who sees and paints objects in relation to their past and future history, who gets so far *within* the person or the thing as to have glimpses behind and before about it, as if he belonged to it, like a memory or a conscience; and the fifth is the universal describer, who sees the object set in the shining sea of its total bearings, representing in it more or less fully the great whole of which it is one significant part. Thus, suppose the object a tree, one will slump up its character as large or beautiful—words which really mean nothing; another will, with the accuracy of a botanist, analyze it into its root, trunk, branches, and leaves; a third will make its rustle seem the rhythm of a poem; a fourth will see in it, as Cowper in Yardley Oak, its entire history, from the acorn to the axe, or perchance from the germ to the final conflagration; and a fifth will look on it as a mouth and mirror of the Infinite—a slip of *Igdrasil*. Or is the object the ocean—one will describe it as vast, or serene, or tremendous, epithets which burden the air but do not exhaust the ocean; another will regard it as a boundless solution of salt; a third will be fascinated by its terrible beauty, as of a chained tiger; a fourth, with a far look into the dim records of its experience, will call it (how different from the foregoing appellations!) the "*melancholy* main;" and the fifth will see in it the reflector of man's history, the shadow and mad sister of earth—the type of eternity!

These last three orders, if not one, at least slide often into each other, and Dr. Croly appears to us a combination of the third and the fourth. His descriptions are rather those of the poet than of the seer. They are rapid, but always clear, vivid, strong, and eloquent, and over each movement of his *pen*, an invisible *pencil* seems to hang and to keep time.

Searching somewhat more accurately for a classification of *minds*, they seem to us to include five orders—the prophet, the artist, the analyst, the copiast, and the combination in part of all the four. There is, first, the prophet, who receives immediately and gives out unresistingly the torrent of the breath and power of his own soul, which has become touched by a high and holy influence from behind him. This is no MECHANICAL office; the fact that he is chosen to be such an instrument, itself proclaims his breadth, elevation, power, and patency. There is next the artist, who receives the same influence in a less measure, and who, instead of implicitly obeying the current, tries to adjust, control, and get it to move in certain bounded and modulated streams. There is, thirdly, the analyst, who, in proportion to the faintness in which the breath of inspiration reaches him, is the more desirous to *turn round upon it*, to reduce it to its elements and to trace it to its source. There is, fourthly, the copiast—we coin a term, as *he* would like to form the far-off *sigh* of the aboriginal thought, which alone reaches him, into a new and powerful spoken word—but in vain. And there is, lastly, the combination of the whole *four*—the clever, nay, gifted mimic, whose light energy enables him to circulate between, and to be sometimes mistaken for, them all together.

Dr. Croly is the artist, and in general an accomplished and powerful artist he is. There is sometimes a little of the slap-dash in his manner, as of one who is in haste to be done with his subject. His style sometimes sounds like the horse-shoes of the belated traveller, "spurring apace to gain the timely inn." He generally, indeed, goes off at a gallop, and continues at this generous, breakneck pace to the close. He consequently has too few pauses and rests. He and you rush up panting, and arrive breathless at the summit. And yet there is never any thing erratic or ungraceful about the motion of the thought or style. If there be not classical repose there is classical rapture. It is no vulgar intoxication—it is a debauch of nectar; it is not a Newmarket, but a Nemean race.

Dr. Croly's intellectual distinction is less philosophic subtlety, than strong, nervous, and manly sense. This, believed with perfect assurance, inflamed with passion, surrounded with the rays of imagination, and pronounced with a dogmatic force and dignity peculiarly his own, constitutes the circle of his literary character—a circle which also includes large and liberal knowledge, but which has been somewhat narrowed by the influence of views, in our judgment, far too close and conservative. Especially, as we have elsewhere said, whenever he nears the French Revolution he loses temper, and speaks of it in a tone of truculence, as if it were a virulent ulcer and not a salutary blood-letting to the social system—the stir of a dunghill and not the explosion of a volcano—a few earthworms crawling out of their lair, and producing a transient agitation in their native mud, and not a vast Vesuvius moved by internal torments to cast out the central demon and with open mouth to appeal to Heaven. To Croly this revolution seems more a ray from hell, shooting athwart our system, than a mysterious part of it through which earth must roll as certainly as through its own shadow—night; more a retribution of unmitigated wrath than a sharp and sudden surgical application, severe and salutary as cautery itself. Now that we have before us a trinity of such revolutions, we have better ground for believing that they are no anomalous convulsions, but the periodical fits of a singular subject, whom it were far better to watch carefully and treat kindly than to stigmatize or assault. Bishop Butler, walking in his garden with his chaplain, after a long fit of silent thought, suddenly turned round and asked him, if he did not think that nations might get mad as well as individuals. What answer the worthy chaplain made to this question we are not informed, but we suspect that few now would coincide with the opinion of the bishop. Nations are never mad, though often mistaken and often diseased; or if mad, it is a fine and terrible frenzy, partaking of the character of inspiration, and telling, through all its blasphemy and blood, some great truth otherwise a word unutterable to the nations. What said, through its throat of thunder, that first revolution of France? It said that men are men, that "God hath made of one blood all nations who dwell upon the face of the earth," and it proved it, alas! by *mingling* together in one tide the blood of captains and of kings, of rich and poor, of bond and free: it shattered for ever the notion of men being ninepins for the pleasure of power, and showed them at the least to be gunpowder, a substance always dangerous, and always, if trode on, to be trode on warily. What said the three days of July, 1830? They said, that if austere unlimited tyranny exceed in guilt, diluted and dotard despotism excels in folly, and that the contempt of a people is as effectual as its anger in subverting a throne. And what is the voice with which the world is yet vibrating, as if the sun had been struck audibly and stunned upon his mid-day throne? It is that, as a governing agent, the days of expediency are numbered, and that henceforth not power, not cunning, not conventional morality, not talent, but truth has been crowned monarch of France, and, if the great experiment succeed, of the world.*

It is of Dr. Croly as a prose writer principally that we

* Alas! alas! This was too evidently written in 1848.

mean to speak. His poetry, though distinguished, and nearly to the same extent, by the qualities of his prose, has failed in making the same impression. The causes of this are various. In the first place, it appeared at a time when the age was teeming to very riot with poetry. Scott, indeed, had betaken himself to prose novels; Southey to histories and articles; Coleridge to metaphysics; Lamb to "Elia;" and Wordwsorth to his "Recluse," like the alchemist to his secret furnace. But still with each new wound in Byron's heart, a new gush of poetry was flowing, and all eyes watching this martyr of the many sorrows, with the interest of those who are waiting silent or weeping for a last breath; and at the same time a perfect crowd of true poets were finding audience, "fit though few." Wilson, Barry, Cornwall, Hogg, Hood, Clare, Cunninghame, Milman, Maturin ,Bowles, Crabbe, Montgomery, are some of the now familiar names which were then identified almost entirely with poetical aspirations. Amid such competitors Dr. Croly first raised his voice, and only shared with many of them the fate of being much praised, considerably abused, and little read. Secondly, more than most of his contemporaries, he was subjected to the disadvantage which in a measure pressed on all. All were stars seeking to shine ere yet the sun (that woful blood-spattered sun of "Childe Harold") had fairly set. Dr. Croly suffered more from this than others, just because he bore in some points a strong resemblance to Byron, a resemblance which drew forth, both for him and Milman, a coarse and witless assault in "Don Juan." And, thirdly, Dr. Croly's poems were chargeable, more than his prose writings, with the want of continuous interest. They consisted of splendid passages, which rather stood for themselves than combined to form a whole. The rich "bugle blooms" were trailed rather than trained about a stick scarce worthy of supporting them, and this, with the monotony inevitable to rhyme, rendered it a somewhat tedious task to climb to the reward which never failed to be met with at last. "Paris in 1815," however, was very popular at first; and "Cataline" copes worthily, particularly in the closing scene of the play, with the character of the gigantic conspirator, whose name even yet rings terribly, as it sounds down from the dark concave of the past.

His prose writings may be divided into three classes; his

fictions, his articles in periodicals, and his theological works. We have not read his "Tales of the Great St. Bernard," but understand them to be powerful though unequal. His "Colonna, the painter," appeared in "Blackwood," and, as a tale shadowed by the deadly lustre of revenge, yet shining in the beauty of Italian light and landscape, may be called an unrhymed "Lara." His "Marston, or Memoirs of a Statesman," is chiefly remarkable for the sketches of distinguished characters, here and in France, which are sprinkled through it, somewhat in the manner of Bulwer's "Devereux," but drawn with a stronger pencil and in a less capricious light. To Danton, alone, we think he has not done justice. On the principle of *ex pede Herculem*, from the power and savage truth of those calossal splinters of expression, which are all his remains, we had many years ago formed our unalterable opinion, that he was the greatest and by no means the worst man, who mingled in the melée of the Revolution—the Satan, if Dr. Croly will, and not the Moloch of the Paris Pandemonium—than Robespierre abler—than Marat, that squalid, screeching, out-of-elbows demon, more merciful—than the Girondin champions more energetic—than even Mirabeau stronger and less convulsive; and are glad to find that Lord Brougham has recently been led, by personal examination, to the same opinion. The Danton of Dr. Croly is a hideous compound of dandyism, diabolism, and power—a kind of coxcomb butcher, who with equal coolness arranges his moustaches and his murders, and who, when bearded in the Jacobin Club, proves himself a bully and a coward. The real Danton, so broad and calm in repose, so dilated and Titanic in excitement, who, rising to the exigency of the hour, seemed like Satan, starting from Ithuriel's spear, to grow *into armor*, into power and the weapons of power—now uttering words which were "half battles," and now walking silent, and unconscious alike of his vast energies and coming doom, by the banks of his native stream—now pelting his judges with paper bullets, and now laying his head on the block proudly, as if that head were the globe—was long since pointed out by Scott as one of the fittest subjects for artistic treatment, either in fiction or the drama, "worthy," says he, "of Schiller or Shakspeare themselves."

Dr. Croly's highest effort in fiction is unquestionably

"Salathiel." And it is verily a disgrace to an age, which devours with avidity whatever silly or putrid trash popular authors may be pleased to issue—such inane commonplace as "Now and Then," where the only refreshing things are the "glasses of wine" which are poured out at the close of every third page to the actors (alas, why not to the readers!), naturally thirsty amid such dry work, or the coarse greasy horrors which abound in the all-detestable "Lucretia"—that "Salathiel" has not yet, we fear, more than reached a second edition. It has not, however, gone without its reward. By the ordinary fry of circulating library readers neglected, it was read by a better class, and by none of those who read it forgotten. None but a "literary divine" could have written it. Its style is steeped in Scripture.

But Croly does more than snatch "live coals from off the altar" to strew upon his style; his spirit as well as his language is oriental. You feel yourselves in Palestine, the air is that through which the words of prophets have vibrated and the wings of angels descended—the ground is scarcely yet calm from the earthquake of the crucifixion—the awe of the world's sacrifice, and of the prodigies which attended it, still lowers over the land—still gapes unmended the ghastly rent in the vail—and still are crowds daily convening to examine the fissure in the rocks, when one lonely man, separated by his proper crime to his proper and unending woe, is seen speeding, as if on the wings of frenzy, toward the mountains of Napthali. It is Salathiel, the hero of this story—the Wandering Jew—the heir of the curse of a dying Saviour, "Tarry thou till I come."

As an artistic conception, we cannot profess much to admire what the Germans call the "Everlasting Jew." The interest is exhausted to some extent by the very title. The subject predicts an eternity of sameness, from which we shrink, and are tempted to call him an everlasting bore. Besides, we cannot well realize the condition of the wanderer as very melancholy, after all. What a fine opportunity must the fellow have of seeing the world, and the glory and the great men thereof! Could one but get up behind him, what "pencillings" could one perpetrate by the "way!" What a triumph, too, has he over the baffled skeleton, death! What a new fortune each century, by selling to advantage his rich "reminiscences!" What a short period at most to wander—a few thousand years, while yonder, the true wanderers, the stars, can hope for no rest! And what a jubilee dinner might he not expect, ere the close, as the "oldest inhabitant," with perhaps Christopher North in the chair, and De Quincy (whom some people suspect, however, of *being* the said personage himself) acting as croupier! Altogether, we can hardly, without ludricous emotions, conceive of such a character, and are astonished at the grave face which Shelley, Wordsworth, Mrs. Norton (whose "Undying One"' by the way, is dead long ago, in spite of a review, also dead, in the "Edinburgh"), Captain Medwyn (would he too had died ere he murdered the memory of poor Shelley!), Lord John Russell (who in his "Essays by a Gentleman who had left his Lodgings, has taken a very, very faint sketch of the unfortunate Ahashuerus), and Dr. Croly put on while they talk of his adventures.

The interest of "Salathiel," beyond the first splendid burst of immortal anguish with which it opens, is almost entirely irrespective of the character of the Wandering Jew. It is chiefly valuable for its pictures of Oriental scenery, for the glimpses it gives of the cradled Hercules of Christianity, and for the gorgeous imagery and unmitigated vigor of its writing. Plot necessarily there is none; the characters, though vividly depicted, hurry past, like the rocks in the "Walpurgis Night"—are seen intensely for a moment, and then drop into darkness; and the crowding adventures, while all interesting individually, do not gather a deepening interest as they grow to a climax. It is a book which you cannot read quickly, or with equal gusto at all times, but which, like "Thomson's Seasons," "Young's Night Thoughts," and other works of rich massiveness, yield intense pleasure, when read at intervals, and in moments of poetic enthusiasm.

Dr. Croly's contributions to periodicals are, as might have been expected, of various merit. We recollect most vividly his papers on Burke (since collected into a volume), on Pitt, and a most masterly and eloquent outline of the career of Napoleon. This is as rapid, as brief almost and eloquent, as one of Bonaparte's own bulletins, and much more true. It constitutes a rough, red, vigorous chart of his fiery career, without professing to complete philosophically the analysis of his character. This task Emerson lately, in our hearing, accomplished with much ingenuity, His lecture was the *portable essence* of Napoleon. He indicated his points with the ease and precision of a lion-showman. Napoleon, to Emerson, apart from his splendid genius, is the representative of the faults and the virtues of the *middle class* of the age. We heard some of his auditors contend that he had drawn two portraits instead of one; but in fact Napoleon was two, if not more men. Indeed, if you draw first the bright and then the black side of any character, you have two beings, which the skin and brain of the one actual man can alone fully reconcile. The experience of every one demonstrates at the least a dualism, and who might not almost any day sit down and write a letter, objurgatory, or condoling, or congratulatory, to "my dear yesterday's self?" Each man, as well as Napoleon, forms a sort of Siamese twins—although, in his case, it was matter of thankfulness that the cord could not be cut. Two Napoleons at large had been *too* much.

Of Dr. Croly's book on the "Revelation" we have spoken formerly. Under the shadow of that inscrutable pyramid it stands, one of the loftiest attempts to scale its summit and explain its construction; but to us all such seem as yet ineffectual. A more favorable specimen of his thelogical writing is to be found in his volume of "Sermons" recently published. The public has reason to congratulate itself on the little squabble which led to their publication. Some conceited persons, it seems, had thought proper to accuse Dr. Croly of preaching sermons above the heads of his audience, and suggested greater simplicity; and, after a careful perusal of them, we would suggest, even without a public phrenological examination of those auditors' heads, that, whatever be their situation in life, they are, if unable to understand these discourses, incapable of their duties, are endangering the public, and should be remanded to school. Clearer, more nervous, and in the true sense of the term, simpler discourses, have not appeared for many years. Their style is in general pure Saxon—their matter strong, manly, and his own—their figures always forcible, and never forced—their theology sound and scriptural—and would to God such sermons were being preached in every church and chapel throughout Britain! They might recall the many wanderers, who, with weary heart and foot, are seeking rest elsewhere in vain, and might counteract that current which is drawing away from the sanctuaries so much of the talent, the virtue, and the honesty of the land.

Dr. Croly, as a preacher, in his best manner, is faithfully represented in those discourses, particularly in his sermons on "Stephen," the "Theory of Martyrdom," and the "Productiveness of the Globe." We admire, in contrast with some modern and ancient monstrous absurdities to the contrary, his idea of God's purpose in making his universe—not merely to display his own glory, which, when interpreted, means just, like the stated purpose of Cæsar, to extend his own *name*, but to circulate his essence and image—to proclaim himself merciful, even through punishment—and even in hell-flames to write himself down Love, is surely, as Dr. Croly proclaims it, "the chief end" of God! His sermon on Stephen is a noble picture—we had almost said a daguerreotype—of that first martyrdom. His "Productiveness of the Globe" is richer than it is original. His "Theory of Religion" is new, and strikingly illustrated. His notion is, that God, in three different dispensations—the Patriarchal, the Mosaic, and the Christian—has developed three grand thoughts: first, the being of God; secondly, in shadow, the doctrine of atonement; and thirdly, that of immortality. With this arrangement we are not entirely satisfied, but reserve our objections till the "conclusion of the whole matter," in the shape of three successive volumes on each of these periods, and the idea of each, has appeared, as we trust it speedily shall.

We depicted, some time since, in a periodical, our visit to Dr. Croly's chapel, and the impression made by his appearance, and the part of his discourse we heard. It seemed to us a shame to see the most accomplished clergyman in London preaching to so thin an audience; but perhaps it is accounted for partly by the strictness of his Conservative principles, and partly by the stupid prejudice which exists against all literary divines.

We are sorry we cannot, ere we conclude, supply any particulars about his history. Of its details we are altogether ignorant. In conversation, he is described as powerful and commanding. Hogg, the Ettrick Shepherd, we remember, describes him as rather disposed to take the lead, but so exceedingly intelligent that you entirely forgive him. He has been, as a literary man, rather solitary and self-asserting —has never properly belonged to any clique or coterie— and seems to possess an austere and somewhat exclusive standard of taste.

It is to us, and must be to the Christian world, a delightful thought, to find such a man devoting the maturity of his mind to labors peculiarly professional; and every one who has the cause of religion at heart must wish him God speed in his present researches. Religion has in its abyss treasures yet unsounded and unsunned, though strong must be the hand, and true the eye, and retentive the breath, and daring yet reverent the spirit of their successful explorer— and such we believe to be qualities possessed by Dr. Croly.

SIR EDWARD BULWER LYTTON.

Perhaps the leading authors of the age may be divided into three classes. 1st, Those who have written avowedly and entirely for the few. 2ndly, Those who have written principally for the many. And, 3dly, Those who have sought their audience in both classes, and have succeeded in forming, to some extent, at once an exoteric and an esoteric school of admirers. Of the first class, Coleridge and Wordsworth are the most distinguished specimens. Scott and Dickens stand at the head of the second; and Byron and Bulwer are *facile principes* of the third. Both these last named writers commenced their career by appealing to the sympathies of the multitude; but by and by, either satiated by their too easy success, or driven onward by the rapid and gigantic progress of their own minds, they aimed at higher things, and sought, nor sought in vain, a more select audience. Byron's mind, in itself essentially unspeculative, was forced upwards upon those rugged and dangerous tracts of thought, where he has gathered the rarest of his beauties, by intimacy with Shelley, by envious emulation of his Lake contemporaries, and, above all, by the pale hand of his misery, unveiling to him heights and depths in his nature and genius, which were previously unknown and unsuspected, and beckoning him onward through their grim and shadowy regions. He grew, at once, and equally, in guilt, misery, and power. An intruder, too, on domains where some other thinkers had long fixed their calm and permanent dwelling, his appearance was the more startling. Here was a dandy discussing the great questions of natural and moral evil; a *roué* in silk stockings meditating suicide and mouthing blasphemy on an Alpine rock; a brilliant and popular wit and poet, setting Spinoza to music, and satirizing the principalities and powers of heaven, as bitterly as he had done the bards and reviewers of earth. Into those giddy and terrible heights where Milton had entered a permitted guest, in "privilege of virtue;" where Goethe had walked in like a passionless and prying cherub, forgetting to worship in his absorbing desire to know; and on which Shelley was wrecked and stranded, in the storm of his fanatical unbelief; Byron is upborne by the presumption and the despair of his mental misery. Unable to see through the high walls which bound and beset our limited faculties and little life, he can at least dash his head against them. Hence, in "Manfred," "Cain," "Heaven and Earth," and "The Vision of Judgment," we have him calling upon the higher minds of his age to be as miserable as he was, just as he had in his first poems addressed the same sad message, less energetically, and less earnestly, to the community at large. And were it not unspeakably painful to contemplate a noble mind engaged in this profitless "apostleship of affliction," this thankless gospel of proclamation to men, that because they are miserable, it is their duty to become more so; that because they are bad, they are bound to be worse; we might be moved to laughter by its striking resemblance to the old story of the fox who had lost his tail.

In the career of Bulwer, we find a faint yet traceable resemblance to that of Byron. Like him he began with wit, satire, and persiflage. Like him, he affected, for a season, a melodramatic earnestness. Like him, he was at last stung into genuine sincerity, and shot upwards into a higher sphere of thought and feeling. The three periods in Byron's history are distinctly marked by the three works, "English Bards," "Childe Harold," and "Cain." So "Pelham," "Eugene Aram," and "Zanoni," accurately mete out the stages in Bulwer's progress. Minor points of resemblance might be noted between the pair. Both sprung from the aristocracy; and one, at least, was prouder of what he deduced from Norman blood, than from nature. Bulwer, like Byron, is a distinguished dandy. Like him, too, he has been separated from his wife; like him, he is liberal in his politics. And while Byron, by way of doing penance, threw his jaded system into the Greek war, Bulwer has with better result leaped into a tub of cold water!

Point and brilliance are at once perceived to be the leading qualities of Bulwer's writing. His style is vicious from excess of virtue, weak from repletion of strength. Every word is a point, every clause a beauty, the close of every sentence a climax. He is as sedulous of his every stroke, as if the effect of the whole depended upon it. His pages are all sparkling with minute and insulated splendors; not suffused with a uniform and sober glow, nor shown in the reflected light of a few solitary and surpassing beauties. Some writers peril their reputation upon one long difficult leap, and, it accomplished, walk on at their leisure. With others, writing is a succession of hops, steps, and jumps. This in general is productive of a feeling of tedium. It teases and fatigues the mind of the reader. It is like crying perpetually upon a hearer, who is attending with all his might, to attend more carefully. It at once wearies and provokes, insults the reader, and betrays a certain weakness on the part of the author. If in Bulwer's writings we weary less than in others, it is owing to the artistic skill with which he intermingles his points of humor with those of sententious reflection or vivid narrative. All is point: but the point perpetually varies "from gay to grave, from lively to severe;" including in it raillery and reasoning, light dialogue and earnest discussion, bursts of political feeling and raptures of poetical description; here a sarcasm, almost worthy of Voltaire, and there a passage of pensive grandeur, which Rousseau might have written in his tears. To keep up this perpetual play of varied excellence, required at once great vigor and great versatility of talents: for Bulwer never walks through his part, never proses, is never tame, and seldom indeed substitutes sound for sense, or mere flummery for force and fire. He generally writes his best; and our great quarrel, indeed, with him is, that he is too uniformly erect in the stirrups, too conscious of himself, of his exquisite management, of his complete equipment, of the speed with which he devours the dust; and seldom exhibits the careless grandeur of one who is riding at the pace of the whirlwind, with perfect self-oblivion, and with perfect security.

Bulwer reminds us less of an Englishman Frenchified, than of a Frenchman partially Anglicized. The original powers and tendencies of his mind, his eloquence, wit, sentiments, and feelings, his talents and his opinions, his taste and style, are those of a modern Frenchman. But these, long subjected to English influences, and long trained to be candidates for an English popularity, have been modified and altered from their native bent. In all his writings, however, you breathe a foreign atmosphere, and find very slight sympathy with the habits, manners, or tastes of his native country. Not Zanoni alone, of his heroes, is cut off from country, as by a chasm, or if held to it, held only by ties, which might with equal strength bind him to other planets; all his leading characters, whatever their own pretensions, or whatever their creator may assert of them, are in reality citizens of the world, and have no more genuine relation to the land whence they spring, than have the winds, which linger not over its loveliest landscapes, and hurry past its most endeared and consecrated spots. Eugene Aram is not an Englishman; Rienzi is hardly an Italian. Bulwer is perhaps the first instance of a great novelist obtaining popularity without a particle of nationality in his spirit, or in his writings.

We do not question his attachment to his own principles or his native country; but of that tide of national prejudice which, Burns says, "shall boil on in his breast till the floodgates of life shut in eternal rest," he betrays not one drop.

His novels might all have appeared as translations from a foreign language, and have lost but little of their interest or verisimilitude. This is the more remarkable, as his reign exactly divides the space between that of two others, who have obtained boundless fame, greatly in consequence of the very quality, in varied forms, which Bulwer lacks. Scott's knowledge and love of Scotland, Dickens' knowledge and love of London, stand in curious antithesis to Bulwer's intense cosmopolitanism and ideal indifference.

Akin to this, and connected either as cause or as effect with it, is a certain dignified independence of thought and feeling, inseparable from the notion of Bulwer's mind. He is not a great original thinker; on no one subject can he be called profound, but on all, he thinks and speaks for himself. He belongs to no school either in literature or in politics, and he has created no school. He is too proud for a Radical, and too wide-minded for a Tory. He is too definite and decisive to belong to the mystic school of letters; too impetuous and impulsive to cling to the classical; too liberal to be blind to the beauties of either. He has attained, thus, an insulated and original position, and may be viewed as a separate, nor yet a small estate, in our intellectual realm. He may take up for motto, "*Nullius jurare addictus in verba magistri*;" he may emblazon on his shield "Desdichado." Some are torn, by violence from the sympathies and attachments of their native soil, without seeking to take root elsewhere; others are early transplanted, in heart and intellect, to other countries; a few, again, seem born, rooted up, and remain so for ever. To this last class we conceive Bulwer to belong. In the present day, the demand for earnestness, in its leading minds, has become incessant and imperative. Men speak of it as if it had been lately erected into a new test of admission into the privileges alike of St. Stephen's and of Parnassus. A large and formidable jury, with Thomas Carlyle for foreman, are diligently occupied in trying each new aspirant, as well as *back-speiring* the old, on this question: "Earnest or a sham? Heroic or hearsay? Under which king, Bezonian? speak, or die." Concerning this cry for earnestness, we can only say, *en passant*, that it is not, strictly speaking, new, but old; as old, surely, as that great question of Deborah's to recreant

Reuben,—"Why abodest thou among the sheep-folds to hear the bleating of the flocks?" or that more awful query of the Tishbite's,—"How long halt ye between two opinions?" that it is, in theory, a robust truth; and sometimes, in application, an exaggeration and a fallacy; and that, unless preceded by the words "enlightened" and "virtuous," earnestness is a quality no more intrinsically admirable, nay, as blind and brutal, as the rush of a bull upon his foeman, or as the foaming fury of a madman. Bulwer is not, we fear, in the full sense of the term, an earnest man: nay we have heard of the great modern prophet of the quality, pronouncing him the most thoroughly false man of the age; and another of the same school, christens him "a double-distilled scent-bottle of cant." In spite of this, however, we deem him to possess, along with much that is affected, much, also, that is true, and much that is deeply sympathetic with sincerity, although no devouring fire of purpose has hitherto filled his being, or been seen to glare in his eye. And, as we hinted before, his later writings exhibit sometimes, in mournful and melancholy forms, a growing depth and truth of feeling. Few, indeed, can even sportively wear, for a long time, the yoke of genius, without its iron entering into the soul, and eliciting that cry which becomes immortal.

Bulwer, as a novelist, has, from a compound of conflicting and imported materials, reared to himself an independent structure. He has united many of the qualities of the fashionable novel, of the Godwin philosophical novel, and of the Waverley tale. He nas the levity and thoroughbred air of the first; much of the mental anatomy and philosophical thought which often overpower the narrative in the second; and a portion of the dramatic liveliness, the historical interest, and the elaborate costume of the third. If, on the other hand, he is destitute of the long, solemn, overwhelming swell of Godwin's style of writing, and of the variety, the sweet, natural, and healthy tone of Scott's, he has some qualities peculiar to himself—point, polish—at times a classical elegance—at times a barbaric brilliance and a perpetual mint of short sententious reflections—compact, rounded, and shining as new-made sovereigns. We know no novelist from whose writings we could extract so many striking sentences containing fine thoughts, chased in imagery, "apples of gold in pictures of silver." The wisdom of Scott's sage reflections is homely but commonplace; Godwin beats his gold thin, and you gather his philosophical acumen rather from the whole conduct and tone of the story, and his commentary upon it, than from single and separate thoughts. Dickens, whenever he moralizes, in his own person, becomes insufferably tame and feeble. But it is Bulwer's beauty that he abounds in fine, though not far gleams of insight; and it is his fault that sometimes, while watching these, he allows the story to stand still, or to drag heavily, and sinks the character of novelist in that of brilliant essay-writer, or inditer of smart moral and political apophthegms. In fact his works are too varied and versatile. They are not novels or romances so much as compounds of the newspaper article, the essay, the political squib, the gay and rapid dissertation; which, along with the necessary ingredients of fiction, combine to form a junction, without constituting a true artistic whole.

Reserving a few remarks upon one or two other of his works till afterwards, we recur to the three which seem to typify the stages of his progress; "Pelham," "Eugene Aram," and "Zanoni." "Pelham," like "Anastasius," begins with a prodigious affectation of wit. For several pages the reading is as gay and as wearisome as a jest-book. You sigh for a simple sentence, and would willingly dig even for dulness as for hid treasure. The wit, too, is not an irrepressible and involuntary issue, like that from the teeming brain of Hood; it is an artificial and forced flow; and the author and his reader are equally relieved, when the clear path of the tale at length breaks away from the luxuriant shrubbery in which it is at first buried, and strikes into more open and elevated ground. It is the same with "Anastasius;" but "Pelham," we must admit, does not reach those heights of tenderness, of nervous description, and of solemn moralizing, which have rendered the other the prose "Don Juan," and something better. It is, at most, a series, or rather string, of clever, dashing, disconnected sketches; and the moral problem it works out seems to be no more than this, that, under the corsets of a dandy, there sometimes beats a heart.

In "Eugene Aram," Bulwer evidently aims at a higher mark; and, in his own opinion, with considerable success.

We gather his estimate of this work from the fact that he inscribes a labored and glowing panegyric on Scott with the words, "The Author of Eugene Aram." *Now*, probably, he would exchange this for "The Author of Zanoni." Nor should we, at least, nor, we think, the public, object to the alteration. "Eugene Aram" seems, to us, as lamentable a perversion of talent as the literature of the age has exhibited. It is one of those works in which an unfortunate choice of subject neutralizes eloquence, genius, and even interest. It is with it as with the "Monk" and the "Cenci," where the more splendid the decorations which surround the disgusting object, the more disgusting it becomes. It is, at best, deformity jewelled and enthroned. Not content with the native difficulties of the subject—the triteness of the story—its recent date—its dead level of certainty—the author has, in a sort of daring perversity, created new difficulties for himself to cope withal. He has not bid the real pallid murderer to sit to his pencil, and trusted for success to the severe accuracy of the portraiture. Him he has spirited away, and has substituted the most fantastic of all human fiends, resembling the more hideous of heraldic devices, or the more unearthly of fossil remains. Call him rather a graft from Godwin's Falkland, upon the rough reality of the actual "Eugene Aram;" for the worst of the matter is, that, after fabricating a being entirely new, he is compelled, at last, to clash him with the old pettifogging murderer, till the compound monstrosity is complete and intolerable. The philosopher, the poet, the lover, the sublime victim fighting with more "devils than vast hell can hold," sinks, in the trial scene, where precisely he should have risen up like a "pyramid of fire," into a sophister so mean and shallow, that you are reminded of the toad into which the lost archangel dwindled his stature. The morality, too, of the tale, seems to us detestable. The feelings with which you rise from its perusal, or, at least, with which the author seems to wish you to rise, are of regret and indignation, that, for the sin of an hour, such a noble being should perish, as if he would insinuate the wisdom of quarrel (how vain!) with those austere and awful laws, by which moments of crime expand into centuries of punishment! It is not wonderful that, in the struggle with such self-made difficulties, Bulwer has been defeated. The wonder is, that he has been able to cover his retreat amid such a cloud of beauties; and to attach an interest, almost human, and even profound, to a being whom we cannot, in our wildest dreams, identify with mankind. The whole tale is one of those hazardous experiments which have become so common of late years, in which a scanty success is sought at an infinite peril; like a wild-flower, of no great worth, snatched, by a hardy wanderer, from the jaws of danger and death. We notice in it, however, with pleasure, the absence of that early levity which marked his writing, the shooting germ of a nobler purpose, and an air of sincerity fast becoming more than an air.

In saying that "Zanoni" is our chief favorite among Bulwer's writings, we consciously expose ourselves to the charge of paradox. If we err, however, on this matter, we err in company with the author himself; and, we believe, with all Germany, and with many enlightened enthusiasts at home. We refer, too, in our approbation, more to the spirit than to the execution of the work. As a whole, as a broad and brilliant picture of a period and its hero, "Rienzi" is perhaps his greatest work, and "that shield he may hold up against all his enemies." "The Last Days of Pompeii," on the other hand, is calculated to enchant classical sholars, and the book glows like a cinder from Vesuvius, and most gorgeously are the reelings of that fiery drunkard depicted. The "Last of the Barons," again, as a cautious yet skilful filling up of the vast skeleton of Shakspeare, is attractive to all who relish English story. But we are mistaken, if in that class who love to see the Unknown, the Invisible, and the Eternal, looking in upon them, through the loops and windows of the present; whose footsteps turn instinctively toward the thick and the dark places of the "wilderness of this world;" or who, by deep disappointment or solemn sorrow, have been driven to take up their permanent mental abode upon the perilous verge of the unseen world, if "Zanoni" do not, on such, exert a mightier spell, and to their feelings be not more sweetly attuned, than any other of this writer's books. It is a book not to be read in the drawing-room, but in the fields—not in the sunshine, but in the twilight shade—not in the sunshine, unless indeed that sunshine has been saddened, and sheathed by a recent sorrow. *Then* will its wild and mystic measures, its pathos, and its grandeur, steal in like music, and mingle with the soul's emotions, till, like music, they seem a part of the soul itself.

No term has been more frequently abused than that of religious novel. This, as commonly employed, describes an equivocal birth, if not a monster, of which the worst and most popular specimen is "Cœlebs in Search of a Wife." It is amusing to see how its authoress deals with the fictitious part of her book. Holding it with a half shudder, and at arms-length, as she might a phial of poison, she pours in the other and the other infusion of prose criticism, commonplace moralizing, sage aphorism, &c., till it is fairly diluted down to her standard of utility and safety. But a religious novel in the high and true sense of the term, is a noble thought: a parable of solemn truth, some great moral law, written out as it were in flowers: a principle old as Deity, wreathed with beauty, dramatized in action, incarnated in life, purified by suffering and death. And we confess, that to this ideal we know no novel in this our country that approaches so nearly as "Zanoni." An intense spirituality, a yearning earnestness, a deep religious feeling, lie like the "soft shadow of an angel's wing upon its every page. Its beauties are not of the "earth earthy." Its very faults, cloudy, colossal, tower above our petty judgment-seats, towards some higher tribunal.

Best of all is that shade of mournful grandeur which rests upon it. Granting all its blemishes, and the improbabilities of its story, the occasional extravagances of its language, let it have its praise for its pictures of love and grief—of a love leading its votary to sacrifice stupendous privileges, and reminding you of that which made angels resign their starry thrones for the "daughters of men;" and of a grief too deep for tears, too sacred for lamentation, the grief which he increaseth that increaseth knowledge, the grief which not earthly immortality, which death only can cure. The tears which the most beautiful and melting close of the tale wrings from our eyes are not those which wet the last pages of ordinary novels: they come from a deeper source; and as the lovers are united in death, to part no more, triumph blends with the tenderness with which we witness the sad yet glorious union. Bulwer, in the last scene, has apparently in his eye the conclusion of the "Revolt of Islam," where Laon and Laone, springing in spirit from the funereal pile, are united in a happier region, in the "calm dwellings of the mighty dead," where on a fairer landscape rests a "holier day,' and where the lesson awaits them, that

> "Virtue, though obscured on earth, no less
> Survives all mortal change, in lasting loveliness."

Amid the prodigious number of Bulwer's other productions, we may mention one or two "dearer than the rest." The "Student," from its disconnected plan, and the fact that the majority of its papers appeared previously, has seemed to many a mere published portfolio, if not an aimless collection of its author's study-sweepings. This, however, is not a fair or correct estimate of its merits. It in reality contains the cream of Bulwer's periodical writings. And the "New Monthly Magazine," during his editorship, approached our ideal of a perfect magazine; combining, as it did, impartiality, variety, and power. His "Conversations with an Ambitious Student in ill health," though hardly equal to the dialogues of Plato, contain many rich meditations and criticisms, suspended round a simple and affecting story. The word "ambitious," however, is unfortunate; for what student is not, and should not be, ambitious? To study is to climb "higher still, and higher, like a cloud of fire." Talk of an ambitious chamois or of an ambitious lark, as lief as of an ambitious student. The allegories in the "Student" strike us as eminently fine, with glimpses of a more creative imagination than we can find in any of his writings save "Zanoni." We have often regretted that the serious allegory, once too much affected, is now almost obsolete. Why should it be so? Shall truth no more have its mounts of transfiguration? Must Mirza no more be overheard in his soliloquies? And is the road to the "Den" lost for ever? We trust, we trow not. In the "Student," too, occurs his far-famed attack upon the anonymous in periodical writing. We do not coincide with him in this. We do not think that the use of the anonymous either could or should be relinquished. It is, to be sure, in some measure relinquished as it is. The tidings of the authorship of any article of consequence, in a Review or

Magazine, often now pass with the speed of lightning through the literary world, till it is as well known in the book-shop of the country town, or the post-office of the country village, as in Albermarle or George Street.

But, in the first place, the anonymous forms a very profitable exercise for the acuteness of our young critics, who become, through it, masters in the science of internal evidence, and learn to detect the fine Roman hand of this and the other writer, even in the strokes of his t's, and the dots of his i's. Besides, secondly, the anonymous forms for the author an ideal character, fixes him in an ideal position, projects him out of himself; and hence many writers have surpassed themselves, both in power and popularity, while writing under its shelter. So with Swift, in his "Tale of a Tub;" Pascal, Junius, Sydney Smith, Isaac Taylor, Walter Scott; Addison, too, was never so good as when he put on the short face of the "Spectator." Wilson is never so good, as when he assumes the glorious *alias* of Christopher North. And, thirdly, the anonymous, when preserved, piques the curiosity of the reader, mystifies him into interest; and, on the other hand, sometimes allows a bold and honest writer, to shoot folly, expose error, strip false pretension, and denounce wrong, with greater safety and effect. A time may come when the anonymous will require to be abandoned: but we are very doubtful if that time has yet arrived.

In pursuing, at the commencement of this paper, a parallel between Byron and Bulwer, we omitted to note a stage, the last in the former's literary progress. Toward the close of his career, his wild shrieking earnestness subsided into Epicurean derision. He became dissolved into one contemptuous and unhappy sneer. Beginning with the satiric bitterness of "English Bards, he ended with the fiendish gayety of "Don Juan." He laughed at first that he "might not weep;" but ultimately this miserable mirth drowned his enthusiasm, his heart, and put out the few flickering embers of his natural piety. The deep tragedy dissolved in a "poor pickle herring," yet mournful farce. We trust that our novelist will not complete his resemblance to the poet, by sinking into a satirist. 'Tis indeed a pitiful sight that, of one who has passed the meridian of life and reputation, grinning back, in helpless mockery and toothless laughter, upon the brilliant way which he has traversed, but to which he can return no more. We anticipate for Bulwer a better destiny. He who has mated with the mighty spirit, which had almost reared again the fallen Titanic form of republican Rome; whose genius has travelled up the Rhine, like a breeze of music "stealing and giving odor;" who, in "England and the English," has cast a rapid but vigorous glance upon the tendencies of our wondrous age; who, in his verse, has so admirably pictured the stages of romance in Milton's story; who has gone down a "diver lean and strong," after Schiller, into the "innermost main," lifting with a fearless hand the "veil that is woven with night and with terror;" and in "Zanoni," has essayed to relume the mystic fires of the Rosicrucians, and to reveal the dread secrets of the spiritual world; must worthily close a career so illustrious.*

RALPH WALDO EMERSON.

Elsewhere we have spoken shortly, but sincerely, of Emerson, and even at the risk of egotism, we must say, that we have been not a little amused at the treatment which our remarks have met with from the press of America. So far

* Since the above was written, Bulwer has published three works of consequence, all very different from each other: "Lucretia," a detestable imitation of a detestable school; "Harold," a fine historical romance; and "The Caxtons," the sweetest, simplest, most genuine and natural of all his productions. An ingenious friend in "Hogg" has charged us with having painted an incongruous and inconsistent portrait of Bulwer, asserting that our original feeling toward him was that of enthusiastic admiration, but had been modified upon the mere dictum of some eminent friend. This is a total misapprehension. Our feelings of admiration toward Bulwer have rather grown than otherwise. In the year 1840 we wrote rather slightingly of him in the "Dumfries Herald," but we had not then read "Zanoni." To piece together an old and new opinion, is, indeed, an absurd attempt, and leads to an absurd result; but it is an attempt we have never made, and let the public judge whether it be a result which we have reached. We could retort upon our clever friend, by proving that within one year he expressed *two* opinions of *this very article.*

as we can judge from periodicals and newspapers, from Baltimore to Boston, a cry of universal reprobation has assailed that article. It has fallen between two stools—on the one hand, Emerson's detractors are furious with us, for placing him at the head of American literature, and so far they are right—though a most national writer, to American literature he does not belong. He is among them, but not of them—a separate state, which no Texas negotiation will ever be able to annex to their territory. On the other hand, the school of Transcendentalists contend that we do him less than justice; that our lines are unable to measure or to hold this leviathan; and the opinion of one American author to this effect deeply humiliated us, till accidentally falling in with her own criticisms, and finding that, among other judgments of the same kind, she preferred Southey, as a poet, to Shelley, we were not a little comforted, and began to think that, perhaps, we had as good a right to think and speak about Emerson as herself. "Verily, a prophet hath honor, save in his own country, and among those of his own house"—an expression containing much more truth in it than it at first seems to imply; for, indeed, the honor given in one's own country is often as worthless as the neglect or abuse; and, notwithstanding the well-known French adage, the vilest and commonest of hero-worship is that of valets and parasites, who measure their idol by the standard of his superiority to their own littleness. Hero-worship, however, even in its worst form, is preferable to that spirit of jealousy which pervades much of the American press in reference to Emerson, which, at the mention of his name, elicits in each journal a long list of illustrious-obscure (like a shower of bats from the roof of a barn on the entrance of a light), in its judgment superior to him—as though a Cockney, insulted by a panegyric on Carlyle, as one of the principal literary ornaments of London, were to produce and parade the names of the subordinate scribblers in the "Satirist," "Literary Gazette," &c, as the genuine galaxy of her mental firmament. With occasional exceptions, the great general rule is—how does a name sound afar?—does it return upon us from the horizon?—what impression does it make upon those who, unprejudiced either for or against the author personally—uncircumscribed by clique or coterie—unaltered by adverse, unsoftened by favorable criticism, have fairly brought his works to the test of their own true-feeling and true-telling souls?

This has been eminently the case with Emerson. To him Britain is beginning to requite the justice which America, to her honor, first awarded to Carlyle. Sincere spirits, in every part of the country, who have, many of them, no sympathy with Emerson's surmised opinions, delight, nevertheless, to do him honor, as an earnest, honest, and gifted man, caught, indeed, and struggling in a most alien element, standing almost alone in a mechanical country, and teaching spiritual truth to those to many of whom Mammon—not Moses—has become the lawgiver, and Cant—not Christ—the God, but as yet faithful to the mission with which he deems himself to be fraught.

Alike careless and fearless of the judgment which may be passed by any man here or in America on our opinions, we propose now to extend our former estimate of Emerson—an estimate which has at once been strengthened and modified by the volume of poems he has recently issued.

And first of his little volume of poems. They are not wholes, but extracts, from the volume of his mind. They are, as he truly calls some of them, "Woodnotes," as beautiful, changeful, capricious, and unfathomable often as the song of the birds. On hearing such notes we sometimes ask ourselves, "What *says* that song which has lapped us in such delicious reverie, and made us almost forget the music in the sweet thoughts which are suggested by it?" Vain the question, for is not the suggestion of such sweet thoughts saying enough, saying all that it was needed to say? It is the bird that speaks—our own soul alone can furnish the interpretation. So with many of the poems of Emerson. They mean absolutely nothing—they are mere nonsense-verses—except to those who have learned their cipher, and whose heart instinctively dances to their tune. It is often a wordless music—a wild wailing rhythm—a sound inexplicable, but no more absurd or meaningless than the note of the flute or the thrill of the mountain bagpipe. Who would, or who, though willing, could, translate into common, into *all* language, that train of thought and emotion, long as the life of the soul, and wide as the firmament, which one inarticulate melody can awaken in the mind? So some of Emerson's verses float us away, listening and lost, on their stream of sound, and of dim suggestive meaning. Led himself, as he repeatedly says, "as far as the incommunicable," he leads us into the same mystic region, and we feel that even in Nature there are things unutterable, which it is not possible for the tongue of man to utter, and which yet are real as the earth and the heavens. Coleridge remarks, that wherever you find a sentence musically worded, of true rhythm, and melody in the words, there is something deep and good in the meaning too. Mere no-meaning will not wed with sweet sound. We do not profess to be in the secret of some of the more mystic poems in this volume, such as "Uriel" and the "Sphynx." Nor can we think that there is much *room* behind the mystic screen—where the poet stands—between his song and the "Oversoul;" but we are ready to apply the old Socratic rule in his behalf—what we understand is excellent, what we do not understand is likely to be excellent too.

A man is often better than his theory, however good and comparatively true that theory be; and this holds especially true of a poet s creed, which, however dry, hard, and abstract, flushes into beauty at his touch, even as the poet's cottage has charms about it, which are concealed from the vulgar eye; and the poet's bride is often by him prodigally clothed with beauties which niggard nature had denied her. What Mr. Emerson's creed is, we honestly say we do not know—that all we confidently assert concerning it is, that you cannot gather it like apples into baskets, nor grind it like corn into provender, nor wind and unwind it like a hank of yarn, nor even collect it like sunlight into a focus, and analyze it into prismatic points, whether five or seven—nor inclose it within all the vocabularies of all vernacular tongues; and yet that it is not so bad or unholy, but that *in his mind* Beauty pitches her tents around its borders, and Wonder looks up toward it with rapt eye, and Song tunes sweet melodies in its praise, and Love, like the arms of a child seeking to span a giant oak, seeks to draw into her embrace its immeasurable vastness. It is such a creed as a man might form and subscribe in a dream, and when he awoke receive a gentle shrift from wise and gentle confessors. Why criticise or condemn the long nocturnal reverie of a poetic mind, seeking to impose its soft fantasy upon the solid and stupendous universe! We will pass it by in silence, simply retorting the smile with which he regards our sterner theories, as we watch him weaving his network of cobweb around the limbs of the "Sphynx," and deeming that he has her fast.

This, indeed, is the great fault of Emerson. He has a penchant for framing brain-webs of all sorts and sizes; and because they hang beautifully in the sunbeam, and wave gracefully in the breeze, and are to his eye peopled with a fairy race, he deems them worthy of all acceptation, and we verily believe would mount the scaffold, if requisite, for the wildest day-dream that ever crossed his soul among the woods. It was for visions as palpable as the sun that the ancient prophets sacrificed or periled their lives. It was for facts of which their own eyes and ears were cognizant that the apostles of the Lamb loved not their lives unto the death. It was not till this age that "Cloudland," nay, dreamland—dimmer still—sent forth a missionary to testify, with rapt look and surging eloquence, his belief in the shadows of his own thoughts.

Emerson, coming down among men from his mystic altitudes, reminds us irresistibly at times of Rip Van Winkle, with his gray beard and rusty firelock, descending the Catskill Mountains, from his sleep of a hundred years. A dim, sleepy atmosphere hangs around him. All things have an unreal appearance. Men seem "like trees walking.' Of his own identity he is by no means certain. As in the "Taming of the Shrew," the sun and the moon seem to have interchanged places; and yet, arrived at his native village, he (not exactly like honest Rip) sets up a grocer's shop, and sells, not the mystic draught of the mountain, but often the merest commonplace preparations of an antiquated morality.

In fact, nothing is more astounding about this writer than the mingled originality and triteness of his matter. Now he speaks as if from inmost communion with the soul of being; Nature seems relieved of a deep burden which had long lain on her bosom, when some of his oracular words are uttered; and now it is as if the throat of the thunder had announced the rule of three—as if the old silence had been broken, to enunciate some truism which every schoolboy had long ago recorded in his copy-book. The "Essay on Compensation," for example, proves most triumphantly that vice is its own punishment, and virtue its own reward; but, so far as it seeks to show that vice is its own *only* punishment, and virtue is its own *only* reward, it signally fails. The truth, indeed, is this—vice does punish, and terribly punish, its victims, but who is to punish vice? How is it to be gibbeted for the warning of the moral universe? Can a mere undercurrent of present punishment be sufficient for this, if there be such a thing as a great general commonwealth in the universe at all? Must it not receive, as the voluntary act of responsible agents, some public and final rebuke? The compensation which it at present obtains is but comparatively a course of private teaching; and does not the fact, that it is on the whole unsuccessful, create a necessity for a more public, strict, and effectual reckoning and instruction?

Thus, what is true in this celebrated essay is not new; and what is new is not true. This is not unfrequently the manner of Mr. Emerson. To an egregious truism he sometimes suddenly appends a paradox as egregious. Like a stolid or a sly servant at the door of a drawing-room, he calls out the names of an old respected guest and of an intruding and presumptuous charlatan, so quickly and so close together, that they appear to the company to enter as a friendly pair. Of intentional deception on such matters, we cheerfully and at once acquit him; but to his eye, emerging from the strange dreamy abnormal regions in which he has dwelt so long, old things appear new, and things new to very crudity appear stamped with the authority and covered with the hoary grandeur of age.

Emerson's object of worship has been by many called nature—it is, in reality, man; but by man, in his dark ambiguities and inconsistencies, repelled, he has turned round and sought to see his face exhibited in the reflector of nature. It is man whom he seeks every where in the creation. In pursuit of an ideal man, he runs up the midnight winds of the forest and questions every star of the sky. To gain some authentic tidings of man's origin—his nature—past and future history—he listens with patient ear to the songs of birds—the wail of torrents—as if each smallest surge of air were whispering, could he but catch the meaning, about man.

He feels that every enigma runs into the great enigma—what is man? and that if he could but unlock his own heart, the key of the universe were found. Perhaps nature, in some benignant or unguarded hour, will tell him where that key was lost! At all events, he will persist in believing that the creation is a vast symbol of man; that every tree and blade of grass is somehow cognate with his nature, and significant of his destiny; and that the remotest stars are only the distant perspective of that picture of which he is the central figure.

It is this which so beautifies nature to his eye—that gives him more than an organic or associated pleasure in its forms, and renders it to him, not so much an object of love or of admiration as of ardent study. To many nature is but the face of a great doll—a well-painted insipidity; to Emerson it has sculptured on it an unknown but mighty language, which he hopes yet to decipher. Could he but understand its alphabet!—could he but accurately spell out one of its glorious syllables! In the light of that flashing syllable he would appear to himself discovered, explained; and thus, once for all, would be read the riddle of the world!

This, too, prevents his intercourse with nature from becoming either tedious or melancholy. Nature, to most, is a gloomy companion. Sometimes they are tired of it—more frequently they are terrified. "What does all this mean? what would all this teach us? what would those frowning schoolmasters of mountains have us to do or learn?" are questions which, though not presented in form, are felt in reality, and which clear, as by a whip of small cords, the desecrated temple of nature. A few, indeed, are still left standing in the midst alone! And among those few is Emerson, who is reconciled to remain, chiefly through the hope and the desire of attaining one day more perfect knowledge of nature's silent cipher, and more entire communion with nature's secret soul. Like an enthusiastic boy clasping a Homer's "Iliad," and saying, "I shall yet be able to understand this," does he seem to say, "Dear are ye to me, Monadnoc and Agiochook, dear ye Alleghanies and Niagaras, because I yet hope (or at least those may hope who are to follow me) to unfix your clasps of iron—to unroll your sheets of adamant—to deliver the giant truths that are buried and struggling below you—to arrest in human speech the accents of your vague and tumultuous thunder."

As it is, his converse with creation is intimate and endearing. "Passing over a bare common, amid snow-puddles, he almost fears to say how glad he is." He seems (particularly in his "Woodnotes") an inspired tree, his veins full of sap instead of blood; and you take up his volume of poems, clad as it is in green, and smell to it as to a fresh leaf. He is like the shepherd (in Johnson's fine fable) among the Carpathian rocks, who understood the language of the vultures; the sounds—how manifold—of the American forest say to his purged ear what they say to few others, and what even his language is unable fully to express.

Akin to this passionate love of nature is one main error in Emerson's system. Because nature consoles and satisfies him, he would preach it as a healing influence of universal efficacy. He would send man to the fields and woods to learn instruction and get cured of his many wounds. These are the airy academies which he recommends. But, alas! how few can act upon the recommendation! How few entertain a genuine love for nature! Man, through his unhappy wanderings, has been separated, nay, divorced, from what was originally his pure and beautiful bride—the universe. No one feels this more than Emerson, or has mourned it in language more plaintive. But why will he persist in prescribing nature as a panacea to those who, by his own showing, are incapable of apprehending its virtue? They are clamoring for bread, and he would give them rocks and ruins. We hold that between man and nature there is a gulf which nothing but a vital change upon his character, circumstances, and habits can fill up. Ere applying the medicine, you must surely premise the stomach. Man, as a collective being, has little perception of the beauty, and none of the high spiritual meaning of creation; and as well teach the blind religion through the avenue of the eye, as teach average man truth or hope, or faith or purity, through a nature amid which he dwells an alien and an enemy.

On no subject is there so much pretended, and on none so little real feeling, as in reference to the beauties of nature. We do not allude merely to the trash which professed authors, like even Dickens, indite, when, against the grain, it is their cue to fall into raptures with Niagara, or the scenery of the Eternal City, but to the experiences of every-day life. How often have we travelled with parties of pleasure (as they are called) whose faces, after the first burst of animal excitement, produced by fresh air and society, had subsided, it was impossible to contemplate without a mixture of ludicrous and melancholy emotions. Besides, here and there, a young gentleman with elevated eyebrow and conceited side-look, spouting poetry; and a few young ladies looking intensely sentimental during the spoutation, the majority exhibited, so far as pleasure was concerned, an absolute blank —weariness, disgust, insipid disregard, or positive aversion, to all the grander features of the scenery, were the general feelings visible. Still more detestable were their occasional exclamations of forced admiration, nearly as eloquent, but not so sincere, as the enthusiasm of porkers over their provender. And how quickly did a starveling jest or a wretched pun jerk them down from their altitudes to a more congenial region! A *double entendre* told better than the sight of a biforked Grampian. The poppling of a cork was finer music than the roar of a cataract. A silly flirtation among the hazel-bushes was far more memorable than the sudden gleam of a blue lake flashing through the umbrage like another morning. And when the day was over, and the party were returning homewards, it was dismal amid the deepening shadows of earth and the thickening glories of the sky, to witness the jaded looks, the exhausted spirits, the emptied hearts and souls of those vain flutterers about nature, whom the mighty mother had amused herself with tiring and tormenting, instead of unbarring to them her naked loveliness, or hinting to them one of the smallest secrets of her inmost soul. Specimens these of myriads upon myriads of parties of pleasure, which fashion is yearly stranding upon the shores of nature—to them an inhospitable coast—and proofs that man, as a species, must grow, and perhaps grow for ages, ere he be fit, even "on tiptoe standing," to be on a level with that "house not made with hands," of which he is now the unworthy tenant. Surely the beauties of nature are an appliance too refined for the present coarse complaints of degraded humanity, which a fiercer caustic must cure.

Emerson may be denominated emphatically the man of contrasts. At times he is, we have seen, the most commonplace, at other times the most paradoxical of thinkers. So is he at once one of the clearest and one of the most obscure of writers. He is seldom muddy; but either transparent as crystal or utterly opaque. He sprinkles sentences (as divines do Scripture quotations) upon his page, which are not only clear, but cast, like glow-worms, a far and fairy light around them. At other times he scatters a shower of paragraphs, which lie, like elf-knots, insulated and insoluble. Hence reading him has the stimulus of a walk amid the interchanging lights and shadows of the woods, or it is like a game of hide-and-seek, or you feel somewhat like the unlearned reader of Howe and Baxter when he comes upon their Latin and Greek quotations. You skip or bolt his bits of mysticism, and pass on with greater gusto to the clear and the open. Whether there be degrees in biblical inspiration or not, there are degrees in *his*. Now he rays out light, and now, like a black star, he deluges us with darkness. The explanation of all this lies, we think, here—Emerson has naturally a poetic and practical, not a philosophic or subtle mind; he has subjected himself, however, to philosophic culture, with much care, but with partial success; when he speaks directly from his own mind, his utterances are vivid to very brilliance; when he speaks from recollection of his teachers, they are exceedingly perplexed and obscure.

He is certainly, apart altogether from his verse, the truest poet America has produced. He has looked immediately, and through no foreign medium, at the poetical elements which he found lying around him. He has "staid at home with the soul," leaving others to gad abroad in search of an artificial and imperfect inspiration. He has said, "If the spirit of poetry chooses to descend upon me as I stand still, it is well; if not, I will not go a step out of my road in search of it; here, on this rugged soil of Massachusetts, I take my stand, baring my brow in the breeze of my own country, and invoking the genius of my own words." Nor has he invoked it in vain. Words, which are pictures —sounds, which are song—snatches of a deep woodland melody—jubilant raptures in praise of nature, reminding you afar off of those old Hebrew hymns, which, paired to the timbrel or the clash of cymbals, rose like the cries of some great victory to heaven—are given to Emerson at his pleasure. His prose is not upon occasion, and elaborately dyed with poetic hues, but wears them ever about it on its way, which is a winged way, not along the earth, but through the high and liquid air. Why should a man like this write verse? Does he think that truth, like sheep, requires a bell round its neck, ere it be permitted to go abroad? Have his thoughts risen irresistibly above the reaches of prose, and voluntarily moved into harmonious numbers? Does he mean to abandon—or could he, without remorse—that wondrous prose style of his, combining the sweet simplicity of Addison with the force of Carlyle? Is he impatient to have his verses set to music, and sung in the streets or in the drawing-rooms? Let him be assured that, exquisite as many of his poems are, his other writings are a truer and richer voice, their short and mellow sentences moving to the breath of his spirit as musically as the pine-cones to the breeze.

When we take into account this author's poetic tendencies and idealistic training, we are astonished that he should be often the most practical of moralists. And yet so it is. His refined theories frequently bend down like rainbows, and rest their bases on earth. He often seeks to translate transcendental truth into life and action. Himself may be standing still, but it is as a cannon stands still; his words are careering over the world, calling on men to be fervent in spirit, as well as diligent in business. There is something at times almost laughable in the sight of this man living "collaterally or aside"—this quiet, wrapt mystic standing with folded arms, like a second Simon Stylites, and yet preaching motion, progress—fervent motion, perpetual kindling progress to all around him. Motionless as a finger-post, he, like it, shows the way onwards to all passers-by. He is, in this respect, very unlike Wordsworth, who would protect the quiet of his fields as carefully as that of his family vault, or as the peace of his own heart; who, in love for calm, would almost prefer the pacing of the silent streets of a city of the plague to the most crowded thoroughfares of London, and who hates each railway as if, to use the Scripture allusion, its foundation were laid on his first-born, and its terminus were set up over the grave of his youngest child. Emerson, standing on the shore, blesses the steamers that are sweeping past, and cries, "Sweep on to your destination with your freightage of busy thoughts and throbbing purposes, and, as you pass, churn up the waters into poetry;" perched on Monadnoc, he seems to print a path into the cloudland of the future for the rushing railway train, which affects him not with fear, but with hope, for he looks on the machinery of this age as a great scheme of conductors, lying spread and ready for the nobler influences of a coming period. He feels that the real truth is this: railways have not desecrated Nature, but have left *man behind*, and it were well that man's spiritual should overtake his physical progress. The great lessons of a practical kind which Emerson teaches, or tries to teach his countrymen, are faith, hope, charity, and self-reliance. He does not need to teach them the cheap virtues of industry and attention to their own interest; certain distinctions between *meum* and *tuum*, right and wrong, even he has failed to impress upon their apprehension. But he has been unwearied in urging them to faith—in other words, to realize, above the details of life, its intrinsic worth and grandeur as a whole, as well as the presence of divine laws, controlling and animating it all; to hope in the existence of an advance as certain as the motion of the globe (a feeling this which we notice with pleasure to be *growing* in his writings); to love, as the mother of that milder day which he expects and prophesies; and to self-reliance, as the strong girdle of a nation's, as well as of an individual's loins, without which both are "weak as is a breaking wave."

To a country like America, whose dependence upon Britain too often reminds us of an upstart hanging heavily, yet with an air of insolent carelessness, upon the arm of a superior, of what use might the latter lesson be? "Trust thyself. Cut a strong oaken staff from thy own woods, and rest sturdily, like a woodland giant, upon it. Give over stealing from and then abusing the old country. Kill and eat thine own mutton, instead of living on rotten imported *fricassées*. Aspire to originality in something else than national faults, insolences, and brutalities. Dare to be true, honest—thyself, indeed, a *new* country—and the Great Spirit, who loved thee in thy shaggy primeval mantle, will love thee still, and breathe on thee a breath of his old inspiration." Thus, substantially, in a thousand places, does Emerson preach to his native country.

In judging, whether of his faults or merits, we ought never to lose sight of what is his real position—he was, and is a recluse. He has voluntarily retired from society. Like the knights of old, who left the society of their mistresses to meditate in solitary places upon their charms, he, in love to man, has left him, and muses alone upon his character and destiny. His is not the savage grumbling retreat of a Black Dwarf, nor the Parthian flight of a Byron, nor the forced expulsion of a Shelley, who, seeking to clasp all men to his warm bosom, was with loud outcries repelled, and ran, shrieking, into solitude—it has been a quiet, deliberate, dignified withdrawal. He has said, "If I leave you, I shall, perchance, be better able to continue to love you—and perhaps, too, better able to understand you—and perhaps, above all, better able to profit you." And so the refined philanthropist has gone away to chew the cud of sweet and bitter fancy, among the blackberry vines or by the "leopard colored rills," or up the long dim vistas of the forest glades. A healthier and happier Cowper, his retreat made, at the time, as little noise as that of the solitary of Olney. London knew not that one, soon to be the greatest poet of that age, and the most powerful satirist of its own vices, was leaving for the country, in the shape of a poor, timid hypochondriac. None cried "stole away" to this wounded hare. So Boston nor New England imagined not that their finest spirit had forsaken his chapel for the cathedral of the woods—and they would have laughed you to scorn had you told them so.

In this capacity of recluse he has conducted himself in a way worthy of the voice which came to him from the heart of the forest, saying, "Come hither and I will show thee a thing." By exercise and stern study he has conquered that tendency to aimless and indolent reverie, which is so apt to assail thinking men in solitude. By the practice of bodily temperance and mental hope, he has, in a great measure, evaded the gloom of vexing thoughts and importunate cravings. His mind has, "like a melon," expanded in the sunshine.

"The outward forms of sky and earth,
Of hill and valley, he has view'd;
And impulses of deeper birth
Have come to him in solitude."

Still we cannot say that he has entirely escaped the drawbacks to which the recluse is subject. He has been living in a world of his own—he has been more conversant with principles than with facts—and more with dreams than either. His writing sometimes wants the edge and point which can be gained only by rough contact with the world; as it is, it is often rather an inarticulate murmur as of a brook, careless whether it be heard or understood or not, than the sharp voice of a living man. Perhaps, also, like most solitaries, he has formed and nursed an exaggerated idea of himself and his mission. In despite to the current of general opinion, he sometimes throws in rugged and crude absurdities, which have come from some other source than of the "Oversoul!" And, altogether, through the mist of the sweet vision, which seems the permanent abode of his own mind, he has but imperfect glimpses of the depth and intensity of that human misery, which is but another name for human life.

There is another subject where, we humbly think, his views are still more egregiously in error. We refer to human guilt. We agree with him in thinking that there is a point of view from which this dark topic may be a theme of gratulation. But we deem him premature and presumptuous in imagining that he has already reached that high angle of vision. If Foster's discolored sight, on the one hand, gave "hell a murkier gloom," and made sin yet uglier than it is, Emerson refines it away to nothing, and really seems to regard the evil committed by man in precisely the same light as the cunning of the serpent and the ferocity of the tiger. Who has anointed his eyes with eye-salve, so that he can look complacently, and with incipient praise on his lips, upon the loathsome shapes of human depravity? What Genius of the western mountains has taken him to an elevation, whence the mass of man's wickedness, communicating with hell, and growing up toward retribution, appears but a mole-hill, agreeably diversifying the monotony of this world's landscape? The sun may, with his burning lips, kiss and gild pollution, and remain pure; but that human spirit ought to be supernal which can touch and toy with sin. And if, in his vision of the world, there be barely room for guilt, where is there space left or required for atonement?

It was once remarked by us of John Foster, "pity but he had been a wickeder man;" the meaning of which strange expression was this—pity but that, instead of standing at such an austere distance from human frailty, he had come nearer it, and in a larger measure partaken of it himself; for, in this case, his conceptions of it would have been juster, mellower, and less terribly harsh. We may parallel this by saying, pity almost but Emerson had been a worse and an unhappier man; for thus might he have felt more of the evil of depravity, from its remorse and its retribution, and been enabled to counteract that tendency, which evidently exists in his sanguine temperament, to underrate its virulence.

Like every really original mind, Emerson has been frequently subjected to and injured by comparison with others. Because he bears certain general resemblances to others, he must be their imitator or feebler alias. Because he is as tall as one or two reputed giants, he must be of their progeny! He has been called, accordingly, the American Montaigne—the American Carlyle—nay, a "Yankee pocket edition of Carlyle." Unfortunate America! It has been so long the land of mocking-birds, that when an eagle of Jove at last appears, he must have imported his scream, and borrowed the wild lustre of his eye! A great original standing up in an imitative country looks so sudden and so strange, that men at first conceive him a forced and foreign production. We will, on the contrary, cling to our belief, that Emerson is himself, and no other; and has learned that piercing yet musical note to which nations are beginning to listen, directly from the fontal source of all melody. We are sure that he would rather be an owl, hooting his own hideous monotone, than the most accomplished of the imitative race of mocking-birds or parrots.

We think that we can observe in many of Emerson's later essays, and in some of his poems, symptoms of deepening obscurity; the twilight of his thought seems rushing down into night. His utterances are becoming vaguer and more elaborately oracular. He is dealing in deliberate puzzles—through the breaks in the dark forest of his page you see his mind in full retreat toward some remoter Cimmerian gloom. That retreat we would arrest if we could, for we are afraid that those who will follow him thither will be few and far between. Since he has gathered a large body of *exoteric* disciples, it is his duty to seek to instruct, instead of perplexing and bewildering them.

Of Emerson's history we have little to tell. He was one of several brothers—all men of promise and genius—who died early, and whose loss, in one of his little poems, he deplores, as the "strong star-bright companions" of his youth. He officiated for some time as a clergyman in Boston. An American gentleman, who attended his chapel, gave us lately a few particulars about his ministry. Noted for the amiability of his disposition, the strictness of his morals, and attention to his duties, he became, on these accounts, the idol of his congregation. His preaching, however, was not generally popular, nor did it deserve to be. Our informant declared, that while Dr. Channing was the most, Emerson was the least, popular minister in Boston, and confessed that he never heard him preach a first rate sermon till his last, in which he informed his congregation that he could conscientiously preach to them no more. The immediate cause of his resignation was his adoption of some peculiar views of the Lord's Supper. In reality, however, the pulpit was not his pride of place. Its circle not only confined his body, but restricted his soul. He preferred rather to stray to and fro along the crooked serpent of eternity! He went away to think, farm, and write (as the Hutchinsons so sweetly sing) in the "old granite state." Thence, save to lecture, he has seldom issued, till his late pilgrimage to Britain. One trial, he has himself recorded to have shot like lightning through the haze of his mystic tabernacle, and to have pierced his soul to the quick. It was the death of a dear child of rare promise, whose threnody he has sung as none else could. It is the most touching of his strains to us, who have felt how the blotting out of one fair young face (albeit not so nearly related) is for a season the darkening of earth and of heaven.

Since beginning to write, we have had the opportunity of hearing Emerson the lecturer, as well as of meeting Emerson the man, and we shall close by a few jottings on him. Of Emerson the private individual, it were indelicate to say much; suffice it that he has neither tail nor cloven foot, has indeed nothing very remarkable or peculiar about him, but is simply a mild and intelligent gentleman, with whom you might be hours and days in company, without suspecting him to be a philosopher or a poet. His manners are those of one who has studied the graces in the woods, unwittingly learned his bow from the bend of the pine, and his air and attitudes from those into which the serviceable wind adjusts the forest trees, as it sweeps across them. His conversation is at times a sweet rich dropping, like honey from the rock. He is a great man, gracefully disguised under sincere modesty and simplicity of character; is totally free from those go-ahead crotchets and cants which disgust you in many Americans; and it is impossible for the most prejudiced to be in his society, and not be impressed with respect for the innocence of his life, and regard for the unaffected sincerity of his manners. Plain and homely he may be as a wooden bowl, but not the less rich and ethereal is the nectar of thought by which he is filled. A lecturer, in the common sense of the term, he is not; call him rather a public monologist, talking rather to himself than to his audience—and what a quiet, calm, commanding conversation it is! It is not the seraph, or burning one that you see in the midst of his wings of fire—it is the naked cherubic reason thinking aloud before you. He reads his lectures without excitement, without energy, scarcely even with emphasis, as if to try what can be effected by the pure, unaided momentum of thought. It is soul totally unsheathed that you have to do with; and you ask, is this a spirit's tongue that is sounding on its way? so solitary and severe seems its harmony. There is no betrayal of emotion, except now and then when a slight tremble in his voice proclaims that he has arrived at some spot of thought to him peculiarly sacred or dear, even as our fellow-traveller along a road sometimes starts and looks round, arrived at some landmark of passion and memory, which to us has no interest; or as an earthly steed might be conceived to shiver under the advent of a supernal horseman—so his voice must falter here and there below the glorious burden it has to bear. There is no emphasis, often, but what is given by the eye, and this is felt only by those who see him on the side view; neither standing behind nor before can we form any conception of the rapt living flash which breaks forth athwart the spectator. His eloquence is thus of that highest kind which produces great effects at small expenditure of means, and without any effort or turbulence; still and strong as gravitation, it fixes, subdues, and turns us around. To be more popular than it is, it requires only two elements—first, a more artistic accommodation to the tastes and understandings of the audience; and, secondly, greater power of personal passion, in which Emerson's head as well as his nature seems deficient. Could but some fiery breath of political zeal or religious enthusiasm be let loose upon him, to create a more rapid and energetic movement in his style and manner, he would stir and inflame the world.

His lectures, as to their substance, are very comprehensive. In small compass, masses of thought, results of long processes, lie compact and firm; as 240 pence are calmly inclosed in one bright round sovereign, so do volumes manifold go to compose some of Emerson's short and Sibyline sentences. In his lecture on Napoleon, as we have already seen, he reduces him and the history of his empire to a strong jelly. Eloquence, that ample theme, in like manner he condenses into the hollow of one lecture—a lecture for once which proved as popular as it was profound. His intellectual tactics somewhat resemble those of Napoleon. As he aimed at, and broke the heart of opposing armies, Emerson loves to grasp and tear out the trembling core of a subject, and show it to his hearers. In both of these lectures we admired his selection of instances and anecdotes; each stood for a distinct part of the subject, and rendered it at once intelligible and memorable. An anecdote thus severely selected answers the end of a bone in the hand of an anatomical lecturer: it appeals to sense as well as soul. We liked, too, his reading of a passage from the "Odyssey," descriptive of the eloquence of Ulysses. It was translated into prose—the prose of his better essays—by himself, and was read with a calm classical power and dignity, which made a thousand hearts still as the grave. For five minutes there seemed but two things in the world—the silence, and the voice which was passing through it.

If men, we have often exclaimed, would but listen as attentively to sermons, as they do to the *intimations* at the end! Emerson generally commands such attention; especially, we are told, that during his first lecture in Edinburgh on Natural Aristocracy it was fine to see him, by his very bashfulness, driven not out of, but *into* himself, and speaking as if in the forest alone with God and his own soul. This was true self-possession. The audience, too, were made to feel themselves as much alone as their orator. To give a curdling sense of solitude in society, is a much higher achievement than to give a sense of society in solitude. It is among the mightiest acts of spiritual power, thus to insulate the imagination or the conscience of man, and suggests afar off the proceedings of that tremendous day, when in the company of a universe each man will feel himself alone.

In the three lectures *we* heard from Mr. Emerson there did not occur a single objectionable sentence. But there was unquestionably a blank in all, most melancholy to contemplate. We have no sympathy with the attempts which have been made to poison the popular mind, and to rouse the popular passions against this gentleman, whether by misrepresenting his opinions or by blackening his motives. He does not believe himself—whatever an ignorant and conceited scribbler in the "United Presbyterian Magazine" may say—to be God. He is the least in the world of a proselytiser. He visited this country solely as a literary man, invited to give literary lectures. Whatever be his creed, he has not, in Scotland at least, protruded it; and even if he had, it would have done little harm; for as easily transfer and circulate Emerson's brain as his belief. But, when we think of such a mind owning a faith seemingly so cold, and vague, and shadowy; and when, in his lectures, we find moral and spiritual truths of such importance robbed of their awful sanctions, separated like rays cut off from the sun—from their parent system and source—swung from off their moorings upon the Rock of ages—the Infinite and the Eternal—and supported upon his own authority alone—when, in short, the Moon of genius comes between us and the Sun of God, we feel a dreariness and desolation of spirit inexpressible; and, much as we admire the author and love the man, we are tempted to regret the hour when he first landed upon our shores. Our best wishes, and those of thousands, went with him on his homeward way; but coupled with a strong desire that a better, clearer, and more definite light might dawn upon his soul, and create around him a true "forest sanctuary." Long has he been, like Jacob, dreaming in the desert: surely the ladder cannot be far off.

GEORGE DAWSON.

The office of an interpreter, if not of the highest order, is certainly very useful, honorable, and, at certain periods, particularly necessary. There are times when the angle at which the highest minds of the age stand to the middle and lower classes is exceedingly awkward and uncertain. Their names and their pretensions are well known; even a glimmer of their doctrine has got abroad; some even of their books are read with a maximum of avidity, and a minimum of understanding; but a fuller reflection of their merits and their views—a farther circulation of their spirit, and a more complete discharge of their electric influences, are still needed. For these purposes, unless the men will condescend to interpret themselves, we must have a separate class for the purpose. Indeed, such a class will be created by the circumstances. As each morning we see a grand process of interpretation, when the living light leaps downwards from heaven to the mountain summits, and from these to the low-lying hills, and from these to the deep glens—each mountain and hill taking up in turn its part in the great translation, till the landscape is one volume of glory—so mind after mind, in succession, and in the order of their intellectual stature, must catch and reflect the empyrean fire of truth.

Chief among the interpreters of our time stands Thomas Carlyle. He has not added any new truth to the world's stock, nor any artistic work to the world's literature, nor is he now likely to do so; but he has stood between the British mind and the great German orbs, and flung down on us their light, with a kind of contemptuous profusion, colored, too, undoubtedly, by the strange rugged idiosyncrasy on which it has been reflected. This light, however, has fallen short of the middle class, not to speak of the masses of the community. This translation must itself be translated. —For some time it might have been advertised in the newspapers—"Wanted, an intrepreter for Sartor Resartus." Without the inducement of any such advertisement, but as a volunteer, has Mr. George Dawson stepped forward, and has now for two years been plying his profession with much energy and very considerable success.

It were not praise—it were not even flattery—it were simply insult and irony, to speak of Mr. Dawson in any other light than as a clever, a very clever translator, or, if he will, interpreter, of a greater translator and interpreter than himself. In all the lectures we have either heard or read of, his every thought and shade of thought was Carlyle's. The matter of the feast was, first course, Carlyle; second, do.; dessert, do.; *toujours*, Carlyle: the dishes, dressing, and sauce only, were his own. Nor do we at all quarrel with him for this. Since the public are so highly satisfied, and since Carlyle himself is making no complaint, and instituting no hue and cry, it is all very well. It is really, too, a delightful *hachis* he does cook, full of pepper and spice, and highly palatable to the majority. Our only proper ground of quarrel would be, if he were claiming any independent merit in the thought, apart from the illustrations, the wit, and the easy vigorous talk of the exhibition. We have again and again been on the point of exclaiming, when compelled to contrast description with reality. We shall henceforth believe nothing till we have seen it with our eyes, and heard it with our ears. The most of the pictures we see drawn of celebrated people seem, after we have met with the originals, to have been painted by the blind. So very many determinedly praise a man for qualities which he has not—if a man is tall, they make him short; if dark, they give him fair hair; if his brow be moderate in dimensions, they call it a great mass of placid marble; if he be an easy, fluent speaker, they dignify him with the name of orator; if his eye kindle with the progress of his theme, they tell us that his face gets phosphorescent, and as the face of an angel. Hence the mortifying disappointments which are so common—disappointments produced less by the *inferiority* than by the *unlikeness* of the reality of the description. A distinguished painter who visited Coleridge was chagrined to find his forehead, of which he had read ravings innumerable, of quite an ordinary size. We watched Emerson's face very narrowly, but could not, for our life, perceive any glow mounting up its pale and pensive lines. We had heard much of Dawson's eloquence, but found that while there was much fluency there was little fire, and no enthusiasm. Distance and dunces together had metamorphosed him, even as a nobler cause of deception sometimes changes a village steeple into a tower of rubies, and plates a copse with gold.

To call this gentleman a Cockney Carlyle, a transcendental bagman, were to be too severe; to call him a combination of Cobbett and Carlyle were to be too complimentary. But while there is much in the matter which reminds you of Carlyle, as the reflection reminds you of the reality, there is much in his style and manner which recalls William Cobbett. Could we conceive Cobbett by any possibility forswearing his own nature, converted to Germanism, and proclaiming it in his own way, we should have had George Dawson anticipated and forestalled. The Saxon style, the homely illustrations, the conversational air, the frequent appeals to common sense, the broad Anglicanisms, and the perfect self-possession, are common to both, with some important differences, indeed; since Dawson is much terser and pointed—since his humor is dry, not rich—and since he is, as to substance, rather an echo than a native, though rude voice.

To such qualities as we have now indirectly enumerated, we are to attribute the sway he has acquired over popular, and especially over English audiences. They are not, while hearing him, called profoundly either to think or feel. They are not painfully reminded that they have not *read*. Enthusiastic appeal never warms their blood. A noble self-contempt and forgetfulness is never inculcated. Of reverence for the ancient, the past, and the mysterious, there is little or none. They are never excited even to any fervor of destructive zeal. A strong, somewhat rough voice is heard pouring out an even, calm, yet swift torrent of mingled paradoxes and truisms, smart epigrammatic sentences, short, cold, hurrying sarcasms, deliberate vulgarisms of expression, quotations from "Sartor Resartus," and Scripture, and from no other book—never growing and never diminishing in interest—never suggesting an end as near, nor reminding us of a beginning as past—every one eager to listen, but no one sorry when it is done; the purpose of the whole being to shake, we think too much, respect for formulas, creeds, and constituted authorities—to inculcate, we think too strongly, a sense of independence and individualism—and to give to the future, we think, an undue preponderance over the past.

Mr. George Dawson has read with considerable care and accuracy the signs of his time. He has watched the direction and the rate of the popular tide, and has cast himself on it with an air of martyrdom. His has been the desperate determination at all hazards to sail with the stream. He sees, what only the blind do not, that a new era is begun, in which, as Napoleon said, "there shall be no Alps," when they threatened to impede his march; our young mind has in like manner sworn there shall be no past, no history, no Bible, no God even, if such things venture to stand across *our* way, and curb *our* principle of progress, and is rushing on heroically with this daring multitude. One is amused at the cry of persecution which he raises on his way. The term, to us, in such cases as his, sounds supremely ludicrous. What, in general, does persecution for conscience-sake now mean? It means, if the subject be a clergyman, the trembling of his audience and the doubling of his income; if an author, the tenfold sale of his works; if a man in business, three customers instead of one—not to speak of the pleasures of notoriety lecturing engagements, gold watches, and pieces of plate Pleasant and profitable persecution! even when it is diversified by a little newspaper abuse—the powerless hatred of the deserted party—and some strictures in the magazines! What comparison between this species of persecution and the treatment which a Wordsworth or a Shelley received? or what comparison between it and the neglect, contempt, and poverty which now befall many a worthy and conscientious supporter of the *Old?* We knew an elderly neglected clergyman, who came to a brother minister and said, "I wish you would preach against me; it might bring me into notice." Mr. Dawson has been preached, placarded, and prayed into notice—a notice in which he has expanded and bourgeoned like a peach-tree in the sunshine, and yet of which he thinks proper to complain as persecution! Pretty exchange! an elegant pulpit for a barrel of burning coals—fifteen hundred admiring auditors for a thousand exulting foes—the "Church" instead of the "Cross" of the Saviour. We really cannot, in this world of woe, find in our hearts one particle of pity to spare for Mr. Dawson, nor for any such mellifluous martyrs.

No eagle soaring and screaming in the teeth of the storm —no thunder-cloud moving up the wind, do we deem our hero; but, on the whole, a most complacent and beautiful peacock's feather, sailing adown the breeze, yet with an air as if it had created and could turn it if he chose; or shall we say, a fine large bubble descending with dignity, as if it were the cataract? or, shall we try it once more? a straw, imagining that because it shows the direction, it is directing the wind. If these figures do not give satisfaction, we have fifty more at the service of Mr. Dawson's admirers; after all, we must blame his admirers and his enemies more than himself. He has much about him that is frank, open, and amiable. A clever young man, endowed with a rare talent for talk, he began to talk in a manner that offended his party. Many, on the other hand, of no party, were struck with surprise at hearing such bold and liberal sentiments uttered from such a quarter. Pure unmixed Carlylism coming from a Baptist pulpit sounded in their ears sweet and strange, as a "voice from a loftier climate." The rest might have been expected. Between the dislike of his foes, the wild enthusiasm of his friends, the ill-calculated pounce of the Archbishop of York, the real, though borrowed merit of many of his sentiments, and the real native force of his speech—he found himself all at once on a giddy eminence which might have turned stronger heads; for here was the *rarissima avis* of a liberal Baptist—a Carlylistic clergyman—a juvenile sage, and a transcendentalist talking English—there was no bird in all Knowesley Park that could be named in comparison. Here, besides, was positively the first Dawson (except Peel's friend) that had, as an intellectual man, been known beyond his own doorway. Such circumstances, besides a felt want in the public mind, which he professed to supply, account for the rapid rise of one who had written and done nothing, except a few lectures and sermons, to the summit of notoriety.

So far as Dawson is a faithful renderer or doer into English of Thomas Carlyle's sentiments, we have, we repeat, no quarrel with him. But in some points we dislike his mode of expounding and illustrating these, or if he be in all things an accurate expounder of his principal, why, then, we must just venture to question his principal's infallibility.

Mr. Dawson, for instance, sets himself with all his might to inculcate the uselessness of the clergy as teachers of truth, and the superiority of the lecturing class, or prophets, as he modestly calls them. Samuel, he told us, was a much greater personage than the priests of his day. We do not, in all points, "stand up for our order." We are far from thinking that the clergy, as a whole, are awake to the necessities of the age, or fully alive to all its tendencies. We know that Dr. Tholuck, when in this country, was grieved at the want of learning he found in some of our greatest men, and especially at their ignorance of the state of matters in Germany. We know that he advised two eminent Doctors of different denominations to read Strauss's "Life of Christ;" and that, while one of them declined, in very strong language, the other, Dr. Chalmers (how like him!) said, "Well, I will read it, Dr. Tholuck; *is't a big book?*" Strauss, of course, he recommended, not from sympathy with its theory, but because it is a book as necessary to be read now by the defenders of Christianity as was Gibbon's "History" fifty years ago. But while granting much to Mr. Dawson, we are far from granting all. Ministers do not profess to be prophets, except in so far as they are *declarers* of the divine will, as exhibited in the Scriptures, or as they may be endowed with that deep vision of truth and beauty which is now, by courtesy, called prophetic sight. But who are prophets, pray, in any other sense? Who can now pretend to stand to ministers in the relation, in which thatSamuel, who had, in his youth, been awakened by the voice of God, and who, in his manhood, had, by his call, aroused the slumbering thunder, and darkened the heavens by the waving of his hand, stood to the priesthood of Israel? Not surely George Dawson, Esq., A.M., nor yet Thomas Carlyle—no, nor Fichte and Goethe themselves. Alas! may we not now, all of us, take up the complaint of the Psalmist?—

> "Our signs we do not now behold,
> There is not us among
> A Prophet more, nor any one
> That knows the time how long."

It is, as it was at the close of Saul's guilty and inglorious reign, when God refused to answer by dreams, by Urim, or by prophets; and when, in defect of the true vision, he went to consult with wizards and *quack salvers.* We are, indeed, rather more favored—we have still among us wise and gifted men; but if we would find prophets, in the highest sense of the word, we must just go back and sit at the feet of those awful bards of Israel—those legislators of the future—whose words are full of eyes, and the depth of whose insight communicates with the omniscience of God. As poets, as seers, as teachers, as truthful and earnest men, not to speak merely of their august supernatural pretensions, they still tower alone unsurmounted and unapproached, the Himalayan mountains of mankind.

It is easy for a popular lecturer, primed and ready with his three or his six polished and labored efforts, to sneer at the ministers of Jesus. But it is not so easy for one of this, now calumniated class, to keep up for long years a succession of effective appeals to the conscience and to the heart, in season and out of season—through good report and through bad report. And it is not particularly kind or graceful in a gentleman, who must have experienced the peculiar difficulties of the order to which he still belongs, to turn again and rend them; enjoying, as he does, even yet, some of the immunities of the class, it is mean in him to shirk its responsibilities, and, meaner still, to try to shake its credit in the estimation of his countrymen.

He draws, to be sure, a distinction between a preacher and a man preaching—a distinction as obvious nearly as that between a fiddling man and a man fiddling, a barking puppy and a puppy barking. He is not a preaching man, but a man preaching. What a miserable quibble! Who means by a preacher any thing else than a man who has voluntarily assumed the task of declaring the truth of God to his fellows? Does one necessarily cease to be a man in becoming a preacher? Or does one necessarily become a man by ceasing to be, or wishing it to be thought that he has ceased to be, a preacher? Nay, verily. In fact, a considerable share of Mr. Dawson's popularity, with a certain class at least, springs from the preacher-air, and the preacher-phrases, which still cling to his delivery and style. He is little else than a clever lecturer, made out of the elements or ruins of a second-rate preacher.

In Mr. Dawson's lectures we find no variety of thought. Two or three ideas, imported into his mind, are rattled like peas over and over, into a thousand different sounds or discords. The same terms, too, such as subjective and objective, dynamical and mechanical, are perpetually repeated, with a parrot-like iteration. There is in some minds, and in some styles, a gigantic monotony, as in the ocean surges, or in the beams of the sun. But there is also a small mannerism arising from the mimicry of a model—itself, in part, a copy, which can with difficulty be endured for a few nights, and for no more.

Of course he proclaims warfare against conventionalisms of speech, and of thought: to call, in prayer, a woman a handmaiden, the sea the great deep, &c., is with him a grave offence. Words are things. Things ought to be called by their right names. A spade should be a spade: and not, with Dr. Johnson, a "broad, semi-wooden, semi-iron, instrument for tearing the bosom of *terra firma*, the pioneer of the advenient seed." Shade of Dr. Johnson! then, art thou not provoked to ask, What in the name of wonder, George Dawson, art thou? what callest thou thyself? Art thou infidel, pagan, or Christian, or any thing more than a man preaching? I know not how to entitle thee, positively; but, negatively, depend upon it, *I* shall never call *thee*, by any accident, "a great deep."

Too often in Mr. Dawson's prelections what is new is not true, and what is true is not new. In proclaiming the stern truth that there is something higher than happiness—namely, blessedness—he only repeated the finest sentence in that abysmal volume, "Sartor Resartus." But who in structed him for once to go beyond his master, and to ridicule the phrase, "luxury of doing good?" Because duty can play its high part at times without public fee or reward, has it not always, in its own exercise, "a joy beyond the name of pleasure?" Does not Scripture often appeal to the desire and to the prospect of happiness as stimulants to duty? Has not the Divine Being annexed even to sacrifice and to martyrdom, a feeling which we may appropriately term "luxury," if luxury mean something at once delicious and rare? "To be good for good's sake," is the noblest reach of man; but what does good imply in its very conception? Surely some severe but real delight, partly in present feeling, and partly in future prospect. We know right well the tendency of Mr. Dawson's sneer—it is an attempt to scoff out the golden candlestick of celestial blessedness, as the reward of the good; although as well might he seek to puff away to-morrow's sun.

We notice, in connection with all his allusions to religion, a want of moral reverence for the subject. Suppose it were true, what he so often intimates, that God has abandoned our present forms of worship, in what spirit should he tread the deserted shrine? In what spirit did (we beg pardon for the reference) the Son of Man walk in the desecrated and doomed Temple of Jerusalem? It was not, certainly, with contemptuous disregard any more than with the cry on on his lips, Raze, raze it to its foundation! It was, doubtless, with tears in his eyes, as he remembered, "Here God once dwelt." With what coolness, with what propensity to sneer, with what ill-suppressed joy, at these long desolations, do some now walk through what they call a ruin, as forsaken as the temple of Jupiter Palatinus. Shame to thee, George Dawson, if this be thy feeling, as we fear it is! This is not, rely on it, the feeling of thy Master, though he never took the vows of the ministry upon his soul. If we have not totally misconstrued the nature of Thomas Carlyle, he passes through the sanctuary, which he deems now forsaken, nay, a den of thieves, with emotions of profoundest sorrow, because, to use the language of Howe, the broken arches, the mouldering inscriptions, and the extinct fire, seem to him but too plainly to testify that the Great Inhabitant is gone.

Mr. Dawson's *forte* lies, unquestionably, in his lively and amusing illustrations. His is a species of proverbial philosophy. He abounds both in "old saws and modern instances." He accommodates the results of philosophy to every-day life, and translates its technicalities into the loose conversation, almost into the slang, of every-day language.

It may be questioned whether in this he does men much service; for, in the first place, in such a process a great deal that is most valuable necessarily escapes. There are thoughts in every high philosophy which will not bear translation into ordinary speech. Our English vernacular will only look ludicrous as it attempts to girth their greatness; and these thoughts are, of course, the deepest and noblest. Secondly, apart from this aboriginal difficulty, the translator, when also a popular lecturer, is under strong temptation to dilute what truth he does tell too much, and to give his babes, instead of milk, milk and water. And, thirdly, those babes will be exceedingly apt to fancy, after a few such diluted preparations, that they have suddenly shot up into men of full age. In the short space of four or five amusing hours, they are quite qualified to chatter Carlylese—to dogmatize on the characteristics and tendencies of the age, and to look with sovereign contempt on ministers, and on all who are weak enough to put their trust in them. We met, some time ago, in a London omnibus, a good-natured, amusing old lady, at whom we inquired if she had ever been in Edinburgh. She answered, "No; but I saw a *panoramar* of it, which gave me a very good *hidear* of it." Such a satisfactory panoram*ar*ic *hidear* does Mr. Dawson give his auditors of the German philosophy, and of Plato.

When I hear such a preacher, said one, I go home well pleased with him; when I hear such another, I go home ill pleased with myself. Mr. Dawson sends home most of his audience well pleased with him and with themselves, and thinking more of him and of themselves than of his theme. They carry away no stings with them—none of that fine humility, of that divine despair, which contemplation of nature's vastness and of man's littleness inevitably produces, and yet which never fails afterwards to excite genuine aspiration. From hearing Professor Nichol, you come home with but one thought, the grandeur of his subject; in which almost the thought of the lecturer has been lost, to which he has but served meekly to point, like the rod which he holds in his hand. In hearing Samuel Brown you have a similar feeling, blended, however, owing to his youth, with still more admiration for the man, who, at such an age, seems conversant with mysteries so profound, as if he had commenced his studies in an ante-natal state of being. The masterly ease, self-possession, clearness, interest, and fluency of Mr. Dawson's talk, give you an hour's, or perchance a night's pleasure, and that is all; for, indeed, he is rather a talker than a teacher. To those who have read Carlyle's Miscellanies and other works, he tells nothing new; and those who have not, are in general more amused by the novel and vivid illustrations, than impressed and subdued by what to them ought to be the startling truths. The enthusiast alone can teach, because he alone can feel up to that point where feeling overflows, burning, and sometimes scalding into other minds. Mr. Dawson may be, we trust is, at heart, a sincere man, but he is not an enthusiast; he has no self-forgetfulness, no rapt emotion of any kind; he manages his instrument but too dexterously, and too consciously well. We have no conception what he can have made of Switzerland—what shape its rocks, torrents, and glaciers have assumed in his mind—what *gingerbread cast* of the Alps he has contrived to form, or how his essentially cold and clever style has managed to rise to cope with the magnificent field. Were there any barn-fowl flutterings, any ghastly contortions of imaginative penury and weakness? or did he, as we rather suspect, with his wonted tact, avoid the grander features of his subject, and turn aside into paths equally pleasing, less hackneyed, and for him less dangerous? Let our Glasgow friends, who heard him on this subject, answer the question. Altogether, Mr. Dawson's mission seems to us exceedingly uncertain, both as to its purpose and its probable results. We do not see any distinct reason or call why he should have separated himself to that gospel of negations which he preaches. We have asked him already, what is he? we ask him now what he wishes us to be? A man who has started from the ranks, who has done so as if in obedience to a voice, "Come out, and be thou separate," ought to be able to tell with some explicitness what he would give us in exchange for what we are in effect required to resign. But "story," like the knife-grinder, "he has none to tell, sir." He offers, it is true, relief to doubters—nay, builds a chapel for them, and calls it by the *unpretending* name, the "Church of the Saviour;" but in truth his teaching only adds fire to fever, and seems to us a masterly machinery for creating or confirming doubt. We grant him readily that doubters—the most interesting and one of the most numerous of classes of men in the present day, including, not now as formerly, merely the vain and the vicious, but many of the sincere, the intelligent, the virtuous and the humble—including, especially, so many of the young and rising spirits of the time—are not sufficiently attended to in the daily ministrations. Their feelings are not respected, their questions are not fairly answered, their motives and characters are misrepresented, their doubts are flung back unresolved, contemptuously, in their face; and hence, many of them are carrying their questions to other oracles, and getting their Gordian knots cut by other swords than that of the Spirit.*

But let those who have done, repair the injury. Let the various churches of the country set to work with greater zeal, with greater unanimity, and, above all, with greater intelligence, and greater charity, to attend to this most important and neglected class. Let them not dream that merely to abuse Germanism is to answer it. Let them no longer waste their strength and breath in calling Carlyle or Emerson by hard names. Let them demonstrate that their charges against Christianity as dead, are untrue, by showing that its ancient spirit is still alive. Let them remember that the front of skeptical battle is changed since the days of Voltaire and Volney—that the character of the leaders is changed too—and that there must be a corresponding change in the tactics of Christian defenders. Such books as Paley, Watson, Hall on Modern Infidelity, or Olinthus Gregory, the leviathan of German skepticism takes up but as straw or rotten wood. They split upon his adamantine scales. The onset of Paine and Volney was from below—from the hell of mean passions, politics, and low conceptions of man; the onset of the German philosophers is from above—from the height of transcendental thought. From a higher eminence ought their onset to be repelled. Dr. Chalmers, from that lofty watch-tower which he occupied, and round which, alas! the shades of evening were gathering fast, saw the big

* We refer our readers for a more particular elucidation of our views on this subject, to our subsequent paper on Sterling.

bulking danger—and it was his all but last act to set the trumpet to his mouth, and blow an alarm to the Christian world. Would it had been more widely echoed and obeyed! Such a tender, general, and enlightened attention to the doubting Thomases of the day, would produce numerous good consequences. It would show religion in her most amiable aspect—having compassion upon the ignorant, and upon those that are out of the way. It would arrest the doubts of many, ere they were hardened into a fierce and aggressive infidelity. It would change every church into a refuge for those who are tossed with tempest, and not comforted—a true "Church of the Saviour;" and it would proclaim to those officious "flatterers," who would rid men of their burdens elsewhere than at the Cross and the Sepulchre, that their occupation was gone. We are not, however, at all sanguine of such results as near. Our wretched divisions and partyisms—the bigoted battle we are still disposed to do for the smallest minutiæ of our different creeds, while its main pillars are so powerfully assailed—our general deadness and coldness, seem to augur that some mighty regenerating process is needed by all churches ere they can fully meet wants which are yearly becoming more and more imperious. "Good religious people," writes to us one of the most eminent evangelical ministers in a sister country, "have a great deal to learn, and some of them will never learn any thing. They are unconscious of the new world in which they live. They do not know what a different thing the pulpit is, and how different the preacher ought to be, since the new and mighty preacher in the form of the Press has risen up, and occupied so much of the preacher's old ground. The Press and the Pulpit might, and ought to understand each other better than they do." Coinciding in such views, we do not, however, expect that Mr. Dawson's pulpit will do much to promote the reconciliation of those two rival powers. He is verily not a preacher, but a man preaching magazine articles sprinkled with Scripture texts. He belongs to an amphibious order of beings neither in nor out of the church. We cannot conceive himself long to remain at ease in such an ambiguous position, nor that the public can continue to place much confidence in him as a clergyman. It is whispered already that he is sinking as rapidly as he rose. We are not afraid that he will ever be totally overlooked. He is young, ready, fluent, ambitious, with much power of mental assimilation, a fertile, teeming brain, and a tongue and pair of lungs perfectly first rate. Such qualities in bustling times can never fail of their reward, although we should imagine that the lecture-room, instead of the chapel, will by and by become the favorite field for their exhibition.

We venture to conclude this from the perusal of his sermon—the opening one of his new chapel—entitled, "The Demands of the Age upon the Church." If this be an average specimen of Mr. Dawson's writing or preaching powers, we must warn the public that they are not to expect him to become a Hall in the pulpit, or a Foster at the desk. As a composition, it is loose, careless, even vulgar. Think of an expression like this, occurring in a discourse on such a solemn occasion: "*We do not unite on the sly.*" The style is an odd compound of Carlylisms and Pickwickisms. The bond of union it proposes is no bond at all. A union of common doubts and disbeliefs may form a vast moral infirmary, but not a church. We forewarn him, that it is difficult now as of old to make bricks without straw, and build a house without cement. That the doubters deserve special tending, he proves satisfactorily. He does not prove the adaptation of his chapel to their case. The spirit of Christianity he would divorce from its eternal principles and facts—an attempt as hopeless as to separate the life of a tree from its leaves, branches, and trunk. The only part of the discourse at all valuable is its statement of the admitted fact, that vital religion is at a low ebb; but even this he exaggerates, and his notion, that it has passed over to the free-thinkers, is simply not true. We would just beg the public to compare this specimen of the new style of preaching with some of Dr. Croly's recently published sermons, where they will find vast and varied erudition, burning genius, an eloquent severe, classical and grand, Scriptural sentiment—all the qualities, in short, which Dawson's writing has not—in order to learn what exchange they are required to make, and to be convinced that although his church be called the Church of the Saviour, he is not destined to be the saviour of the Church.

We know full well that such a frank expression of our

sentiments will, as did our strictures on Macaulay and Burns, create against us a number of opponents. We are perfectly indifferent. Whenever the trigger of the gun, Truth, is drawn, by however feeble a hand, and a report follows, multitudes of timorous or stupid creatures are sure to rise up alarmed or enraged, and to rend the air with their screams. It will be said that we are actuated by some *animus* against Mr. Dawson, just as a few blockheads accused us of hating a man who had been dead for half a century, and whose genius we had taken fifty opportunities of lauding in terms little short of downright idolatry. We must simply disown any such feeling. We gave Mr. Dawson constant attendance and earnest attention. We were occasionally delighted, and testified it by no feeble or niggardly applause. We saw much about him in private that was pleasing. But a sense of duty, coupled, we grant, with a certain feeling of indignation at the undue prominence which is partly given him, and which in part he assumes, and to which no man possessed merely of mechanical gifts, however extraordinary, is entitled, has urged us to write as we have written. "It is intolerable," said one, "to think of the literary coteries of London being over-crowed in the accent of an Ecclefechan carter." This may be, and is, and ought to be borne, when that accent stirs, warbles, and inflames, under the words of genius. But it is intolerable, that a glib and flowing tongue, conveying borrowed sentiments, in the language of the Pickwick papers, should be listened to as if behind it were flashing the eye of a Burns, or towering the brow of a Shakspeare. And it is still more intolerable, that a man without depth, learning, originality, or enthusiasm, should be swaying opinion, or shaking the faith of any in the great inspirations of the past.

If Isaiah, Ezekiel, and Daniel are to be blotted out, let the blank be filled up with names of a somewhat higher calibre—and mighty to start a nobler spirit—than that of George Dawson.

Our faith in popular lecturing has never been great, and has been lessened by the experiences of several past winters. In the course of them, we have heard five or six of the most distinguished of the class, and have not only listened carefully to them, but have watched the effects of their prelections on their audiences. So far as the lecturers are concerned, our expectations have been exceeded rather than the reverse. All, in different styles, were excellent. All, through very different avenues, found their way to the attention and to the applause of their hearers. One, by a rich anecdotage, and the clear and copious detail of facts, nailed the ears of his audience to his lips. Another gathered them around him, talking though he was in an unknown tongue, through the cloudy grandeur of his speculation. Another took them captive by the enthusiasm which shone in his face and quivered on his lips. Another passed across them, like a rapid snow-drift, showering on their passive spirits a thick succession of clear, cold sentences. All exerted power; all gave a certain amount of pleasure. Did any much more? Was any permanent elevation given, or lasting effect produced? Had Scotland, England, and America, been ransacked for their choicest spirits, only to produce a certain tickling gratification, at most amounting to a high intellectual treat? We do not wish to speak dogmatically on the point, but it is our distinct impression that in a spiritual, not in a pecuniary sense, the cost outwent the profit. The great ends of teaching were not, and in the space, and in the circumstances, could hardly have been answered. Multitudes, unprepared by previous reading and training, were brought out by curiosity, or in some cases by a better principle, to hear some of the first men of the age; listened with most exemplary attention, were thrilled or tickled, but we fear not *fed*. We are convinced that steady attendance upon one plain single month's course on geology, or modern history, would have done more good than whole years spent in hearing such brilliant birds of passage.

ALFRED TENNYSON.

The subject of the following sketch seems a signal example of the intimate relation which sometimes exists between original genius, and a shrinking, sensitive, and morbid nature. We see in all his writings the struggle of a strong intellect to "turn and wind the fiery Pegasus" of a most capricious, volatile, and dream-driven imagination. Tennyson is a curious combination of impulse, strength, and delicacy approaching to weakness. Could we conceive, not an Eolian harp, but a grand piano, played on by the swift fingers of the blast, it would give us some image of the sweet, subtle, tender, powerful, and changeful movements of his verse, in which are wedded artificial elegance, artistic skill, and wild, impetuous impulse. It is the voice and lute of Ariel; but heard not in a solitary and enchanted island, but in a modern drawing-room, with beautiful women bending round, and moss-roses breathing, in their faint fragrance, through the half-opened windows. Here, indeed, lies the paradox of our author's genius. He is haunted, on the one hand, by images of ideal and colossal grandeur, coming upon him from the isle of the Syrens, the caves of the Kraken, the heights of Ida, the solemn cycles of Cathay, the riches of the Arabian heaven; but, on the other hand, his fancy loves, better than is manly or beseeming, the tricksy elegancies of artificial life—the "white sofas" of his study—the trim walks of his garden—the luxuries of female dress—and all the tiny comforts and beauties which nestle round an English parlor. From the sublime to the snug, and *vice versa*, is with him but a single step. This moment toying on the carpet with his cat, he is the next soaring with a roc over the valley of diamonds. We may liken him to the sea-shell which, sitting complacently and undistinguished amid the commonplace ornaments of the mantelpiece, has only to be lifted to give forth from its smooth ear the far-rugged boom of the ocean breakers. In this union of feminine feebleness and imaginative strength, he much resembles John Keats, who at one time could hew out the vast figure of the dethroned Saturn, "quiet as a stone," with the force of a Michael Angelo, and, again, with all the gusto of a milliner, describe the undressing of his heroine in the "Eve of St. Agnes." Indeed, although we have ascribed, and we think justly, original genius to Tennyson, there is much in his mind, too, of the imitative and the composite. He adds the occasional languor, the luxury of descriptive beauty, the feminine tone, the tender melancholy, the grand aspirations, perpetually checked

9

and chilled by the access of morbid weakness, and the mannerisms of style which distinguish Keats, to much of the simplicity and the philosophic tone of Wordsworth, the peculiar rhythm and obscurity of Coleridge, and a portion of the quaintness and allegorizing tendency which were common with the Donnes, Withers, and Quarleses, of the seventeenth century. What is peculiar to himself is a certain carol, light in air and tone, but profound in burden. Hence his little lyrics—such as "Oriana," "Mariana at the Moated Grange," the "Talking Oak," the "May Queen"—are among his most original and striking productions. They tell tales of deep tragedy, or they convey lessons of wide significance, or they paint vivid and complete pictures, in a few lively touches, and by a few airy words, as if caught in dropping from the sky. By sobs of sound, by half-hints of meaning, by light, hurrying strokes on the ruddy chords of the heart, by a ringing of changes on certain words and phrases, he sways us as if with the united powers of music and poetry. Our readers will, in illustration of this, remember his nameless little song, beginning

> "Break, break, break,
> On thy cold gray crags, O sea!"

which is a mood of his own mind, faithfully rendered into sweet and simple verse. It is in composition no more complicated or elaborate than a house built by a child, but melts you, as that house would, were you to see it after the dear infant's death. But than this he has higher moods, and nobler, though still imperfect aspirations. In his "Two Voices," he approaches the question of all ages.—Whence evil? And if he, no more than other speculators, unties, he casts a soft and mellow light around this Gordian knot. This poem is no fancy-piece, but manifestly a transcript from his own personal experience. He has sunk into one of those melancholy moods incident to his order of mind, and has become "aweary of the sun," and of all the sun shines upon—especially of his own miserable idiosyncrasy. There slides in at that dark hour a still small voice: how different from that which thrilled on Elijah's ear in the caves of Horeb! It is the voice of that awful lady whom De Quincey calls *Mater tenebrarum*, our lady of darkness. It hints at suicide as the only remedy for human woes.

"Thou art so full of misery,
Were it not better not to be!"

And then there follows an eager and uneasy interlocution between the "dark and barren voice," and the soul of the writer, half spurning and half holding parley with its suggestions. Seldom, truly, since the speech by which Despair in Spenser enforces the same sad argument, did misanthropy breathe a more withering blight over humanity and human hopes; seldom did unfortunate by a shorter and readier road reach the conclusion, "there is one remedy for all," than in the utterance of this voice. Death in it looks lovely; nay, the one lovely thing in the universe. Again and again the poet is ready to yield to the desire of his own heart, thus seconded by the mystic voice, and, in the words of one who often listened to the same accents, to "lie down like a tired child, and weep away this life of care." But again and again the better element of his nature resists the temptation, and beats back the melancholy voice. At length, raising himself from his lethargy, he rises, looks forth—it is the Sabbath morn, and, as he sees the peaceful multitudes moving on to the house of God, and as, like the Anciente Mariner, he "blesses them unaware," straightway the spell is broken, the "dull and bitter voice is gone," and, hark!

"A second voice is at his ear,
A little whisper, silver-clear."

and it gives him a hidden and humble hope, which spreads a quiet heaven within his soul. Now he can go forth into the fields, and

"Wonder at the bounteous hours,
The slow result of winter showers,
You scarce can see the grass for flowers."

All nature calls upon him to rejoice, and to the eye of his heart, at least, the riddle is read. Nay, we put it to every heart if this do not, more than many elaborate argumentations, touch the core of the difficulty. "Look up," said Leigh Hunt to Carlyle, when he had been taking the darker side of the question, and they had both come out under the brilliance of a starry night—"look up, and find your answer there!" And although the reply failed to convince the party addressed, who, looking aloft at the sparkling azure, after a deep pause, rejoined, with a sigh, and in tones we can well imagine, so melancholy and far withdrawn, "Oh! it's a sad sight;" yet, apart from the divine discoveries, it was the true and only answer. The beauty, whether of Tennyson's fields—where we "scarce can see the grass for flowers"—or of Leigh Hunt's skies, "whose unwithered countenance is young as on creation's day," and where we find an infinite answer to our petty cavils—is enough to soothe, if not to satisfy, to teach us the perfect patience of expectancy, if not the full assurance of faith.

Tennyson, in some of his poems as well as this, reveals in himself a current of thought tending towards very deep and dark subjects. This springs partly from the metaphysical bias of his intellect, and partly from the morbid emotions of his heart. And yet he seems generally to toy and trifle with such tremendous themes—to touch them lightly and hurriedly, as one might hot iron—at once eager and reluctant to intermeddle with them. Nevertheless, there is a perilous stuff about his heart, and upon his verse lies a "melancholy compounded of many simples." He is not the poet of hope, or of action, or of passion, but of sentiment, of pensive and prying curiosity, or of simple stationary wonder, in view of the great sights and mysteries of Nature and man. He has never thrown himself amid the heats and hubbub of society, but remained alone, musing with a quiet but observant eye upon the tempestuous pageant which is sweeping past him, and concerning himself little with the political or religious controversies of his age. There are, too, in some of his writings, mild and subdued vestiges of a wounded spirit, of a heart that has been disappointed, of an ambition that has been repressed, of an intellect that has wrestled with doubt, difficulty, and disease.

In "Locksley Hall," for instance, he tells a tale of unfortunate passion with a gusto and depth of feeling, which (unless we misconstrue the mark of the branding-iron) betray more than a fictitious interest in the theme. It is a poem breathing the spirit of, and not much inferior to, Byron's "Dream," in all but that clear concentration of misery which bends over it like a bare and burning heaven over a bare and burning desert. "Locksley Hall," again, is turbid and obscure in language, wild and distracted in feeling. The wind is down, but the sea still runs high. You see in it the passion pawing like a lion who has newly missed his prey, not fixed as yet in a marble form of still and hopeless disappointment. The lover, after a season of absence, returns to the scene of his early education and hapless love, where of old he

> "Wander'd, nourishing a youth sublime
> With the fairy tales of science, and the long result of time."

A feeling, cognate with, and yet more imperious than those of his high aspirations, springs up in his mind. It arises in spring like the crest of a singing-bird. It is the feeling of love for Amy his cousin, sole daughter of her father's house and heart. The feeling is mutual, and the current of their true love flows smoothly on, till interrupted by the interference of relatives. Thus far he remembers calmly; but here recollection strikes the fierce chord of disappointment, and he bursts impetuously forth—

> "O, my cousin, shallow-hearted. O, my Amy, mine no more.
> O, the dreary, dreary moorland. O, the barren, barren shore."

Darting then one hasty and almost vindictive glance down her future history, he predicts that she shall lower to the level of the clown she has wedded, and that he will use his victim a little better than *his dog or his horse.* Nay, she will become

> "Old and formal, suited to her petty part;
> With her little hoard of maxims, preaching down a daughter's heart."

But himself, alas! what is to become of him? Live he must—suicide is too base an outlet from existence for his brave spirit. But what to do with this bitter boon of being? There follow some wild and half-insane stanzas expressive of the ambitions and uncertainties of his soul. It is the Cyclops mad with blindness, and groping at the sides of his cave He will hate and despise all women, or, at least, all British maidens. He will return to the orient land, whose "larger constellations" saw a father die. He will, in his despair, take some savage woman who shall rear his dusky race. But no—the despair is momentary—he may not mate with a squalid savage; he will rather revive old intellectual ambitions, and renew old aspirations, for he feels within him that the "crescent promise of his spirit has not set." It is resolved—but, ere he goes, let every ray of remaining love and misery go forth in one last accusing, avenging look at the scene of his disappointment and the centre of his wo.

"Howsoever these things be, a long farewell to Locksley Hall.
Now, for me, the woods may wither; now, for me, the roof-tree fall.
Comes a vapor from the margin, blackening over heath and holt;
Cramming all the blast before it, in its breast a thunderbolt.
Let it fall on Locksley Hall, with rain, or hail, or fire, or snow,
For a mighty wind arises, roaring seaward, and I go."

And thus the ballad closes, leaving, however, with us the inevitable impression that the unfortunate lover is not done with Locksley Hall nor its bitter memories—that Doubting Castle is not down, nor giant Despair dead—that the calls of the curlews around it will still resound in his ears, and the pale face of its Amy, still unutterably beloved, will come back upon his dreams—that the iron has entered into his soul—and that his life and his misery are henceforth commensurate and the same.

Among the more remarkable of Tennyson's poems, besides those already mentioned, are "The Poet," "Dora," "Recollections of the Arabian Nights," "Œnone," "The Lotos Eaters,' "Ulysses," "Godiva," and "The Vision of Sin." "The Poet" was written when the author was young, and when the high ideal of his heart was just dawning upon his mind. It is needless to say that his view of the powers and influences of poetry is different with what prevails with many in our era. Poetry is, with him, no glittering foil to be wielded gayly on gala days. It is, or ought to be, a sharp two-edged sword. It is not a baton in the hand of coarse authority—it is a magic rod. It is not a morning flush in the sky of youth, that shall fade in the sun of science—it is a consuming and imperishable fire. It is not a mere amusement for young love-sick men and women—it is as serious as death, and longer than life. It is tuned philosophy—winged science—fact on fire—"truth springing from earth" —high thought voluntarily moving harmonious numbers.

His "Poet" is "dowered with the hate of hate, the scorn of scorn, the love of love," and his words "shake the world."

The author, when he wrote "The Poet," was fresh from school, and from Shelley, his early idol. Ere writing "Dora" he had become conversant with the severer charms of Wordsworth; and that poem contains in it not one figure or flower—is bare, literal, and pathetic as the book of Ruth. Its poetry is that which lies in all natural life, which, like a deep quiet pool, has only to be disturbed in the slightest degree to send up in dance those bells and bubbles which give it instantly ideal beauty and interest, and suddenly the pool becomes a poem!

His "Recollections of the Arabian Nights" is a poem of that species which connects itself perpetually, in feeling and memory, with the original work, whose quintessence it collects. It speaks out the sentiments of millions of thankful hearts. We feel in it what a noble thing was the Arabian mind—like the Arabian soil, "all the Sun's"—like the Arabian climate, fervid, golden—like the Arabian horse, light, elegant, ethereal, swift as the wind. "O, for the golden prime of good Haroun Alras-chid!" O, for one look—though it were the last—of that Persian maid, whom the poet has painted in words vivid as colors, palpable almost as sense. Talk of enchantment! The "Thousand-and-One Nights is one enchantment—more powerful than the lamp of Aladdin, or the "Open Sesame" of Ali Baba. The author, were he *one*—not many—is a magician—a geni—greater than Scott, than Cervantes, equal to Shakspeare himself. What poetry, passion, pathos, beauty of sentiment, elegance of costume, ingenuity of contrivance, wit, humor, farce, interest, variety, tact in transition, sunniness of spirit, dream-like wealth of imagination, incidental but precious light cast upon customs, manners, history, religion—every thing, in short, that can amuse or amaze, instruct or delight, the human spirit! Like the "Pilgrim's Progress"—devoured by boys, it is a devout study for bearded men.

Tennyson has expressed, especially, the moonlight volup tuousness of tone and spirit which breathes around those delicious productions, as well as the lavish magnificence of dress and decoration, of furniture and architecture, which were worthy of the witch element, the sunny climate, and the early enchanted era, where and when they were written. But we doubt if he mates adequately with that more potent and terrible magic which haunts their higher regions, as in the sublime picture of the Prince's daughter fighting with the Enchanter in mid air, or in the mysterious grandeur which follows all the adventures of Aboulfaouris. With this, too, indeed, he must have sympathy; for it is evident that he abundantly fulfils Coleridge's test of a genuine lover of the "Arabian Nights." "Do you admire," said the author of "Kubla Khan" to Hazlitt, "the Thousand-and-one Nights?" "No," was the answer. "That's because you *don't dream.*" But, surely, since the "noticeable man, with large gray eyes," awoke in death from his long life-dream, no poet has arisen of whom the word were more true than of Tennyson, whether in reproach or commendation, asleep or awake—"Behold this dreamer cometh."

In "Œnone," we find him up on the heights of Ida, with the large foot-prints of gods and goddesses still upon its sward, and the citadel and town of Troy, as yet unfallen, as yet unassailed, visible from its summit. Here the poet sees a vision of his own—a vision which, recorded in verse, forms a high third with Wordsworth's "Laodamia" and Keats's "Hyperion," in the classical style. Less austere and magnificent than the poem of Keats, which seems not so much a torso of earthly art as a splinter fallen from some other exploded world—less chaste, polished, and spiritual than "Laodamia," that Elgin marble set in Elysian light, it surpasses both in picturesqe distinctness and pathetic power. The story is essentially that of "Locksley Hall," but the scene is not the flat and sandy moorland of Lincolnshire, but the green gorges and lawns of Ida. The deceived lover is Œnone, the daughter of a river god. She has been deceived by Paris, and her plaint is the poem. Melancholy her song, as that of a disappointed woman—melodious, as that of an aggrieved goddess. It is to Ida, her mother mountain, that she breathes her sorrow. She tells her of her lover's matchless beauty—of her yielding up her heart to him—of the deities descending to receive the golden apple from his hands—of his deciding it to Venus, upon the promise of the "fairest and most loving wife in Greece"—of his abandonment of Œnone, and of her despair. Again and again, in her agony, she cries for Death; but the grim shadow, too busy in hewing down the happy, will not turn aside at her miserable bidding. Her despair at last becomes fury; her tears begin to burn; she will arise; she will leave her dreadful solitude—

> "I will rise, and go
> Down into Troy, and, ere the stars come forth,
> Talk with the wild Cassandra; for she says
> A fire dances before her, and a sound
> Rings ever in her ears of armed men.
> What this may be I know not; but I know
> That, whereso'er I am, by night and day
> All earth and air seems only burning fire."

And fancy follows Œnone to Ilium, and sees the two beautiful broken-hearted maidens meeting, like two melancholy flames, upon one funeral pile, mingling their hot tears, exchanging their sad stories, and joining, in desperate exultation, at the prospect of the ruin which is already darkening, like a tempest, round the towers and temples of Troy. It is pleasant to find from such productions that, after all, the poetry of Greece is not dead—that the oaks of Delphos and Dodona have not shed all their oracular leaves—that the lightnings in Jove's hand are still warm—and the snows of Olympus are yet clear and bright, shining over the waste of years—that Mercury's feet are winged still—and still is Apollo's hair unshorn—that the mythology of Homer, long dead to belief, is still alive to the airy purposes of poetry—that, though the "dreadful infant's hand" hath smitten down the gods upon the capitol, it has left them the freedom of the Parnassian Hill; and that a Wordsworth, or a Tennyson, may, even now, by inclining the ear of imagination, hear the river god plunging in Scamander—Œnone wailing upon Ida—Old Triton blowing his wreathed horn; for never was a truth more certain than that "a thing of beauty is a joy for ever."

We had intended to say something of his "Lotos-eaters." but are afraid to break in upon its charmed rest—to disturb its sleepy spell—to venture on that land "in which it seemed always afternoon"—or to stir its melancholy, mild-eyed inhabitants. We will pass it by, treading so softly that the "blind mole may not hear a footfall." We must beware of slumbering, and we could hardly but be dull on the enchanted ground.

While the "Lotos-eaters" breathes the very spirit of luxurious repose, and seems, to apply his own words, a perfect poem in "perfect rest," "Ulysses" is the incarnation of restlessness and insatiable activity. Sick of Ithaca, Argus, Telemachus, and (*sub rosa*) of Penelope too, the old, much enduring Mariner King, is again panting for untried dangers and undiscovered lands.

> "My purpose holds,
> To sail beyond the sunset, and the baths
> Of all the western stars, until I die."

Tennyson, with his fine artistic instinct, saw that the idea of Ulysses at rest was an incongruous thought, and has chosen rather to picture him journeying ever onwards toward infinity or death—

> "It may be that the gulphs will wash us down—
> It may be, we shall reach the happy isles,
> And see the great Achilles, whom we knew."

And with breathless interest, and a feeling approaching the sublime, we watch the gray-headed monarch stepping, with his few aged followers, into the bark, which is to be their home till death, and stretching away toward eternity; and every heart and imagination cry out after him—"Go, and return no more."

"Godiva" is an old story newly told—a delicate business delicately handled—the final and illuminated version of an ancient and world-famous tradition. Its beauty is, that, like its heroine, it is "clothed on with chastity." It represses the imagination as gently and effectually as her naked virtue did the eye. We hold our breath, and shut every window of our fancy, till the great ride be over. And in this trial and triumph of female resolution and virtue, the poet would have us believe that Nature herself sympathized—that the light was bashful, and the sun ashamed, and the wind hushed, till the sublime pilgrimage was past—and that, when it ended, a sigh of satisfaction, wide as the circle of earth and heaven, proclaimed Godiva's victory.

The "Vision of Sin" strikes, we think, upon a stronger,

though darker, chord than any of his other poems. There are in it impenetrable obscurities, but, like jet black ornaments, some may think them dearer for their darkness. You cannot, says Hazlitt, make "an allegory go on all fours." A vision must be hazy—a ghost should surely be a shadow. Enough, if there be a meaning in the mystery, an oracle speaking through the gloom. The dream is that of a youth, who is seen riding to the gate of a palace, from which

> "Came a child of sin,
> And took him by the curls and led him in."

He is lost straightway in mad and wicked revel, tempestuously yet musically described. Meanwhile, unheeded by the revellers, a "vapor, (*the mist of darkness!*) heavy, hueless, formless, cold," is floating slowly on toward the palace. At length it touches the gate, and the dream changes, and such a change!

> "I saw
> A gray and gap-toothed man, as lean as Death,
> Who slowly rode across a wither'd heath,
> And lighted at a ruined inn."

And, lighted there, he utters his bitter and blasted feelings in lines, reminding us, from their fierce irony, their misanthropy, their thrice-drugged despair, of Swift's "Legion Club;" and—as in that wicked, wondrous poem—a light sparkle of contemptuous levity glimmers with a ghastly sheen over the putrid pool of malice and misery below, and cannot all disguise the workings of that remorse which is not repentance. At length this sad evil utterance dies away in the throat of the expiring sinner, and behind his consummated ruin there arises a "mystic mountain range," along which voices are heard lamenting, or seeking to explain the causes of his ruin. One says—

> "Behold it was a crime
> Of sense, avenged by sense, that wove with time."

Another—

> "The crime of sense became
> The crime of malice, and is equal blame."

A third—

> "He had not wholly quenched his power—
> A little grain of conscience made him sour."

And thus, at length, in a darkness visible of mystery and grandeur, the "Vision of Sin" closes:—

> "At last I heard a voice upon the slope
> Cry to the summit, Is there any hope?
> To which an answer peal'd from that high land,
> But in a tongue no man could understand;
> And on the glimmering limit, far withdrawn,
> God made himself an *awful rose of dawn.*"

A reply there is; but whether in the affirmative or negative we do not know. A revelation there is; but whether it be an interference in behalf of the sinner, or a display, in ruddy light, of God's righteousness in his punishment, is left in deep uncertainty. Tennyson, like Addison in his "Vision of Mirza," ventures not to withdraw the veil from the left side of the eternal ocean. He leaves the curtain to be the painting. He permits the imagination of the reader to figure, if it dare, shapes of beauty, or forms of fiery wrath, upon the "awful rose of dawn," as upon a vast back-ground. It is his only to start the thrilling suggestion.

After all, we have considerable misgivings about placing Tennyson—for what he has hitherto done—among our great poets. We cheerfully accord him great powers; but he is, as yet, guiltless of great achievements. His genius is bold, but is waylaid at almost every step by the timidity and weakness of his temperament. His utterance is not proportionate to his vision. He sometimes reminds us of a dumb man with important tidings within, but only able to express them by gestures, starts, sobs, and tears. His works are loopholes, not windows, through which intense glimpses come and go, but no broad, clear, and rounded prospect is commanded. As a thinker, he often seems like one who should perversely pause a hundred feet from the summit of a lofty hill, and refuse to ascend higher. "Up! the breezes call thee—the clouds marshal thy way—the glorious prospect waits thee, as a bride for her husband—angels or gods may meet thee on the top—it may be thy Mountain of Transfiguration." But, no; the pensive or wilful poet chooses to remain below.

Nevertheless, the eye of genius is flashing in Tennyson's head, and his ear is unstopped, whether to the harmonies of nature, or to the still sad music of humanity. We care not much in which of the tracks he has already cut out he may choose to walk; but we would prefer if he were persuaded more frequently to see visions and dream dreams—like his "Vision of Sin"—imbued with high purpose, and forming the Modern Metamorphoses of truth. We have no hope that he will ever be, in the low sense, a popular poet, or that to him the task is allotted of extracting music from the railway train, or of setting in song the "fairy tales of science"—the great astronomical or geological discoveries of the age. Nor is he likely ever to write any thing which, like the poems of Burns, or Campbell, can go directly to the heart of the entire nation. For no "Song of the Shirt" even, need we look from him. But the imaginativeness of his nature, the deep vein of his moral sentiment, the bias given to his mind by his early reading, the airy charm of his versification, and the seclusion in which he lives, like a flower in its own peculiar jar, all seem to prepare him for becoming a great spiritual dreamer, who might write not only "Recollections of the Arabian Nights," but Arabian Nights themselves, equally graceful in costume, but impressed with a deeper sentiment, chastened into severer taste, and warmed with a holier flame. Success to such pregnant slumbers! soft be the pillow as that of his own "Sleeping Beauty;" may every syrup of strength and sweetness drop upon his eyelids, and may his dreams be such as to banish sleep from many an eye, and to people the hearts of millions with beauty!

On the whole, perhaps Tennyson is less a prophet than an artist. And this alone would serve better to reconcile us to his silence, should it turn out that his poetic career is over. The loss of even the finest artist may be supplied—that of a prophet, who has been cut off in the midst of his mission, or whose words some envious influence or circumstance has snatched from his lips, is irreparable. In the one case, it is but a painter's pencil that is broken; in the other it is a magic rod shivered. Still, even as an artist, Tennyson has not yet done himself full justice, nor built up any structure so shapely, complete, and living, as may perpetuate his name.*

Alfred Tennyson is the son of an English clergyman in Lincolnshire. He is of a retiring disposition, and seldom, though sometimes, emerges from his retirement into the literary coteries of London. And yet welcome is he ever among them—with his eager physiognomy, his dark hair and eyes, and his small, black tobacco pipe. Some years ago, we met a brother of his in Dumfries, who bore, we were told, a marked, though miniature resemblance to him, a beautiful painter and an expert versifier, after the style of Alfred.

The particulars of his literary career are familiar to most. His first production was a small volume of poems, published in 1831. Praised in the "Westminster" elaborately, and extravagantly eulogized in the Englishman's Magazine" (a periodical conducted by William Kennedy, but long since defunct, and which, according to some malicious persons, died of this same article)—it was sadly mangled by less generous critics. "Blackwood's Magazine" doled it out some severely sifted praise; and the author, in his next volume, rhymed back his ingratitude in the well-known lines to "Rusty, musty, fusty, crusty Christopher," whose blame he forgave, but whose praise he could not. Meanwhile, he was quietly forming a small but zealous cohort of admirers; and some of his poems, such as "Mariana," &c., were universally read and appreciated. His second production was less successful, and deserved to be less successful, than the first. It was stuffed with wilful impertinencies and affectations. His critics told him he wrote ill, and he answered them by writing worse. His third exhibited a very different spirit. It consisted of a selection from his two former volumes, and a number of additional pieces—the principal of which we have already analyzed. In his selection, he winnows his former works with a very salutary severity; but what has he done with that delectable strain of the "Syrens?" We think he has acted well in stabling and shutting up his "Krakens" in their dim, ocean mangers; but we are not so willing to

* His "Princess," published since the above, is a medley of success, failure, and half-success—not even an attempt towards a whole.

part with that beautiful sisterhood, and hope to see them again at no distant day, standing in their lovely isle, and singing—

> "Come hither, come hither, and be our lords,
> For merry brides are we.
> We will kiss sweet kisses and speak sweet words.
>
> . . . . .
>
> Ye will not find so happy a shore,
> Weary mariners all the world o'er.
> Oh fly, oh fly no more."

PROFESSOR NICHOL.

This is the age of public lecturing, and we might spend a long time in discussing its *pros* and *cons*, its advantages and its evils. The open and legitimate objects which popular lecturing proposes to itself are chiefly the three following: instruction, excitement, and communication between the higher minds of the age and those of a lower grade. Now, in reference to its utility as an organ of instruction, much may be said on both sides. In public lecturing, truth is painted to the eye; it is enforced and illustrated by voice, gesture, and action; it stands in the person of the orator as in an illumined window. The information thus given, attended by a personal interest, and accompanied by a peculiar emphasis, is more profoundly impressed upon the memory: and many, by the fairy aspect of truth which is presented, are induced to love and learn, who otherwise would have remained indifferent and distant. On the other hand, the quantity of knowledge communicated by lecturing is seldom large; and as to its quality, lecturers are under strong temptations to dilute it down to the capacities of their audience; and, instead of conducting them from first principles to details, to give them particular facts, and tell them to travel back themselves to leading principles, an advice which they seldom, if ever, follow. Too often the hearers, however strongly urged to the contrary by their instructors, forget to pursue profounder researches, to seek after higher sources; and the close of the six or seven lectures is the close of their studies, and furnishes the complement of their knowledge. Often too, the class who have least access to books have also least access to lectures, or even when privileged to attend them, find their *special* wants but indifferently supplied.

In the excitement produced by good public lecturing, its advocates find a more plausible argument in its favor. It is an amusement so happy and so innocent; it withdraws so many from the theatre, the card-table, and the tavern; it gives such a stimulus to nascent intellects; it creates around the lecturer such circles and semicircles of shining faces; it rouses in so many breasts the spark of literary and scientific genius; it commences the manufacture of so many incipient Miltons, no longer mute and inglorious; and of whole generations of young Arkwrights, worthy of their illustrious progenitor. Nay, we would go a little farther still: we would "better the instruction." Its excitement and pleasure do not stop here. The lecture-room promotes a great many matches; it brings young ladies and gentlemen into close and intimate propinquity; it excites active and animated flirtations; it forms, besides, a pleasant interchange to one class with the card-table—to another, an agreeable lounge on the road to the afterpiece; and to a third, a safe and decent half-way house to a quiet social talk in a quiet alehouse. It is also a nursery for the numerous sprigs of criticism which abound—faithfully figured by the immortal "Punch," in those specimens of the rising generation who deem that, as "for that ere Shakspeare, he has been vastly overrated." And last, not least, it permits many a comfortable nap to the hard-wrought doctor, or schoolmaster, or artizan—to whom it matters not whether the lecturer be in the moon or in the clouds, as they are only, like their instructor, absent and lost.

Joking, however, apart, popular lecturing is undoubtedly a source both of much entertainment and excitement, though we are not sure but that that entertainment is more valued by the luxurious as a variety in their pleasures, than by the middle and lower classes as a necessity in their intellectual life; and although we are sure that an undue portion of that excitement springs from the glare of lights, the presence of ladies, the mere "heat, and stare, and pressure" of which Chalmers complained; and that comparatively little of it can be traced to the art, less to the genius, and least of all to the subject, of the discourser.

As a means of communication between men of science and literature and the age, it is, we are afraid, what Mr. Horne would call a "false medium." You have in it the prophet, shorn, dressed, perhaps scented, perhaps playing miserable monkey-tricks to divert the audience—and not the Moses coming down the Mount, with face shining, but with lips stammering, from that dread communion on the summit; or if the prophet do preserve his integrity, and speak to the souls instead of the eyes and ears of his audience, it is at his proper peril; wild yawnings, slumbers both loud and deep, not to speak of the more polite hints conveyed in the music of slapping doors and rasping floors, are the reward of his fidelity. We are aware, indeed, that a few have been able to overcome such obstacles, and, in spite of stern adherence to a high object to gain general acceptance. But these are the exceptions. Their success, besides, has greatly resulted from other causes than the truth they uttered. Certain graces of manner—certain striking points in delivery—a certain melody, to which their thoughts were set—created at the first an interest which gradually, as the enthusiasm of the speaker increased, swelled into a brute wonder, which made you fancy the words "Orpheus no fable," written in a transparency over the speaker's head. But clear steady visions of truth, true and satisfying pleasure, and any permanent or transforming change, were not given. The audience were lifted up for a season, like an animal caught in a whirlwind, by the sheer power of eloquence; they were not really elevated one distinct step—they came down precisely the same creatures, and to the same point, as before, and the thing would be remembered by them afterwards as a dream.

Minds, again, somewhat inferior to the prophetic order, find a far freer and more useful passage to the public ear and intellect, and succeed in giving not only a vague emotion of delight, but some solid knowledge, and some lasting result. Such a mind is that of our admirable friend, Professor Nichol; and even at the apparent risk of indelicacy, we propose to analyze its constituent qualities, as well as the special causes of his great success as a lecturer.

The first time we heard of Professor Nichol was on the publication of his "Views of the Architecture of the Heavens," and the first thing that struck us about the production was the felicity and boldness of its title. The words "Architecture of the Heavens" suggested, first, the thought that the heavens were the building of a distinct divine architect; secondly, that the building was still in progress; and, thirdly, that from even this low and distant platform, we are permitted glimpses of its gradual growth toward perfection. The essence, in fact, of the nebular hypothesis was contained in the title; and although that hypothesis is now commonly thought exploded, it is only so far as the visible evidence is concerned—as a probable and beautiful explanation of phenomena, the original of which is lost in the darkness of immeasurable antiquity, it retains its value. But how suggestive to us at the time was the expression, "Architecture of the Heavens!" Formerly we deemed that when man awaked into existence, the building, indeed, was there in all its magnitude, but that the scaffolding was down—all trace and vestige of the operation elaborately removed—and that the almighty Architect had withdrawn and hid himself. But now we had come upon the warm footprints of omnipotence—the Power was only a few steps in advance; nay, thrilling thought! we had only to lift our telescopes to behold him actually at work up there, in the midnight sky. The telescope enabled us to stand behind the processes of the Eternal—it was a wing by which we overtook the great retreat of the Deity, if indeed a retreat it was, and not rather a perpetual progress—a triumphal march onwards into the infinite dark. It brought us ever new, electric, telegraphic tidings of Him whose goings forth were of *old*—from everlasting—and which were *new* to everlasting as well. Such were the dim, yet high suggestions, of the nebular hypothesis. If we relinquished them recently with a sigh, we now sigh no more; for now we have been taught, in a manner most impressive, the immense *age* of the universe, whose orbs seem hoary in their splendor, and have thus found a new measure for computing our knowledge, or rather for more accurately estimating our ignorance, of the days, of the years, of the right hand of him that is the Most High. How long, we now exclaim, it must be since the Great Artist put his finishing touch to that serene gallery of paintings we call the stars, and yet how perfect and how godlike their execution; since their lustre, their beauty, and their holy calm are this night as fresh and unfaded as at the beginning. And how solemn the thought, if these works, in the hiding of their Creator, be so magnificent, how great must himself be, and how great must he have been, especially as he travailed in birth with such an offspring, amid the jubilant shouts of all-awakening intelligence!

It is very common to skip the preface in order to get at the book. In this case, we skipped the book to get at the pictures. We read, nay, devoured, the plates—the poems shall we call them—ere we read a word of the letter-press. And most marvellous to us was their revelation of those starry sprinklings, relieved against the dark background—those wild capricious shapes, which reminded you of rearing steeds under the control of perfect riders—seeming at once to spurn and to be subject to immutable laws—those unbanked rivers of glory flowing through the universe—why, we seemed standing on a Pisgah, commanding the prospect of immensity itself. But still more striking to overlook, as we then imagined, the laboratory of God, and to see his work in every stage of its progress—the six demiurgic days presented to us contemporaneously and at once. No wonder that such plates enchanted us, and that we seemed gazing on rough copies from the paintings of the Divine hand itself. What a triumph, too, to mind over matter, and to a poor sun-illumined worm, over his haughty torch—to be able, *with a pin-point*, to indicate, and, if necessary, to hide his place in the firmament! It was, indeed, an hour much deserving of memory. The folding-doors of the universe seemed to open upon us in musical thunder; and if we could not as yet enter, yet we could wish, like Mirza, for the wings of a great eagle to fly away within them. It was one of those apocalyptic moments that occur, or that can occur so seldom in life, for it is not every day that we can see, for the first time, in the expanded page of immensity, the charter of our soul's freedom, and feel ourselves "enlarged" to the extent of the length and breadth, the depth and the height of the creation.

Returning from a reverie, in which we saw our sun and his thousand neighbor stars quenched like a taper in the blaze of that higher noon, we found ourselves on earth again, and remembered that we had yet to read Dr. Nichol's book. And it is the highest compliment we can pay it, to say that it did not dissipate or detract from the impressions which the eloquent pictures had produced, and that it gave them a yet clearer and more definite form. It bridged in the foaming torrent of our enthusiasm. It translated (as Virgil does Homer) the stern and literal grandeurs of night into a mild and less dazzling version. We liked, in the first place, its form. It consisted of letters, and of letters to a lady. This held out a prospect of ease, familiarity, clearness, and grace. Most expounders, hitherto, of astronomical truth, had been either too stilted in their style, or too scientific in their substance. But here was a graceful conversation, such as an accomplished philosopher might carry on with an intelligent female, under the twilight canopy, or in the window recess, as the moon was rising. It in no way transcended female comprehension, or if it did, it was only to slide into one of those beautiful, bewitching mists, which the imagination of women so much loves. There were, too, a warmth and a heartiness about the style and manner, which distinguished the book favorably from the majority of scientific treatises. These, generally, are cold and dry. Trusting, it would seem, to the intrinsic grandeur of the subject, they convey their impressions of it in a didactic and feeble style, and catalogue stars as indifferently as they would the withered leaves of the forest. Nichol, on the contrary, seems to point to them, not with a cold rod, but with a waving torch. He never "doubts that the stars are fire"—no immeasurable icebergs they, floating in frozen air, but glowing, burning, almost living orbs; and his words glow, burn, and nearly start from the page in unison. We will not deny that this heat and enthusiasm sometimes betray him into *splendida vitia*—into rhetorical exaggerations—into passages which sound hollow, whether they are so or not—and worse, into dim and vague obscurities, copied too closely from his own nebulæ, where you have misty glimmer, instead of clear, solid land; but his faults are of a kind which it is far more easy to avoid than to reach, which no sordid or commonplace mind, however accomplished, durst commit; and the spirit which animates his most tasteless combinations of sound, and peeps through his swelling intricacies of sentence, is always beautiful and sincere. Beyond most writers, too, on this theme, he has the power of giving, even to the uninitiated, a clear and memorable idea of his subject—the truths of Astronomy he paints upon the eye and soul of the reader. And this he is enabled to do—first, because he has a clear vision himself, which his enthusiasm is seldom permitted to dull or to distort; and, secondly, because he seeks—labors—is not satisfied till he has transferred this entire to the minds of his readers, and of his auditors. Thus far of the mere manner of his writing. In considering its spirit, we shall find metal more attractive. This is distinguished by its sincere enthusiasm, its joyous hope, and by its religious reverence.

What field for enthusiasm can be named in comparison with the innumerous and ever-burning stars—the first objects which attract the eyes of children, who send up their sweetest smiles, and uplift their tiny hands to pluck them down as playthings—the beloved of solitary shepherds, who, lying on the hillside, try to count them in their multitudes, call them by names of their own, love those "watchers and holy ones," as if they were companions and friends, and sometimes exclaim, with the great shepherd king of Israel, "When I consider thy heavens, the work of thy fingers, the moon and the stars, which thou hast ordained, what is man!"—the beloved of the mariner, who, pacing his midnight deck, turns often aloft his eye to those starry sparklers, shining on him through the shrouds, or—

"Mirrored in the ocean vast—
A thousand fathoms down,"—

the loved of the wakeful, especially of those who are awake through sorrow, who, as they see them trembling through the lattice, feel, or fancy, that they are sympathizing with their agonies, and would, if they could, send down a message from their far thrones that might wipe away their tears—the loved of the astronomer, who, a friendly spy, watches their every motion, and through the tube of his telescope distils into himself the essence of their beauty, their meaning, and their story—the loved of the poet's soul, who snatches many a live-coal of inspiration from their flaming altars—the loved of the Christian, who sees in them the reflection of his Father's glory, the milestones on the path of his Redeemer's departure, and of his return—the loved of all who have eyes to see, understandings to comprehend, and souls to feel their grandeur so unspeakable, their silence so profound, their separation from each other, and from us so entire, their multitude so immense, their lustre so brilliant, their forms so singular, their order so regular, their motions so dignified, so rapid, and so calm. "If," says Emerson, "the stars were to appear one night in a thousand years, how would men believe and adore, and preserve for many generations the remembrance of the city of God which had thus been shown. But night after night come out these preachers of beauty, and light the universe with their admonishing smile."

It is singular, that while the theory of the stars has been perpetually changing, the conception of their sublime character has, under every theory, remained nearly the same. While they are believed to be, as in the darker ages, absolutely divine, incorruptible, and perfect in their essence, they were not regarded with more enthusiasm, alluded to with more frequency, or lauded with more eloquence, than now, when we know that imperfection, and inequality, decay, and destruction, snow, and perhaps sin, have found their way thither, as well as here; and Dante, amid his innumerable descriptions of the heavenly bodies—and no poet has so many—has said nothing finer in their praise than we find in some of the bursts of Bayly. If science has, with rude hand, torn off from the stars that false lustre of supernaturalism which they bore so long, it has immeasurably multiplied their numbers, unlocked their secrets, at once brought them nearer and thrown them farther off, and supplied the glitter of superstition by the severe light of law. If they seem no longer the thrones of angels, they are at least porch-lamps in the temple of Almighty God. If no longer the regents of human destiny, they are the Urim and Thummim upon the breast of the Ancient of Days. If not now regarded as a part of the highest heaven, they at least light the way that leadeth to honor, glory, and immortality. From sparks they have broadened into suns; from thousands they have multiplied into millions. It is ever thus with the progress of genuine truth. Remorselessly, as it rushes on, it scatters a thousand beautiful dreams, slumbering like morning dew-drops among the branches of the wood, but from the path of its progress there rises, more slowly, a stern, but true and lasting glory, before which, in due time, the former "shall no more be remembered, neither come into mind."

A collection of all the descriptions of the stars, in the poetry and prose of every age, would constitute itself a galaxy. It would include Homer's wondrous one-lined allusions to them—so rapid and so strong, as they shone over Ida, or kept still watch above the solitary Ulysses in his sea-wanderings—the crown they wove over the bare head of the sleepless Prometheus—the glances of power and sympathy which they shed in, through rents in the night of the Grecian tragedies—the ornate and labored pictures of Virgil and Lucretius—the thick imagery they supply to the Scripture bards—their perpetual intermingling with the *Divina Comedia*, darting down through crevices in the descending circles of damnation, circling the mount of purgatory, and paving the way to the vision of essential Deity—Shakspeare's less frequent but equally beautiful touches—Milton's plaintive, yet serene references to their set glories—Young's bursts of wonder, almost of longing and desire, for those nearer neighbors to the eternal throne, which appeared to him to see so far and to know so much—Byron's wild and angry lashing at them, like a sea, seeking to rise, and reach and quench them, on a thousand shipwrecks—Wordsworth's love to them, *for* loving and resting on his favorite mountains—Bayly's hymnings of devotion—Chalmers' long-linked swells of pious enthusiasm—and last, not least, our author's raptures, more measured, more artistic, but equally sincere.

There occurs a passage in one of Byron's letters, written in Venice, where he describes himself, after a debauch, looking out at the night, when he exclaims, "What nothings we are before these stars!" and adds, that he *never sufficiently felt their greatness*, till he looked at them through Herschel's telescope, and *saw that they were worlds.* We rather wonder at this, for we have always thought that, to a highly imaginative mind, it mattered little whether it looked to the stars through the eye or the telescope. Who does not see and feel that they are worlds, if he has a heart and an imagination, as well as an eye? Who cares for the size of algebraic symbols? A star, at largest, is but a symbol, and the smaller it seems, the more scope it leaves for imagination. The telescope tends rather to crush and overwhelm than to stimulate—to fill than to fire—some souls. It necessarily, too, deprives the seeing of the stars, so far as they are regarded individually, of many of its finest accessories. The mountain which the star seems to touch—the tree through which it trembles—the soft evening air on which it seems silently to feed—the quick contrasts between it and its neighboring orbs—its part as one of a constellated family—such poetical aspects of it are all lost, and the glare of illumination falls upon one vast unit, insulated at once from earth, and from the other parts of heaven. It is as though we should apply a magnifying-glass to a single face in a group of painted figures, thereby enlarging one object at the expense of the others, which are not diminished, but blotted out. While, of course, acknowledging the mighty powers and uses of the telescope, and confessing that from no *dream* did we ever more reluctantly awake than from one which lately transported us to Parsonstown, and showed us the nebula in Orion just dropping to pieces, like a bright dissolving cloud, yet we venture to assert that many derive as much pleasure and excitement from the crescent moon still as in Shakspeare's time, a silver bow new bent in heaven—from round, shivering Venus in the green west—from the star of Jove suspended high over head, like the apparent king of the sky—and from those glorious jewels, hanging like two pendents, of equal weight and brilliance, from the ear of night, Orion and the Great Bear, as they could from any revelation of the telescope. This very night we saw what probably impressed our imagination as much as a glimpse of the Rossian glories would have done. The night has been dark and drifting till a few minutes ago. We went out to the door of our dwelling, looking for nothing but darkness, when suddenly, as if flashing out through and from the gloom, and meeting us like a gigantic ghost at our very threshold, we were aware of the presence of *Orion*, and involuntarily shuddered at the sight.

All astronomers of high name have been led at first to

their science by the workings of an enthusiasm as strong as passion and as high as poetry. We cannot doubt that Newton was from his boyhood fascinated by the beauty of the heavenly bodies, and that his wistful boyish glances at their serene splendor and mystic dance formed the germs of his future discoveries. To some *Woolsthorpe* reverie of twilight, we may trace the fall of the keys of the universe at the feet of his matured manhood! Surely a loftier principle was stirring in him than that which renders the juvenile mechanician uneasy till he has analyzed the construction of a toy. It was not, in the first instance, the mathematical puzzles connected with them that attracted him to those remote regions; but it was their remoteness, magnitude, and mystery, which roused him to grapple with their secrets. Ordinary children love to see, and would like to join, the march of soldiers, as they step stately by. The boy Newton burned to accompany, as an intelligent witness and companion, the steps of planets and suns. This enthusiasm never altogether subsided, as many well-known anecdotes prove. But too soon it ceased to express itself otherwise than by silent study and wonder; it retired deep into the centre of his being, and men, astonished at the lack-lustre look with which the eye of the sage was contemplating the stars, knew not that his spirit was the while gazing at them as with the insatiate glance of an eagle. Thus frequently has it been with astronomers. Their ardor diving beyond human sight or sympathy has failed to attract the minds of others, and by coating itself in the ice of cold formulæ and petrified words, has repelled many a poetical enthusiast, whose imagination was not his only faculty. We look on professor Nichol as an accomplished mediator between the two classes of mind, or, as we have formerly called him, an Aaron to many an ineloquent Moses of astronomy.

How he has preserved his child-like love for his subject-matter we do not know, but certainly we always feel, when reading him, that we are following the track of suns, burning and beneficent as footsteps of God, and not of "cinders of the element," whirled round in a mere mechanical motion, and chiefly valuable as lively and cheap illustrations of "Euclid's Elements!" It is said that he has sacrificed powers of original discovery to popular effect; but what if this popular effect, in which so many are now participating, should be to rouse the slumbering energies of still mightier geniuses, and give us a few Newtons, instead of one fully developed Nichol! "Ha! I think there be *six* Richmonds in the field."

We like next to, and akin to this, in Professor Nichol, his spirit of hope and joy. This, we think, ought to be, but is not always the result of starry contemplations. We quoted before Carlyle's celebrated exclamation, "Ah, it's a sad sight," as he looked up to a sparkling January sky. Whether we join with him in this, or with Emerson in expressions of jubilant praise, may depend partly upon our state of feeling. In certain moods the stars will appear hearths, in others hells. The moon is bayed at not by dogs alone. The evening star awakens the gloomy hour of the misanthrope, and shines the signal to the murderer, as well as lights the lover to his assignation with his mistress, and the poet to his meeting with the muse. It seems now, besides, evident to most, that the universe being made of one material, struggle, uncertainty, woe, and the other evils to which finitude is heir, are, in all probability, extended to its remotest limits, and that thus the stars are no islands of the blest, but, like our own world, stern arenas of contest, of defeat or of victory. Still, there are many reasons why the heavenly bodies should be a permanent spring of cheering, if pensive, thought. There is, first, their unfathomable beauty. Is it nothing to the happiness of man that God has suspended over his head this book of divine pictures, talking to him in their own low but mighty speech, spotting his nights with splendor, and filling his soul with an inspiring influence which no earthly object can communicate? Doubts and difficulties may occupy part of the intervening time, but the first and the last feeling of humanity is, "Thanks, endless and boundless, to Heaven for the stars." Secondly, They give us a sense of liberty which no other external cause can do, and which must enhance the happiness of man. This was one great good of the discovery of America. *It* did not, when found, fulfil the dreams of navigators; it was not a cluster of fortunate isles, filled with happy spirits—the worst passions of man were found among the most beautiful scenery in the world; but its discovery shivered the fetters of usage and prejudice, burst the old *mœnia mundi;* and man, the one-eyed giant, found himself groping and pawing, to say the least, in a wider dungeon, and breathing a freer air. But the modern astronomy has broken down stronger walls, and made man, in a sense, free of the universe. What though he has good reason to believe that these many mansions of his Father's house are not, as yet, peopled with the perfect and the happy. To him, height and depth have unbarred many of their sacred marvels—new provinces, pointing to innumerable others behind, have expanded in the kingdom of the Infinite—every limit and barrier have fled away, and the surprised prisoner feels his spirit at large, unbounded in a boundless universe. Surely the telescope, in infusing into the mind such a sense of freedom, has been a benefactor to the heart of man, who may exclaim to it, in the language of the sword-song, "Joy-giver, I kiss thee." But, thirdly, the stars diffuse happiness through the thoughtful mind, as revealing a whole so vast that all our partial and gloomy views of it are straightway stamped with imperfection and imbecility. How little and idle our most plausible theories look under the weight of that beaming canopy! Imagine the shellfish, amidst its sludge, dreaming of the constitution of that world of waters which rolls above! So insignificant appears a Locke, a Kant, or a Spinoza, exalted each some five or six feet above his grave, and theorizing so dogmatically on the principles of the starry ocean. We seem to see the mighty mother bending down, listening to each tiny but pompous voice, smilingly measuring the size of the sage, and saying, in the irony of the gods, "And is this really thy opinion, my little hero, and hast thou, within that pretty new thimble of thine, actually condensed the sea of truth? *Perge Puer.*" Thus the midnight sky teaches us at once the greatness and the littleness of man—his greatness by comparison with his past self—his littleness by comparison with the expanse of the universe, and with his future being; and by both lessons it summonses us to joy; because from the one we are obviously advancing upwards, and because from the other our doubts are seen to be as little as our resolution of them; our darkness yet pettier than our light. Why, to one who could from a high point of view overlook the general scheme of things, the darkest and broadest shadow that ever crossed the mind of man—that ever made him dig for death or leap howling into perdition—may appear no larger than one dim speck upon a mountain of diamond.

We stand up, therefore, with Leigh Hunt and Emerson *versus* Carlyle and Foster, for the old name—the happy stars; and Professor Nichol will come in and complete the majority. Without specially, or at large, arguing the question, he takes it for granted, and sees human immortality and infinite progress legibly inscribed on the sky. The words "onwards" and "to come" are to him the rung changes of the sphere-music, and fearlessly, and as in dance, he follows them into the hoary deep.

We admire, still more, Professor Nichol's spirit of reverence. Religion as a human feeling is so natural a deduction from the spectacles of night, that we sometimes fancy, that did man live *constantly* in a sunless world, and under a starry canopy, he would be a wiser and holier, if a sadder being. One cause, we imagine, why people in the country are more *serious* than the same class in towns, is, that they are brought more frequently, with less interruption, and often alone, into contact with the night sky, which falls sometimes on the solitary head heavy as a mantle with studs of gold. "An undevout astronomer," says Young, "is mad." Nor will the case of La Place disprove this poetic adage—if we understand him to mean, by devotion, that general sense of the Infinite in the imagination which passes as worship into the heart, and comes out as praise upon the lips. In this sense La Place was a worshipper—and that not merely, as Isaac Taylor intimates, of a law which had frozen into a vast icy idol, but of the warm creation as it shone around him. Still, his worship did not reach the measure, or deserve the name, of piety; it was the worship of an effect, not of its living, personal, and father-like cause. Nichol, on the other hand, never loses sight of the universe as an instant, ever-rushing emanation of the Deity. "God," he says, quoting a friend of kindred spirit, "literally creates the universe every moment." He is led by Boscovich's theory of atoms to suppose an infinite Will, producing incessantly all force and motion. And thus the beauty of things seems to him, as it were, an immediate flush upon the cheek of the

Maker, and their light a lustre in his eye, and their motion the circulation of his untiring energies; and yet, withal, the works are never lost in the conception of their Creator, nor the Creator pantheistically identified with the works. The mighty picture, and its mightier background and source, are inseparably connected, but are never confused.

He takes up, in short, precisely the view and the attitude of the ancient Hebrew prophets, in regard to the external universe. To them, that is just a bright or black screen concealing God. "Whither can they go from his Spirit? whither can they flee from his presence?" At every step, and in every circumstance, they feel themselves God-inclosed, God-filled, God-breathing men, with a spiritual Presence lowering or smiling on them from the sky, sounding in wild tempest, or creeping in panic stillness across the surface of the earth; and if they turn within, lo! it is there also —an Eye hung in the central darkness of their own heart. This sublime consciousness a cold science had in a great measure extinguished. Deity, for a season, was banished from the feeling of men; but we are mistaken if a higher and better philosophy have not brought *him* back!—brought back the sun to the earth, in bringing back sight to the blind! Say, rather, a better philosophy, of which our author is not the least eloquent expounder, is bringing back *man* to a perception of the overhanging Deity.

On the relations which connect astronomy with revealed religion, Professor Nichol, though not silent, is somewhat less explicit than we could have wished. In the absence of the powerful light which he could have cast upon this topic, we must permit ourselves a few cursory remarks constituting an outline, which may or may not afterwards be filled up. The Christian Scriptures were, of course, never intended to teach astronomy, any more than to teach botany, or zoology, or conchology, or any other ology, but theology; their main object is to bear a message of mercy to a fallen race, and their allusions to other subjects are necessarily incidental, brief, glancing for a moment to a passing topic, and then rapidly returning to the main and master theme. It follows, therefore, that if we look into them for a systematic statement of truth on any secular subject, we may look long, and look in vain. Nay, we need not have been surprised, although they had in every point coin cided with floating popular notions of physical subjects, provided they did not fail, by their wonted divine alchemy, to deduce from them eternal lessons of moral truth and wisdom. But as "all things are known to the soul"—as even the mind of genius, in its higher hour, has rare glimpses of subjects lying round about, as well as within, the sphere of its thought—so, much more we might have expected that the divinely inspired soul should have hints and intimations, occasional and imperfect, of other fields besides its own. Working in ecstasy, was the prophetic mind never to overleap its barriers?

We affirm, and could, we think, prove the following propositions:—1st, We find in the Scripture-writers not only a feeling of the grandeur of the heavenly bodies, but a sense, obscure, indeed, yet distinct, of their vast magnitude; 2dly, No real contradiction to the leading principles of the modern astronomy; 3dly, One or two hints, that, whether by revelation or otherwise, the true scheme of the universe was understood by more than one of their number; 4thly, The recognition, especially, of the principle of a plurality of worlds; and, 5thly, The recognition of the operation of decay, change, convulsion, and conflagration, among the stars. "He hangeth," says Job, "the earth upon nothing." What a clear and noble gleam of astronomical insight was this in that dark age! In the deep wilderness of Edom did this truth, the germ of the Copernican hypothesis, flash upon the soul of the lonely herdsman, as he turned up his eye to a heaven of far more brilliance than ours, through whose serene and transparent air night looked down in all her queen-like majesty. There wandering, the inspired herdsman, and seeing that those orbs which his heart told him were worlds, were suspended and balanced in the mere void, his mind leaped to the daring conclusion, that so, too, was the firm earth beneath his feet; and with like enthusiasm to that of Archimedes, when he cried "*Eureka! eureka!*" did he exclaim, "He hangeth the earth upon nothing, and stretcheth out the north over the *empty* place."

In like manner, striking is the relation between some admitted facts of astronomy, and some recent speculations in metaphysics, and those remarkable declarations of Scripture concerning the non-permanence of this material framework. We will not soon forget a little circumstance of curious coincidence which occurred in our own experience, in reference to this subject. We had returned from hearing, in Dundee, a lecture by a brilliant friend, in which, in his own inimitable way, and as a deduction from his own daring theory, he had described the dissolution of the universe. At family prayers that very evening, in the course of our ordinary reading, occurred the third chapter of Peter, prophesying the same event. We were all, particularly the lecturer himself, struck with it. It seemed a sublime commentary from the written word upon the lesson we had heard read us from the stars. So far from looking on it as a mere chance coincidence, we all appeared to hear in it God's own whisper—that we had not been hearing or believing a lie.

We are aware that the magnitude and multitude of the stars have furnished a theme of objection to the skeptic, and have elsewhere attempted to show, that Dr. Chalmers has not fully or satisfactorily answered that objection. His "Sermons on the Modern Astronomy"—certainly of this century the most brilliant contribution to the *oratory* of religion—are not distinguished by his usual originality and force of argument. They repel assumptions by assumptions; and, in the exuberant tide of eloquence, the sophism in question is lost sight of, but not drowned. The objection of the skeptic was—Would the Proprietor of a universe so vast have given his Son to die for a world so small? and, perhaps the best reply might be condensed in three questions asked in return to the infidel's one. 1st, What is material magnitude compared to mind? 2dly, Can you *prove* that the vast magnitude on which you found your objection is peopled by moral beings? and, 3dly, What has magnitude to do with a moral question? What, for instance, has the size of a city to do with the moral character of its inhabitants? What has the extent of a country to do with the intellectual or moral interest which may or may not be connected with its plains? Whether is Ben Mac Dhui or Bannockburn the dearer to the Scottish heart, though the one be the prince of Scottish hills, and the other only a poor plain, undistinguished save by an humble stone, and by the immortal memories of patriotism and courage which gather around that field, where "those who had wi' Wallace bled" bade "welcome to their gory bed, or to victory?" Whether is more glorious the gay city of Madrid, or the lonely cape of Trafalgar, where the guns of Nelson, from their iron lips, spake destruction to the united fleets of France and Spain? Whether is Mont Blanc or Morgarten the nobler object, though the one be the

"Monarch of mountains—
They crown'd him long ago,
On a throne of rocks, in a robe of clouds,
With a diadem of snow"—

and the other only a humble field where the Swiss baffled their Austrian oppressors, and where "first in the shock with Xuri's spear was the arm of William Tell?" Whether is more beloved by the Christian's heart Caucasus or Calvary? and yet the one is the loftiest of Asia's mountains, and the other a little hill—a mere dot upon the surface of the globe. So, may there not issue from this remote earth of ours—from the noble deeds it has witnessed—from the nobler aspirations which have been breathed upon it—from the high thoughts which have been thought upon its surface—from the eloquent words which have stirred its air into music—from the poets who have wrought its language into undying song—from the philosophers who have explored the secrets of its laws—from the men of God who have knelt in its temples—from the angels who have touched its mountains—from the footsteps of Incarnate Deity, which have imprinted its plains—a burst of glory, before which the lustre of suns, constellations and firmaments, must pale, tremble, and melt away?

Another consideration is important and obvious. If the greatness of the creation and of its God dwindles earth and man, it must dwindle also every separate section of the universe, and each separate family—for all sections and families, compared to infinity, are less than nothing; and if special circumstances in man's history called for a special interposition in his behalf, surely the urgency of the demand justifies the interference. And as to the question of condescension, the very term involves a false and human conception of God; or if God did condescend to come down to man's condition, it was, in fact, little more than had he condescended to care for and die for angels—the gulf between both ranks of being and himself being boundless. Besides, if, as many suppose, misery and sin extend throughout the universe, may not the scheme of human redemption be only a part of a general process—as Chalmers says, "May not the redemption of many guilty worlds have been laid on the Redeemer's shoulders;" or if, on the other hand, ours be the sole world that has fallen, would not this alone account for the importance attached to, and the sacrifices made for it? Just as, let the meanest man in a kingdom commit a high crime, his insignificance is forgotten—he rises instantly into importance—he is summoned to solemn trial, and on his trial the interest and eyes of an entire nation are suspended; or let the tiniest hill in a country, so tiny that it was not thought worth while to give it a name, but break out into a volcano, and that fire will become to it as a crown—men will flock from every quarter to see it—it will become the principal feature, the terrible tongue of the region—and the old snow-clad mountains will appear diminished in its presence. So (*this* view Dr. Chalmers has admirably amplified, but has not sought to prove the *premise* on which it would require to be founded), if we should call earth the only blot on the fair page of God's universe, we can thus account why angels have rested on its summits—the voice of God been heard in its groves—and the Son of God, for thirty-three years, ate its bread, walked on its surface, and at last died for its sins.

But, in seeking partially to fill up Dr. Nichol's blanks, let us not forget his redundant merits—the genial glow of his spirit—the rich yet nice exuberance of his language—his tremulous and prolonged sympathy with every note of his theme—the clear telescopic light he casts on what is dark—the fine chiaroscuro in which he often bathes what is clear—the choice flowers of poesy which he culls and wreaths around the drier and barer corners of his discourse—and the rich steam of pious feeling which rises irresistibly from each of his closes, as from a censer of incense. Such qualities we find not only in his first work, but even more finely displayed, we think, in his book on the "Solar System." "We would indite," says Charles Lamb, "something on the solar system. Betty, bring the candles." How the gentle Elia fared in this candle-light excursion he does not inform us. In the absence of authentic details concerning this expedition, we have willingly accepted Dr. Nichol's more scientific guidance. We have stood with him on the shining summits of the Moon, looked around on the glazed desolation, gone down into the dreader than Domdaniel caverns, and, coming up, asked at the huge overhanging Earth and the stripped stony Sun, the unanswered question—is this a choas or a ruin? We have climbed the tall cliffs of Venus—been motes in Mercury, itself a mote in the near blaze of the Sun—pressed our footprints in the snows of Mars—swam across the star of Jove, so beautiful and large—paused, and wished to pause for ever, under the divine evenings of Saturn, wishing his ring that of eternity—saluted, from Herschel, the Sun, as the "*Star* of Day," far, faint, diminished, discrowned—and from Neptune, as from a promontory, have looked out into the empire of a night like day, while behind us lay a day like night. A winged painter, with bold pinion and bolder pencil, did he lead us from world to world, and his wing seemed to get stronger, and his vision clearer, and his colors more vivid, the dimmer the region, and the farther the flight.

If we have, in speaking at such length of Dr. Nichol as a writer, left ourselves less room to descant on his merits as a lecturer, our reason is, in both characters he is substantially the same. His writings are just undelivered lectures—his lectures are just spoken books. There are some in whom speaking developes new powers, and who are more at home behind the desk of the lecture-room than behind that of the study. There are others in whom speaking discovers new deficiencies, and who, from want of practice, or diffidence, or contempt for their audience, lecture below their general powers. Professor Nichol belongs to neither of those classes. Both in the study and the lecture-room, he is the same clear expounder, vivid describer, and tempered enthusiast. His manner, without detracting aught from, adds little or nothing to, the impression of his thought or style, of which it is simply the medium. Its principal quality is ease—an ease not materially impaired by a certain hesitation. Hesitation, we need scarcely say, has often a great charm. How fine sometimes it is accompanying the prattle of a beautiful child! And we know some popular divines who have stammered themselves into pulpit celebrity, proving that a fault dexterously managed, is worth *two* merits left in a state of nature. Dr. Nichol's hesitation is not great, is confined to his extempore speech, and seems rather to spring from an excess than a deficiency of matter or words. Every little while, too, he resorts to his notes, and reads his fine passages with much gusto and effect. We must say, however, that we prefer him when carrying on his conversations—so lively, explicit, and entertaining—with his hearers.

In this combined character of lecturer and popular writer, Dr. Nichol has done more than any man living to uncase science from its mummy confinements, and to make it walk abroad as a free and living thing. And though he should never accomplish much in the walks of positive discovery, nor even build up any solid systematic treatise of scientific exposition, he shall not have labored in vain, nor spent his strength for nought. He has, in his various works and progresses through the country, scattered the profuse seeds of what shall yet be an abundant harvest of astronomical enlightenment and enthusiasm. We have been amazed and delighted to witness the impression he contrives to make upon even humble minds, by the joint effect of his subject—his gorgeous style—his gigantic diagrams, and the enthusiasm which speaks through his pallid visage and large gray eyes; and how many "ready-made astronomers" he leaves behind him wherever he goes.

At the commencement of this century, the popular literature of astronomy was in no very palmy condition. Fontenelle, indeed, had defended, with much acuteness and elegance, the doctrine of a "plurality of worlds." Addison, like a "child-angel," had prattled a wondrous prattle about the stars in some of his Saturday "Spectators." But the real text-book of popular prose instruction on this subject was "Hervey's Meditations"—a book written by a good man, but feeble writer, and chiefly distinguished by its inane glitter. But now, not to speak of Dr. Dick, whose lucid, interesting, and widely-read books have done so much to popularize the theme, the genius of Chalmers, Isaac Taylor, and others, has made up for the indifference of ages. Still, Nichol is the *prose* laureate of the stars. From his writings ascends hitherto the richest tribute of mingled intelligence of their laws—love for their beauty—admiration of their still strong order—hope in the prospects of mankind, as reflected in their mirror—and sense, ever profound and near, of that unseen Power, who counts their numbers, sustains their motions, and makes their thousand eyes the organs and the symbols of his omniscience.

In some of the Professor's recent works, such as his "Observations on the System of the World," and his Preface to Willm's "Education," we have been a little annoyed at the quantity of careless writing they contain—at once loose, obscure, and incorrect—and have been tempted to lay the blame now upon his printers, and now upon his own most incomprehensible and *nebulous handwriting.*

We take our leave of this subject with considerable regret, both because we are always sorry to part from a frank, friendly, and intelligent companion like Dr. Nichol, and because we are even yet sorrier to leave a theme so fascinating, even to an unscientific writer, as the "star-eyed science." We cannot close without alluding to the recent death of Miss Herschel, long the associate of Sir William, in his midnight observations, and to whom our author pays an elegant compliment, in his "Architecture of the Heavens." After long enjoying the brilliant reputation of her brother, and the equally wide and true, if not so brilliant, reputation of her nephew—retaining, amid the chills of extreme age, all the ardor of her enthusiasm, and engaged, it is said, to the last in her favorite pursuit—she has fallen asleep. Every astronomer, surely, is ready to envy her fate, so far as her retaining to the end her post is concerned. To die at the telescope is surely a nobler destiny than to die at the can non, or on the throne.*

* Since this was written, the Professor has been in America, and the public may soon expect the result in a separate, and, we doubt not, most interesting work.

MRS. HEMANS.

Female authorship is, if not a great, certainly a singular fact. And if a singular fact in this century, what must it have been in the earlier ages of the world—when it existed as certainly as now, and was more than now a phenomenon, standing often insulated and alone? If, even in this age, *blues* are *black*-balled, and homespun is still the "only wear," and music, grammar, and *gramarye* are the three elements legitimately included and generally expected in the education of woman, in what light must the Aspasias and the Sapphos of the past have been regarded? Probably as *lusus naturæ*, in whom a passionate attachment to literature was pardoned as a pleasant peccadillo, or agreeable insanity; just as a slight squint in the eye of a beauty, or even a far-off *faux pas* in her reputation, is still not unfrequently forgiven. But alas! in our age the exception is likely soon to become the rule—the *lusus* the law; and, at all events, of female authorship the least gallant of critics is compelled now to take cognizance; and without absolutely admitting this as *our* characteristic, we must confess the diffidence as well as the good-will wherewith we approach a subject where respect for truth and respect for the sex are sometimes apt to jostle and jar.

The works of British women have now taken up, not by courtesy but by right, a full and conspicuous place in our literature. They constitute an elegant library in themselves; and there is hardly a department in science, in philosophy, in morals, in politics, in the belles-lettres, in fiction, or in the fine arts, but has been occupied, and ably occupied, by a lady. This certainly proclaims a high state of cultivation on the part of the many which has thus flowered out into composition in the case of the few. It exhibits an extension and refinement of that element of female influence which, in the private intercourse of society, has been productive of such blessed effects—it mingles with the harsh tone of general literature, "as the lute pierceth through the cymbal's clash."—it blends with it a vein of delicate discrimination, of mild charity, and of purity of morals—gives it a healthy and happy tone, the tone of the fireside; it is in the chamber of our literature, a quiet and lovely presence; by its very gentleness, overawing as well as refining and beautifying it all. One principal characteristic of female writing in our age is its sterling sense. It is told of Coleridge, that he was accustomed, on important emergencies, to consult a female friend, placing implicit confidence in her first instructive suggestions. If she proceeded to add her reasons, he checked her immediately. "Leave these, madam, to me to find out." We find this rare and valuable sense—this short-hand reasoning—exemplified in our lady authors—producing, even in the absence of original genius, or of profound penetration, or of wide experience, a sense of perfect security, as we follow their gentle guidance. Indeed, on all questions affecting proprieties, decorums, what we may call the *ethics* of sentimentalism, minor as well as major morals, their verdict may be considered oracular, and without appeal. We remark, too, in the writings of females, a tone of greater generosity than in those of men. They are more candid and amiable in their judgments of authors and of books. Commend us to female critics. *They* are not eternally consumed by the desire of being witty, astute, and severe, of carping at what they could not equal—of hewing down what they could or *would* not have built up. The principle, *nil admirari*, is none of theirs; and whether it be that a sneer disfigures their beautiful lips, it is seldom seen upon them. And in correspondence with this, it is curious that (in our judgments, and, we suspect, theirs) the worst critics are persons who dislike the sex, and whom the sex dislikes—musty, fusty old bachelors, such as Gifford, or certain pedantic prigs in the press of the present day. Ladies, on the other hand, are seldom severe judges of any thing, except each other's dress and deportment; and in defect of profound principles, they are helped out by that fine instinctive sense of theirs, which partakes of the genial nature, and verges upon genius itself.

Passing from such preliminary remarks, we proceed to our theme. We have selected Mrs. Hemans as our first specimen of Female Authors, not because we consider her the best, but because we consider her by far the most feminine writer of the age. All the woman in her shines. You could not (unknowing of the author) open a page of her writings without feeling this is written by a lady. Her inspiration always pauses at the feminine point. It never "oversteps the modesty of nature," nor the dignity and decorum of womanhood. She is no sibyl, tossed to and fro in the tempest of furious excitement, but ever a "deep, majestical, and high-souled woman"—the calm mistress of the highest and stormiest of her emotions. The finest compliment we can pay her—perhaps the finest compliment that it is possible to pay to woman, as a moral being—is to compare her to "one of Shakspeare's women," and to say, had Imogen, or Isabella, or Cornelia become an author, she had so written.

Sometimes, indeed, Mrs. Hemans herself seems seduced, through the warmth of her temperament, the facility and rapidity of her execution, and the intensely lyrical tone of her genius, to dream that the shadow of the Pythoness is waving behind her, and controlling the motions of her song. To herself she appears to be uttering oracular deliverances. Alas! "oracles speak," and her poetry, as to all effective utterance of original truth, is silent. It is emotion only that is audible to the sharpest ear that listens to her song. A bee wreathing round you in the warm summer morn her singing circle, gives you as much new insight into the universe as do the sweetest strains which have ever issued from this "voice of spring." We are reluctantly compelled, therefore, to deny her, in its highest sense, the name of poet—a word often abused, often misapplied in mere compliment or courtesy, but which ought ever to retain its stern and original signification. A *maker* she is not. What dream of childhood has she ever, to any imagination, reborn? whose slumbers has she ever peopled with new and terrible visions? what new form or figure has she annexed, like a second shadow, to our own idiosyncracy, to track us on our way for ever? to what mind has she given such a burning stamp of impression as it feels eternity itself unable to efface? There is no such result from the poetry of Mrs. Hemans. She is less a maker than a *musician*, and her works appear rather to rise to the airs of the piano than to that still sad music of humanity—the adequate instrument for the expression of which has not yet been invented by man. From the tremulous movement, the wailing cadences, the artistic pauses, and the conscious-swelling climaxes of her verse, we always figure her as modulating, inspiring, and controlling her thoughts and words to the tune of some fine instrument, which is less the vehicle than the creator of the strain. In her poetry, consequently, the music rather awakens the meaning, than does the meaning round and mellow off into the music.

With what purpose does a lady, in whom perfect skill and practice have not altogether drowned enthusiasm, sit down to her harp, piano, or guitar? Not altogether for the purpose of display—not at all for that of instruction to her audience—but in a great measure that she may develop, in a lawful form, the sensibilities of her own bosom. Thus sat Felicia Hemans before her lyre—not touching it with awful reverence, as though each string were a star, but regarding it as the soother and sustainer of her own high-wrought emotions—a graceful *alias* of herself. Spring, in its vague joyousness, has not a more appropriate voice in the note of the cuckoo than feminine sensibility had in the more varied but hardly profounder song of the authoress before us.

We wish not to be misunderstood. Mrs. Hemans had something more than the common belief of all poets in the existence of the beautiful. She was a genuine woman, and, therefore, the sequence (as we shall see speedily) is irresistible, imbued with a Christian spirit. Nor has she feared to set her creed to music in her poetry. But it was as a betrayal, rather than as a purpose, that she so did. She was more the organ of sentiment and sensibility than of high and solemn truth—more a golden morning mist, now glittering and then gone in the sun, than a steady dial at once meekly reflecting and faithfully watching and measuring his beams.

She was, as Lord Jeffrey well remarks, an admirable writer of *occasional* verses. She has caught, in her poetry, passing moods of her own mind—meditations of the sleepless night—transient glimpses of thought, visiting her in her serener hours—the "silver lining" of those cloudy feelings which preside over her darker—and the impressions made upon her mind by the more remarkable events of her every-day life—and the more exciting passages of her reading. Her works are a versified *journal* of a quiet, ideal, and beautiful life—the life at once of a woman and a poetess, with just enough, and no more, of romance to cast around it a mellow autumnal coloring. The songs, hymns, and odes in which this life is registered, are as soft and bright as atoms of the rainbow; like them, tears transmuted into glory, but, no more than they, are great or complete. In many poets, we see the germ of greatness, which might, in happier circumstances, or in a more genial season, have been developed. But no such germ can the most microscopic survey discover in her, and we feel that at her death her beautiful but tiny task was done. Indeed, with such delicate organization, and such intense susceptiveness as hers, the elaboration, the long reach of thought, the slow *cumulative* advance, the deep-curbed, yet cherished ambition which a great work requires and implies, are, we fear, incompatible.

It follows, naturally from this, that her largest are her worst productions. They labor under the fatal defect of tedium. They are a surfeit of sweets. Conceive an orchard of rose-trees. Who would not, stupefied and bewildered by excess and extravagance of beauty, prefer the old, sturdy, and well-laden boughs of the pear and pippen, and feel the truth of the adage—"The *apple* tree is the fairest tree in the wood?" Hence few, comparatively, have taken refuge in her "forest sanctuary," reluctant and rare the ears which have listened to her "Vespers of Palermo," her "Siege of Valencia" has stormed no hearts, and her "Skeptic" made, we fear, few converts. But who has not wept over her "Graves of a Household," or hushed his heart to hear her "Treasures of the Deep," in which the old Sea himself seems to speak, or wished to take the left hand of the Hebrew child and lead him up, along with his mother, to the temple service; or thrilled and shouted in the gorge of "Morgarten," or trembled at the stroke of her "Hour of Death?" Such poems are of the kind which win their way into every house, and every collection, and every heart. They secure for their authors a sweet garden plot of reputation, which is envied by none, and with which no one intermeddles. Thus flowers smile, unharmed, to the bolt which levels the pine beside them. The tapers live while suns sink and disappear. Even a single sweet poem, flowing from a gentle mind in a happy hour, is as "ointment poured forth," and carries a humble name in fragrance far down into futurity, while the elaborate productions of loftier spirits rot upon the shelves. A Lucretius exhausts the riches of his magnificent mind in a stately poem, which is barely remembered, and never read. A Wolfe expresses the emotions of every heart at the recital of Sir John Moore's funeral in a few rude rhymes, and becomes immortal. A Shelley, dipping his pen in the bloody sweat of his lonely and agonized heart, traces voluminous lines of "red and burning" poetry, and his works are known only to some hardy explorers. A Michael Bruce transfers one spring-joy of his dying frame, stirred by the note of the cuckoo, to a brief and tear-stained page; and henceforth the voice of the bird seems vocal with his name, and wherever, from the "engulphed navel" of the wood, you hear its strange, nameless, tameless, wandering, unearthly voice, you think of the poet who sighed away his soul and gathered his fame in its praise. A Bayley constructs a work "before all ages," lavishes on it imagination that might suffice for a century of poets; and it lies, on some recherché tables, like a foreign curiosity, to be seen, shown, and lifted, rather than to be read and pondered. A William Miller sings, one gloaming, his "Wee Willie Winkie," and the nurseries of an entire nation re-echo the simple strain, and every Scottish mother blesses, in one breath, her babe and his poet. We mention this, not entirely to approve, but in part to wonder at it. It is not just that one strain from a lute or a pan's pipe should survive a thunder-psalm—that effusions should eclipse works.

Mrs. Hemans's poems are strictly effusions; and not a little of their charm springs from their unstudied and extempore character. This, too, is in fine keeping with the sex of the writer. You are saved the ludicrous image of a double-dyed Blue, in papers and morning wrapper, sweating at some stupendous treatise or tragedy from morn to noon, and from noon to dewy eve—you see a graceful and gifted woman, passing from the cares of her family and the enjoyments of society, to inscribe on her tablets some fine thought or feeling, which had throughout the day existed as a still sunshine upon her countenance, or perhaps as a quiet unshed tear in her eye. In this case, the transition is so natural and graceful, from the duties or delights of the day to the employments of the desk, that there is as little pedantry in writing a poem as in writing a letter, and the authoress appears only the lady in *flower*. Indeed, to recur to a former remark, Mrs. Hemans is distinguished above all others by her intense womanliness; and as her own character is so true to her sex, so her sympathies with her sex are very peculiar and profound. Of the joys and the sorrows, the difficulties and the duties, the trials and the temptations, the hopes and the fears, the proper sphere and mission of woman, and of those peculiar consolations which the "world cannot give nor take away," that sustain her even when baffled, she has a true and thorough appreciation; and her "Records of Woman," and her "Songs of the Affections," are just audible beatings of the deep female heart. In our judgment, Mrs. Ellis's idea of woman is trite, vulgar, and limited, compared with that of "Egeria," as Miss Jewsbury used fondly to denote her beloved friend. What a gallery of Shakspeare's female characters would the author of the "Mothers, Daughters, and Women of England" have painted! What could she have said of Juliet? How would she have contrived to twist Beatrice into a pattern Miss? Perdita! would she have sent her to a boarding-school? or insisted on *finishing*, according to the Hannah More pattern, the divine Miranda? Of that pretty Pagan Imogen, what would she make? Imagine her criticism on Lady Macbeth, or on Ophelia's dying speech and confession, or her revelation of the "Family Secrets" of the "Merry Wives of Windsor!"

Next to her pictures of the domestic affections stand Mrs. Hemans's pictures of nature. These are less minute than passionate, less sublime than beautiful, less studies than free, broad, and rapid sketches. Her favorite scenery was the woodland, a taste in which we can thoroughly sympathize. In the wood there is a fulness, a roundness, a rich harmony, and a comfort, which soothe and completely satisfy the imagination. There, too, there is much life and motion. The glens, the still moorlands, and the rugged hills, will not move, save to one master finger, the finger of the earthquake, who is chary of his great displays; but before each lightest touch of the breeze the complacent leaves of the woodland begin to stir, and the depth of solitude seems instantly peopled, and from perfect silence there comes a still small voice, so sweet and sudden that it is as if every leaf were the tongue of a separate spirit. Her favorite season was the autumn, though her finest verses are dedicated to the spring. Here, too, we devoutly participate in her feelings. The shortening day—the new out-bursting from their veil of daylight of those, in summer, neglected tremblers, the stars—the yellow corn—the gray and pensive light—the joy of harvest—the fine firing of all—the groves (not the "fading but the kindling of the leaf")—the frequent and moaning winds—the spiritual quiet in which, at other times, the stubble-fields are bathed—the rekindling of the cheerful fires upon the hearth—the leaves falling to their own sad music—the rising stackyards—the wild fruit, ripened at the cold sun of the frost—the "ineffable gleams of light dropping upon favorite glens or rivers, or hills that shine out like the shoulder of Pelops"—the beseeching looks with which, trembling on the verge of winter, the belated season seems to say, "Love me well, I am the last of the sisterhood that you can love"—in short, that indescribable charm which breathes in its very air and colors its very light, and sheds its joy of grief over all things, have concurred with some sweet and some sad associations to render autumn to us the loveliest and the dearest of all seasons. As Mrs. Hemans loved woodland scenery for its kindly "looks of shelter," so she loved the autumn principally for its correspondence with that fine melancholy which was the permanent atmosphere of her being. In one of her letters, speaking of an autumn day, she says, "The day was one of a kind I like—soft, still, and gray, such as makes the earth appear a 'pensive but a happy place.'" We have sometimes thought that much of Wordsworth's poetry should always be read and can never be so fully felt as in the autumn, when "Laodamia," at least, must have been written. Should not poems, as well as pictures, have their peculiar light, in which alone they can properly be seen? Should not Scott be read in spring, Shelley in the fervid summer, Wordsworth in autumn, Cowper and Byron in the winter, Shakspeare all the year round?

In many points Mrs. Hemans reminds us of a poet just named, and whom she passionately admired, namely Shelley. Like him, drooping, fragile, a reed shaken by the wind, a mighty wind, in sooth, too powerful for the tremulous reed on which it discoursed its music; like him, the victim of exquisite nervous organization; like him, verse flowed on and from her, and the sweet sound often overpowered the meaning, kissing it, as it were, to death; like him, she was melancholy, but the sadness of both was musical, tearful, active, not stony, silent, and motionless, still less misanthropical and disdainful; like him, she was gentle, playful, they could both run about their prison garden, and dally with the dark chains which, they knew, bound them till death. Mrs. Hemans, indeed, was not like Shelley, a *vates;* she has never reached his heights nor sounded his depths, yet they are, to our thought, so strikingly alike as to seem brother and sister in one beautiful but delicate and dying family. Their very appearance must have been similar. How like must the girl, Felicia Dorothea Browne, with the mantling bloom of her cheeks, her hair of a rich golden brown, and the ever-varying expression of her brilliant eyes, have been to the noble boy, Percy Bysshe Shelley, when he came first to Oxford, a fair-haired, bright-eyed enthusiast, on whose cheek and brow, and in whose eye was already beginning to burn a fire, which ultimately enwrapped his whole being in flames!

In Mrs. Hemans's melancholy, one "simple" was wanting, which was largely mixed in Shelley's, that of faithless despondency. Her spirit was cheered by faith—by a soft and noble form of the softest noblest faith—a form, reminding us much from its balance of human, poetical, and celestial elements, of that Jeremy Taylor—the "Shakspeare of divines." Although, as we have said, her poetry is not, of prepense and purpose, the express image of her religious thought, yet it is a rich illustration of the religious tendency of the female mind. Indeed, females may be called the natural guardians of morality and faith. These shall always be safe in the depths of the female intellect, and of the female heart—an intellect, the essence of which is worship—a heart, the element of which is love. Unhired, disinterested, spontaneous is the aid they give to the blessed cause; leaning, indeed, in their lovely weakness on the "worship of sorrow," they, at the same time, prop it up through the wide and holy influences which they wield. Their piety, too, is no fierce and foul polemic flame—it is that of the feelings—the quick instinctive sense of duty—the wonder-stricken soul and the loving heart—often it is not even a conscious emotion at all—but in Wordsworth's language—they lie in

> "Abraham's bosom all the year,
> And God is with them, and they know it not."

In Mrs. Hemans's writings you find this pious tendency of her sex unsoiled by an atom of cant, or bigotry, or exclusiveness; and shaded only by so much pensiveness as attests its divinity and its depth: for as man's misery is said to spring from his greatness, so the gloom which often overhangs the earnest spirit arises from its more immediate proximity to the Infinite and the Eternal. And who would not be ready to sacrifice all the cheap sunshine of earthly success and satisfaction for even a touch of a shadow so sublime?

After all, the nature of this poetess is more interesting than her genius, or than its finest productions. These *descend* upon us like voices from a mountain summit, suggesting to us an elevation of character far higher than themselves. If not, in a transcendent sense, a poet, her life was a poem. Poetry colored all her existence with a golden light—poetry presided at her needlework—poetry mingled with her domestic and her maternal duties—poetry sat down with her to her piano—poetry fluttered her hair and flushed her cheek in her mountain rambles—poetry quivered in her voice, which was a "sweet sad melody"—poetry accompanied her to the orchard as she read the "Talisman," in that long glorious summer day which she has made immortal—and poetry attended her to the house of God, and listened with her to the proud pealing organ, as to an echo from within the veil. Poetry performed for her a still tenderer ministry; it soothed the deep sorrows, on which we dare not enter, which shaded the tissue of her history—it mixed its richest cupful of the "joy of grief" for her selected lips—it lapped her in a dream of beauty, through which the sad realities of life looked in, softened and mellowed in the medium. What could poetry have done more for her, except, indeed, by giving her that sight "as far as the incommunicable"—that supreme vision which she gives so rarely, and which she bestows often as a curse, instead of a blessing? Mrs. Hemans, on the other hand, was too favorite a child of the Muse to receive any such baneful boon. Poetry beautified her life, blunted and perfumed the thorns of her anguish, softened the pillow of her sickness, and combined with her firm and most feminine faith to shed a gleam of soft and tearful glory upon her death.

Thus lived, wrote, suffered, and died "Egeria." Without farther seeking to weigh the worth, or settle the future place of her works, let us be thankful to have had her among us, and that she did what she could, in her bright, sorely-tried, yet triumphant passage. She grew in beauty; was blasted where she grew; rained around her poetry, like bright tears from her eyes; learned in suffering what she taught in song; died, and all hearts to which she ever ministered delight, have obeyed the call of Wordsworth, to

> "Mourn rather for that holy spirit,
> Mild as the spring, as ocean deep;—
> For her who, ere her summer faded,
> Has sunk into a dreamless sleep."

MRS. ELIZABETH BARRETT BROWNING.

In selecting Mrs. Hemans as our first specimen of Female Authors, we did so avowedly, because she seemed to us the most feminine writer of the day. We now select Mrs. Browning for the opposite reason, that she is, or at least is said by many to be, the most masculine of our female writers.

To settle the respective spheres and calibres of the male and the female mind, is one of the most difficult of philosophical problems. To argue, merely, that because the mind of woman has never hitherto produced a "Paradise Lost," or a "Principia," it is therefore for ever incapable of producing similar masterpieces, seems to us unfair, for various reasons. In the first place, how many ages elapsed ere the *male* mind realized such prodigies of intellectual achievement? And do not they still stand unparalleled and almost unapproached? And were it not as reasonable to assert that man as that woman can renew them no more? Secondly, because the premise is granted—that woman *has* not—does the conclusion follow, that woman cannot excogitate an argument as great as the "Principia," or build up a rhyme as lofty as the "Paradise Lost?" Would it not have been as wise for one who knew Milton only as the Milton of "Lycidas" and "Arcades," to have contended that he was incapable of a great epic poem? And is there nothing in Madame De Stael, in Rahel the Germaness, in Mary Somerville, and even in Mary Wollstonecraft, to suggest the idea of heights, fronting the very peaks of the Principia and the Paradise, to which woman may yet attain? Thirdly, has not woman understood and appreciated the greatest works of genius as fully as man? Then may she in time equal them; for what is true appreciation but the sowing of a germ in the mind, which shall ultimately bear similar fruit? There is nothing, says Godwin, which the human mind can conceive, which it cannot execute; we may add, there is nothing the human mind can understand which it cannot equal. Fourthly, let us never forget that woman, as to intellectual progress, is in a state of infancy. Changed as by malignant magic, now into an article of furniture, and now into a toy of pleasure, she is only as yet undergoing a better transmigration, and "timidly expanding into life."

Almost all that is valuable in female authorship has been produced within the last half-century, that is, since the female was generally recognized to be an intellectual creature; and if she has in such a short period, so progressed, what demi-Mahometan shall venture to set bounds to her future advancement? Even though we should grant that woman, more from her bodily constitution than her mental, is inferior to man, and that man, having got, shall probably keep, his start of centuries, we see nothing to prevent woman overtaking, and outstripping with ease, his *present* farthest point of intellectual progress. We do not look on such productions as "Lear," and the "Prometheus Vinctus," with the despair wherewith the boy who has leaped in vain to seize, regards ever after the moon and the stars; they are, after all, the masonry of men, and not the architecture of the gods;

and if man may surpass, why may not woman, "taken out of his side," equal them?

Of woman, we may say, at least, that there are already provinces where her power is incontested and supreme. And in proportion as civilization advances, and as the darker and fiercer passions which constitute the *feræ naturæ* subside, in the lull of that milder day, the voice of woman will become more audible, exert a wider magic, and be as the voice of spring to the opening year. We stay not to prove that the *sex* of genius is *feminine*, and that those poets who are most profoundly impressing our young British minds, are those who, in tenderness and sensibility—in peculiar power, and peculiar weakness, are all but females. And whatever may be said of the effects of culture, in deadening the genius of man, we are mistaken if it has not always had the contrary effect upon that of woman, (where do we find a female Bloomfield or Burns?) so that, on entering on the far more highly civilized periods which are manifestly approaching, she will but be breathing the atmosphere calculated to nourish and invigorate, instead of weakening and chilling, her mental life. Our admirable friend, Mr. De Quincey, has, we think, conceded even more than we require, in granting that woman can die more nobly than man.* For whether is the writing or the doing of great tragedy the higher achievement? Poor the attitude even of Shakspeare, penning the fire-syllables of Macbeth, to that of Joan of Arc, entering into the flames as into her wedding suit. What comparison between the face inflamed of a Mirabeau or a Chalmers, as they thundered; and the blush on the cheek of Charlotte Corday, still extant, as her head was presented to the people? And who shall name the depicter of the death of Beatrice Cenci with that heroine herself; or with Madame Roland, whose conduct on the scaffold might make one in "love with death?" If to die nobly demand the highest concentration of the moral, intellectual, and even artistic powers—and if woman has *par excellence* exemplified such a concentration, there follows a conclusion to which we should be irresistibly led, were it not that we question the minor proposition in the argument—we hold that man has often as

* See in "Tait" a paper on Joan of Arc.

fully as woman risen to the dignity of death, and met him not as a vassal, but as a superior.

To say that Mrs. Browning has more of the man than any female writer of the period, may appear rather an equivocal compliment; and its truth even may be questioned. We may, however, be permitted to say, that she has more of the *heroine* than her compeers. Hers is a high, heroic nature, which adopts for the motto at once of its life and of its poetry, "Perfect through suffering." Shelley says:—

> "Most wretched men
> Are cradled into poetry by wrong;
> They learn in suffering what they teach in song."

But wrong is not always the stern schoolmistress of song. There are sufferings springing from other sources—from intense sensibility—from bodily ailment—from the loss of cherished objects, which also find in poetry their natural vent. And we do think that such poetry, if not so powerful, is infinitely more pleasing and more instructive than that which is inspired by real or imaginary grievance. The turbid torrent is not the proper mirror for reflecting the face of nature; and none but the moody and the discontented will seek to see in it an aggravated and distorted edition of their own gloomy brows. The poetry of wrong is not the best and most permanent. It was not wrong alone that excited, though it unquestionably directed, the course of Dante's and Milton's vein. The poetry of Shakspeare's wrong is condensed in his sonnets—the poetry of his forbearance and forgiveness, of his gratitude and his happiness, is in his dramas. The poetry of Pope's wrong (a scratch from a thorn hedge!) is in his "Dunciad," not in his "Rape of the Lock." The poetry of Wordsworth's wrong is in his "Prefaces," not in his "Excursion." The poetry of Byron's wrong is in those deep curses which sometimes disturb the harmony of his poems; and that of Shelley's in the maniacal scream which occasionally interrupts the pæans of his song. But all these had probably been as great, or greater poets, had no wrong befallen them, or had it taught them another lesson, than either peevishly to proclaim or furiously to resent it.

Mrs. Browning has suffered, so far as we are aware, no

wrong from the age. She might, indeed, for some time have spoken of neglect. But people of genius should now learn the truth, that *neglect* is not *wrong;* or if it be, it is a wrong in which they often set the example. Neglecting the tastes of the majority, the majority avenges itself by neglecting them. Standing and singing in a congregation of the deaf, they are senseless enough to complain that they are not heard. Or should they address the multitude, and should the multitude not listen, it never strikes them that the fault is their own; they ought to have compelled attention. Orpheus was listened to: the thunder is: even the gentlest spring shower commands its audience. If neglect means wilful winking at claims which are *felt*, it is indeed a wrong; but a wrong seldom if ever committed, and which complaint will not cure—if it means, merely, ignorance of claims which have never been presented or enforced, where and whose is the criminality?

To do Mrs. Browning justice, she has not complained of neglect nor injury at all. But she has acknowledged herself inspired by the genius of suffering. And this seems to have exerted divers influences upon her poetry. It has, in the first place, taught her to rear for herself a spot of transcendental retreat, a city of refuge in the clouds. Scared away from her own heart, she has soared upwards, and found a rest elsewhere. To those flights of idealism in which she indulges, to those distant and daring themes which she selects, she is urged less, we think, through native tendency of mind, than to fill the vacuity of a sick and craving spirit. This is not peculiar to her. It may be called, indeed, the "Retreat of the Ten Thousand;" though strong and daring must be those that can successfully accomplish it. Only the steps of sorrow—we had almost said only the steps of despair—can climb such dizzy heights. The healthy and the happy mind selects subjects of a healthy and a happy sort, and which lie within the sphere of every-day life and every-day thought. But for minds which have been wrung and riven, there is a similar attraction in gloomy themes, as that which leads them to the side of dark rivers, to the heart of deep forests, or into the centre of waste glens. Step forth, ye giant children of Sorrow and Genius, that we may tell your names, and compute your multitudes. First, there is the proud thundershod Æschylean family, all conceived in the "eclipse" of that most powerful of Grecian spirits. Then follows Lucretius—

> "Who cast his plummet down the broad
> Deep universe, and said, No God;
> Finding no bottom, he denied
> Divinely the divine, and died,
> Chief poet upon Tiber side."—(*Mrs. Browning.*)

There stalk forward, next in the procession, the kings, priests, popes, prelates, and the yet guiltier and mightier shapes of Dante's Hell. Next, the Satan of Milton advances, champing the curb, and regarding even Prometheus as no mate for his proud and lonely misery. Then comes, cowering and shivering on, the timid Castaway of Cowper. He is followed by Byron's heroes, a haughty yet melancholy troop, with *conscious madness* animating their gestures and glaring in their eyes. The Anciente Marinere succeeds, now fearfully reverting his looks, and now fixing his glittering eye forward on a peopled and terrible vacancy. And, lastly, a frail shadowy and shifting shape, looking now Laon, now like Lionel, and now like Prometheus, proclaims that Alastor himself is here, the Benjamin in this family of tears.

"Whither shall I wander," seems Mrs. Browning to have said to herself, "to-day to escape from my own sad thoughts, and to lose, to noble purpose, the sense of my own identity? I will go eastward to Eden, where perfection and happiness once dwelt. I will pass, secure in virtue, the far-flashing sword of the cherubim; I will knock at the door and enter. I will lie down in the forsaken garden; I will pillow my head where Milton pillowed his, on the grass cool with the shadow of the Tree of Life; and I will dream a vision of my own, of what this place once was, and of what it was to leave it for the wilderness." And she has passed the waving sword, and she has entered the awful garden, and she has dreamed a dream, and she has, awaking, told it as a "Drama of Exile." It were vain to deny that the dream is one full of genius—that it is entirely original; and that it never once, except by antithesis, suggests a thought of Milton's more passive and palpable vision. Her Paradise is not a garden, it is a flush on a summer evening sky. Her Adam is not the fair large-fronted man, with all manlike qualities meeting unconsciously in his full clear nature—he is a German metaphysician. Her Eve is *herself*, an amiable and gifted blue stocking, not the mere meek motherly woman, with what Aird beautifully calls the "broad, ripe, serene, and gracious composure of love about her." Her spirits are neither cherubim nor seraphim—neither knowing nor burning ones—they are fairies, not, however, of the Puck or Ariel species, but of a new metaphysical breed; they do not ride on, but split hairs; they do not dance, but reason; or if they dance, it is on the point of a needle, in cycles and epicycles of mystic and mazy motion. There is much beauty and power in passages of the poem, and a sweet inarticulate melody, like the fabled cry of mandrakes, in the lyrics. Still we do not see the taste of turning the sweet open garden of Eden into a maze—we do not approve of the daring precedent of trying conclusions with Milton on his own high field of victory—and we are, we must say, jealous of all encroachments upon that fair Paradise which has so long painted itself upon our imaginations—where all the luxuries of earth mingled in the feast with all the dainties of the heavens—where celestial plants grew under the same sun with terrestrial blossoms, and where the cadences of seraphic music filled up the pauses in the voice of God. Far different, indeed, is Mrs. Browning's from Dryden's disgusting inroad into Eden—as different, almost, as the advent of Raphael from the encroachment of Satan. But the poem professed to stand in the lustre of the fiery sword, and this should have burnt up some of its conceits, and silenced some of its meaner minstrelsies. And all such attempts we regard precisely as we do the beauties of the Apocrypha, when compared tc the beauties of the Bible. They are as certainly beauties, but beauties of an inferior order—they are flowers, but not the roses which grew along the banks of the Four Rivers, or caught in their crimson cups the "first sad drops wept at committing of the mortal sin." "One blossom of Eden outblooms them all."

Having accepted from Mrs. Browning's own hand sadness, or at least seriousness, as the key to her nature and genius, let us continue to apply it in our future remarks. This at once impels her to, and fits her for, the high position she has assumed, uttering the "Cry of the Human." And whom would the human race prefer as their earthly advocate, to a high-souled and gifted woman? What voice but the female voice could so softly and strongly, so eloquently and meltingly, interpret to the ear of him whose name is Love, the deep woes and deeper wants of "poor humanity's afflicted will, struggling in vain with ruthless destiny?" Some may quarrel with the title, "The Human," as an affectation; but, in the first place, if so, it is a very small one, and a small affectation can never furnish matter for a great quarrel; secondly, we are not disposed to make a man, and still less a woman, an offender for a word, and thirdly, we fancy we can discern a good reason for her use of the term. What is it that is crying aloud through her voice to Heaven? It is not the feral or fiendish element in human nature? That has found an organ in Byron—an echo in his bellowing verse. It is the human element in man—bruised, bleeding, all but dead under the pressure of evil circumstances, under the ten thousand tyrannies, mistakes, and delusions of the world, that has here ceased any longer to be silent, and is speaking in a sister's voice to Time and to Eternity—to Earth and Heaven. The poem may truly be called a prayer for the times, and no collect in the English liturgy surpasses it in truth and tenderness, though some may think its tone daring to the brink of blasphemy, and piercing almost to anguish.

Gracefully from this proud and giddy pinnacle, where she has stood as the conscious and commissioned representative of the human race, she descends to the door of the factory, and pleads for the children inclosed in that crowded and busy hell. The "Cry of the Factory Children" moves you, because it is no poem at all—it is just a long sob, veiled and stifled as it ascends through the hoarse voices of the poor beings themselves. Since we read it we can scarcely pass a factory without seeming to hear this psalm issuing from the machinery, as if it were protesting against its own abused powers. But, to use the language of a writer quoted a little before, "The Fairy Queen is dead, shrouded in a yard of cotton stuff made by the spinning-jenny, and by that other piece of new improved machinery, *the souls and bodies of British children*, for which death alone holds the patent." From Mrs. Browning, perhaps the most imaginative and intellectual of British females, down to a pale-faced, thick-voiced, degraded, hardly human, factory girl, what a long and precipitous descent! But though hardly, she is human; and availing herself of the small, trembling, but eternally indestructible link of connection implied in a common nature, our author can identify herself with the cause, and incarnate her genius in the person of the poor perishing child. How unspeakably more affecting is the pleading in behalf of a particular portion of the race, than in behalf of the entire family! Mrs. Browning might have uttered a hundred "cries of the human," and proved herself only a sentimental artist, and awakened little save an echo dying away in distant elfin laughter; but the cry of a factory child, coming through a woman's, has gone to a nation's heart.

Although occupied thus with the sterner wants and sorrows of society, she is not devoid of interest in its minor miseries and disappointments. She can sit down beside little Ella (the miniature of Alnaschar) and watch the history of her day-dream beside the swan's nest among the reeds, and see in her disappointment a type of human hopes in general, even when towering and radiant as summer clouds. Ella's dream among the reeds! What else was Godwin's Political Justice? What else was St. Simonianism? What else is Young Englandism. And what else are the hopes built by many now upon *certain* perfected schemes of education, which, freely translated, just mean the farther sharpening and furnishing of knaves and fools; and now upon a "Coming Man," who is to supply every deficiency, reconcile every contradiction, and right every wrong. Yes, he will come mounted on the red-roan horse of sweet Ella's vision!

Shadowed by the same uniform seriousness are the only two poems of her which we shall farther at present mention —we mean her "Vision of Poets," and her "Geraldine's Courtship." The aim of the first is to present, in short compass, and almost in single lines, the characteristics of the greater poets of past and present times. This undertaking involved in it very considerable difficulties. For, in the first place, most great poets possess more than one distinguishing peculiarity. To select a single differential point is always hazardous, and often deceptive. 2dly, After you have selected the prominent characteristic of your author, it is no easy task to express it in a word, or in a line. To compress thus an Iliad in a nutshell, to imprison a giant geni in an iron pot, is more a feat of magic than an act of criticism. 3dly, It is especially difficult to express the differentia of a writer in a manner at once easy and natural, picturesque and poetical. In the very terms of such an attempt as Mrs. Browning makes, it is implied that she not only defines, but describes the particular writer. But to curdle up a character into one noble word, to describe Shakspeare, for instance, in such compass, what sun-syllable shall suffice; or must we renew Byron's wish?—

> "Could I unbosom and embody now
> That which is most within me; could I wreak
> My thought upon expression!
> * * * * * * *
> And that *one word were Lightning*, I would speak;
> But as it is, I live and die unheard,
> With a most voiceless thought, sheathing it as a sword."

Accordingly, this style of portraiture (shall we call it, as generally pursued, the thumb-nail style?) has seldom been prosecuted with much success. Ebenezer Elliot has a copy of verses after this fashion, not quite worthy of him. What, for example, does the following line tell us of Shelley?

> "Ill-fated Shelley, vainly great and brave."

The same words might have been used about Sir John Moore, or Pompey. Mrs. Browning's verses are far superior. Sometimes, indeed, we see her clipping at a character, in order to fit it better into the place she has prepared for it. Sometimes she crams the half of an author into a verse, and has to leave out the rest for want of room. Sometimes over a familiar face she throws a veil of words and darkness. But often her one glance sees, and her one word shows, the very heart of an author's genius and character. Our readers may recur to the lines already quoted in reference to Lucretius, as one of her best portraitures. Altogether this style, as generally prosecuted, is a small one, not much better than anagrams and acrostics—ranks, indeed, not much higher than the ingenuity of the persons who transcribe the "Pleasures of Hope" on the breadth of a crown-piece, and should be resigned to such praiseworthy personages. By far the best specimen of it we remember, is the very clever list involving a running commentary of the works of Lord Byron, by Dr. M'Ginn; unless, indeed, it be Gay's "Catalogue Raisonné" of the portentous poems of Sir Richard Blackmore. Who shall embalm, in a similar way, the endless writings of James, Cooper, and Dickens?

"Lady Geraldine's Courtship," as a transcript from the "red-leaved tablets of the heart"—as a tale of love, set to the richest music—as a picture of the subtle workings, the stern reasonings, and the terrible bursts of passion—is above praise. How like a volcano does the poet's heart at length explode! How first all power is given him in the dreadful trance of silence, and then in the loosened tempest of speech! What a wild, fierce logic flows forth from his lips, in which, as in that of Lear's madness, the foundations of society seem to quiver like reeds, and the mountains of conventionalism are no longer found; and in the lull of that tempest, and in the returning sunshine, how beautiful, how almost superhuman, seem the figures of the two lovers seen now and magnified through the mist of the reader's fast-flowing tears. It is a tale of successful love, and yet it melts you like a tragedy, and most melts you in the crisis of the triumph. On Geraldine we had gazed as on a star, with dry-eyed and and distant admiration; but when that star dissolves in showers at the feet of her poet lover, we weep for very joy. Truly a tear is a sad yet beautiful thing; it constitutes a link connecting us with distant countries, nay, connecting us with distant worlds. Gravitation has, amid all her immensity, wrought no such lovely work as when she rounded a tear.

From this beautiful poem alone, we might argue Mrs. Browning's capacity for producing a great domestic tragedy. We might argue it, also, from the various peculiarities of her genius—her far vision into the springs of human conduct—into those viewless veins of fire, or of poison, which wind within the human heart—her sympathy with dark bosoms—the passion for truth, which pierces often the mist of her dimmer thought, like a flash of irrepressible lightning—her fervid temperament, always glowing round her intellectual sight—and her queen-like dominion over imagery and language. We think, meanwhile, that she has mistaken her sphere. In that rare atmosphere of transcendentalism which she has reached, she respires with difficulty, and with pain. She is not "native and endued" into that element. We would warn her off the giddy region, where tempests may blow as well as clouds gather. Her recent sonnets in "Blackwood" are sad failures—the very light in them is darkness—thoughts, in themselves as untangible as the films upon the window pane, are concealed in a woof of words, till their thin and shadowy meaning fades utterly away. Morbid weakness, she should remember, is not masculine strength. But can she not, through the rents in her cloudy tabernacle, discern, far below in the vale, fields of deep though homely beauty, where she might more gracefully and successfully exercise her exquisite genius? She has only to stoop to conquer. By and by we may—using unprofanely an expression originally profane—be tempted to say, as we look up the darkened mountain, with its flashes of fire hourly waxing fewer and feebler, "As for this poetess, we wot not what has become of her."

While we are venturing on accents of warning, we might also remind her that there are in her style and manner peculiarities which a wicked world will persist in calling affectations. On the charge of affectation, generally, we are disposed to lay little stress—it is a charge so easily got up, and which can be so readily swelled into a cuckoo cry; it is often applied with such injustice, and it so generally attaches to singularities in manner, instead of insincerities in spirit and matter. But why should a true man, or a true woman, expose themselves needlessly to such a charge? We think in general, that true taste in this, as in matters of dress and etiquette, dictates conformity to the present mode, provided that does not unduly cramp the freedom and the force of natural motions. There is, indeed, a class of writers who are chartered libertines—who deal with language as they please—who toss it about as the autumn wind leaves; who, in the agony of their earnestness, or in the fury of their excitement, seize on rude and unpolished words, as Titans on rocks and mountains, and gain artistic triumphs in opposition to all the rules of art. Such are Wilson and Carlyle, and such were Burke and Chalmers. These men we must just take as they are, and be thankful for them as they are. We must just give them their own way. And whether such a permission be given or not, it is likely to be taken. "Canst thou draw out Leviathan with a hook, or his tongue with a cord which thou lettest down? will he make many supplications unto thee? will he speak soft words unto thee? Will the Unicorn be willing to serve thee, or abide by thy crib? canst thou bind him with his band in the furrow? will he harrow the valleys after thee? wilt thou believe that he will bring home thy seed, and gather into thy barn?" No: like the tameless creatures of the wilderness—like the chainless elements of the air—such men obey a law, and use a language, and follow a path of their own.

But this rare privilege Mrs. Browning cannot claim. And she owes it to herself and to her admirers to simplify her manner—to sift her diction of whatever is harsh and barbarous—to speak whatever truth is in her, in the clear articulate language of men—and to quicken, as she well can, the dead forms of ordinary verbiage, by the spirit of her own superabundant life. Then, but not till then, shall her voice break fully through the environment of coteries, cliques, and magazine readers, and fall upon the ear of the general public, like the sound, sweet in its sublimity, simple amid its complex elements, earthly in its cause and unearthly in its effect upon the soul, of a multitude of waters.

MRS. SHELLEY.

Much as we hear of Schools of Authors, there has, properly speaking, been but one in British literature—at least, within this century. There was never, for example, any such thing as a Lake school. A school supposes certain conditions and circumstances which are not to be found among the poets referred to. It supposes, first of all, a common master. Now, the Lake poets had no common master, either among themselves or others. They owned allegiance neither to Shakspeare, nor Milton, nor Wordsworth. Each stood near, but each stood alone, like the stars composing one of the constellations. A school, again, implies a common creed. But we have no evidence, external or internal, that though the poetical diction of the Lakers bore a certain resemblance, their poetical creed was identical. Indeed, we are yet to learn that Southey had, of any depth or definitude, a poetical creed at all. A school, again, supposes a similar mode of training. But how different the erratic education of Coleridge, from the slow, solemn, silent degrees by which, without noise of hammer or edge-tool, arose, like the ancient temple, the majestic structure of Wordsworth's mind! A school, besides, implies such strong and striking resemblances as shall serve to overpower the specific differences between the writers who compose it. But we are mistaken if the dissimilarities between Wordsworth, Coleridge, and Southey be not as great as the points in which they agree. Take, for example, the one quality of speculative intellect. That, in the mind of Coleridge, was restless, discontented, and daring—in Wordsworth, still, collected, brooding perpetually over narrow but profound depths—in Southey, almost totally quiescent. The term Lake School, in short, applied at first in derision, has been retained, principally because it is convenient—nay suggests a pleasing image, and gives both the public and the critics "glimpses that do make them less forlorn," of the blue peaks of Helvellyn and Skiddaw, and of the blue waters of Derwent and Windermere.

The Cockney School was, if possible, a misnomer more absurd—striving, as it did, in vain to include, within one term, three spirits so essentially distinct as Hazlitt, Keats and Leigh Hunt—the first a stern metaphysician, who had fallen into a hopeless passion for poetry; the second, the purest specimen of the ideal—a ball of beautiful foam, "cut off from the water," and not adopted by the air; the third, a fine tricksy medium between the poet and the wit, half a sylph and half an Ariel, now hovering round a lady's curl, and now stirring the fiery tresses of the sun—a fairy, fluctuating link, connecting Pope with Shelley. We need not be at pains to cut out into little stars the Blackwood constellation, or dwell on the differences between a Wilson, a Lockhart, and a James Hogg.

One school, however, there has appeared within the last fifty years, answering to all the characteristics we have enumerated, namely, the Godwin school, who, by a common master—the old man eloquent himself—a common philosophical as well as poetical belief, common training, that of warfare with society, and many specific resemblances in manner and style, are proclaimed to be one. This cluster includes the names of William Godwin, Mary Wollstonecroft, Brockden Brown of America, Shelley, and Mrs. Shelley.

Old Godwin scarcely got justice in Tait's Magazine from Mr. De Quincey. Slow, cumbrous, elephantine as he was, there was always a fine spirit animating his most lumpish movements. He was never contemptible—often commonplace, indeed, but often great. There was much in him of the German cast of mind—the same painful and plodding diligence, added to high imaginative qualities. His great merit at the time—and his great error, as it proved afterwards—lay in wedding a partial philosophic system with the universal truth of fiction. Hence the element which made the public drunk with his merits at first rendered them oblivious afterwards. So dangerous it is to connect fiction (the finer alias of truth) with any dogma or mythus less perishable than the theogony of Homer, or the catholicism of Cervantes. After all, what was the theory of Godwin but the masque of Christianity? Cloaking the leading principle of our religion, its disinterested benevolence, under a copy of the features of Helvetius and Volney, he went a mumming with it in the train on the philosophers of the Revolution. But when he approached the domain of actual life and of the human affections, the ugly disguise dropped, and his fictions we hesitate not to characterize as among the noblest illustrations of the Sermon on the Mount. But to the public they seemed the reiterations of exploded and dangerous errors—such a load of prejudice and prepossession had been suspended to their author's skirts. And now, the excitement of danger and disgust having passed away from his theories, interest in the works which propounded them has also subsided. "Caleb Williams," once denounced by Hannah More as a cunning and popular preparation of the poison which the "Political Justice" had contained in a cruder form, is now forgotten, we suspect, by all but a very select class. "St. Leon,"

"Fleetwood," "Mandeville," and "Cloudesley," with all their varied merits, never attracted attention, except through the reflex interest and terror excited by their author's former works. Thus political excitement has been at once a raising and a ruining influence to the writings of a great English author—ruining, we mean, at present—for the shade of neglect has yet to be created which can permanently conceal their sterling and imperishable worth. After the majority of the writings of Dickens have perished—after one-half of Bulwer's, and one-fourth of Scott's novels have been forgotten—shall some reflective spirits be found following the fugitive steps of Caleb Williams, or standing by the grave of Marguerite de Damville, or sympathizing with the gloom of Mandeville, or of Bethlem Gabor, as they do well to be angry even unto death. If sincerity, simplicity, strength of thought, purity of sentiment and power of genius can secure immortality to any productions, it is to the fictions of Godwin.

Mary Wollstonecroft—since we saw her countenance prefixed to her husband's memoir—a face so sweet, so spiritual, so far withdrawn from earthly thoughts, steeped in an enthusiasm so genuine—we have ceased to wonder at the passionate attachment of Southey, Fuseli, and Godwin, to the gifted being who bore it. It is the most feminine countenance we ever saw in picture. The "Rights of Women" seem in it melted down into one deliquium of love. Fuseli once, when asked if he believed in the immortality of the soul, replied in language rather too rough to be quoted verbatim, "I don't know if *you* have a soul, but I am sure that *I* have." We are certain that he believed in the existence of at least one other immortal spirit—that of the owner of the still, serene, and rapt countenance on which he hopelessly doted. It is curious that on the first meeting of Godwin and his future wife, they "interdespised"—they recoiled from each other, like two enemies suddenly meeting on the street, and it required much after-intercourse to reconcile them, and ultimately to create that passion which led to their union.

Mary Wollstonecroft shone most in conversation. From this to composition she seemed to descend as from a throne. Coleridge describes her meeting and extinguishing some of Godwin's objections to her arguments with a light, easy, playful air. Her fan was a very falchion in debate. Her works—"History of the French Revolution," "Wanderer of Norway," "Rights of Women," &c.—have all perished. Her own career was chequered and unhappy—her end was premature—she died in childbed of Mrs. Shelley (like the sun going down to reveal the evening star); but her name shall live as that of a deep, majestical, and high-souled woman—the Madame Roland of England—and who could, as well as she, have paused on her way to the scaffold, and wished for a pen to "record the strange thoughts that were arising in her mind." Peace to her ashes! How consoling to think that those who in life were restless and unhappy, sleep the sleep of death as soundly as others—nay, seem to sleep more soundly—to be hushed by a softer lullaby, and surrounded by a profounder peace, than the ordinary tenants of the grave. Yes, sweeter, deeper, and longer is the repose of the *truant* child, after his day of wandering is over, and the night of his rest is come.

Another "wanderer o'er eternity" was Brockden Brown, the Godwin of America. And worse for him, he was a wanderer, not from, but among men. For Cain of old, it was a relief to go forth from his species into the virgin empty earth. The builders of the Tower of Babel must have rejoiced as they saw the summit of their abortive building sinking down in the level plain; they fled from it as a stony silent satire on their baffled ambition, and as a memorial of the confusion of their speech—it scourged them forth into the wilderness, where they found peace and oblivion. A self-exiled Byron or Landor is rather to be envied; for though "how can your wanderer escape from his own shadow?" yet it is much if that shadow sweep forests and cataracts, fall large at morning or evening upon Alps and Apennines, or swell into the Demon of the Brockan. In this case misery takes a prouder, loftier shape, and mounts a burning throne. But a man like Brockden Brown, forced to carry his incommunicable sorrow into the press and thick of human society, nay, to coin it into the means of procuring daily bread, he is the true hero, even though he should fall in the struggle. To carry one's misery to market, and sell it to the highest bidder, what a necessity for a proud and sensitive spirit! Assuredly Brown was a brave struggler, if not a successful one. Amid poverty, neglect, non-apprecia tion, hard labor, and the thousand *niaiseries* of the crude country which America then was, he retained his integrity; he wrote on at what Godwin calls his "story books;" he sought inspiration from his own gloomy woods and silent fields; and his works appear, amid what are called "standard novels," like tall wind-swept American pines amid shrubbery and brushwood. His name, after his untimely death (at the age of thirty-nine), was returned upon his ungrateful country —from Britain, where his writings first attained eminent distinction, while even yet Americans, generally, prefer the adventure and bustle of Cooper to the stern Dante-like simplicity, the philosophical spirit, and the harrowing and ghost-like interest of Brown.

Of Shelley, having spoken so often, what more can we say? He seems to us as though the most beautiful of beings had been struck blind. Mr. De Quincey, in unconscious plagiarism from ourselves, compares him to a "lunatic angel." But perhaps, after all, his disease might be better denominated blindness. It was not because he saw falsely, but as if seeing and delaying to worship the glory of Christ and his religion, that delay was punished by a swift and sudden darkness. Imagine the Apollo Belvidere, animated and fleshed, all his dream-like loveliness of form retained, but his eyes remaining shut! Thus blind and beautiful stood Shelley on his pedestal, or went wandering, an inspired sleep-walker, among his fellows, who, alas! not seeing his melancholy plight, struck and spurned, instead of gently and soothingly trying to lead him into the right path. We still think, notwithstanding Mr. De Quincey's eloquent strictures in reply, that if pity and kind-hearted expostulation had been employed, they might have had the effect, if not of weaning him from his errors, at least of modifying his expressions and feelings—if not of opening his eyes, at least of rendering him more patient and hopeful under his eclipse. What but a partial clouding of his mind could have prompted such a question as he asked upon the following occasion? Haydon, the painter, met him once at a large dinner party in London. During the entertainment, a thin, cracked, shrieking voice was heard from one end of the table, "You don't believe, do you, Mr. Haydon, in that execrable thing, Christianity? The voice was poor Shelley's, who could not be at rest with any new acquaintance till he ascertained his impressions on that one topic.

Poets, perhaps all men, best understand themselves. Thus no word so true has been spoken of Shelley, as where he says of himself, that "an adamantine veil was built up between his mind and heart." His intellect led him in one direction —the true impulses of his heart in another. The one was with Spinosa; the other with John. The controversy raged between them like fire, and even at death was not decided. We rejoice, in contrast with the brutal treatment he met with while living, to notice the tenderness which the most evangelical periodicals (witness a late number of the "North British Review") extend to the memory of this most sincere, spiritual, and unearthly of modern men. It is to us a proud reflection, that for at least seventeen years our opinion of him has remained unaltered.

It is not at all to be wondered at, that two such spirits as Shelley and Mary Godwin, when they met, should become instantly attached. On his own doctrine of a state of pre-existence, we might say that the marriage had been determined long before, while yet the souls were waiting in the great antenatal ante-chamber! They met at last, like two drops of water—like two flames of fire—like two beautiful clouds which have crossed the moon, the sky, and all its stars, to hold their midnight assignation over a favorite and lonely river. Mary Godwin was an enthusiast from her childhood. She passed, by her own account, part of her youth at Broughty Ferry, in sweet and sinless reverie among its cliffs. The place is, to us, familiar. It possesses some fine features—a bold promontory crowned with an ancient castle jutting far out the Tay, which here broadens into an arm of the ocean—a beach, in part smooth with sand, and in part paved with pebbles—cottages lying artlessly along the shore, clean, as if washed by the near sea—sandy hillocks rising behind—and westward, the river, like an inland lake, stretching around Dundee, with its fine harbor and its surmounting Law, which, in its turn, is surmounted by the far blue shapes of the gigantic Stuicknachroan and Benvoirlich. Did the bay of Spezia ever suggest to Mrs. Shelley's mind the features of the Scottish scene? That scene, seen so often, seldom fails to bring before us her image—the child, and soon to be the bride, of genius. Was she ever, like Mirza, overheard in her soliloquies, and did she bear the shame, accordingly, in blushes which still rekindle at the recollection? Did the rude fishermen of the place deem her wondrous wise, or did they deem her mad, with her wandering eye, her rapt and gleaming countenance, her light step moving to the music of her maiden meditation? The smooth sand retains no trace of her young feet—to the present race she is altogether unknown; but we have more than once seen the man of genius, and its lover, turn round and look at the spot, with warmer interest, and with brightening eye, as we told them that she had been there.

We have spoken of Mrs. Shelley's similarity of genius to her husband—we by no means think her his equal. She has not his subtlety, swiftness, wealth of imagination, and is never caught up (like Ezekiel by his lock of hair) into the same rushing whirlwind of inspiration. She has much, however, of his imaginative and of his speculative qualities—her tendency, like his, is to the romantic, the ethereal, and the terrible. The tie detaining her, as well as him, to the earth, is slender—her protest against society is his copied out in a female hand—her style is carefully and successfully modelled upon his—she bears, in brief, to him, the resemblance which Laone did to Laon, which Astarte did to Manfred. Perhaps, indeed, intercourse with a being so peculiar, that those who came in contact with, either withdrew from him in hatred, or fell into the current of his being, vanquished and enthralled, has somewhat affected the originality, and narrowed the extent of her own genius. Indian widows used to fling themselves upon the funeral pyre of their husbands: she has thrown upon that of hers her mode of thought, her mould of style, her creed, her heart, her all. Her admiration of Shelley was, and is, an idolatry. Can we wonder at it? Separated from him in the prime of life, with all his faculties in the finest bloom of promise, with peace beginning to build in the crevices of his torn heart, and with fame hovering ere it stooped upon his head—separated, too, in circumstances so sudden and cruel—can we be astonished that from the wounds of love came forth the blood of worship and sacrifice? Wordsworth speaks of himself as feeling for "the Old Sea some reverential fear." But in the mind of

"Mary" there must lurk a feeling of a still stronger kind toward that element which *he*, next to herself, had of all things most passionately loved—which he trusted as a parent—to which he exposed himself, defenceless (he could not swim—he could only soar)—which he had sung in many a strain of matchless sweetness, but which betrayed and destroyed him—how can she, without horror, hear the boom of its waves, or look without a shudder, either at its stormy or its smiling countenance? What a picture she presents to our imagination, running with dishevelled hair, along the sea-shore, questioning all she met if they could tell her of her husband—nay, shrieking out the dreadful question to the surges, which, like a dumb murderer, had done the deed, but could not utter the confession!

Mrs. Shelley's genius, though true and powerful, is monotonous and circumscribed—more so than even her father's—and, in this point, presents a strong contrast to her husband's, which could run along every note of the gamut—be witty or wild, satirical or sentimental, didactic or dramatic, epic or lyrical, as it pleased him. She has no wit, nor humor—little dramatic talent. Strong, clear description of the gloomier scenes of nature, or the darker passions of the mind, or of those supernatural objects which her fancy, except in her first work, somewhat *laboriously* creates, is her forte. Hence her reputation still rests upon "Frankenstein;" for her "Last Man," "Perkin Warbeck," &c., are far inferior, if not entirely unworthy of her talents. She unquestionably made him; but, like a mule or a monster, he has had no progeny.

Can any one have forgot the interesting account she gives of her first conception of that extraordinary story, when she had retired to rest, her fancy heated by hearing ghost tales; and when the whole circumstances of the story appeared at once before her eye, as in a camera obscura? It is ever thus, we imagine, that truly original conceptions are produced. They are cast—not wrought. They come as wholes, and not in parts. It was thus that "Tam o'Shanter" completed, along Burns' mind, his weird and tipsy gallop in a single hour. Thus Coleridge composed the outline of his "Ancient Marinere," in one evening walk near Nether Stowey. So rapidly rose "Frankenstein," which, as Moore well remarks, has been one of those striking conceptions which take hold of the public mind at once and for ever.

The theme is morbid and disgusting enough. The story is that of one who finds out the principle of life, constructs a monstrous being, who, because his maker fails in forming a female companion to him, ultimately murders the dearest friend of his benefactor, and, in remorse and despair, disappears amid the eternal snows of the North Pole. Nothing more preposterous than the meagre outline of the story exists in literature. But Mrs. Shelley deserves great credit, nevertheless. In the first place, she has succeeded in her delineation; she has painted this shapeless being upon the imagination of the world for ever; and beside Caliban, and Hecate, and Death and Life, and all other weird and gloomy creations, this nameless, unfortunate, involuntary, gigantic unit stands. To succeed in an attempt so daring, proves at once the power of the author, and a certain value even in the original conception. To keep verging perpetually on the limit of the absurd, and to produce the while all the effects of the sublime, takes and tasks very high faculties indeed. Occasionally, we admit, she does overstep the mark. Thus the whole scene of the monster's education in the cottage, his overhearing the reading of the "Paradise Lost," the "Sorrows of Werter," &c., and in this way acquiring knowledge and refined sentiments, seems unspeakably ridiculous. A Caco-demon weeping in concert with Eve or Werter is too ludicrous an idea—as absurd as though he had been represented as boarded at Capsicum Hall. But it is wonderful how delicately and gracefully Mrs. Shelley has managed the whole prodigious business. She touches pitch with a lady's glove, and is not defiled. From a whole forest of the "nettle danger" she extracts a sweet and plentiful supply of the "flower safety." With a fine female footing, she preserves the narrow path which divides the terrible from the disgusting. She unites, not in a junction of words alone, but in effect, the "horribly beautiful." Her monster is not only as Caliban appeared to Trinculo—a very pretty monster, but somewhat poetical and pathetic withal. You almost weep for him in his utter insulation. Alone! dread word, though it were to be alone in heaven! Alone! word hardly more dreadful if it were to be alone in hell!

"Alone, all, all, alone.
Alone on a wide, wide sea;
And never a saint took pity on
My soul in agony."

Wrapt around by his loneliness, as by a silent burning chain, does this gigantic creature run through the world, like a lion who has lost its mate, in a forest of fire, seeking for his kindred being, but seeking for ever in vain. He is not only alone, but alone because he has no being like him throughout the whole universe. What a solitude within a solitude!—solitude comparable only to that of the Alchemist in St. Leon, when he buries his last tie to humanity in his wife's grave, and goes on his way, "friendless, friendless, alone, alone."

What a scene is the process of his creation, and especially the hour when he first began to breathe, to open his ill-favored eyes, and to stretch his ill-shapen arms toward his terrified author, who, for the first time, becomes aware of the enormity of the mistake he has committed; who has had a giant's strength, and used it tyrannously like a giant, and who shudders and shrinks back from his own horrible handiwork! It is a type whether intended or not, of the fate of genius, when it dares either to revile or to resist the common laws and obligations and conditions of man and the universe. Better, better far be blasted with the lightnings of heaven, than by the recoil, upon one's own head, of one false, homeless, returning, revenging *thought*.

Scarcely second to her description of the moment when, at midnight, and under the light of a waning moon, the monster was born, is his sudden apparition upon a glacier among the high Alps. This scene strikes us the more, as it seems the fulfilment of a fear which all have felt, who have found themselves alone among such desolate regions. Who has not at times trembled lest those ghastlier and drearier places of nature, which abound in our own Highlands, should bear a different progeny from the ptarmigan, the sheep, the raven, or the eagle—lest the mountain should suddenly crown itself with a Titanic sceptre, and the mist, disparting, reveal demoniac forms, and the lonely moor, discover its ugly dwarf, as if dropped down from the overhanging thunder cloud —and the forest of pines show unearthly shapes sailing among their shades—and the cataract overboil with its own wild creations? Thus fitly, amid scenery like that of some dream of nightmare, on a glacier as on a throne, stands up before the eye of his own maker, the miscreation, and he cries out, "Whence and what art thou, execrable shape?"

In darkness and distance, at last, the being disappears, and the imagination dares hardly pursue him as he passes amid those congenial shapes of colossal size, terror, and mystery, which we fancy to haunt those outskirts of existence, with, behind them at midnight, "all Europe and Asia fast asleep, and before them the silent immensity and palace of the Eternal, to which our sun is but a porch-lamp."

Altogether the work is wonderful as the work of a girl of eighteen. She has never since fully equalled or approached its power, nor do we ever expect that she shall. One distinct addition to our original creations must be conceded her—and it is no little praise; for there are few writers of fiction who have done so much out of Germany. What are they, in this respect, to our painters—to Fuseli, with his quaint brain, so prodigal of unearthly shapes—to John Martin, who has created over his head a whole dark, frowning, but magnificent *world*—or to David Scott, our late dear friend, in whose studio, while standing surrounded by pictured poems of such startling originality, such austere selection of theme, and such solemn dignity of treatment (forgetting not himself, the grave, mild, quiet, shadowy enthusiast, with his slow, deep, sepulchral tones), you were almost tempted to exclaim, "How dreadful is this place!"

Of one promised and anticipated task we must, ere we close, respectfully remind Mrs. Shelley; it is of the life of her husband. That, even after Captain Medwyn's recent work, has evidently yet to be written. No hand but hers can write it well. Critics may anatomize his qualities—she only can paint his likeness. In proclaiming his praise, exaggeration in her will be pardoned; and in unveiling his faults, tenderness may be expected from her; she alone, we believe, after all, fully understands him; she alone fully knows the particulars of his outer and inner history; and we hope and believe, that her biography will be a monument to his memory, as lasting as the Euganean hills; and her lament over his loss as sweet as the everlasting dirge, sung in their "late remorse of love," by the waters of the Italian sea.*

WILLIAM COBBETT.

William Cobbett, we may, without fear of contradiction, call the father of cheap literature. His self-styled "twopenny trash" was the strong seed whence a progeny has sprung, manifold and thick as the "leaves of Vallambrosa;" and a portion of whatever honor or shame attaches to our present cheap publications must redound to his credit or to his disgrace. And although he was by no means a timid or a squeamish man, we are certain that, could he now raise his head from the dust, it were to look with withering scorn and pity, not unmingled with remorse, upon those myriads of low and loathsome publications at present pouring from the English press—making up for their minuteness by their mischief—for their want of point, by their profanity—for their stupidity, by their licentiousness—absolutely monopolizing millions of readers, and reminding us of that plague of frogs which swept Egypt, "till the land stank, so numerous was the fry."

William Cobbett has been often ably, but never, we think, fully or satisfactorily criticised. We do not refer merely to his political creed and character: these topics we propose to avoid, permitting ourselves, however, the general remark that he was just as able and just as consistent a politician as some of his most formidable opponents (such as Peel, Burdett, and Brougham) have *since* proved themselves to be. Of his literary merits, we remember only three striking pictures, all of which, however, slide into his political aspects. The first is that very eloquent, though somewhat sketchy and one-sided character by Robert Hall, ending with the words

* Since writing this, we have read more carefully the "Last Man." Though the gloomiest, most improbable, and most hopeless of books, it abounds in beautiful descriptions, has scenes of harrowing interest, and depicts delicately the character of Shelley, who is the hero of the story.

—"a firebrand, not a luminary—the Polyphemus of the mob—the one-eyed monarch of the blind." Hall, we imagine, however, was too different a man from Cobbett to appreciate him entirely—too attentive to the construction of his sentences to relish Cobbett's easy, rambling style—too fastidious in his taste to bear with Cobbett's blunt picturesque expressions—too fond of the elegant abstractions of thought to sympathize with Cobbett's passion for, and power over, facts; still he must have often admired his vigorous dissections of character, and often chuckled, and even roared, over his rough native humor. Another attempt to contain Cobbett in a crown-piece was made by Lockhart, in what, we think, was the last "Noctes" he contributed to "Blackwood," appearing somewhere about the close of the year 1832. It is put into the mouth of Jeffrey, and is very smart, snappish, and pointed, pouring out as briskly as bottled beer, but is not peculiarly characteristic. It is rather an inventory than a picture; and such an inventory of this modern "man Mountain" as the Lilliputians made of Gulliver when they emptied his *pockets.* It is not such a masterly full length as Lockhart could have executed, and as he has executed of a kindred spirit, John Clerk. The third and best character is by Hazlitt in his "Table-Talk," and is written with all his wonted discrimination. We remember that he calls him a "very honest man, with a total want of principle," speaks of his "Register" as a "perpetual prospectus," and draws a striking parallel between him and Paine. Our object is somewhat more minutely and in detail to bring this brawniest of men before our readers.

And, first, of his personal appearance. That was, as generally happens, a thorough, though not an ostentatious index to his character. Those who expected to find in Cobbett a rude, truculent barbarian, were, as they deserved to be, disappointed. They found, instead, a tall, stout, mild-faced, broad-shouldered, farmer-looking man, with a spice of humor lurking in his eye, but without one vestige of fierceness or malignity either in his look or demeanor. His private manners were simple, unaffected—almost gentlemanly. His mode of addressing an audience was quiet, clear, distinct, and conversational; and the fury and the fervor of the demagogue alike were wanting. The most sarcastic and provoking things oozed out at his lips like milk or honey. Add to this, perfect self-possession, his usual vein of humor somewhat subdued into keeping with his audience, and a certain cajolery in his manner, as the most notable features in his mode of public address. We heard him repeatedly in Edinburgh, during his visit in 1832. He came to the Modern Athens with as much fear and trembling as could befall a man of his sturdy temperament. He expected, he said, ere he arrived, that the Edinburgh people would 'throw him into a ditch," but went away highly gratified with his reception. The truth is, they welcomed him as a curiosity, and went to see and hear him as a rarée show. They showed no genuine appreciation of his talents; and if they did not lift from the dirt and pelt him with the common calumnies, it was because they thought it not worth while. He came, tickled their midriffs—they laughed, applauded, and forgot him, as soon as his back was turned.

It is dangerous to seek to include a whole character in a single epithet, otherwise we might call William Cobbett "the genius of common sense." Common sense, possessed in an uncommon degree, and backed by powerful passion, often verges, in its effects and in its nature, on genius. Like genius, it works by intuition; it does not creep nor walk, but leaps to its conclusion. It is to genius an inferior system of shorthand—as swift, but not so beautiful; or it may be called, genius applied to meaner subjects, and guided by impulses as free but less lofty. Such a homespun but masculine spirit had perched upon the shoulder of Swift, and came directly from him to Cobbett.

If ever man deserved, in a subordinate acceptation, the name of "seer," it was the author of the "Register." He did not ratiocinate or inquire; he saw, and saw at the first opening of his sagacious eye. Sometimes his sight was true, and sometimes false—sometimes healthy, and sometimes jaundiced—but it was always sight, and not hearsay; and as well argue with the testimony of the eye as dispute with him his convictions. This was at once his power and his weakness; it accounted for his true and strong perception of public characters, and of the tendency and issues of public events; it accounted for his dogmatism, his inconsistency, and his caprice. It was this strong personal sight which made Cobbett maintain his ground against his many far more accomplished and learned rivals. While they were reading, reflecting, deflecting, and circumspecting, he was looking straight forward and right down into the very heart and marrow of his theme. Whilst they were wasting time in trying on pairs of spectacles belonging to others, he was using his own piercing pair of eyes. Thus, though taken at tremendous odds, the old sergeant seldom failed of a complete triumph. We own it pleases us—it stirs our blood—to think that there has been, even in our time, native vigor enough, in a half-taught man of talent, to neutralize the most accomplished, to level the most learned, to "turn wise men backward and make diviners mad," to startle an age anxious to hide its weakness under the variety of its studies and the multiplicity of its accomplishments, by the tidings that there is yet something better than education—that an "ounce of mother wit" retains its original value—that genius still claims its ancient privileges—and that the breed of intellectual Spartaci and Toussaints is not extinct, amid all the cultivated fribbles and martinets of the day.

Cobbett, if he wanted learning, possessed what was far more valuable—he possessed experience. How few writers have it! Voltaire speaks of some astonishingly wise young hero who seemed born with experience; but, as Campbell remarks, "how few of our heads come into the world with this valuable article!" Most authors, indeed, go through a certain routine, which is dignified with this name. They pass through school and college; write their first sonnet or epigram; fall in love—are received or rejected; publish their first volume—it is puffed or abused, according to the state of the critic's temper or stomach; fall into a sulk or a syncope—gradually cool and calm as they rise or fall to their proper level: and this is called experience. Abused, outraged term! Has an author of almost Miltonic genius run the gauntlet of abusive or detracting criticism for many long years, and yet retained his integrity, his magnanimity, the calm purpose of his soul? Then let him speak of experience, for assuredly experience has spoken to him. Or, has a man of whom the world was not worthy been driven, for his conscientious convictions, forth from the society of men, and died gray-haired and all but broken-hearted at twenty-nine? *He* might have spoken of experience. And did one who could, from native talent, have led armies, cabinets, his country, spend years as a private soldier, visit various lands, and undergo many privations and hardships? What a different course of experience this —and it was Cobbett's—from the flea-bites of so-called criticism, or the night-mare of an unsold edition!

Our strong, burly sergeant carried his eye with him into the ranks, in all his travels—in the choice of a wife. Wherever he went, he "saw and conquered"—(what need, after all, of this last word? To see, in the true sense, is always, in the true sense, to conquer. The want of sight is the same thing with the want of success; and thus Cæsar, in his celebrated bulletin, "Veni, vidi, vici," was, for the first and last time, a tautologist)—and home he came, a giant furnished and trained, by an irregular but gigantic education, for becoming a "fourth estate" in the political and literary world.

One quality strikingly manifest in Cobbett, and which had been nurtured by his training, is health. He was essentially a healthy man. He did not, it is true, want his peevish and peculiar humors, but the general tone of his mind as well as body was sound and clear. He signally exemplified the words, "Sana mens in sano corpore." Without the border blood and the minstrel spirit of Scott, he had much of his soundness, geniality, and broad strength. Morbidity was a word he did not recognize as English. Mawkish sentimentalism, in all its shapes, he abhorred; and cant found in him an inexorable foe. Hence we account for his celebrated criticisms on Shakspeare and Milton. In his heart, perhaps, he appreciated both, but was indignant at the false and wholly conventional admiration paid them by the multitude. Or, even granting that his taste was bad, and that, from native inaptitude, he could not feel the more delicate and spiritual beauties of either poet, was he not better to avow it openly than to wear a "foolish face of praise," and pretend to what he had not? In his nonsense of abuse there is something infinitely more racy and refreshing than in others' nonsense of commendation. We prefer him making a football of the "Paradise Lost," and kicking at it with all his might—impotently indeed, and to the damage of nothing but his own toes—than to see it shining in illustrated editions in the libraries of those whose simpering imbecilities of affected eu thusiasm convince you that they have neither understood nor really read it. Much as we admire Shakspeare and Milton, we are not disposed to sacrifice Cobbett as a whole burnt-offering at their shrine.

In keeping with this quality of health was that of good-humor. He was the best-natured of political writers. Even when abusing his opponents, there was a kindly twinkle in his eye, and you never were sure that he heartily hated them. His high animal spirits, his fine constitution, and his undisturbed self-complacency, all served to carry off and qualify his rage. He dealt with his foes as a kitten with a mouse. They furnished him with so much amusement, and he made others so merry with them, that he began rather to like them than otherwise. The most of them, besides, were so far his inferiors in intellect, that they exerted no magnetism sufficient to draw forth the full riches of his wrath. If he felt deep and deadly animosity to any, it was to the three formerly mentioned, Peel, Burdett, and Brougham, which might suggest, to an ill-natured person, the proverb, "Two of a trade," &c. How different from Junius! Cobbett at most hates; Junius loathes. Cobbett splashes pails of dirty water over his enemies; Junius deals in drops, but they are drops of prussic acid. Cobbett, with loud outcries, knocks down his opponents; Junius steps up and softly whispers in their ear a sentence, an insinuation, a syllable, which withers the very heart within them. To express, by a change of figure, a change of mood and manner in both, Cobbett often covers his enemy with nicknames, which stick but do not scorch: such toys are beneath the deep long hate of Junius; he scatters firebrands, arrows, and death.

From health and good-humor, blended with a keen sense of the ridiculous, sprung his faculty of humor, one of the most curious of all his gifts. It is in him at one time the power of singling out minute absurdities in the conduct, character, style of writing, appearance, or names of his opponents, and by endless repetitions enlarging their ridiculous aspect, till you, the reader, become a mere *alias* of laughter holding both his sides. It is at another time produced by culling the oddest and lowest figures and allusions from the barn-yard or the dunghill, and hanging those mud-garlands about the necks of dignitaries, prelates, statesmen, of majesty itself, till they look supremely ridiculous. Some times he secures his ludicrous effects by the mere daring effrontery of his onset, as in his celebrated chapter, "Errors and Nonsense in a King's Speech;" often by the unexpected introduction of political or personal allusions amid serious or indifferent subjects; sometimes, as we have seen, by the dexterous use of nicknames and slang; and often by the sheer power of exuberant and dauntless egotism.

He had very little of what is strictly called wit, or the power of perceiving unexpected resemblances and contrasts, and no dry severe irony. Coleridge defined Swift as the soul of Rabelais in a dry place. Cobbett may perhaps be defined the soul of Swift in a softer, sunnier, *sappier*, place. Swift was a machine of humor; he himself derived neither good nor pleasure from the lavish mirth he distributed to others. Cobbett, on the contrary, was compelled by his own tickling sensations to tickle the whole world besides; his humor was not a voluntary exercise of power, but a vent for surcharged emotion.

His gift, as Shakspeare has it, of "iteration" he turned to account for more purposes than those of humor. His arguments, his facts, as well as his favorite nicknames, such as the "Wen," "Old Bloody," the "Press-gang," &c., he repeated again and again. He sat, like a "starling," opposite the treasury and the bank, and hallooed out what he deemed offensive truths, and recounted untoward events, the more pertinaciously that the truths were offensive, and that the events had been untoward. And then, worst of all, his croaking was so unlike that of all other croakers, it was so funny, so far from a dull monotony, founded so much on fact, and so widely listened to, that government, between amusement and provocation were "perplexed in the extreme." They durst neither openly laugh nor cry. For here was no hunger-bitten scribbler, no lean Cassius, no wild-eyed emaciated fanatic, but a joyous jolly prophet, six feet high and proportionably broad, whom it was difficult either to bribe or to kill, pouring out his endless predictions and warnings under the sign of a gridiron, on which it was quite as likely that they as that he should be roasted alive.

Was it from this practice of incessant repetition that there sprung that egotism with which he has been so often charged? Was it that, as he could not help talking about other things over and over again, so he could not help, much more, talking about himself? Cobbett, in fact, was not more an egotist than the majority of writers, only he spoke of himself directly and not by implication. Some speak of themselves while praising their idols, and others while indulging their hobbies. But William Cobbett, a plain blunt man, instead of veiling his egotism under the guise of sentimental sonnets, or working it up into imaginary conversations, or throwing it out into imaginary heroes, writes it down as plain "as downright Shippen or as old Montaigne." We must say we like this trait in his character, believing that there is often more of the spirit of egotism discovered in avoiding than in using its language. Why, the editorial word "we" contains in it the *double*-distilled essence of egotism, modest as it looks. And how much intolerable self-conceit is concealed under the phrases "we humbly think," "it appears to us," and "our feeble voice," &c. Cobbett was as great an enemy to shams as Carlyle. He had a vast notion of himself, and he took every opportunity, proper and improper, of declaring it. Unlike the boy Tell, "he was great, *and* knew how great he was." His opinion, at any rate, was perfectly sincere, and as such required, nay, demanded expression. He felt himself, and was, a reality among mewing and moping, painted and gilded, starred, gartered, and crowned phantoms; and who shall quarrel with him because ever and anon he touched his strong sides and brow with his strong arms, and said, "Here I am, this is solid, were all else the shadow of a shade." Bulwer, our readers are aware, thought proper, many years ago, to quarrel with the use of the anonymous in periodical literature. We think that Cobbett had been a worthier champion for supporting this quarrel than Sir Edward. No mask or visor would ever have become or fitted him. His personality seen at every turning in the lane, every opening in the hedge of his argument—his abuse or his humor—was his power. He was not a knight of chivalry, bearing no device upon his shield, and covering his face in the hollow of his helm, but a Tom Cribb or Spring, open-faced, strong, stripped, and ready to do battle with all comers. The anonymous seemed to him anti-English, and he resigned it to the Italians, the "press-gang," and the author of Junius.

As Scott seemed to draw into his single self the last national spirit of his country, as Byron was our last purely English poet, so Cobbett was our all but last purely English prose writer. He seemed, next to Churchill, the most striking personification of John Bull. There were the brawny form, the swagger, the blustering temper, the broad humor, the pertinacity, the variability, the dogmatic prejudice, the rudeness, the common sense, the sagacity, the turbulence, the gullosity, and the pugnacity of a genuine Englishman as ever drank beer, bolted bacon, or flourished singlestaff. How he could upon occasion flatter national prejudices and prepossessions! How he could stir up into absolute springtide the English blood! How he used to pelt, when he pleased, the French and the Scotch! What a chosen champion to the chaw-bacons! It is not too much to say that he understood his countrymen as well as Napoleon did the French, and, had he possessed the fighting talent, could, in the event of a revolution, have led it and risen upon its wave. As it was, for a season he was the real king of the masses, and even after, through want of discretion, he lost his sovereignty, his rebel subjects, as often has happened in the history of rebellions, frequently felt their hearts palpitating, their ears tingling, and their knees instinctively bending to the voice of their ancient leader.

A pleasing feature in Cobbett's character was his love for the country. We remember him, in one of his "Registers," expressing his wonder that one like himself, who relished intensely all rural sights and sounds, should have passed so large a portion of his life amid the smoke and din and strife of cities. It was not, indeed, the great features of nature that he admired; its more ethereal aspects, and that mysterious symbolic relation which it bears to the nature and history of man, he did not comprehend, and would have laughed at any one who pretended to do. We can fancy him thus criticising Emerson—"Wonders will never cease. Here comes a Yankee prophet—yes, a Yankee prophet—talking transcendental (query, transcendent?) nonsense by the yard, and trying to get the gullible goose

John Bull to listen to him, at the rate of seven guineas for each hour's lecture. He'd better—for us, at any rate—have stopped at home, and fed his pigs, or prophesied to his henroost. May I be roasted on a gridiron, if there's not more sense in this one number of the 'Twopenny Trash' than in all that this man Emerson ever wrote or ever will write till his last breath. And yet who'll pay me seven guineas for each of my lectures? This half-crazy quack, I am told, pulls down the old prophets, Jeremy, Daniel, and the rest, and sets himself up in their stead as prophet Ralph Waldo. I venture to predict to prophet Ralph, that he won't see Boston Bay again ere his gulls would rather by twenty times have their guineas in their pockets than his lectures in their memories. But I beg Ralph's pardon, for it's not in the power of any mortal man, I'm told, to mind one word that Ralph says to them, or to come off with any thing but a general notion that they have been quacked out of their sixpences. They say that the fellow is rather good-looking, a glib talker, and has a smattering of the German, but never gives his hearers one good round *fact* in all his lectures: has no statistics or arguments either; and you would never guess, while hearing him, whether you were in America or England, the earth or the moon. But enough of prophet *Raff*. I hope I have settled his hash as effectually as I did that of a much cleverer fellow, sqinting prophet Ned, of Hatton Garden."

Thus Cobbett would have thought and said. Others, with Cobbett's prejudices, but destitute of his powers and his outspoken directness, have recently thought, but have not courage to say the same. And yet, while utterly incapable of feeling, and of affecting to feel, a high ideal view of nature, he loved sincerely and passionately this green earth, its fresh breezes, its soft waters, and its spring sky, blue, as if newly dyed, as the bridal-curtain of the youthful season. He cared nothing for the stars; these, which are rather like paintings than works of nature, he disregarded nearly as much as he did the pictures of man's pencil; he loved the moon only as it lighted up the harvest-field; but the hedgerows, the trees, and the cornfields, of merry England grew in his heart, and waved over, and cooled the stream of his life's blood. It is pleasant to come upon such passages in his pages. We linger and coo over them, like a breeze caught amid the woods which surround some spot of insulated loveliness. They raise and soften our opinion of the man; and whenever we are disposed to think or speak harshly of William Cobbett, we are calmed by remembering his dying moments, when he requested to be carried round his farm, that he might see for the last time the fields which he loved so dearly. The fact that this desire was so strong at death itself proved that it, and no lower or fiercer feeling, was his ruling passion.

From this love of homely, English nature, and from his minute habits of observation, sprang that abundant and picturesque imagery with which his writings abound. A fresh breeze from the "farm" is always felt passing over his driest discussions, and mingling with his bitterest personalities. It is this which prevents him from being ever vulgar; for, as Hazlitt has remarked, Cobbett is never vulgar, though often coarse. And why? Because nature, though often coarse, is never vulgar—though often common, is never mean; and because Cobbett is never himself, and will never permit his reader to be, long or far away from the sweet, balmy breath of nature. Coleridge, in one of his little poems, speaks of trying, by abstruse research, to steal from himself "all the natural man"—a process difficult, we suspect, in any case, but in Cobbett's, even had he made the attempt, impossible; for he was nothing, if not natural. Like Caliban, he seems newly dug out, and smelling strongly of the virgin earth.

What shall we say of his style? That it was a forcible and fit expression to his thought—little more. It did not pretend to be elegant; it was not so accurate as it pretended to be. It were not difficult retorting upon many passages of his own writing the lynx-eyed system of criticism which he directed against the slovenly compositions of Sidmouth and Wellington. In fact, no style can stand minute criticism, just as the most beautiful countenance shrinks before the eye of the microscope. And let Blair's contemptible cavillings at the style of Addison—whose very errors, like the blunders of a beautiful child, are graceful and interesting—stand a perpetual monument of the folly of going too near to the masterpieces of literature. Cobbett's style is composed of the purest Saxon, and proves, as well as Bunyan's (as Macaulay has remarked), what purposes that simple speech can serve. Subtle distinctions it could not have conveyed; but Cobbett had none such to convey. Under certain grandeurs of thought, it might, like Charon's boat, have creaked and trembled; but Cobbett required it only to express clear, common sense logic, strong facts, and strong passions; to beat down his foes, and to cut his own way—and for such work it never failed him. Its general tone was that of a long rambling conversation; its principal design seemed to be to make every smallest shade of his meaning perfectly clear; its windings and turnings so distinct and vivid in their variety, reminded you of the *branching veins*—with all the repetitions of a law-paper, it was as lively and interesting as a novel. You might grin over it, or guffaw over it, or frown at it, or fling it from you in a fit of fury; but it was impossible to sleep over it, or to yawn over it, or to refrain from thinking over it. While statesmen amused themselves with the "Register" (amusement reminding you of the games in Pandemonium!) at their breakfast-tables; while the "press-gang," their lips the while smacking, and their eyes glistening with delight, proceeded to answer and abuse it, the country parson was reading it in his after-dinner easy-chair, the Paisley weaver had it lying on his loom, and the weary ploughman in his cottage kept himself awake with its quaint and rich humors. Since the works of Burns, no writings were so much appreciated by all ranks and conditions of men. And the reason of this was to be found in their corresponding qualities. Clearness; simplicity; picturesque description; racy, reckless humor; big-boned, brawny strength; contempt of conventionalisms; rugged, self-trained reason—in one word, nature—were common to both. The "hairbrained sentimental trace," which was the peculiar poetic differentia of Burns, of course was wanting in Cobbett.

One curious but unquestionable cause of Cobbett's popularity we must also mention. It was his intense sympathy with that organ which those "masters of the mint," phrenologists, have, with their usual felicity of coinage, called "gustativeness." How he expands and rejoices in describing all sorts of savory food! The droppings of Hermon's dew or of Hybla's honey, are to him nothing compared to the droppings from the sausage-pan or the roasting-jack of an English fireside! With what lively logic he undertakes the quarrel of "beer *versus* tea!" with what a deep bass he trolls out the old stave—"Oh, the roast-beef of Old England!" how profound and edifying his contempt for swipes and potatoes! how sublime he waxes over a sirloin; how pathetic his reminiscences of the good old days, when "mutton, veal, and lamb were the food of the commoner sort of people!" what a whet his "Register" made before dinner! and what a digestive after it! Here again he resembles Burns—who describes the homely food of Caledonia—her "souple scones"—her "curny ingans, mixed wi' spice," and the other ingredients of the haggis, "great chieftain o' the puddin' race"—not to speak of her tippenny and usqueba—with such infinite gusto; and Scott, whose books are the best appetizers in the world, and whose good digestion constituted, we venture to say, one-half of his physical, and one-fourth of his mental power.

In connection with this, we notice a vital defect in Cobbett's theory of man. He scarcely seems to have risen higher than the conception of him as an animal—a beef-bolting and beer-bibbing animal. If government, and his own strong hand, found him in those articles; and if William Cobbett were permitted to supply him with amusement, besides a little instruction in grammar, in arithmetic, and in the evil effects of priestcraft and potatoes, of gin and tea, he might consider himself satisfied. And this was his theory of human life! this his recipe for human woes! this his mode of filling the infinite cravings of the human heart! And yet, ere laughing at this "Gospel, according to St. Cobbett," and calling it a piggish panacea for a race of erect pigs, let us remember that the utilitarians of our own day do not rise much higher. They trace man's origin from the brutes; they, by implication, deny his natural superiority to the brutes; and, consequently, his natural immortality. Denying he was made in God's image, how can they conceive he is ever to reach it? They systematically overlook his relation to his Maker. They would cut—the puny insects!—that awful tie which from the beginning has bound our race to the throne of the Eternal! They would, with insane but impotent hands, quench the only authentic fire of revela tion which ever shone from heaven! They would arrest, if they could, the wheels of that coming One, before whose throne every knee shall bow, and whose authority every tongue shall confess! They would indeed clothe man with more accomplishments than Cobbett's rude nature recognized; they would teach man (on the brink of annihilation) to dance, and sing, and play, and recite verses, and babble of green fields, and chatter science, as well as to eat and to drink; but no more than he would they have him to expand in the prospect, and to shine in the radiance of the future destinies of his immortal being! In fact, we value Cobbett's theory as the *reductio ad absurdum* of the utilitarian view; and we fancy we hear the old sergeant growling out to those bastards of Bentham—"If you believe that man is to perish to death, like a pig, why bother yourselves with teaching him languages, music, and science? *fill his belly, you fools, and send him to sleep.*"

But we must not part in bad humor with Cobbett, nor with any body else. Pity, after all, is the most appropriate feeling to entertain towards those who judge so meanly of man. And for Cobbett, especially, there are many grounds of excuse—from his early circumstances—from his want of a spiritual education—from the sight of human nature, in its worst forms, which he had in the army—and from the scrambling and precarious life he was compelled to lead afterwards.

Besides those separate works of his which are so well known, such as his "Cottage Economy," "Legacy to Parsons," his "Life" of himself, and his "English and French Grammars," &c., we should like to see some judicious hand employed in making selections from the "Register." We despair, indeed, of ever finding the "Beauties of Cobbett" collected into such a nosegay as ladies would like to handle and to smell. Indeed, the term "Beauties of Cobbett" would seem sufficiently affected and inappropriate. But some one, surely, might give us a collection of Cobbett's "*good, strong, and true things.*" Nay, let us have some of his shadows, as well as his lights; some of his racier and more characteristic faults, a prudent selection from his vocabulary of slang, some of his richer passages of egotism, a few of his predictions that have not, and *others that have been* fulfilled—such a book, in short, as he himself would have acknowledged as a faithful likeness, and as should convey to posterity a just impression of a great English author.

JAMES MONTGOMERY.

Some seven or eight years ago, the inhabitants of a large city in the north of Scotland were apprised, by handbills, that James Montgomery, Esq., of Sheffield, the poet, was to address a meeting on the subject of Moravian missions. This announcement, in the language of Dr. Caius, "did bring de water into our mouth." The thought of seeing a live poet, of European reputation, arriving at our very door, in a remote corner, was absolutely electrifying. We went early to the chapel where he was announced to speak, and ere the lion of the evening appeared, amused ourselves with watching and analyzing the audience which his celebrity had collected. It was not very numerous, and not very select. Few of the grandees of the city had condescended to honor him by their presence. Stranger still, there was but a sparse supply of clergy, or of the prominent religionists of the town. The church was chiefly filled with females of a certain age, one or two stray "hero worshippers" like ourselves, a few young ladies who had read some of his minor poems, and whose eyes seemed lighted up with a gentle fire of pleasure in the prospect of seeing the author of those "beautiful verses on the Grave, and Prayer," and two or three who had come from ten miles off to see and hear the celebrated poet. When he at length appeared, we continued to marvel at the aspect of the platform. Instead of being supported by the *élite* of the city, instead of forming a rallying centre of attraction and unity to all who had a sympathy with piety or with genius for leagues round it, a few obscure individuals presented themselves, who seemed rather anxious to catch a little *eclat* from him, than to delight to do him honor. The evening was rather advanced ere he rose to speak. His appearance, as far as we could catch it, was quite in keeping with the spiritual cast of his poetry. He was tall, thin, bald, with face of sharp outline, but mild expression; and we looked with no little reverence on the eye which had shot fire into the Pelican Island, and on the hand (skinny enough we ween), which had written "The Grave." He spoke in a low voice, sinking occasionally into an inaudible whisper: but his action was fiery and his pantomime striking. In the course of his speech he alluded, with considerable effect, to the early heroic struggles of Moravianism, when she was yet alone in the death-grapple with the powers of Heathen darkness, and closed (when *did* he ever close a speech otherwise?) by quoting a few vigorous verses from himself.

We left the meeting, we remember, with two wondering questions in our ears: first, Is this fame? of what value reputation, which, in a city of seventy thousand inhabitants, is so freezingly acknowledged? Would not any empty, mouthing charlatan, any "twopenny tear-mouth," any painted, stupid savage, any clever juggler, any dexterous player upon the fiery harp-strings of the popular passions, have enjoyed a better reception than this true, tender, and holy poet? But secondly, Is not this true, tender, and holy poet partly himself to blame? Has he not put himself in a false position? Has he not too readily lent himself as an instrument of popular excitement? Is this progress of his altogether a proper, a poet's progress? Would Milton, or Cowper, or Wordsworth, have submitted to it? And is it in good taste for him to eke out his orations by long extracts from his own poems? Homer, it is true, sang his own verses; but he did it for food. Montgomery recites them, but it is for fame.

We pass now gladly—as we did in thought then—from the progress to the poet-pilgrim himself. We have long admired and loved James Montgomery, and we wept under his spell ere we did either the one or the other. We will not soon forget the Sabbath evening—it was in golden summer tide—when we first heard his "Grave" repeated, and wept as we heard it. It seemed to come, as it professed to come, from the grave itself—a still small voice of comfort and of hope, even from that stern abyss. It was a fine and bold idea to turn the great enemy into a comforter, and elicit such a reply, so tender and submissive, to the challenge, "O Grave, where is thy victory?" Triumphing in prospect over the sun himself, the grave proclaims the superiority and immunity of the soul—

"The Sun is but a spark of fire,
A transient meteor in the sky;
But thou! immortal as his Sire,
Shalt never die."

Surely no well in the wilderness ever sparkled out to the thirsty traveller a voice more musical, more tender, and more cheering, than this which Montgomery educes from the jaws of the narrow house. Soon afterwards we became acquainted with some of his other small pieces, which then seized and which still occupy the principal place in our regards. Indeed, it is on his little poems that the permanency of his fame is likely to rest, as it is into them that he has chiefly shed the peculiarity and the beauty of his genius. James Montgomery has little inventive or dramatic power; he cannot write an epic; none of his larger poems, while some are bulky, can be called great; but he is the best writer of hymns (understanding a hymn simply to mean a short religious effusion) in the language. He catches the transient emotions of the pious heart, which arise in the calm evening walk, where the saint, like Isaac, goes out into the fields to meditate; or under the still and star-fretted midnight; or on his "own delightful bed;" or in pensive contemplations of the "Common Lot;" or under the Swiss heaven, where evening hardly closes the eye of Mont Blanc, and stirs lake Leman's waters with a murmur like a sleeper's prayer; wherever, in short, piety kindles into the poetic feeling, such emotions he catches, refines, and embalms in his snatches of lyric song. As Wordsworth has expressed sentiments which the "solitary lover of nature was unable to utter, save with glistening eye and faltering tongue," so Montgomery has given poetic form and words to breathings and pantings of the Christian's spirit, which himself never suspected to be poetical at all, till he saw them reflected in verse. He has caught and crystallized the tear dropping from the penitent's eye; he has echoed the burden of the heart, sighing with gratitude to Heaven; he has arrested and fixed in melody the "upward glancing of an eye, when none but God is near." In his verse, and in Cowper's, the poetry of ages of devotion has broken silence, and spoken out. Religion, the most poetical of all things, had, for a long season, been divorced from song, or had mistaken pert jingle, impudent familiarity, and doggerel, for its genuine voice. It was reserved for the bards of Olney and Sheffield to renew and to strengthen the lawful and holy wedlock.

Montgomery, then, is a religious lyrist, and as such, is distinguished by many peculiar merits. His first quality is a certain quiet simplicity of language, and of purpose. His is not the ostentatious, elaborate, and systematic simplicity of Wordsworth; it is unobtrusive, and essential to the action of his mind. It is a simplicity, which the diligent student of Scripture seldom fails to derive from its pages, particularly from its histories and its psalms. It is the simplicity of a spirit which religion has subdued as well as elevated, and which consciously spreads abroad the wings of its imagination, under the eye of God. As if each poem were a prayer, so is he sedulous that its words be few and well ordered. In short, his is not so much the simplicity of art, nor the simplicity of nature, as it is the simplicity of faith. It is the virgin dress of one of the white-robed priests in the ancient temple. It is a simplicity which, by easy and rapid transition, mounts into bold and manly enthusiasm. One is reminded of the artless sinkings and soarings, lingerings and hurryings of David's matchless minstrelsies. Profound insight is not peculiarly Montgomery's forte. He is rather a seraph than a cherub; rather a burning than a knowing one. He kneels; he looks upward with rapt eye; he covers at times his face with his wing; but he does not ask awful questions, or cast strong though baffled glances into the solid and intolerable glory. You can never apply to him the words of Gray. He never has "passed the bounds of flaming space, where angels tremble as they gaze." He has never invaded those lofty but dangerous regions of speculative thought, where some have dwelt till they have lost all of piety, save its grandeur and gloom. He does not reason, far less doubt, on the subject of religion at all; it is his only to wonder, to love, to weep, and to adore. Sometimes, but seldom, can he be called a sublime writer. In his "Wanderer of Switzerland," he blows a bold horn, but the echoes and the avalanches of the highest Alps will not answer or fall to his reveillé. In his "Greenland," he expresses but faintly the poetry of Frost; and his line is often cold as a glacier. His "World before the Flood" is a misnomer. It is not the young virgin undrowned world it professes to be. In his "West Indies," there is more of the ardent emancipator than of the poet; you catch but dimly, through its correct and measured verse, a glimpse of Ethiopia—a dreadful appellant, standing with one shackled foot on the rock of Gibraltar, and the other on the Cape of Good Hope, and "stretching forth her hands" to an avenging God. And although, in the horrors of the middle passage, there were elements of poetry, yet it was a poetry which our author's genius is too gentle and timid fully to extract. As soon could he have added a story to Ugolino's tower, or another circle to the Inferno, as have painted that pit of heat, hunger, and howling despair, the hold of a slave vessel. Let him have his praise, however, as the constant and eloquent friend of the negro, and as the laureate of his freedom. The high note struck at first by Cowper in his lines, "I would not have a slave," &c., it was reserved for Montgomery to echo and swell up, in reply to the full diapason of the liberty of Ham's children, proclaimed in all the isles which Britain claims as hers. And let us hope that he will be rewarded, before the close of his existence, by hearing, though it were in an ear half-shut in death, a louder, deeper, more victorious shout springing from emancipated America, and of saying, like Simeon of old, "Lord, now let thy servant depart in peace, for mine eyes have seen thy salvation."

The plan of "The Pelican Island" was an unfortunate one, precluding as it did almost entirely human interest, and rapid vicissitude of events; and resting its power principally upon the description of foreign objects, and of slow though majestic processes of nature. Once, and once only, in this and perhaps any of his poems, does he rise into the rare region of the sublime. It is in the description of the sky of the south, a subject which indeed is itself inspiration. And yet, in that solemn sky, the great constellations, hung up in the wondering evening air, the Dove, the Raven, the Ship of Heaven, "sailing from eternity;" the Wolf, "with eyes of lightning watching the Centaur's spear; the Altar blazing, "even at the footsteps of Jehovah's throne; the Cross, "meek emblem of Redeeming love," which bends at midnight as when they were taking down the Saviour of the world, and which greeted the eye of Humboldt as he sailed over the still Pacific, had so hung and so burned for ages, and no poet had sung their praises. Patience, ye glorious tremblers. In a page of this "Pelican Island," a page bright as your own beams, and like them immortal, shall your splendors be yet inscribed. This passage, which floats the poem, and will long memorize Montgomery's name, is the more remarkable, as the poet never saw but in imagination that unspeakable southern midnight. And yet we are not sure but, of objects so transcendent, the "vision of our own" is the true vision, and the vision that ought to be perpetuated in song. For our parts, we, longing as we have ever done to see the Cross of the South, would almost fear to have our longings gratified, and to find the reality, splendid as it must be, substituted for that vast image of bright, quivering stars, which has so long loomed before our imaginations, and so often visited our dreams. Indeed, it is a question, in reference to objects which must, even when seen, derive their interest from imagination, whether they be not best seen by its eye alone.

Among Montgomery's smaller poems, the finest is the "Stanzas at Midnight," composed in Switzerland, and which we see inserted in Longfellow's romance of Hyperion, with no notice or apparent knowledge of their authorship. They describe a mood of his own mind while passing a night among the Alps, and contain a faithful transcript of the emotions which, thick and sombre as the shadows of the mountains, crossed his soul in its solitude. There are no words of Foster's which to us possess more meaning than that simple expression in his first essay, "solemn meditations of the night." Nothing in spiritual history is more interesting. What vast tracts of thought does the mind sometimes traverse when it cannot sleep! What ideas, that had bashfully presented themselves in the light of day, now stand out in bold relief and authoritative dignity! How vividly appear before us the memories of the past! How do, alas! past struggles and sins return to recollection, rekindling on our cheeks their first fierce blushes unseen in the darkness!

How new a light is cast upon the great subjects of spiritual contemplation! What a "browner horror" falls upon the throne of death, and the pale kingdoms of the grave! What projects are then formed, what darings of purpose conceived, and how fully can we then understand the meaning of the poet,

> "In lonely glens, amid the roar of rivers,
> When the still nights were moonless, have I known
> Joys that no tongue can tell; my pale lip quivers
> When thought revisits them!"

And when, through the window, looks in on us one full glance of a clear large star, how startlingly it seems, like a conscious, mild, yet piercing eye; how strongly it points, how soothingly it mingles with our meditations, and, as with a pencil of fire, points them away into still remoter and more mysterious regions of thought! Such a meditation Montgomery has embodied in these beautiful verses: but then HE is up amid the midnight and all its stars; he is out amid the Alps, and is catching on his brow the living breath of that rarest inspiration which moves amid them, then and then alone.

We mentioned Cowper in conjunction with Montgomery in a former sentence. They resemble each other in the pious purpose and general simplicity of their writings, but otherwise are entirely distinct. Cowper's is a didactic, Montgomery's a romantic piety. Cowper's is a gloomy, Montgomery's a cheerful religion. Cowper has in him a fierce and bitter vein of satire, often irritating into invective; we find no traces of any such thing in all Montgomery's writings. Cowper's withering denunciations seem shreds of Elijah's mantle, torn off in the fiery whirlwind. Montgomery is clothed in the softer garments, and breathes the gentler genius of the new economy. And as poets, Montgomery, with more imagination and elegance, is entirely destitute of the rugged strength of sentiment, the exquisite keenness of observation, the rich humor and the awful personal pathos of Cowper.

Montgomery's hymns (properly so called), we do not much admire. They are adapted, and seem written, for such an assemblage of greasy worshippers, such lank-haired young men, such virgins wise and foolish, such children, small and great, as meet to lift up their "most sweet voices" within certain well-known sanctuaries. They have in them often a false gallop of religious sentimentalism. Their unction has been kept too long, and has a savor not of the sweetest: they abound less indeed than many of their class, in such endearing epithets as "dear Lord," "dear Christ," "sweet Jesus," &c.; but are not entirely free from these childish decorations. That one song, sung by the solitary Jewish maiden in "Ivanhoe" (surely the sweetest strain ever uttered since the spoilers of Judah did by Babel's streams require of its captives a song, and were answered in that melting melody which has drawn the tears and praises of all time), is worth all the hymn-books that ever were composed. Montgomery's true hymns are those which bear not the name, but which sing, and for ever will sing, their own quiet tune to simple and pious spirits.

Of Montgomery's prose we might say much that was favorable. It is truly "Prose by a Poet," to borrow the title of one of his works. You see the poet every now and then dropping his mask, and showing himself in his true character. It is enough of itself to confute the vulgar prejudice against the prose of poets. Who indeed but a poet has ever written, or can ever write good prose, prose that will live? What prose, to take but one example, is comparable to the prose of Shakspeare, many of whose very best passages—as Hamlet's description of man, Falstaff's death, the speech of Brutus, or that dreadful grace before meat of Timon, which is of misanthropy the quaintest and most appalling quintessence, and seems fit to have preceded a supper in Eblis—are not in verse? Montgomery's prose criticism we value less for its exposition of principles, or for its originality, in which respects it is deficient, than for its generous and eloquent enthusiasm. It is delightful to find in an author, who had so to struggle up his way to distinction, such a fresh and constant sympathy with the success and the merits of others. In this point he reminds us of Shelley, who, hurled down at one time, by universal acclamation, into the lowest abyss of contempt, both as an author and a man, could look up from it, to breathe sincere admiration toward those who had usurped the place in public favor to which he was, and knew he was, entitled. We are not reminded of the Lakers, whose tarn-like narrowness of critical spirit is the worst and weakest feature in their characters. Truly a great mind never looks so contemptible as when, stooping from its pride of place, it exchanges its own high aspirations after fame for poor mouse-like nibblings at the reputation of others.

Many tributes have been paid of late years to the "Pilgrim's Progress." The lips of Coleridge have waxed eloquent in its praise; Southey and Macaulay have here embraced each other; Cheever, from America, has uttered a powerful sound in proclamation of its unmatched merits: but we are mistaken if its finest panegyric be not that contained in Montgomery's preface, prefixed to the Glasgow edition. In it all the thankfulness cherished from childhood, in a poet's and a Christian's heart, toward this benign and beautiful book, comes gushing forth; and he closes the tribute with the air of one who has relieved himself from a deep burden of gratitude. Indeed, this is the proper feeling to be entertained toward all works of genius; and an envious or malign criticism upon such is not so much a defect in the intellect as it is a sin of the heart. It is a blow struck in the face of a benefactor. A great author is one who presents us with a priceless treasure; and if we at once reject the boon and spurn the giver, ours is not an error simply, it is a deadly crime.

The mention of Bunyan and Montgomery in conjunction, irresistibly reminds us of a writer who much resembles the one, and into whom the spirit of the other seems absolutely to have transmigrated: we mean Mary Howitt. She resembles Montgomery principally in the amiable light in which she presents the spirit of Christianity. Here the Moravian and the Friend are finely at one. Their religion is no dire fatalism, like Foster's; it is no gloomy reservoir of all morbid and unhappy feelings, disappointed hopes, baffled purposes, despairing prospects, turning toward heaven, in their extremity, for comfort, as it is with a very numerous class of authors. It is a glad sunbeam from the womb of the morning, kindling all nature and life into smiles. It is a meek, womanlike presence in the chamber of earth, which meanwhile beautifies, and shall yet redeem and restore it—by its very gentleness righting all its wrongs, curing all its evils, and wiping away all its tears. Had but this faith been shown more fully to the sick soul of Cowper! were it but shown more widely to the sick soul of earth,

> "Soon
> Every sprite beneath the moon
> Would repent its envy vain,
> And the earth grow young again."

And how like is Mary Howitt to Bunyan! Like him, she is the most sublime of the simple, and the most simple of the sublime; the most literal and the most imaginative of writers. Hers and his are but a few quiet words: but they have the effect of "Open Sesame;" they conduct into deep caverns of feeling and of thought, to open which ten thousand mediocrists behind are bawling in vain. In "Marien's Pilgrimage" (thanks to the kind and gifted young friend who lately introduced us to this beautiful poem), we have a minor "Pilgrim's Progress," where Christianity is represented as a child going forth on a mission to earth, mingling with and mitigating all its evils; and is left, at the close, still wandering on in this her high calling. The allegory is not, any more than in Bunyan, strictly preserved; for Marien is at once Christianity personified and a Christian person, who alludes to Scripture events, and talks in Scripture language; but the simplicity, the child-likeness, and the sweetness, are those of the gentle dreamer of Elstowe.

We return to James Montgomery only to bid him farewell. He is one of the few lingering stars in a very rich constellation of poets. Byron, Coleridge, Southey, Crabbe, Campbell, Shelley, Keats, are gone; some burst to shivers by their own impetuous motion; others, in the course of nature, have simply ceased to shine. Three of that cluster yet remain, in Wordsworth, Moore, and Montgomery. Let us, without absurdly and malignantly denying merit to our rising luminaries, with peculiar tenderness cherish these both for their own sakes, and as still linking us to a period in our literary history so splendid.

SIDNEY SMITH.

It is melancholy to observe how speedily, successively, nay, almost simultaneously, our literary luminaries are disappearing from the sky. Every year another and another member of the bright clusters which arose about the close of the last, or at the beginning of this century, is fading from our view. Within nineteen years, what havoc, by the "insatiate archer," among the ruling spirits of the time! Since 1831, Robert Hall, Andrew Thomson, Goethe, Cuvier, Mackintosh, Crabbe, Foster, Coleridge, Edward Irving, Sir Walter Scott, Charles Lamb, Southey, Thomas Campbell, &c., have entered on the "silent land;" and latterly has dropped down one of the wittiest and shrewdest of them all—the projector of the "Edinburgh Review"—the author of "Peter Plymley's Letters"—the preacher—the politician—the brilliant converser—the "mad-wag"—Sidney Smith.

It was the praise of Dryden that he was the best reasoner in verse who ever wrote; let it be the encomium of our departed Sidney that he was one of the best reasoners in wit of whom our country can boast. His intellect—strong, sharp, clear, and decided—wrought and moved in a rich medium of humor. Each thought, as it came forth from his brain, issued as "in dance," and amid a flood of inextinguishable laughter. The march of his mind through his subject resembled the procession of Bacchus from the conquest of India—joyous, splendid, straggling—to the sound of flutes and hautboys—rather a victory than a march—rather a revel than a contest. His logic seemed always hurrying into the arms of his wit. Some men argue in mathematical formulæ; others, like Burke, in the figures and flights of poetry; others in the fire and fury of passion; Sidney Smith in exuberant and riotous fun. And yet the matter of his reasoning was solid, and its inner spirit earnest and true. But though his steel was strong and sharp, his hand steady, and his aim clear, the management of the motions of his weapon was always fantastic. He piled, indeed, like a Titan, his Pelion on Ossa, but at the oddest of angles; he lifted and carried his load bravely, and like a man, but laughed as he did so; and so carried it that beholders forgot the strength of the arm in the strangeness of the attitude. He thus sometimes disarmed anger; for his adversaries could scarcely believe that they had received a deadly wound while their foe was roaring in their face. He thus did far greater execution; for the flourishes of his weapon might distract his opponents, but never himself, from the direct and terrible line of the blow. His laughter sometimes stunned, like the cachination of the Cyclops, shaking the sides of his cave. In this mood—and it was his common one—what scorn was he wont to pour upon the opponents of Catholic emancipation—upon the enemies of all change in legislation—upon any individual or party who sought to obstruct measures which, in his judgment, were likely to benefit the country. Under such, he could at any moment spring a mine of laughter; and what neither the fierce invective of Brougham nor the light and subtle railery of Jeffrey could do, his contemptuous explosion effected, and, himself crying with mirth, saw them hoisted toward heaven in ten thousand comical splinters. Comparing him with other humorists of a similar class, we might say, that while Swift's ridicule resembles something between a sneer and a spasm (half a sneer of mirth, half a spasm of misery)—while Cobbett's is a grin—Fonblanque's a light but deep and most significant smile—Jeffrey's a sneer, just perceptible on his fastidious lip—Wilson's a strong, healthy, hearty laugh—Carlyle's a wild unearthly sound, like the neighing of a homeless steed—Sidney Smith's is a genuine guffaw, given forth with his whole heart, and soul, and mind, and strength. Apart from his matchless humor, strong, rough, instinctive, and knotty sense was the leading feature of his mind. Every thing like mystification, sophistry, and humbug, fled before the first glance of his piercing eye; every thing in the shape of affectation excited in him a disgust "as implacable" as even a Cowper could feel. If possible, with still deeper aversion did his manly nature regard cant in its various forms and disguises; and his motto in reference to it was, "spare no arrows." But the mean, the low, the paltry, the dishonorable, in nations or in individuals, moved all the fountains of his bile, and awakened all the energy of his invective. Always lively, generally witty, he is never eloquent, except when emptying out his vials of indignation upon baseness in all its shapes. His is the ire of a genuine "English gentleman, all of the olden time." It was in this spirit that he recently explained, in his own way, the old distinctions of Meum and Tuum to Brother Jonathan, when the latter was lamentably inclined to forget them. It was the same sting of generous indignation which, in the midst of his character of Mackintosh, prompted the memorable picture of that extraordinary being who, by his transcendant talents and his tortuous movements —his head of gold, and his feet of miry clay—has become the glory, the riddle, and the regret of his country, his age, and his species.

As a writer, Smith is little more than a very clever, witty, and ingenious pamphleteer. He has effected no permanent *chef d'œuvre;* he has founded no school; he has left little behind him that the "world will not willingly let die;" he has never drawn a tear from a human eye, nor excited a thrill of grandeur in a human bosom. His reviews are not preserved by the salt of original genius, nor are they pregnant with profound and comprehensive principle; they have no resemblance to the sibylline leaves which Burke tore out from the vast volume of his mind, and scattered with imperial indifference among the nations; they are not the illuminated indices of universal history, like the papers of Macaulay; they are not specimens of pure and perfect English, set with modest but magnificent ornaments, like the criticism of Jeffrey or of Hall; nor are they the excerpts, rugged and rent away by violence, from the dark and iron tablet of an obscure and original mind, like the reviews of Foster; but they are exquisite *jeux d'esprit*, admirable occasional pamphlets, which, though now they look to us like spent arrows, yet assuredly have done execution, and have not been spent in vain. And as, after the lapse of a century and more, we can still read with pleasure Addison's "Old Whig and Freeholder," for the sake of the exquisite humor and inimitable style in which forgotten feuds and dead logomachies are embalmed, so may it be, a century still, with the articles on Bentham's Fallacies and on the Game Laws, and with the letters of the witty and ingenious Peter Plymley. There is much at least in those singular productions—in their clear and manly sense—in their broad native fun—in their rapid, careless, and energetic style—and in their bold, honest, liberal, and thoroughly English spirit—to interest several succeeding generations, if not to secure the "rare and regal" palm of immortality.

Sidney Smith was a writer of sermons as well as of political squibs. Is not their memory eternized in one of John Foster's most ponderous pieces of sarcasm? In an evil hour the dexterous and witty critic came forth from behind the fastnesses of the Edinburgh Review, whence, in perfect security he had shot his quick glancing shafts at Methodists and Missions, at Christian Observers and Eclectic Reviews, at Owens and Styles, and (what the more wary Jeffrey, in the day of his power, always avoided) became himself an author, and, *mirabile dictu*, an author of sermons. It was as if he wished to give his opponents their revenge; and no sooner did his head peep forth from beneath the protection of its shell than the elephantine foot of Foster was prepared to crush it in the dust. It was the precise position of Saladin with the Knight of the Leopard, in their memorable contest near the Diamond of the Desert. In the skirmish Smith had it all his own way; but when it came to close quarters, and when the heavy and mailed hand of the sturdy Baptist had confirmed its grasp on his opponent, the disparity was prodigious, and the discomfiture of the light horseman complete. But why recall the memory of an obsolete quarrel and a forgotten field? The sermons—the *causa belli*—clever but dry, destitute of earnestness and unction—are long since dead and buried; and their review remains their only monument.

Even when, within his own stronghold, our author intermeddled with theological topics, it was seldom with felicity or credit to himself. His onset on missions was a sad mistake; and in attacking the Methodists, and poor, pompous John Styles, he becomes as filthy and foul-mouthed as Swift himself. His wit forsakes him, and a rabid invective ill supplies its place; instead of laughing, he raves and foams at the mouth. Indeed, although an eloquent and popular preacher, and in many respects an ornament to his cloth, there was one radical evil about Smith; *he had mistaken his profession.* He was intended for a barrister, or a literary man, or a member of parliament, or some occupation into which he could have flung his whole soul and strength. As it was, but half his heart was in a profession which, of all others, would require the whole. He became consequently a rather awkward medley of buffoon, politician, preacher, literateur, divine. and diner-out. Let us grant, however, that the ordeal was severe, and that, if a very few have weathered it better, many more have ignominiously broken down. No one coincides more fully than we do with Coleridge in thinking that every literary man should have a profession; but in the name of common sense let it be one fitted for him, and for which he is fitted—one suited to his tastes as well as to his talents—to his habits as well as to his powers—to his heart as well as to his head.

As a conversationist, Sidney Smith stood high among the highest—a Saul among a tribe of Titans. His jokes were not rare and refined, like those of Rogers and Jekyll; they wanted the slyness of Theodore Hook's inimitable equivoque; they were not poured forth with the prodigal profusion of Hood's breathless and bickering puns; they were rich, fat, unctuous, always bordering on farce, but always avoiding it by a hair's-breadth. No finer cream, certes, ever mantled at the feasts of Holland House than his fertile brain supplied; and, to quote himself, it would require a "forty-parson power" of lungs and language to do justice to his convivial merits. An acquaintance of ours sometimes met him in the company of Jeffrey and Macaulay—a fine concord of first-rate performers, content, generally, to keep each within his own part, except when, now and then, the author of the "Lays" burst out irresistibly, and changed the concert into a fine solo.

Sidney Smith, we never saw, and his *personnel*, therefore, we cannot describe. We always figure him, however, to ourselves as a "round, fat, oily man of God," with a strongly marked forehead, and an unspeakable twinkle in his eye. How far this resembles the original, we leave others to determine. Altogether "we could have better spared a better man." Did not his death "eclipse the gayety of nations?" Did not a Fourth Estate of Fun expire from the midst of us? Did not even Brother Jonathan drop a tear when he thought that the scourge that so mercilessly lashed him was broken? And shall not now all his admirers, unite with us in inscribing upon his grave—"Alas! poor Yorick!"

WILLIAM ANDERSON, GLASGOW.

Amid our profusion of sketches, we have never yet permitted ourselves to draw a likeness of our venerable father, Samuel Gilfillan of Comrie. We feel at present a strong impulse to do so shortly; and we know Mr. Anderson too well to doubt that he will stand aside gladly for a little, till we limn a yet dearer countenance than his, and analyze a character equally upright and sincere.

Our father was indeed a very remarkable man. He was not what this fastidious age would call a man of genius, learning, or eloquence; but for genius he had a genial and impulsive heart—for learning, extensive information—for eloquence, unequalled ease of plain effective address. His form was erect and manly—his brow lofty and marked—his eye quick to restlessness—his hair, as we remember it, tinged with gray—his whole aspect denoting the utmost activity of mind and ardor of character. Though naturally impetuous in his temper, and hasty in its expressions, he was one of the most delightful of companions. He was frank to excess—guile had been forgotten in his composition; he had a childlike gayety and warmth of manner, from which he rose gently—not, like some, rebounded violently—into dignity; he was full of talk, and especially of anecdote and allusion, culled from a wide extent of miscellaneous reading; he had a nack, altogether his own, in bringing in his religious views, not like staring strangers, but like welcome and respected guests, into any company and any conversation. He was admirable, too, at adapting himself to all kinds of persons, and had one manner for the peasant, another for his brother-minister, a third for the literary man, a fourth for the religious and high-bred lady, and a fifth for the mere man of the world—yet all natural, easy, and ranking themselves gracefully under the one idiosyncrasy of his character. As a husband and parent, he was affectionate to indulgence. His beaming eye betrayed his deep love—his faltering tones in his Sabbath-evening addresses to the little circle—the warm pressure of his welcoming hand, when any of his family came home from the distant city—his all but last look to us as, a few days before his death, he met us returning from the village-library with a precious volume of "Plutarch's Lives" in our hand—his walks with us through the ripe corn-fields of autumn, pouring out the while a stream of information and interesting comment on the objects around—the hope and preference, but faintly disguised—even his occasional inequalities of temper, shall all be dear "while memory holds a seat on this distracted globe." As a preacher, he was plain, earnest, serious, always animated, sometimes vehement. All this is true of many preachers besides him; but few possessed the inexpressible charm, the naïveté, the exquisite power of adapting his discourse to every little incident which occurred in the history of his audience, to every smallest surge which took place in its stream. He did not stand up before them as a sublime orator, to fulminate, and fiercely and contemptuously sway—as an eager aspirant for their favorable suffrages, to tickle and to soothe—as the primed mouthpiece of an elaborate discharge—as a being piercing a lonely way through the thick of his hearers, wondered at, looked after, but not followed (a description this last which some will know how to fit on); but as a plain, honest, well-informed, warm-hearted man, conversing on the level of his people, solemnly yet easily, about the matters of their eternity; and, as the conversation went on, allowing himself the widest range, now beseeching, now threatening, gathering illustrations from every remarkable aspect of the sky above, or any singular incident in his audience below—here quoting a verse of poetry which evidently occurred at the moment, there applying an anecdote from his multifarious stores, and here again snatching a shaft from the newspapers of the day, watching the while every countenance, and obliging every one to return the eager glance; and doing all this with such perfect mastery, and in such evident good faith, as to secure undivided attention, when he did not, as was often the case, awaken deeper emotions—the tears of penitence, the thrill of conviction, the spasm of remorse, the eager light, forming itself on the upturned countenance, of the "joy that is unspeakable and full of glory."

As a writer, he enjoyed more extensive and valuable popularity than perhaps any man in his own body. His works, consisting of papers printed in the "Christian Magazine," and occasional small volumes on religious subjects, were read from Maidenkirk to John o'Groat's, welcomed in many an humble cottage as monthly messengers of gladness, and, besides passing through a multitude of impressions in this country, translated into French, Dutch, and Russ. Nor was their popularity to be wondered at, considering their unostentatious and pleasing merits. They were somewhat loosely and illogically composed; but so easy in their style, so lucid in their meaning, so short in their structure of sentence, so child-like and Bunyan-like in their tone, so evidently the effusions of an earnest spirit, and sprinkled so knackily with anecdote, and allusion, and verse, and bits of historic lore, all steeped in genuine Gospel-savor, that we can at once account why readers of all classes and intellects perused them with pleasure and profit. They had no pretension to acute argumentation, or original imagery, or searching thought; but, full of Gospel-marrow and affectionate earnestness, won their way to thousands of pious hearts, and lighted up a *lowe* of delight on many a cheek, bending at once over the ingle-*bleeze* and the pleasant page of *Leumas*. This was his favorite signature, consisting of the letters of his Christian name reversed.

His death we do well remember, and frequently roll over with melancholy pleasure. He had gone from Comrie to a country hamlet, on a *diet* (as those occasions were then called) of pastoral visitation. The good people had provided a basket of *sloes*, knowing his partiality for them. Of these he ate largely, and had scarcely reached home till they affected his system in the shape of severe inflammation. This was on Wednesday, the 11th of October, 1826. All Thursday and Friday he was in violent anguish, absolutely shouting for pain, expecting immediate dissolution, and giving advices to his family with all the earnestness of a dying man. On Saturday there was a delusive pause in the tragedy; his pains subsided, though the foundation of the disease was not reached; and he spent the day reading in bed. It was a quiet gray autumn day, and we see him still, self-propped on his pillow, and with eager eye reading "Hervey's Letters," and the Bible. On Sabbath the 15th the dark disease returned to his charge, and would now permit no farther delay. Severe was the struggle, dire the tossings, deep the groans, of this strong man caught in the embrace of one stronger than he. The medical men did their utmost. We remember seeing a basin of a father's blood, which they had drawn; we remember overhearing a consultation among them, the result of which was they could *do no more;* we remember the sad silence with which they left the house; we remember the entrance of members of the family, who had been summoned from a distance to see him ere he died, coming in with red eyes to swell the general grief; we remember his last exclamation to his nearest earthly relative—"You will be a widow, and a poor widow!" and her look of calm, speechless sorrow, like that of one seeing from the shore a friend rushing down a remorseless rapid, and his answering glance, expressing, long after he could not speak, a deep interest in her he was leaving, as if even more than his wonted love were glowing in his eye; we remember the awful hush which reigned throughout the chamber till the presence of death was authentically proclaimed, and the wild sobs which burst out afterwards; we remember turning round from the death-bed, and looking with a sick and strange emotion to the golden autumn day, the stubble-fields, the lonely hills, the solemn silence of the Sabbath, which seemed to lie in sympathy without; we remember our first feelings, dreary and desolate beyond expression, on awakening the next morning, and finding ourselves *fatherless;* and a burst of wild grief at the coffining, which shook our young being to its foundations; and of turning round, in our agony, and gazing through a window northwards, and praying for and almost expecting to see his spirit appearing amid the still moonlight. We need not record how that tumultuous grief gradually subsided into a pensive recollection, seated in the heart as much as in the memory, of his dear image—an image which a thousand sunbeams, and showers, and shadows, and sorrows, and joys, have left uneffaced upon the soul—"It trembles, but it cannot pass away."

Samuel Gilfillan was a broad-minded, kind-hearted, and thoroughly Christian being. To a greater extent than almost any contemporary in his own church, he had swallowed formulas, forgotten points of distinction, and fastened on points of resemblance, between various bodies. Add to this a love of literature, then, as now, rare among Scottish dissenting ministers—a knowledge of many departments of the arts and sciences—an impetuous yet holy philanthropy—a generous, self-forgetting enthusiasm—a sympathy with the poor, the neglected and the forgotten—the principles of a "Whig and something more"—the head, heart, and life of a man and a Christian, and you have the outline of *Leumas.*

The parish kirk, near where he lies, is rather a striking object. It stands on a small knoll above the river Earn. It is a whitewashed structure, and its churchyard commands a noble prospect. This churchyard, however, would be greatly improved by a circle of trees around it; for although we do not greatly like the modern style of taste in burying-places—a taste transplanted from the country of Victor Hugo and Voltaire—a taste which has converted graveyards into gardens, sought in vain to disguise death and his horrors, and would allow Hervey, were he alive now, to carry on his "Meditations on a Flower-Garden and on the Tombs" in the same place, yet we do stand up for a diadem of trees as the crown of the departed, for a living company over the congregation of the dead, for a speaking as the guardians of a silent multitude—their very murmur in the wind, and the ever-renewing green of their spring garniture, preaching better than a thousand homilies the truth of resurrection, and returning to the question, "Shall these dead live?" an emphatic and everlasting "Yea." Would that Comrie kirkyard had its synod of trees to whisper this over *his* dust, whose memory is still cherished amid those pastoral regions with an enthusiasm which is attested by the beaming eye and kindling countenance with which his name is uttered—of one who in all respects realized the poetical pictures of "the good minister"—of one to whom we feel in his sepulchre all the tenderness of filial affection, and all the reverence of profound esteem—of one who "having turned many to righteousness, shall shine as the brightness of the firmament, and as the stars, for ever and ever."

William Anderson, like the author of this sketch, was born and brought up under the roof and amid the influences of a quiet country Dissenting manse, with this difference, that his excellent father is still alive, and that we lost ours while yet a boy. In Kilsyth, under the shadow of the Campsie Hills, Mr. Anderson first breathed the air of life.

Mr. Anderson is a man who has many eccentricities, but all whose oddnesses are cognate with his nature, and do only slenderly disguise it. It is vain to object to the *queerness* of the attitude or action by which the strong man levels you to the dust. In such a case, the smile of laughter might contend with the grin of death. All Glasgow has felt and owned in William Anderson the presence of a strong, simple-minded, clear-visioned, and earnest man, at whom fools might laugh, but whom cold men wondered at, ardent men admired, and wise men understood.

The Germans were wont to say of Jean Paul Richter that he was the *only one.* Among his class, connection, and contemporaries, William Anderson is the *only one.* He stands beside or collaterally—quietly, collectedly, and modestly himself. Nor is he a mere made original, a modern antique; he is one through whose mind all things and thoughts, as they pass, receive a distinct and peculiar tinge, just as light flowing through a painted window accomplishes the prophecy of the medium, and becomes something finer than itself. Be it that some say that his mind is bended, it is no bend sinister—that his brain is *cracked*, it is neither the crack of *duncedom* nor of *doom*—save to his opponents.

William Anderson possesses the rare quality of power. If he does not *make*, nor seek to make, he *moves*, often without seeking to move. There is sometimes a stormy force about him, which seems superfluous whenever you witness the calm of his better and higher manner, which seems to fold around his audience as completely, irresistibly, and tenderly as the blue sky of spring over the mountains and the clouds. Artistic polish or beauty is not often *his*, but there shines out not unfrequently a stranger and a rarer beauty, that of holiness, from his pages. Something of the sacred fervor, and boldness, and fierceness of the ancient Hebrew mind breathes and burns about him. He has more of the vehemence of the Baptist than of the charity and mildness of the new dispensation, save ever and except when *children* are concerned. Then the old love, which shone in the eye of the Saviour as he said, "Suffer the little children to come unto me, and forbid them not," sparkles in his; and lo! it is one weaned child discoursing to other weaned children, and from the mouths of babes and sucklings seeking to perfect praise.

When we speak of Anderson as having more of the old than of the new dispensation, we refer not so much to his views as to his spirit. His views are singularly wide and catholic, so far as the dark and disputed questions in theology are concerned. His heart, too, is warm and generous to a degree. But somehow or other, whether owing to the intense purity of his nature, or to the fervor of his temperament, he has fallen at times into outrageous and violent extremes of abuse and invective against those unfortunate men who have been led astray by error or vice, particularly if they have published the results of their perverted powers, and has not unfrequently, instead of leaving them and their sins in the hands of their "Father and their God," burst across the limits of the world, anticipated their dooms, and sought to stir into fiercer energy the surge of Almighty vengeance, as if it were slow, sleepy, and reluctant in its movements. He loves, as Charles Lamb says of Southey, "to paint a given king in bliss, and a given chamberlain in torment, even to the eternizing of a cast of the eye in the latter;" loves to stand by the burning bedsteads of Voltaire, Volney, Rousseau, Burns, and Byron, and interpret the wild Babel of their confused blasphemies and piercing lamentations, forming out of the vague clamors the treble, tenor, counter, and bass of the music of hell. Now, this you might have expected in a fierce inquisitor, forgiven in the worn and desperate Dante, pitied in the narrow and stung Southey; but in the robust, liberal, and kind-hearted William Anderson, you, or at least we, cannot account for and cannot away with.

Let us grant, however, that in thus dealing round damnation, he is quite impartial. Southey's "Vision of Judgment" is just a monstrous binding up of the "Court Calendar" with the Book of Life. Our hero does not go over the "Directory" of his city, and jot down his candidates for destruction or salvation, according to their streets or squares. He does not spare the rich transgressor for his wealth, nor the poor sinner for his poverty. Much as he adores genius, he will not permit its painted screen to stand, when it would shade the fierceness of the unquenchable fire—he hurls it down straightway. Since Edward Irving died, there has not been pouring from any pulpit such a stream of *purged perdition.* "It is fire and brimstone *from the Lord out of heaven.*" Still we much prefer, what Mr. Anderson also often distils upon his hearers, the soft-dropping dew of the Gospel Hermon.

In many points, Anderson bears a resemblance to Edward Irving. His rich scripturality of quotation, his antique cast of phraseology, his long unmeasured sentences, his personal appeals, his sudden short bursts of eloquence, his fearless and sometimes fierce spirit blended with much gentleness, his mixture of *cajolerie* and real simplicity, his occasional wildness, his sincere and burning enthusiasm, not to speak of his millennial views, render him a striking though smaller similitude of that "Shakspeare of preachers"—that embodied flame of meteoric fire, who, like the wondrous tent or temple of electric light we saw lately suspended in the sky, hung, broadened, fluctuated, shivered, faded, went out in darkness —the pride, wonder, and terror of our ecclesiastical heavens.

One quality Mr. Anderson possesses, the want of which in Irving was pernicious—we mean, strong manly common sense. An old divine was wont to say, that if you wanted learning—if you wanted even the grace of God—if you wanted any thing else, in short, you might get it; but if you want common sense, you will never get it. The most splendid endowments do not compensate for its want; the most extensive and bitter experience does not communicate it. This *pocket-map* of man Mr. Anderson always carries about with him; and next to the inestimable divine chart, which no man values more, it has been his most valuable directory, and has saved him harmless where many have sunk to ruin, either been inflated and burst by vanity, or stiffened into salt statues of pride, or gone down the steep places of semi-spiritual semi-sensual destruction. In reading Mr. Anderson's works, and particularly his volume of sermons issued a few years ago, their main characteristic appears to be akin to this—vigorous, independent, yet cautious judgment. The volume contains in it, besides many artistic merits and literary beauties, some highly finished passages, both of reasoning, of fancy, of sarcasm, and of practical appeal. There is, for example, a description of the hypocrite, which might have come from Foster's pen. Passages of similar power has he sprinkled throughout his "Good Works," on the "Duty of loving God," on the "Evil of Sin," and on the "Reunion of Christian Friends in the Heavenly World." From this last, throughout a piece of fine fancy and feeling, we quote the following touch of real genius:—"Many a mother will not find her son in heaven, and yet the Saviour will make her happy; there can be no grief in the Paradise of God, no not even for a perished son. She could not now endure him, and Christ will bring her some other woman's child, who has been seeking for his *mother* in vain, and He will say, 'Woman behold thy son,' and to him, 'Behold thy mother,' and the wounds of the hearts of both will be healed." Nothing can be a simpler, yet nothing a finer application of our Saviour's dying words.

We think, indeed, that if Mr. Anderson, in his published works, had been less of a controversialist, and more of an utterer of sweet, musical, and poetical thoughts, such as this we have now quoted, his fame as a writer had been greater than it is. How soon polemical writings die! No one seeks to preserve them, after a certain date, any more than to prop up a fallen thistle or thorn; but let a flower or a hedge of roses begin to totter to its fall, every passing beggar will become its patron, and discover that there is in his heart some dim instinct of beauty unknown even to himself. Thus Clark's *a priori* argument (supposing its credit to fall) would fall amid utter silence, while an attack on the "Romeo and Juliet" of Shakspeare would make thousands eloquent, whose very tongues had been problematical before. Many even of Protestants would mourn less the want of Chillingworth's work than that of some of the sublime hymns of the Catholic Litany, such as the *Dies Irae;* and so we would cheerfully have wanted some of Mr. Anderson's defences against those who thought him heterodox on the points of the "organ" and the "personal reign," rather than those numerous tender and beautiful passages, which illustrate in an uncommon way points common to all Christians.

Mr. Anderson, as a writer, is noted for nerve, contempt of conventionalities, and daring selection of all the words, thoughts, and images which will serve his purpose, culled be they from whatever quarter—from earth, air, sea, heaven, or that "other place." He knows that a true thought, like a true prism, will reflect light of all kinds and from every quarter. You occasionally find him *recollecting* but never imitating other writers. They are *in*, but not *on* and *over* his eye. Strong and startling as he is sometimes in his expressions, he is seldom wrong in his conclusions. We hear of writers—

> "Ne'er so sure our favor to create,
> As when they tread the brink of all we hate."

Mr. Anderson is one of this class. He drives his chariot along the brink of a whole chain of precipices, with a success as perfect as the way is perilous. He seems to love that border-land between truth and error. As you are about to call him an Arminian, he turns round and throws a *blash* of Calvinism in your face; as you are about to charge him with leaning to "universal salvation," he so paints perdition that you seem to hear the roar of its sleepless fires, and the tossing of the victims on the unmade beds of despair. He does not consider himself bound to reconcile apparently opposite truths, though he is bound to believe both. *He* cannot cast a bridge between Ayr and Arran, but he knows that some god or giant yet may.

Mr. Anderson, as a preacher, has a great variety of styles and manners. He can be, and is, either practical or profound—either minute or abstract—either too plain to be pleasant, or too rich and powerful to be plain—either calm or vehement—either commonplace or original. We assisted him lately, and were much interested in the whole services of the day. His congregation is very large, and is almost—thanks to him—the best *singing* congregation in Scotland. It was thrilling, almost to the sublime, to hear their morning psalm. His prayers were minute, comprehensive, and earnest; his sermon, though not in his highest vein, was interesting and forcible. But the most striking part was his table-service. During the consecration prayers he holds the elements in his hand. While holding the cup and praying for the coming of Christ—dark, solemn, swarthy as he stood—he reminded us of the "*King's* cup-bearer." The large assembly seemed eating and drinking consciously under the shadow of the coming chariot; and if the morning psalm approached the sublime, the evening anthem, sung by the whole congregation standing, exceeded it, and rose to the sublime of dreams, when our vision of the night is heaven.

Mr. Anderson's delivery does not add at all to the impression of his matter. It is rather slow and drawling; his accent and pronunciation are of Kilsyth in the last century; his tone is rather nasal, his gesture ungraceful. When he rises, however, into his true power, all this is forgotten in the animation, the forceful bursts, the impassioned truth of a genuine natural orator. The air of eld, too, which breathes around his style, language, appearance, and address, adds a tart peculiarity to the whole, and you are carried back to the days of Cameron and Renwick. What a hill-preacher would he have made, as the enemy was coming up, or as a thunder-storm was darkening over the heads of the assembly!

As a public and platform man, William Anderson exerts great power in Glasgow. Every one believes him sincere, and every one knows him to be one of the ablest, readiest, and raciest of speakers. Here, too, all his strength, impetuosity, and earnestness, are under the control of discretion and sound judgment. His appearance is singular, if not fine. His features are plain, his face is slightly marked with the small-pox, his complexion is dark, but his eye, from its expression of blended sagacity and benevolence, redeems the whole. In private he is homely, social, kindly, full of matter, especially of anecdote and incident illustrative of life and character—proner to praise than blame—and, with all his sagacity, simple as a child. Music and infancy are the two mild hobbies he loves to ride, and long may he ride them! Like many other men of mark, he has had to fight his way. He was long a wonder unto many. The foolish laughed at, the malignant defamed, the hypercritical underrated him, and from his peers he received little sympathy or support. But, like all the brave, he struggled on, and was rewarded with victory. His popularity, at first excited by the eccentricities, was at last allowed calmly to rest on the excellence of his preaching and character. "Those who came to laugh remained to pray," personal and party prejudice was gradually subdued, his oddities mellowed and softened with time, and we may now as safely as we can conscientiously declare, that the United Presbyterian Church, with all its host of talented men, possesses scarcely one who equals in genius, and very few who surpass in talent, plain, strong, gifted William Anderson.

We may just add that Mr. Anderson, although not distinguished for pastoral visitation, is most exemplary in waiting on the sick-bed. We heard recently a rather amusing anecdote of him. Some person called, complaining that he had been eighteen years a member of his congregation and had never been visited by his minister. "You should be very thankful," replied Mr. Anderson. "How that, sir?" rejoined Mr. B. "I never visit any but those in whose houses God has entered by affliction. It seems you have been eighteen years without affliction in your family; few are so highly privileged. I trust other eighteen years may elapse ere I be in your house, sir. Good morning, Mr. B." So may all querulous Bs or blockheads be treated!*

LEIGH HUNT.

The present state of poetry is a subject on which a great deal of nonsense has been written, and on which a greater deal still of nonsense is every day spoken. "We have no poets now-a-days," is the chatter at many a tea-table—a chatter which a glance at a few of the present names "flaming on the forehead" of our literary sky, is enough to confute. Beside such veterans as Wordsworth, Wilson, Croly, Montgomery, and our present subject, Leigh Hunt, who are now rather honorary than active members of the corporation of Apollo, there are numerous aspirants of the laurel, of whom high hopes may be entertained. There is especially a little cluster of *earnest* poets whom we are at all times delighted to honor, and some of whom we may now briefly characterize, as an introduction not inappropriate to a notice of one who long ago, and in days darker than these, set them a good example, and who then stood almost singular in adding the spirit of the martyr to the accomplishments of the muses' son.

* Mr. Anderson is just issuing a volume on "Regeneration," which we expect to be quite worthy of him.

We may name, then, Longfellow, Emerson, Bailey, Tennyson, and the Brownings, as the *Dii Majorum Gentum* of this modern class.

We name first the American poet, Longfellow. We know nothing whatever of his theoretical creed, but we are not blind to the marks of sincerity and of high-minded aspiration which pervade his poetry. He feels what Foster uniformly forgets or denies, the worth of man. He looks at the ruins of the human soul in a certain rich moonlight which softens many an asperity, fills up many a chasm, symmetrizes many a disproportion, and sheds a soft golden film, a gossamer of the night, over the whole. His eye, too, is anointed to see innumerable fine and fairy hands repairing the desolation, as well as beautifying its decay. "It is a little thing to be a man." Yes, comparativly it is; but whence springs the smallness? Surely from the greatness of the height whence we have fallen, and to which we are invited to aspire. Life and man, like the Jura in the presence of Mont Blanc, dwindle before a greater, which greater in this case is the grandeur of man's ideal of himself and of God. It is little to be, it is far less to doubt of man. Spring but this one leak, and what a black flood of skepticism rushes in —death is regarded with the avidity of a suicide, and it is well if the Foster does not darken into the Swift.

Hear Longfellow:—

"Not enjoyment and not sorrow
Is our being's destined way;
But to live that each to-morrow
Finds us farther than to-day."

And again:

"Life is real, life is earnest,
And the grave is not its goal;
'Dust thou art, to dust returnest,'
Was not spoken of the soul."

Such manly lines, rising clear, loud, and bold, like the notes of Chanticleer, dissipate a thousand dismal dreams and terrors of the night. They are not the day, but they are its promise. What we miss in Longfellow is a decided acknowledgment of the realization which such sentiments as his find in Christianity. His verses are torn from their proper

Christian context. Now, a few fresh leaves snapped from the bough may tell that spring has come, but we prefer the full tidings of the round tree itself.

In Emerson we find, amid more power, originality, and perhaps equal sincerity, a more palpably vital defect. What the "hope set before" him in his melancholy gospel is we cannot tell. In his "Threnody" he laments most sweetly and plaintively the loss of a favorite son, and hints at some obscure and mystic source of consolation, described in the words, that his child is "Lost in God, in Godhead found!' Alas! can he allow his child, with his glorious personality, to slide away into a vague, vast ocean, even as his own dreams among the "blackberry vines" did leave his soul, with no trace behind? Can he part with a son as with a thought? Can he believe that the soul which, as it looked through the "blue summer" of his child's eyes, seemed to "span the mystic gulf 'tween God and man," is henceforth an unconscious nonentity, somewhere in the eternal spaces, but with no spring of return to him, and no prospect of encounter with him, save in the cold commerce of the waves of the Pantheistic deep? Or if he has, apart from this dreary dream, a principle of hope and comfort, is there no word in the ample tongue of Milton and Coleridge that can *express* this hope? and if there be, why does he delay to inform us what we are to substitute for the simple declaration, "Them that sleep in Jesus shall the Lord bring with him?" Indeed, over all Emerson's poems, and over those of many of his followers, there hangs a deep gloom. His fun, when he attempts to be humorous, is dull and feeble. It is the drone of the "humble bee," which is quite as melancholy as it is mirthful. He is never so eloquent as when expressing the feelings of one who, from the pursuits of ambition, and the company of men, has sought a sad solace in Nature, which yet without a God can only glare and glitter about his eye and imagination, but not touch his heart. His personal purity, which is that of a guarded dewdrop—has saved him from many pains and penalties; but we do think that it is the subtlety which so strangely mingles with the simplicity of his nature, like the eye of the basilisk looking out from the silvery plumage of the dove, which has veiled from many the fact that *he is not a happy man.*

No wonder although, according to a CERTAIN rumor, Emerson does not fully sympathize with Bailey of "Festus." How can he? How can a man who manages his misery so artfully that the deep scar looks like a badge of honor upon his bosom—who can regulate, turn, and wind his madness like a watch—sympathize with one who, with the power and precipitation of a thunder-shower, expresses his whole soul to the world in tumultuous verse? How stiff and measured the extravagances (*madness prepense*) of Emerson look beside Bailey's unpremeditated hallelujahs! In Emerson you hear a man crying "down" to the idea of a personal deity, which is for ever rising in his truly poetical heart; to Bailey the universe is but a reflector for the face of a Saviour and God. In Emerson you find a nature, originally poetic and even devout, chilled and strangled by the frost of an imperfect philosophy (as though an eagle on his way to the sun were killed by the cold of our upper atmosphere); in "Festus" faith is the philosophy, hope is the science, and love the logic of the strain. In Emerson's verse, truth lurks like a guilty thing in single lines, which are rather pinfolds than panoramas; Bailey's broad nature luxuriates in long, interlinked, and magnificent passages, which rise and rise till no wing short of that of imagination can reach and rest upon their summit.

Leaving comparisons, we may simply say that, in the two qualities of impulse and earnestness, we have seldom read a work to be compared with "Festus." We care nothing for its theory—admit its many and monstrous faults—are not careful to answer the charge of imitation in its plan—but the vigor of individual thought, the amplitude of general view, and wealth of imagery—the rough strength of language, and, above all, the deep, sparkling, "blood-power of spirit," so religious and so fervidly sincere, have compelled like a captive, our at first unwilling admiration. It now resounds in our ears like the Pan-pipe of a belated Titan from his lonely rock, at once bewailing the past, and calling, in no measured strains, for the advent of the future.

Of Browning, Mrs. Browning, and Tennyson, we need hardly speak, so well are they known and so thoroughly appreciated by the lovers of poetry in Britain. Tennyson of the three is the most purely poetical, and perhaps the least prophetic in spirit or purpose. He may be compared to Ariel in the "Tempest." Ariel *can* pluck up cedars by the roots, but prefers swinging in the blossom which hangs from the bough. He can back and bridle the fiery steed of the lightning, but prefers sucking in time and tune with the sucking bee. He can "flame amazement" over a crowded ship, but would rather fly on the bat's back in the still evenings of summer. From tasks at once mighty and delicate, requiring both infinite power and infinite tact, he springs gladly to the more congenial pursuits of an eternity of busy and merry idleness. So Tennyson, with powers which, as Carlyle once said, "might move the world," condescends sometimes to play tricks, to sing snatches, to waver in beautiful gyrations, like the down of the thistle, instead of going straight to his mark, like an arrow or a thunderbolt. In both the Brownings, but especially in the lady, we find a more powerful and condensed purpose, united to imagination of almost equal brilliance. There is in her no dallying with her theme—no drawing back from her pictures, as a painter does to try the effect—no "staying her thunder in mid-volley." She is in evident and deep earnest. Each theme sits before her, as a ghost might be supposed to sit before a limner—at once shuddering and admiring; and you fancy her, at the close, falling back exhausted and trembling, after her faculties had been tasked to their utmost in that unearthly sitting. Seldom has woman had a higher or more masculine message to deliver. Yet sorrow hovers over the sublimity of her strains, "like the soft shadow of an angel's wing," and the knowledge she has gained, and the power of moving us she exerts, have been bought at their weight, not in gold, but in *fire*.

It is pleasant, in some moods, to pass from these poets, with their passionate, or fierce, or heroic attitudes, to the blended ease and earnestness of Leigh Hunt. He stands among them like an oak amidst the surrounding pines, or birches, or sensitive plants, less tremulous, dark, drooping, or defiant, to every breath of heaven, but greener, ampler, calmer, albeit ready always to resist strong aggression, as well as to shade unassuming merit. If they aspire to the rank of prophets, he is a patriarch, seated and uttering gentle yet profound responses at his tent-door.

The highest compliment ever paid to Hunt is, perhaps, that of Byron, who, after a furious and vulgar diatribe against him, owns him to be a "good man." This may seem poor praise, but a cold shower-bath from Hecla were less astonishing than the acknowledgment of any human virtue from the mouth of a man who had set himself elaborately to erase each vestige of goodness from his own character, and had well nigh succeeded—who had nearly completed an exchange between his heart and the "nether millstone,"—and whose praises of all but his personal friends came forth rare and reluctant, as do the audible groans of his proud spirit. Hunt's goodness and talent he always admitted—and with regard to the charge of vulgarity, which now, at this distance of time, is the vulgar person of the two? Hunt's vulgarity is that of circumstances and education, Byron's was ingrained in his nature—and neither the Highlands, with their grandeur, nor Holland House, with its varied and brilliant converse, nor Italy, with the *recherchē* society of its better classes, were able to erase the original stamp of the degraded and blackguard lord, which had been transmitted from generations downwards, till it was fortunate in his countenance to meet and contend with the blaze of genius and the pale impress of coming death.

In our notion, Thomas Macaulay is an infinitely more vulgar person than Leigh Hunt or even Lord Byron—if vulgarity mean the want of all those qualities which go to constitute a gentleman. Our readers, in illustration of this, may take the following anecdote, which we know to be correct. A writer who had, some year or two ago, rather severely, although with a friendly feeling, criticised Macaulay in one of our leading periodicals, chanced to read Croker's assault upon his "History of England" in the "Quarterly." Struck with its unfairness and with the *animus* which pervaded it, he wrote Mr. Macaulay a note, couched in the most respectful terms, not retracting his former statements, but expressing a manly sympathy with him under an unjust attack. He was not a little surprised to receive an extremely harsh and contemptuous reply, in which the Edinburgh ex-member told his correspondent that he cared neither for his blame nor his praise. Had the writer been a clamorous petitioner for his pelf or his praise—had he approached him in an unfriendly guise, and with unfriendly language, or had he been base enough to have flattered the man whom he had criticised, he could have accounted for such treatment; as it was, he was forced to regard it as a breach of the laws of common courtesy, as a specimen of the wretched airs of aristocracy which upstarts often assume—as the action of a coxcomb, not a gentleman—and we understand told the historian so in language which he is not likely soon to forget or to forgive. Leigh Hunt is incapable, both from geniality and gentlemanly feeling, of such conduct as this. He always dips his pen in a reservoir compounded of warm blood and of the milk of human kindness. This element, indeed, bathes his whole being and person. It swims in his restless eye—it throbs in his hot hand—it, and not age's winter, seems to have whitened his locks—it gushes out in the jets and sparkles of his conversation, which is yet evidently only the relic of what it was in earlier times—and it is the mild or mirthful inspiration of his various writings.

Had Hunt been a less sincere and simple-minded person than he has been, he might, we think, have been quite as popular a writer as Thomas Moore. He has the *champagne* qualities of that writer, without, indeed, so many or such brilliant bubbles of wit and fancy upon the top—and has a world more of body, solidity, and truth. It is his assuming the fairy shape, that has made some (ourselves at one time included) to underrate his powers. But why did he assume it? Why did he, like the devils in Milton, shrink his stature to gain admission to the halls of Pandemonium? Why did he not rather, in dignified humility, wait without as he was till the great main door was opened, and till in full size and panoply he entered in, and sat down a giant among giants, a god amidst gods? In such figured language we convey our notion at once of Hunt's strength and weakness. He has been, partly owing to circumstances, and partly to himself, little other than a glorious trifler. He has smiled, or lounged, or teased, or translated, away faculties which, with proper concentration and a perpetual view toward one single object, had been incalculably beneficial to the general progress of literature and of man.

Moore again seems made for trifling. It is his element. The window pane being his world, may we not call him the fly? His love is skin-deep; his anger, too, is a mere itch on the surface; his patriotism is easy, beginning and ending at the piano; his friendship all oozes out in a memoir of his departed friend; his hatred is exhausted in a single satire; and even his melody, while suiting the ivory keys of Lady Blessington's harpsichord, shrinks from the full diapason of the organ or the terrible unity of the fife; he has no powers which earnestness would much care to challenge as her own. Hunt, on the contrary, has put martial faculties upon perpetual parade—they have walked to and fro to beautiful music, but they have rarely mounted the breach, or even seen the enemy. This has not sprung either from the want of power or of courage, but from a kind of amiable ease of temperament, and, perhaps, also from a defect of constitutional stamina. A soul of fire has been yoked to a nervous and feeble constitution.

We can hardly charge the author of forty volumes with having written little, but, perhaps there is not one among all those volumes to which you can point as entirely worthy, and fully reflective, of the powers which are visible in all. Throughout them all you have a beautiful diffusion—over many of them hangs a certain weary languor—in some you are saluted with an explosion of wit like the crackers of a birth-night—and the others are full of a pensive poetry, tremulous with sentiment, and starred with the strangest and most expressive *epithets*. Heart, geniality, humanity, and genius pervade the whole.

Altogether, we cannot but look upon Hunt's present position as an enviable and fortunate one. He is in the evening of his days, but at evening time it is light with him; he has outlived many a struggle; he has survived a storm in which many larger ships were wrecked; he has not now a single enemy; his name is a household word throughout the world; his fame is dear to every lover of poetry and of liberty; the government of his country has appreciated and rewarded his services. Whatever of the fierce or bitter circumstances had infused into his mind has now been extracted. Above all, milder and juster views of Christianity, its claims and character, seem entering his mind. We will not, therefore, close by wishing him happiness—it is his, we trust, already—but by wishing him long life to enjoy the meek and bright sunset of his chequered and troublesome day.*

THOMAS MOORE.

To be the poet *par excellence* of Ireland, the cleverest man in the cleverest nation in the world, is to hold no mean position, and that position we claim for Thomas Moore. We do not of course mean that he is by many degrees the greatest poet at present alive; but for sparkle, wit, and brilliance, his country's qualities, he is unsurpassed. The bard of the butterflies, he is restless, gay, and gorgeous as the beautiful creatures he delights to depict. It would require his own style adequately to describe itself. Puck putting a girdle round about the globe in forty minutes—Ariel doing his spiriting gently—the Scotch fairy footing it in the moonlight, the stillness of which seems intended to set off the lively and aerial motion—any of these figures may faintly express to us the elegant activities of Moore's mind and fancy. We are never able to disconnect from his idea that of minuteness. Does he play in the "plighted clouds?" It is as a "creature of the element," as tiny as he is tricksy. . Does he flutter in the sunbeam? It is as a bright mote. Does he hover over the form and face of beauty? It is as a sylph-like sprite, his little heart surcharged and his small wings trembling with passion. Does he ever enter on a darker and more daring flight? It is still rather the flight of a fire-fly than of a meteor or a comet. Does he assail powers and potentates? It is with a sting rather than a spear—a sting small, sharp, bright, and deadly.

Thomas Moore is a poet by temperament, and by intellect a wit. He has the warmth and the fancy of the poet,

* We owe our readers an apology for the brief notices this article contains of authors elsewhere in the book characterized at large. They belonged to the article, and we could not prevail on ourselves to erase them.

It were needless to dilate upon the beauties which he has scattered around him in this unprofitable career. His fancy is prodigious in quantity and variety, and is as elegant as it is abundant. Images dance down about us like hailstones, illustrations breathlessly run after outrun illustrations, fine and delicate shades melt into others still finer and more delicate, and often the general effect of his verse is like that of a large tree alive with bees, where a thousand sweet and minute tones are mingled in one hum of harmony. Add to this his free flow of exquisite versification, the richness of his luscious descriptions, the tenderness of many of his pictures, and the sunny glow, as of eastern day, which colors the whole, and you have the leading features of his poetical idiosyncrasy.

But it is as a wit and a satirist that Moore must survive. There is no "horse play in his raillery." It is as delicate as it is deadly. He carves his foeman as a "dish fit for the gods, not hews him as a carcass meet for hounds." Such a gay gladiator, such a smiling murderer as he is! How small his weapon—how elegant his flourishes—how light but sinewy his arm—and how soon is the blow given—the deed done—the victim prostrate! His strokes are so keen that ere you have felt them you have found death. He is an aristocratic satirist not only in the objects but in the manner of his attack. Coarse game would not feel that fine tremulous edge by which he dissects his highbred and sensitive foes to the quick. We notice, too, in his sarcastic vein, and this very probably explains its superiority, a much deeper and heartier earnestness. When he means to be serious he trifles, when he trifles it is that he is most sincere. His work is play, his play is work. All his political feeling—all the moral indignation he possesses—all the hatred which as an Irishman and a gentleman he entertains for insincerity, humbug, and selfishness in high places—come out through the veil of his witty and elegant verse. Of a great satirist, only one element seems wanting in Moore, namely, that cool concentrated malignity which inspires Juvenal and Junius. He hates, they loathe. He tickles his opponent to death, they tear him to pieces. His arrows are polished, theirs are poisoned. His malice is that of a man, theirs is that of a demon. His wish is to gain a great end over the bodies of his antagonists, their sole object is to destroy or blacken the persons of their foes. His is a public and gallant rencounter, theirs a sullen and solitary assassination.

Moore may be regarded under the four phases of an amatory poet, a narrative poet, a satirical poet, and a prose writer. As an amatory poet he assumed, every one knows, the *nom-de-guerre* of Tommy Little, and as such do not his merits and demerits live in the verse of Byron and in the prose of Jeffrey? These poems, lively, gay, shallow, meretricious, were the sins of youth; they were not, like "Don Juan," the deliberate abominations of guilty and hardened manhood. Their object was to crown vice, but not to deny the existence of virtue. They were unjustifiably warm in their tone and coloring, but they did not seek to pollute the human heart itself. It was reserved for a mightier and darker spirit to make the desperate and infernal attempt, and to include in one "wide waft" of scorn and disbelief the existence of faithfulness in man and of innocence in woman. Little's lyrics, too, were neutralized by their general feebleness; they were pretty, but wanted body, unity, point, and power. Consequently, while they captivated idle lads and lovesick misses, they did comparatively little injury. It is indeed ludicrous, looking back through the vista of forty years, and thinking of the dire puddle and pother which such tiny transgressions produced among the critics and moralists of the time; they seem actually to have dreamed that the morality of Britain, which had survived the dramatists of Queen Elizabeth's day, the fouler fry of Charles II.'s playwrights, the novels of Fielding and Smollett, the numerous importations of iniquity from the Continent, was to fall below a few madrigals and double-entendres. No, like "dew-drops from the lion's mane," it shook them off, and pursued its way without impediment or pause. Whatever mischief was intended, little we are sure was done.

As a narrative poet, Moore aimed at higher things, and, so far as praise and popularity went, with triumphant success. His "Lalla Rookh" came forth amid a hum of general expectation. It was rumored that he had written a great epic poem; that Catullus had matured into Homer. These expectations were too sanguine to be realized. It was soon found that "Lalla Rookh" was no epic—was not a great poem at all—that it was only a short series of Oriental tales, connected by a slight but exquisite framework. Catullus, though stripped of many of his voluptuous graces, and much of his false and florid taste, remained Catullus still. And the greatest admirer of the splendid diction, the airy verse, the melodramatic incident, the lavish fancy of the poem, could not but say, if the comparison came upon his mind at all—"Ye critics, say how poor was this to Homer's style!" The unity, the compactness, the interest growing to a climax, the heroic story, the bare and grand simplicity of style—all the qualities we expect in the epic, were wanting in "Lalla Rookh." It was not so much a poem, indeed, as a rhymed romance. Still its popularity was instant and boundless. If it did not become a great, still, steadfast luminary in the heaven of song, it flashed before the eye of the world brief, beautiful, gorgeous, and frail—

"A tearless rainbow, such as span
The unclouded skies of Peristan."

And even yet, after the lapse of twenty years, there are many who, admiring the fine moral of "Paradise and the Peri," or melted by the delicate pathos of the "Fireworshippers," own the soft seductions of "Lalla Rookh," and in their hearts, if not in their understandings, prefer it to the chaster and more powerful poetry of the age.

The "Loves of the Angels" was a bolder but not a more successful flight. It was a tale of the "Arabian heaven;" and there is nothing certainly, in these wondrous "thousand and one nights," more rich, beautiful, and dream-like in its imagination and pathos, as in those impassioned stories. But it was only a castle in the clouds after all—one of those brilliant but fading pomps which the eye of the young dreamer sees "for ever flushing round a summer's sky." Its angels were mere winged dolls compared to the "celestial ardors" whom Milton has portrayed, or even to those proud and impassioned beings whom Byron has drawn. In fact, the poem was unfortunate in appearing about the same time with Byron's "Heaven and Earth," which many besides us consider his finest production as a piece of art. Mere atoms of the rainbow fluttering round were the pinions of Moore's angels compared to the mighty wings of those burning ones who came down over Ararat, drawn by the loadstars which shone in the eyes of the "daughters of men," and for which, without a sigh, they "lost eternity." And what comparison between the female characters in the one poem and the two whom we see in the other, waiting with uplifted eyes and clasped hands for the descent of their celestial lovers, like angels for the advent of angels? And what scene in Moore can be named beside the deluge in Byron; with the gloomy silence of suspense which precedes it—the earnest whispers heard among the hills at dead of night, which tell of its coming—the waters rising solemnly to their work of judgment, as if conscious of its justice and grandeur—the cries heard of despair, of fury, of blasphemy, as if the poet himself were drowning in the surge—the milder and softer wail of resignation mingling with the sterner exclamations—the ark in the distance—the lost angels clasping their lost loves, and ascending with them from the doom of the waters to what we feel and know must be a direr doom?

We have spoken already of Moore's character as a witty poet, and need only now refer to the titles of his principal humorous compositions, such as the "Fudge Family in Paris;" the "Twopenny Post-Bag;" "Cash, Corn Currency, and Catholics," &c. They constitute a perfect gallery of fun without ferocity, without indecency, and without more malice than serves to give them poignancy and point.

From Moore's "Life of Sheridan" we might almost fancy that, though he had lisped in numbers, and early obtained a perfect command of the language and versification of poetry, yet that he was only beginning, or had but recently begun to write prose. The juvenility, the immaturity, the false glare, the load of useless figure, the ambition and effort of that production, are amazing in such a man at such an age. It contains, of course, much fine and forcible writing; but even Sheridan himself, in his most ornate and adventurous prose, which was invariably his worst, is never more unsuccessful than is sometimes his biographer. Perhaps it was but fitting that the life of such a heartless, faithless, though brilliant charlatan, should be written in a style of elaborate falsetto and fudge.

We have a very different opinion indeed of his "Life of

Byron." It is not, we fear, a faithful or an honest record of that miserable and guilty mistake—the life of Byron. We have heard that Dr. MacGinn, by no means a squeamish man, who was at first employed by Murray to write his biography, and had the materials put into his hands, refused, shrinking back disgusted at the masses of falsehood, treachery, heartlessness, malignity, and pollution which they revealed. The same materials were submitted to Moore, and from them he has constructed an image of his hero, bearing, we suspect, as correct a resemblance to his character as the ideal busts which abound do to his face. When will biographers learn that their business, their sole business, is to tell the truth or to be silent? How long will the public continue to be deceived by such gilded falsehoods as form the staple of obituaries and memoirs? It is high time that such were confined to the corners of newspapers and of churchyards. We like Moore's "Byron," not for its subject or its moral tone, but solely for its literary execution. It is written throughout in a clear, chaste, dignified and manly manner; the criticism it contains is eloquent and discriminating, and the friendship it discovers for Byron, if genuine, speaks much for its author's generosity and heart.

We must not speak of his other prose productions—his "Epicurean," "History of Ireland," &c. The wittiest thing of his in prose we have read is an article in the "Edinburgh Review" on "Boyd's Lives of the Fatherr," where, as in Gibbon, jests lurk under loads of learning, double-entendres disguise themselves in Greek, puns mount and crackle upon the backs of huge folios, and where you are at a loss whether most to chuckle at the wit, to detest the animus, or to admire the erudition.

We had nearly omitted, which had been unpardonable, all mention of the "Irish Melodies"—those sweet and luscious strains which have hushed ten thousand drawing-rooms and drawn millions of such tears as drawing-rooms shed, but which have seldom won their way to the breasts of simple unsophisticated humanity—which are to the songs of Burns what the lute is to the linnet—and which, in their title, are thus far unfortunate that, however melodious, they are not the melodies of Ireland. It was not Moore but Campbell who wrote "Erin Mavourneen." "He," says

Hazlitt, "has changed the wild harp of Erin into a musical snuff-box."

Such is our ideal of Thomas Moore. If it do not come up to the estimate of some of his admirers, it is faithful to our own impressions, and what more from a critic can be required? We only add, that admired by many as a poet, by all as a wit, he is as a man the object of universal regard; and we believe there is not one who knows him but would be ready to join in the words—

> "Were it the last drop in the well,
> 'Tis to thee that I would drink;
> In that water as this wine,
> The libation I would pour
> Would be peace to thee and thine,
> And a health to thee, Tom Moore."

ISAAC TAYLOR.

Christianity has been much indebted to its lay supporters and defenders. Without professing to give a complete list of the illustrious laymen who have either advocated its evidences or expounded its doctrines, we may simply remind the reader of the names of Milton, Newton, Boyle, Locke, Addison, Lord Lyttelton, Charles Leslie, Soame Jenyns, Dr. Johnson, and Cowper, which belong to other ages than the present; while, as respects our own times, it may be enough to mention Coleridge, Southey, Douglas of Cavers, Robert Ainslie, Thomas Erskine of Linlathan, Bowdler, Wilberforce, and Isaac Taylor. Of this latter list, Coleridge, partly in his other writings, but chiefly in his "Table-talk," illustrated the general and more remote bearings of Christianity, the points where it touches upon the other sciences. Southey has stood up bravely for its external bulwarks, and exemplified its consistent morals. Douglas, to use the language of another, "eagle-eyed and eloquent, has anticipated time, and, surveying the world, has laid down the laws of general amelioration." Ainslie has broken down the great leading principles of religion into simple, portable, and pathetic forms, and from the "strong" has educed "sweetness." Erskine has admirably expounded the internal evidences of Christianity. Bowdler has strewn chaste flowers and Addisonian graces around its softer and more spiritual aspects. Wilberforce has laid bare its deep practical bearings. And Isaac Taylor has applied to the exposure of its corruptions and counterfeits, the vigor of a more original genius, and the splendor of a richer, more varied, and more dazzling eloquence, as well as entered with a firm yet gentle tread on some of its more mysterious provinces.

Isaac Taylor styles himself in the title of one of his own chapters, the "Recluse." He has long ago retired from the world into the sanctuary of his own family and his own soul. There aloft, but not aloof—apart, but not askance—separate, but not utterly secluded—regarding the distant crowd more in sorrow than in anger, and more in love than in sorrow—he passes the "noiseless tenor" of his serene and busy days. "He hears the tumult and is still." His mind dwells habitually in a lone and lofty sphere. The cell of his soul is curiously constructed, elaborately adorned, hung with antique tapestry, decked with the rich paintings of the past, and steeped through its gorgeous windows in a dim religious light. There seated, he now muses with half-shut eye upon the history of bygone ages—now erects himself to lift the large folios of the fathers—now swells with righteous indignation as he remembers the corruption and degeneracy which so soon and so long supplanted the first faith and love of the primitive age—now analyzes the palpitating heart of the enthusiast, and now turns to the sterner task of baring the flinty spirit of fanaticism—now maps out the future history of the church and world—and now sinks into sublime reverie, and in the trance of genius sees

> "Hell, hades, heaven—the eternal how and where—
> The glory of the dead, and their despair."

The leading power of Taylor's mind is not argument, though he reasons often acutely and energetically—nor is it imagination, though he has much of this faculty too —nor is it original and native thought, though he strikes out many sparkles of intuition on his way—nor is it eloquence, though his words are often quick and powerful: it is meditation—that refined action of the mind which is softer than ratiocination, more sublime than thought, calmer than passion, and cooler than genius. He is inspired, not by the muses nor by the furies—is neither full of the demon nor of the god; but above him hangs the "cherub Contemplation," and over him broods for ever her still but radiant wing. He evidently emulates that serene motion, or rather, rest of intellect, in which Plato, under the skies of Greece, rejoiced, and which, beneath the profounder firmament of Palestine, "unloosed its golden couplets" over the head of the Essenes and the earlier Christian mystics. While keenly alive to, and indignant at, the errors and abuses of mysticism, he has very strong sympathies with its better spirit—with its voluntary solitude—its abnegation of self—its habits of still, spiritual communion with its own soul, and with the works and word of God. He is, above most modern writers, an orientalist. That "land of the east—that clime of the sun," is the country of his adoption. His learning has been collected in the gardens of eastern literature. His imagination has an oriental vastness and brilliancy npon its wings, and he strings his sentences with "orient pearl." His style, too, seems dyed in the colors of a hotter sun than that of his native land. His views of divine truth, often clear and definite, not unfrequently shade away into the dim, the unformed, and the obscure—into "regions where light glances at an angle only, without diffusing itself over the whole surface." He loves to linger, and it is only a stern sense of duty which prevents him from lingering always, in the dubious and debatable tracts which surround the clear and firm territory of Scripture truth. His piety, too, is peculiar. Though true and sound, it is not the simple, fervid devotion of his father or sister. It is more that of the burning seraph than of the kneeling saint; it is the rapt contemplation of the divine attributes, rather than the awful abasement of a spirit overwhelmed in the view of its own guilt and misery. Blended, however, with this native tendency toward the lofty, the enthusiastic, and the dangerous realms of speculation—a tendency fostered, besides, by the course of his studies and the circumstances of his lot—there are counteracting and balancing elements in his mind, habits of deep submission to the divine testimony, a strong basis of solid judgment and varied knowledge, a distinct though not very deep vein of sarcastic observation, added to all the advantages which natural good sense must ever derive from English blood, birth, and training.

It is a curious fact in literary history, that many writers have surpassed themselves, both in power and popularity, while writing under the shelter of the anonymous. Swift's "Tale of a Tub," which he never acknowledged, so far surpasses his other writings in fertility of invention, richness of humor, and force of style, that Dr. Johnson refused to believe it his. Junius was strong only within the circle of that mysterious shadow which even yet rests on his name. Pascal's "Provincial Letters," the best of his works, were issued anonymously. So were those of Peter Plymley. The admirable newspaper criticisms of "Jonathan," and the eloquent diatribes of O. P. Q., owed not a little of their zest to the obscurity which rested on the names of the authors. Even the Waverley tales lost nothing from the doubt in which their authorship was for a season involved. We cannot tell how much of their power reviewers owe to their position—how much the masking adds to the momentum of their battery. And within a twelvemonth we have witnessed a book, written indeed in an easy and agreeable style, but developing an absurd theory, and swarming with blunders (the "Vestiges of the Natural History of Creation"), rising into popularity upon the twin wings of the mischief of its intention and the mystery of its authorship. Whether this be owing to the greater liberty an anonymous writer enjoys—to the ideal position which, projected as it were out of himself, he for a season occupies—or to the twofold effect of mystification, in stimulating the mind of the writer and provoking the curiosity of the reader—we do not stop to inquire. And perhaps it was in order to take advantage of this principle, that the subject of the present sketch, after having to little purpose wooed the attention of the world in *propria persona*, determined to disguise himself, and walked forth at length in the graceful mask of the author of the "Natural History of Enthusiasm." The issue justified his most sanguine hopes of success. The book was fortunate in the time of its appearance. It came forth when the rage of Rowism and Irvingism was at its height—when in every corner of the land, our old men, and women too, were seeing visions, and our young men and maidens were dreaming dreams. To analyze the subtle steam of enthusiasm when it was rushing from the boiler—to detect and expose its distinct proportions of false and true—was an attempt daring, hazardous, but useful, and loudly demanded by the urgencies of the time. It required, too, peculiar qualifications, which seemed all possessed by the anonymous author: learning—he was manifestly a ripe and good scholar; piety—his work glowed with it; eloquence—it heaved in every sentence; a vantage-ground lifting him above sectarian bias—the most acute were unable to tell to what denomination he belonged; soundness of religious sentiment—the strain of the whole work was strictly evangelical; and last, not least, a sympathy with true enthusiasm, while he exposed and reprobated the false—and the book was no cold analysis, no stern and callous anatomy. The work, besides, was written in an elaborate and ornate style; and though some of the more fastidious objected to its taste, and some of the more lynx-eyed detected marks of a manner affected and a diction studiously disguised, yet, on the whole, the exclamation of the Christian church was—"Behold, a master risen in Israel!" And straightway the question rose and ran, "Who is he?" Some bethought themselves of Douglas of Cavers as the probable author, in despite of the most marked difference in sentiment, style, manner, and cast of thought. Others, even less acute, fancied that here was Foster shaking off his giant sleep, and arising a new man—a new man indeed—with a new intellect, a new learning, a new temperament, and a new vocabulary. In certain circles, there were frequent rumors of some great Christian unknown—some gentler Junius—some wondrous young Titan—who was to astonish, if not revolutionize the religious world. And if here and there a solitary finger pointed to the "Recluse" of Stamford Rivers as the real author, the scornful rejoinder was, "What has he done hitherto—what proportion is there between the 'Elements of Thought' and the 'History of Enthusiasm?' Such a lion-like man of God could never have issued from the still parsonage of Ongar." Popular meanwhile the book became, particularly among students, who did their best to imitate its style, or with greater success to imbibe its spirit. Its main leading proposition, that the difference between true and false enthusiasm is a difference of kind, not of degree—its rich and racy illustration—its familiarity with the primitive and darker ages of the Church—its grand insulated pictures, as of the Romish hierarchy and the monastic system—its cheerful, sanguine, religious spirit—the rose-colored glow which rested on its every page—and not less, with some, its blazing faults and deliberate innovations of language—were among the elements of its first success; and even yet, we believe, in popular estimation, retain it at the head of its author's works.

Dearer to us, however, we confess, is his second work, the "Saturday Evening." It is a series of sublime meditations, bound together by a certain shadowy tie, involving a multitude of topics nearest and dearest to the author's heart, and tinged with the sweet and solemn hues of the approaching Sabbath. "Dreams" they will be, they have been called by the skeptical and the cold; but such an epithet, while it fails fully to express, fails entirely to damage their character. They open up, to the pious and imaginative, tracts of thought, like golden furrows in an evening sea, or like those glorious vistas which endlessly expand in an evening heaven. They are dreams, but dreams of night, of heaven, of immensity, and eternity; and if the dream be there, the ladder whose top reached unto the sky is not far off. Philosophical views of the present and of the past are not wanting; but the mind of the contemplatist is perpetually, as if on the wings of the evening, borne away up through the wilderness of worlds above his head—or on to those bright pages of the earth's story which remain to be read—or in amid the starry circles of the heavenly hosts—nay, at times, a step or two, but no more, up towards

> "The sapphire throne—the living blaze,
> Where angels tremble as they gaze."

And yet, from the most daring of his excursions, he returns undazzled, and with lessons of practical truth, to his native homestead of earth. We like especially his glimpses of the coming Sabbath of the world, which, like a red western heaven seen through trees, perpetually interposes its splendid boundary to the stages of his thought. Next to this, we like his "Vastness of the Material Creation," where to "him the book of night is opened wide"—and where he finds that a page thick with suns is not more true or glorious than one leaf of his Bible, where "voices from the depths of space proclaim a marvel and a secret;" but he discovers the marvel to be the old mystery of godliness, the secret to be only that of the Lord, which "is with them that fear him."

By a strange association, this book of "Saturday Evening" suggests to us the Saturday papers of the "Spectator." They are "alike, but oh, how different!" Their subjects are the same; night, the stars, immortality, God, and heaven. But since Addison's time, how much nearer have the stars approached! and yet, in another sense, how much farther off have they receded! At what a ratio of more than geometric increase has the universe been multiplying to our eyes! And with regard to the other topics, in what deeper channels do the modern's thoughts flow than those of the gentle "Spectator!" Their language is the same; but how different the classic coolness, the careless but inimitable graces, the modest but inestimable ornaments, the ease and sweet simplicity of Addison's English, from the feverish heat and the rich tropical exuberance of Taylor's! Their religion is the same; but how different the faint though true glow of Christianity in Addison's page from that seraphic flame which burns in Taylor's! In what different ages written! The one a low and languid age—feeble in faith, feebler in love, feeblest of all in hope—in which Addison's sanctified genius shines as a sweet solitary star; the other a "juncture of eras"—a period of bustle, and heat, and hope, and progress, and anxious uncertainty, and listening silence; for do not all men expect, sooner or later, the crisis of the earth to be coming—and do not "all creatures sigh to be renewed?"

We must permit ourselves a few observations upon "Fanaticism" and the "Physical Theory of a Future Life." "Fanaticism" was unfortunate in its subject. From the black and malevolent passions, even when portrayed by the hand of a master, men in general shrink. To dissect deformity is a thankless task. And although it is said that the laws of disease are as beautiful as those of health, yet few have the patience or courage to wait till they are initiated in to that terrible kind of beauty. Fanaticism, also, was a topic too like enthusiasm to be susceptible of much novelty in the mode of treatment. And here and there you could detect traces of that mannerism, and self-imitation which betray in authors their fear at least that their vein is nearly exhausted —a fear reminding us of the reluctance of the mariner to take soundings in a suspected shallow. The style too had not improved from the date of his former work, nay, it bore marks of great effort, was uneven and uneasy, and sinned often against the laws of clearness, simplicity, and good taste. Something of the cloudy character of the theme seemed to have infected the writer; and the language was swollen, as if under the "fanaticism of the scourge." Still the book had bold bursts and splendid sweeping pictures; and it were worth while contrasting its estimate of Mahometanism with that of Carlyle, and wondering by what strange possibility a system which appears to the one a vast and virulent ulcer should appear to the other a needful volcano, and through what transfiguring magic Mahomet the monster of the one becomes Mahomet the hero of the other.

We hinted a little before, that there was in Taylor's mind a strong but subdued tendency toward the mystic and supernatural. In all his works, he seems standing on the confines of the spiritual world, leaning over the great precipice, and, with beseeching looks, essaying to commune with the tremendous secrets of the final state. Entirely satisfied with the declarations of Scripture, that there is immortality for man, he yet must "ask that dreadful question at the hills which look eternal"—at the streams which "lucid flow for ever"—at the stars, those bright and pure watchers—at the deepest metaphysics of the human mind—and find in them something more than a faltering perhaps, in addition to the loud, confident, and commanding, "Thus saith the Lord." Nay, in the "Physical Theory of Another Life," he fairly bursts across the barriers, enters like a "permitted guest" within the mighty curtain which divides the living and the dead, and with infinite ingenuity maps out the dim provinces and expounds the mysterious conditions of that strange world. The intention of the work has been often misapprehended. It is no dogmatic dream, like the visions of Swedenborg—no "rushing in where angels fear to tread." Nor is it the more mechanical fancy disporting itself on the theme, as in the reveries of Tucker (to whom Taylor, however, is considerably indebted;) it is a long philosophical, modest and earnest conjecture—a trial, as it were, how far the human mind can go in that shadowy direction, and how far it is possible, by combining psychological principles with Scripture hints, to build up a probable and lifelike scheme of the future existence. How far he has been successful in this attempt we shall, of course, never know till we enter on that solemn state ourselves. But, in the mean time, it is curious to think of this writer's spirit, from the height of eternity, looking back and comparing the continent of glory he has reached with the meagre yet memorable map he drew of it, in the infancy of his being. And yet more curious it were to imagine an actual denizen of that sublime world smiling a gentle smile over this effort of the unborn child to conceive of the green earth, the gay sun, and the ever burning stars!

The reader would be richly rewarded who should sit down and compare the Visions of heaven and hell ascribed to Bunyan with Taylor's theory of a future life. Both are rich, eloquent, and imaginative dreams—but how different in spirit, manner, style, and scientific construction! Between the two, what an interval has the religious mind traversed! What a difference between the "melted gold" and coarse material torments of the one author, and Ariel-like agonies of Taylor's supposed spirit, thrust out naked amid the quick agencies of an angry universe, where the silent night surrounds it as in a sea of fire, and where, through a thousand avenues, rushes in upon it the wrath of Heaven. And yet the author of these visions (Bunyan he certainly was not) was not only a man of high genius, as some magnificent passages prove, but a thorough scholar; for its frequent literary allusions and use of scholastic terms sufficiently evince that he was quite up to, if not before, the spirit and learning of his times. How little, after all, do the revolutions of time and the advancement of the human mind add to our real knowledge, however they may modify our feelings and language, in respect to the awful futurity before us! The path of human progress, on one side so free and boundless, on another is soon met by its uttermost confine on earth, as by a wall of black, solid, and frowning marble!

Isaac Taylor is, as before hinted, of "virtuous father, virtuous son." The praise of Taylor of Ongar was in "all the churches." His daughter, Jane Taylor, a woman of a highly cultivated and most feminine intellect, authoress of several well known works, has long been dead. Isaac, at first designed for the Dissenting pulpit, became a barrister in preference, but has for many years resided in retirement at Stamford Rivers, educating his family, and prosecuting his own delightful and holy studies. A writer in the "Edinburgh Review" has given a description of his early feelings and his present habits of life, displaying at once the warmth of personal friendship and the sympathy of kindred intellect and kindred sentiments. We learn with interest from it, that Taylor is an expert and eager angler as well as the far-famed author of the "Natural History of Enthusiasm;" that he spends his Saturday mornings in directing the sports of his dear children; while his Saturday evenings are devoted to the loftiest meditations which can engross the soul of mortal. He is, moreover, a person of animated bearing, brilliant eye, and incessant and eloquent talk. Altogether, we deem him among the most accomplished of modern religious authors, and heartily wish him life and strength to fulfil that great work of his life, from which the tractarian controversy has for a season drawn him aside—the history of the various corruptions of Christianity, which, if worthily completed, as it has been worthily commenced, shall more assuredly and honorably preserve his name, "than though a pyramid formed his monumental fane."

HENRY WADSWORTH LONGFELLOW.

America has been long looking for its Poet, and has been taught by many sages to believe, that hitherto it has been looking in vain. Each new aspirant to the laurel has been scanned with a watchfulness and jealousy, proportioned to the height of expectation which had been excited, and to the length of time during which that expectation has been deferred; and because the risen Poet did not supply the vacuum of centuries—did not clear all the space by which Britain had got the start of her daughter—did not include in his single self the essence of Shakspeare, Spenser, Milton, and Byron—his genius was pronounced a failure, and his works naught. Tests were proposed to him, from which our home authors would have recoiled. Originalities were demanded of him, which few of ourselves, in this imitative age, have been able to exemplify. As in Macbeth, not the "child's," but the "armed head" was expected to rise first from the vacant abyss. American literature must walk before creeping, and fly before walking. Not unfrequently, our British journals contained programmes of the genius and writings of the anticipated Poet, differing not more from common sense, than from each other. "He must be intensely national," said one authority. "He must be broadly Catholic—of no country," said a second. "He must be profoundly meditative, as his own solitary woods," said a third. "He must be bustling, rapid, and fiery as his own railways," said a fourth. One sighed for an American Milton; another predicted the uprise of another Goethe, "Giant of the Western Star;" and a third modestly confined his wishes within the compass of a second Shakspeare.

Pernicious as, in some measure, such inordinate expectations must have proved to all timid and vacillating minds in America, it did not prevent its bolder and more earnest spirits from taking their own way,—by grafting, upon the stock of imported poetry, many graceful and lovely shoots of native song. In spite of the penumbra of prejudice against American verse, more fugitive floating poetry of real merit exists in its literature than in almost any other. Dana has united many of the qualities of Crabbe to a portion of the weird and haggard power of Coleridge's muse Percival has recalled Wordsworth to our minds, by the pensive and tremulous depth of his strains. Bryant, without a trace of imitation, has become the American Campbell, equally select, simple, chary, and memorable. In reply to Mrs. Hemans, have been uttered a perfect chorus of voices—

"Sweet and melancholy sounds,
Like music on the waters."

Emerson has poured forth notes, sweet now as the murmur of bees, and now strong as the roar of torrents; here cheerful as the pipings of Arcadia, and there mournfully melodious as the groans of Ariel, from the centre of his cloven pine. And with a voice of wide compass, clear articulation, and most musical tones, has Longfellow sung his manifold and melting numbers.

The distinguishing qualities of Longfellow seem to be beauty of imagination, delicacy of taste, wide sympathy, and mild earnestness, expressing themselves sometimes in forms of quaint and fantastic fancy, but always in chaste and simple language. His imagination sympathizes more with the correct, the classical, and the refined, than with that outer and sterner world, where dwell the dreary, the rude, the fierce, and the terrible shapes of things. The scenery he describes best is the storied richness of the Rhine, or the golden glories of the Indian summer, or the environs of the old Nova Scotian village, or the wide billowing prairie; and not those vast forests, where a path for the sunbeams must be hewn, nor those wildernesses of snow, where the storm and the wing of the condor divide the sovereignty. In the midst of such dreadful solitudes, his genius rather shivers and cowers, than rises and reigns. He is a spirit of the Beautiful, more than of the Sublime; he has lain on the lap of Loveliness, and not been dandled, like a lion-cub, on the knees of Terror. The magic he wields, though soft, is true and strong. If not a prophet, torn by a secret burden, and uttering it in wild, tumultuous strains, he is a genuine poet, who has sought for, and found inspiration, now in the story and scenery of his own country, and now in the lays and legends of other lands, whose native vein, in itself exquisite, has been highly cultivated and delicately cherished.

It is to us a proof of Longfellow's originality, that he bears so well and meekly his load of accomplishments and acquirements. His ornaments, unlike those of the Sabine maid, have not crushed him, nor impeded the motions of his own mind. He has transmuted a lore, gathered from many languages, into a quick and rich flame, which we feel to be the flame of Genius.

It is evident that his principal obligations are due to German literature, which over him, as over so many at the present day, exerts a certain wild witchery, and is tasted with all the sweetness of the forbidden fruit. No writer in America has more steeped his soul in the spirit of German poetry, its blended homeliness and romance, its simplicity and fantastic emphasis, than Longfellow. And if he does not often trust himself amidst the weltering chaos of its philosophers, you see him, lured by their fascination, hanging over their brink, and rapt in wonder at their strange, gigantic, and ever-shifting forms. Indeed his "Hyperion" contains two or three most exquisite bits of transcendentalism.

Longfellow is rather a romantic and sentimental, than a philosophical poet. He throws into verse the feelings, moods, and fancies of the young or female mind of genius, not the mature cogitations of profound philosophy. His song is woven of moonlight, not of strong summer sunshine. To glorify abstractions, to flush clear naked truth into beauty, to "build" up poems slowly and solidly, as though he were piling pyramids, is neither his aim nor his attainment. He gathers, on the contrary, roses and lilies,—the roses of the hedge and lilies of the field, as well as those of the garden,—and wreathes them into chaplets for the brow and neck of the beautiful. His poetry is that of sentiment, rather than of thought. But the sentiment is never false, nor strained, nor mawkish. It is always mild, generally manly, and sometimes it approaches the sublime. It touches both the female part of man's mind and the masculine part of woman's. He can at one time start unwonted tears in the eyes of men, and at another kindle on the cheeks of women a glorious glow of emotion, which the term *blush* cannot adequately measure; as far superior to it as is the splendor of a sunset to the bloom of a peach.

We have been struck with the variety of Longfellow's poems. He has written hitherto no large, recondite work. His poems are all short—effusions, not efforts. He has exhibited no traces of a comic vein. His sphere is that of sentiment, moralizing elegantly upon many objects. And yet within that sphere there is little mannerism, repetition, or self-imitation. His sentiment assumes a great variety of aspects. Now it is tender to tears, and now heroic to daring;

now it muses, and now it dreams; now it is a reverie, and now a rapture; now it is an allegory, now a psalm, and again a song; every thing, in short, save a monotony. Nor is this the many-sidedness of a mocking-bird. The sentiment of the varied song, as well as the song of the varied sentiment, is ever *his own*.

One of the most pleasing characteristics of this writer's works is their intense humanity. A man's heart beats in his every line. His writings all

> "Take a sober color from the eye
> That hath kept watch o'er man's mortality."

He loves, pities, and feels with, as well as for, his fellow "human mortal." Hence his writing is blood-warm. He is a brother, speaking to men as brothers, and as brothers are they responding to his voice. Byron addressed men as reptiles or fiends; Wordsworth and others soliloquize, careless whether their voice be listened to or not. But no poet can be loved, as well as admired, who does not speak from the broad level of humanity. If we dare apply the language, "he must be touched with a fellow-feeling of our infirmities, and have been tempted in all points as we are." He must have fallen and risen, been sick and sad, been joyful and pensive, drank of the full cup of man's lot, ere he can so write that man will take his writings to his heart, and appropriate them as part of the great general human stock. A prophet may wrap himself up in austere and mysterious solitude; a poet must come "eating and drinking." Thus came Shakspeare, Dryden, Burns, Scott, Goethe; and thus have come in our day Dickens, Hood, and Longfellow.

Besides this quality of generous, genial manhood, Longfellow is distinguished by a mild religious earnestness. We do not vouch for the orthodoxy of his creed, but we do vouch for the fine Christianity of his spirit. No poet has more beautifully expressed the depth of his conviction, that life is an earnest reality—a something with eternal issues and dependencies; that this earth is no scene of revelry, or market of sale, but an arena of contest, and a hall of doom. This is the inspiration of his "Psalm of Life," than which we have few things finer, in moral tone, since those odes by which the millions of Israel tuned their march across the wilderness, and to which the fiery pillar seemed to listen with com placency, and to glow out a deeper crimson in silent praise. To man's now wilder, more straggling, but still God-guided and hopeful progress towards a land of fairer promise, Longfellow's "Psalm" is a noble accompaniment:

"Life is real! Life is earnest!
And the grave is not its goal;
'Dust thou art, to dust returnest,'
Was not spoken of the soul.

Not enjoyment, and not sorrow,
Is our destined end or way;
But to act, that each to-morrow
Find us farther than to-day.

In the world's broad field of battle,
In the bivouac of Life,
Be not like dumb, driven cattle!
Be a hero in the strife!

Trust no Future, howe'er pleasant!
Let the dead Past bury its dead!
Act—act in the living Present!
Heart within, and God o'erhead!

Lives of great men all remind us
We can make our lives sublime,
And, departing, leave behind us
Footprints on the sands of time,—

Footprints, that perhaps another,
Sailing o'er life's solemn main,
A forlorn and shipwrecked brother,
Seeing, shall take heart again.

Let us, then, be up and doing,
With a heart for any fate;
Still achieving, still pursuing,
Learn to labor, and to wait."

Glancing again critically at Longfellow's poems, we find that his genius is essentially lyrical. Neither the severity of epic power nor the subtlety of the dramatic genius are his. But how swiftly and surely does he respond to those passing impulses which come upon his soul, like winds from the forest, and which, like sudden gusts, are brief, musical,—now swelling into high rapture, and now dying away in tremulous pathos! Mrs. Hemans and Sir Walter Scott once coincided in remarking, that each tree gives forth a peculiar cadence to the wind; and we have ourselves noticed, that from the willow there issues a dry, hissing *eery* sound; from the sycamore a full murmur, as if the tree were one vast bee-hive; from the pine a deep, mellow, lingering tone, as though each cone were an ivory key; and from the oak a strong, sturdy, reluctant rustle, as if it were an unwilling instrument in the hand of the blast. Thus do Longfellow's finer poems play themselves off upon the autumn trees of the Western forest, as upon harps of gold—one being sad and stern—another quiet and full, as of many murmurs rounded into one calm—a third, soft and long-drawn—and a fourth, rough, abrupt, and tormented into music.

Ere speaking of some of his poems in detail, we must permit ourselves a word on the only prose work of his with which we are acquainted—"Hyperion." We shall never forget the circumstances of its first perusal. We took it as our pocket companion with us, on our first walk down the Tweed, by Peebles, Inverleithen, Clovenford, Ashestiel, and Abbotsford. It was fine, at any special bend of the stream, or any beautiful spot along its brink, taking it out, and finding in it a conductor to our own surcharged emotions. In our solitude we felt "we are not alone, for these pages can sympathize with us." The course of "Hyperion," indeed, is that of a river, winding at its own sweet will,—now laughing and singing to itself, in its sparkling progress, and now slumbering in still deep pools,—here laving cornfields and vineyards, and there lost in wooded and sounding glens. Interest it has much—incident, little; its charm is partly in the "Excelsior" progress of the hero's mind, partly in the sketches of the Great German authors, and principally in the sparkling imagery and waving, billowy language of the book. Longfellow, in this work, is Jean Paul Richter, without his grotesque extravagances, or riotous humor, or turbulent force. He seems a lesser and more simple form of the same genus, sprung from him, as the elephant from the mammoth.

We have just alluded to "Excelsior," one of those happy thoughts which seem to drop down, like fine days, from some serener region, or, like moultings of the celestial dove, which meet instantly the ideal of all minds, and run on afterwards, and for ever, in the current of the human heart. We can now no more conceive of a world without "Excelsior," than of a world without the "Iliad," the "Comus," or the "Midsummer Night's Dream." It has expressed in the happiest and briefest way what many minds in the age had been trying in vain to express. Thousands, therefore, were ready to cry out, "That's my thought; that's my desire; that's myself; I bear that banner; I fear not to die that death!" "Excelsior" is the Ledyard of intellectual travellers. He typifies all that is heroic, and high, and disinterested in the age. "Excelsior!" cries the student, as he climbs the steep ascent of science. "Excelsior!" cries the poet, who takes up Parnassus as but a little thing. "Excelsior!" cries the thinker; "I have passed the transcendental, let me have at the divine." "Excelsior!" cries the liver; let me reach virtue, not merely as a law, but as a life." "Excelsior!" cries every where the young time; "let us onward and up ward, though it be into the regions of the storm; we are weary of the past, let us try what the future will do for us." "Excelsior!" cry the dying, who feel that death is but a door into the infinite; "let us up and breathe the atmosphere of the stars." More than one brave spirit has departed singing this noble battle-burst of "Excelsior!"

"Excelsior" is Life and its Psalm *personified.* Longfellow has written in it his glowing hopes of the future, as well as his theory of the past. That figure, climbing the evening Alps, in defiance of danger, of man's remonstrance, and the far deeper fascination of woman's love, is a type of man struggling, triumphing, purified by suffering, perfected in death. And it insinuates strongly the poet's belief in that coming era in human history, when the worth and grandeur of man's regenerated *life* will cast a calm and beauty, at present inconceivable, around his *death*, and when the roses and chaplets and premature rejoicings of his bridal, shall more worthily await his marriage with the infinite. Who pants and prays not for the arrival of such a day, when the sting of death shall thus be taken out—when its grand meaning and porch-like position shall be fully disclosed and vividly realized?

Next to "Excelsior," and the "Psalm of Life," we are

disposed to rank "Evangeline." Indeed, as a work of art, it is superior to both, and to all that Longfellow has written in verse. Save "Hyperion" it is his *only* piece of pure and elaborate art. We began to read it under a certain degree of prejudice at the measure, which has been so vulgarized by Southey, in his lamentable "Vision of Judgment." But soon Southey, "Vision of Judgment," and all were forgotten. Acadia—Arcadia it might be called—and the sweet moonlight of Evangeline's face, crowded the whole sky of our imagination. Nothing can be more truly conceived, or more tenderly expressed, than the picture of that primitive Nova Scotia, and its warm-hearted, hospitable, happy, and pious inhabitants. We feel the air of the "Fore-world" around us. The light of the Golden Age,—itself joy, music, and poetry,—is shining above. There are evenings of summer or autumn tide so exquisitely beautiful, so complete in their own charms, that the entrance of the moon is felt almost as a painful and superfluous addition; it is like a candle dispelling the weird darkness of a twilight room. So we feel at first, as if Evangeline, when introduced, were an excess of loveliness—an amiable eclipser of the surrounding beauties. But even as the moon, by and by, vindicates her intrusion, and creates her own "holier day," so with the delicate and lovely heroine of this simple story—she becomes the centre of the entire scene. She is that noblest of characters, a *lady in grain.* She has borrowed her motions and attitudes from the wind-bent trees; her looks have kindled at the stars; her steps she has unwittingly learned from the moving shadows of the clouds. On her way home from confession, "when she had passed, it seemed like the ceasing of exquisite music." Thus should all lives be led, all steps be tuned; and thus they shall, whenever Love, instead of Law, shall lead the great dance of human life. Purest of virgins, art thou to be sacrificed! Finest of vessels, art thou to be dashed in pieces! It seems almost cruel in the poet to try her so painfully, and to send her to seek her sole redress in heaven.

We think every reader must feel that the first part of "Evangeline" is far superior to the second. Evangeline's search after her lover is beautifully described, but becomes at last oppressive and painful. We cry out, in our sorrow and disappointment, for Acadia, with its crowing cocks, bursting barns, flowery meadows, and happy hearts back again.

The descriptions of American scenery in "Evangeline" are in general extremely picturesque and beautiful. Witness this for example:—

"Now had the season returned, when the nights grew colder and longer,
And the retreating Sun the sign of the Scorpion enters;
Birds of passage sail'd through the leaden air from the icebound
Desolate northern bays, to the shores of the tropical islands.
Harvests were gathered in; and, wild with the winds of September,
Wrestled the trees of the forest, as *Jacob of old with the angel.*"

The picture of the Indian summer is finer still, with the exception of the conceit with which it closes:—

"Array'd in its robes of russet, and scarlet, and yellow;
Bright with the sheen of the dew, each glittering tree of the forest
Flash'd like the *plane-tree the Persian adorned with mantles and jewels.*"

This last line contains a poor and forced memory. What an injury to the glorious forest-tree to compare it to the foolish and contemptible freak referred to. The simile is alike far-fetched and worthless. "I say unto you, that Solomon, in all his glory, was not arrayed like one of these."

By a similar conceit (a mode of writing quite unusual with him) has he spoiled one of his finest passages:—

"Meanwhile apart in the twilight gloom of a window's embrasure,
Sat the lovers, and whispering together, beholding the moon rise
Over the pallid sea, and the silvery mist of the meadows,
Silently, one by one, in the infinite meadows of heaven,
Blossom'd the lovely stars, the *forget-me-nots of the angels.*"

Next to the spectacle of a man destroying a noble constitution, or marring fine faculties, is that of an author deliberately spoiling a passage which otherwise had touched or trembled on perfection. It is a case of literary *felo de se.* What business had the idea of a forget-me-not at such a moment. Gabriel Lajeunesse himself, we are certain, enamored as he was, and even in that most imaginative hour, never could dream of seeing an angel with a knot of stars on his breast while visiting his true love.

Such faults are rare in this writer. Once or twice, indeed, he approaches the brink of the bathos, and snatches one of those few, perilous, and precious flowers which bloom along it. Thus, in "Hyperion," he compares a glacier to a gauntlet of ice, thrown down by winter, in defiance of the sun; a thought so beautiful, that you forget the danger which he has encountered and escaped in finding it for you.

A striking little copy of verses he has entitled "The Light of Stars." His "bright particular star" is not the "star of Jove, so beautiful and large," nor the star of lovers, Venus, nor the star of suicides, Saturn. It is the star of warriors, "the red light of Mars." We share with him in his feelings. Mars has, to men, more points of interest and sympathy than almost any other planet. One frozen band at least binds us to it. One white signal has been hung out by this near vessel; snow and winter are there. And if, as analogy would plead, there be inhabitants, these inhabitants must be somewhat like ourselves. There are *fires*, there are *hearths*, there are *homes* in Mars! There is struggle, there may be sin, there may be death—there is contest, there is mystery, there may be victory! What home sounds, what thrilling tones, what an array of signals, what a sheaf of telegraphic rays, from that red planet! Hear Longfellow—

"Earnest thoughts within me rise,
  When I behold afar,
Suspended in the evening skies,
  The shield of that red star.

O star of strength! I see thee stand
  And smile upon my pain;
Thou beckonest with thy mailed hand,
  And I am strong again.

Within my breast there is no light,
  But the cold light of stars;
I gave the first watch of the night
  To the red planet Mars."

We must not overlook a poem entitled "Footsteps of Angels." Who are the angels who visit and imprint his heart? No cherubim—dim to him amid all their blaze of intelligence. No strange seraphs—cold to him amid all their flames of fire. They are the friends of his youth—the loved of his early heart—now sons and daughters of the grave. The eye of his heart sees them; the ear of his heart hears their soft footsteps, and their voices so low and sweet. Have all of us not at times such angel visits! Are we not at this moment summoned to look up, and see and hear them? Ah! we know that strong deep-furrowed face, that lofty brow, those locks sprinkled with gray, that eye, restless with the fire of intelligence, and with the light of paternal affection. We know too, too well, that young form, that step light as the roe's upon the mountains, that clear blue eye, that brown curling head, that forehead so high, that face so pale and beautiful, over which, ere her ten winters had passed, death had spread a ghastlier paleness——it is our Agnes, at once sister and child! And we cry

> "O God! if it be thus, and thou
> Art not a madness and a mockery,
> We yet might be most happy."

Longfellow's writings are in general prophetic of, and preparatory for, the grand reconciliation of man, both as regards man the individual, and man the species. In his "Arsenal," and his "Occultation of Orion," he shadows forth the "coming of the milder day," when there is

> "Peace! and no longer from its brazen portals
> The blast of War's great organ shakes the skies!
> But beautiful as songs of the immortals,
> The holy melodies of love arise."

And both in "Hyperion" and "Evangeline," the agency of sorrow, in purging the eye, subduing the senses, watering all the stronger plants in the soul's garden, is abundantly recognized. Perhaps still another's "Pilgrim's Progress," cut out through rougher ways, darkened by deeper shadows, and exhibiting more the teaching of error than either "Hyperion" or "Sartor," is still desiderated by the age.

We cannot linger much longer with this delightful writer. He has scattered many other delicious drops of song along his course. Such are—"Rain in Summer," "To a Child,"

"To the Driving Cloud," and "The Old Clock on the Stairs." These are all amiable carols, inspirited with poetic life, decorated with chaste image, and shadowed with pensive sentiment, like the hand of manhood laid gently upon the billowing head of a child.

The character of a translator's own genius may be gathered with considerable accuracy from his selection of pieces to translate. In general, the graceful bends to the graceful, the pensive sighs back to the pensive, and the strong shadows the strong. Longfellow has not dared any lofty heights, or sounded any dark hollows, of foreign poetry. The exquisite patriarchal simplicities of the Swedish ballad have attracted his kindred spirit. It is not "deep calling unto deep." It is one corn-field responding to another, across the hedge, under one soft westerly breeze. Need we do more than allude to "The Children of the Lord's Supper," which, both in verse and spirit, is the model of "Evangeline." Thus he characterizes himself as a translator:—"The translation is literal, perhaps to a fault. In no instance have I done the author a wrong, by introducing into his work any supposed improvements or embellishments of my own. I have preserved even the measure, that inexorable hexameter in which, it must be confessed, the motions of the English muse are not unlike those of a prisoner dancing to the music of his chains; and perhaps, as Dr. Johnson said of the dancing dog, 'the wonder is not that she should do it so well, but that she should do it at all.'"

We close our paper with feelings of gratitude and respect for our transatlantic author It is pleasant, in this melancholy world, to "light upon such certain places," where beautiful dreams, and lofty, generous aspirations, lift us up, on a ladder, into ideal regions, which are yet to become real; for every such aspiration is a distinct step upwards to meet our expected New Jerusalem of man, "coming down as a bride adorned for her husband." Every volume of genuine poetry, besides, constitutes a cool grotto of retreat, with the altar of a bloodless sacrifice standing in the midst. We love, too, even better than the poetry of this volume, its sunny, genial, human, and hopeful spirit. Perhaps there are more depth and power, certainly there are more peculiarity and strangeness, in Emerson's volume, but over many parts of it is suspended a dry, rainless cloud of gloom, which chills and withers you. You become, it may be, a wiser, but certainly a sadder man. Longfellow sheds a chequered autumnal light, under which your soul, like a river, flows forward, serene, glad, strong, and singing as it flows—

"Let us then be up and doing,
With a heart for any fate;
Still achieving, still pursuing,
Learn to labor and to wait."

PHILIP JAMES BAILEY.

These sketches are by no means intended as a complete literary history of the age; yet we believe that in our two "Galleries" few names of great note will be found altogether omitted. We have not, indeed, analyzed at length such writers as Dickens, Thackeray, Horne, Robert Browning, or our admirable friend Marston, partly because we are not fully acquainted with their works, and partly because they have been thoroughly treated by other writers. To omit, however a distinct notice of such a phenomenon as "Festus" were unpardonable, and to this we now address ourselves. "Festus" is, indeed, a phenomenon. "When I read 'Festus,'" said poor David Scott to us, "I was astonished to find such work going on in a mind of the present day." It seemed to him, as Edinburgh on first view was called by Haydon, a "giant's dream." Indeed it much resembles one of Scott's own vast unearthly pictures, the archetypes of which he may have recognized now in that world of shadows, of which he was born and lived a denizen; for surely, if ever walked "phantom amongst men," it was the creator of "Vasco," "Sarpedon," and the "Resurrection of the Cross."

The first feeling which affected many besides us at the perusal of "Festus" was a shock of surprise, mixed with pain, and not free from a shade of disgust. If we did not "believe," we trembled; if we did not sympathize, we shuddered. Every thing was so strange that the whole seemed monstrous. We can compare our feelings to nothing else than Cain's flight with Lucifer through the stars. We found ourselves caught up on dark and mighty wings, through wildernesses of dim and shadowy objects, worlds unpeopled, worlds half-created, worlds peopled by forms so monstrous that solitude seemed sweet in the comparison—"gorgons, and hydras, and chimeras dire." But just as disgust and terror were about to drive us away from this weltering chaos, a light appeared, softer than sunlight, warmer than moonlight —the light of genius—which beckoned us on, and in which, at last, all the abortional shapes and unearthly scenery became beautiful as the landscapes of a dream. It was an angel after all, and not an eccentric demon, who was our conductor, and we yielded ourselves gladly to his gentle guidance, although the path lay over all prodigious and unspeakable regions. We want words to express the wonder which grew upon us, as each page opened like a new star, and we felt that the riches of thought, and imagery, and language scattered through the poem, were absolutely "fineless," and that the poet's mind was as vast as his theme. That vague but thrilling wonder has subsided into a calm but profound sense of the various elements of power and beauty which compose the "one and indivisible" "Festus."

It is, first of all, an original production. Some, indeed, have called it a mere cento from Goethe, Byron, and Shelley. We grant at once that it bears a striking resemblance to some of the productions of those great three; but the resemblance is only that of a kindred subject and a kindred elevation. It is a new comet in an old sky. As well call "Manfred" a copy of "Faust," or "Faust" of Job, as trace "Festus" to a slavish imitation of any preceding poem. It takes its place instantly as the lawful member of a family of sublime eccentrics, who have pierced more or less boldly into forbidden regions "beyond the solar path and milky-way," and whose fiery tresses tell on their return that they have neared the ardors now of the light that is full of glory, and now of the flames that shall never be quenched. In all these, however, the argument and object are different. Job, as we mean to show elsewhere, contains a solution of the grand problem of the reconciliation of individual man to God, and to the difficulties of the universe, through a divine medium. "Faust" is a fragmentary attempt to settle the same question, apart from supernatural aid. "Manfred" howls back to both, that such reconciliation is impossible, and that the riddle of the universe is absolutely illegible by man. Shelley's "Prometheus" is the argument of the "Faust" extended from man the individual to man the species; while Bailey's "Festus" is the argument of Job applied, in like manner, to the whole human family. He takes a similar view to that which Blake has so beautifully developed in his illustrations of the book of Job. "Festus" is to the one as Job to the other—a type of the fall and recovery of all men. The scene of "Faust" and of "Prometheus" is in earth; that of Job and of "Festus" is (essentially) in eternity.

That the book of Job is intended to teach universal restoration we do not, notwithstanding Blake, believe. But one principal object of "Festus" is to promulgate this dream. A lovely dream, verily, it is. That the surprise of a final deliverance should pierce into the darkness of the second death—that heads bowed down on the pillows of despair should be raised up to look and be lightened by the THIRD ADVENT of a more glorious "star of Lethe" than was ever Mercury as he descended into the Pagan shades—that "faces faded in the fire" should glow with the freshness of eternal youth—that the prey should be taken out of the hands of such mighty ones, and the captives from a fate so terrible—that the spring of a sublimer resurrection should reach the remote Hecla of hell, substituting flowers for flames, and for ice sunshine—that the words of the "Devil's Dream" should be fulfilled even in the case of the eldest born of Anarchy and Sin,—

> "Thou shalt walk in soft white light with kings and priests abroad,
> And thou shalt summer high in bliss upon the hills of God"—

is a most captivating notion, and might be credited, had it the slightest ground in the Word of God, or any where but in the poetic fancy or the wild wish of man. As it is, it rises up before us, a brilliant but unsubstantial and fading pomp, like a splendid evening sky; or if it die not altogether away, it must be from its connection with the imperishable fame of "Festus."

We could have wished that the author of this poem had severed its masses of beauty from a moral or theological system. All such unions are dangerous to poems. Milton, indeed, has surmounted the difficulty; and while we spurn Shelley's assertion that the system of Christianity shall by and by only be remembered in Milton's poem, we grant that the "Paradise Lost" is a subordinate evidence of its truth, as well as a rich halo around its central and solid greatness. To Pollok's work, again, his high Calvinism has proved partly a blessing and partly a bane —inwrought, as it is, into the entire structure of the poem, it has created either blind partisans or bitter enemies; only a few have been able to look through the "fire-mist" into the poetical beauties which are hid beneath it. In like manner, while Festus has been adopted and fondled by the large sect (large at least in America) calling itself Universalists, its doctrines have repelled many of the orthodox, who otherwise would have rejoiced in the "wilderness of sweets" and the forest of grandeurs, which its circuit includes. Nor must Mr. Bailey imagine that he has, by his notion of a universal restoration, in any effectual way, recommended religion to the skeptical of the present day. Eternal punishment, fifty years ago, was a great stumbling-block to unquiet spirits. Such have generally now travelled on so far towards Naturalism or Pantheism, that they will not return at the voice of the charmer, charm he never so wisely—they will laugh at the fine dream, as a man would at the offer of sugar-plums for food—and walk on their own ungovernable way. They will ask, must not the reason for a hell at all be an *infinite* one, and if so, is it not likely to be an *eternal* reason too? In every great house is there not a furnace for the dross, as well as a light in the drawing-room? If sin be of an expansive character, will not punishment expand along with it? or, if God means to destroy sin hereafter, why does he not begin by abolishing it here? And what need, they will ask again, of any hell afterwards, when justice is done now? And, again, your theory may prove the book *human*, but does it prove it *divine?*

Thus innocuously will the milk and rose-water of Bailey's

doctrine drop upon the iron scales of modern skepticism, which seeks now not so much to object to our special form of revelation, as to deny revelation altogether.

Bailey's originality is not merely that of plan, but of thought and style. He "hath a demon." He speaks as immediately told from behind. All conventionalisms are spurned—all opposites paired—all contradictions reconciled—all elements mingled—all tenses lost in the holy and glorious hubbub of "Festus." He is evidently a boy at blood-heat, but an inspired boy. We have been as much amazed to find critics treating "Festus"—sometimes with praise, sometimes with blame—as an elaborate piece of art, as Byron was to find his "Don Juan"—the child of gin and sin—treated by the Germans as an artistic work. But Bailey's book is the effect of the intoxication of youth—a powerful and lawful stimulant, which the poor jaded hack of the "Spectator" or "Literary Gazette," or any such small critic, is as incapable of sympathizing with as he is now of imbibing.

These miserable effigies of critics, when they approach books like "Festus," should really read the "Riot Act;" for certainly such works do rebel against all arbitrary authority, and do stir the air and load the wind with extravagant liberties of thought and word, which neither they nor their fathers (Rymer, Dennis, &c.) were able to bear. We have, within the last few years, witnessed (through such critics) the strange phenomena of a Dickens deified and a Christopher North (save in Scotland) forgotten, a Warren's "Now and Then" in its third edition, and Aird's "Poems" scarcely out of their first, Macaulay crowned with the richest laurels of the historic muse, and Thomas De Quincey, with a genius, an intellect, and a learning qualifying him for an historian as far superior to the ex-Edinburgh member as was Tacitus to Suetonius, having "nowhere to lay his head"—a "Course of Time" and a "Silent Love" in their teens of editions, and "Festus," after ten years, in its third; phenomena somewhat substantiating the assertion of an old clever clergyman about the march of intellect, "It has certainly been very rapid of late—it has *marched out of sight.*

The poem of "Festus," however, has by no means lost its reward. Its evident earnestness—its holy yet charitable spirit—its inexhaustible fountain of imagery—its individual thoughts of splendor, like spots of sunshine lost yet living, amid the dark forests around—its long sweeping passages, which seem to *grow* visibly and audibly before you—its infinite variety—the spirit and music of its songs—the living aspect of its characters—the bold but striking generality of its descriptions—the simplicity, or force, or beauty, or languor, of its language—the broad picture of life it presents—prove it, apart from its theological pretensions, the poem of the age's hope, even as "Sartor Resartus" is the prose record of the age's experience. We should, perhaps, forbear to add, that besides the warm verdict of the thinking youth of the country, it has gained the praise of Bulwer, Montgomery, Wilson, Tennyson, Binney, David Scott, Professor Nichol, Samuel Brown, and others of equal note. Partial, or insincere, or interested praise (although we by no means apply these terms to the above), and also malicious censure, may be told here to stand aside, inasmuch as "Festus" has written its own indelible impress upon a very broad, true, and responsive section of the intellectual world. "You may know it by its fruits."

"The young mind of the age!" What a multitude of thoughts crowd on us when we utter these simple words!—What mingled hope and fear—what tremulous anticipations rush in, as we think of what it is, and of what it may become—of the work it has to do, and the sufferings it has to endure. Never was there an age when there were so many young, ardent, and gifted spirits—never was there an age when they more required wise guidance. The desideratum may be thus expressed, "Wanted, a tutor to the rising age; he must be a creedless Christian—full of faith, but full of charity—wise in head and large in heart—a poet and a priest—an 'eternal child,' as well as a thoroughly furnished man."

This advertisement has not yet been fully answered. The work of Carlyle and Emerson has been principally negative, and it seems now nearly perfected. We wait a new teacher, who, by uniting the spirit of Christianity to that of philosophy, shall present us with a satisfactory whole—with nothing less than which our eager inquirers will rest contented. May all the quick and cunning forces of nature combine in forming such an august spirit! Yet are we not at all sanguine of his speedy advent. Things, we fear, must be worse ere they are better. And, perhaps, the deepest hour of the darkness may be cloven by no earthly radiance, but by the wide wings of that advent for which the weary Church and the wearier world, are beginning to pant, with unutterable groanings. Meanwhile, many gifted spirits, besides Bailey, are working a good work. Some poets of uncommon promise are ever and anon appearing. Among these we may mention the author of "Nimrod," a work containing much fine description and exquisitely developed character. Aytoun has given us one admirable ballad on "Montrose," although his vein is not of the deepest; Henry Sutton, A. J. Symington, Strype, and William Allingham, are all gifted and promising persons. But our greatest hope is fixed on Sidney Yendys, of Cheltenham; this young gentleman has written a drama entitled, "The Roman," still in MS., of which Shelley himself would not have been ashamed. With something of the diffusion and exaggeration of youth, it has a richness of thought, a felicity of language, a copiousness of imagery, a music of versification, not easy in any first effort to be paralleled. It contains passages of beauty, of power which absolutely startle you, and specimens of every variety of excellence, from the lofty declamation to the melting ballad. We stake whatever critical reputation we have on the prediction, that no recent poem, save "Festus," shall make a profounder impression upon the lovers of poetry when it appears than "The Roman." It is a very conflagration of genius, as well as in many parts a high triumph of art.*

JOHN STERLING.

The removal of a young man of high performance and still higher promise, is in all circumstances melancholy. It is more so, if with the youth has expired either a new vein of poetry or a new view of truth; and it is scarcely less so when the youth has been unconsciously the type of a large

* Bailey's *theory* is said to be derived, in a great measure, from the writings of that extraordinary man, David Thom of Liverpool.

class of cultivated and earnest minds, and when his partial successes, baffled endeavors—his admitted struggles, and his premature fate—have been in some measure *vicarious.*

These three short and simple sentences appear to us to include, positively and negatively, the essence of the late John Sterling, and shall form the leading heads in our after remarks on his genius and character. He was, in the judgment of all who knew or had carefully read him a person of very distinguished abilities, and of still more singular promise. He did *not*, in *our* view of him, exhibit indications of original insight or of creative genius. But he has, from his peculiar circumstances, from his speculative and practical history, from his exquisitely-tuned and swiftly-responsive symphonies with his age and its progressive minds, acquired a double portion of interest and importance; his experience seems that of multitudes, and in that final look of disappointed yet submissive inquiry which he casts up to heaven, he is but the foremost in a long, fluctuating, and motley file.

The external evidences of his powers and acquirements are numerous and irresistible. In his boyhood he discovered striking tokens of a mind keen, sensitive, and turned in the direction of those high speculations from which his eye, till death, was never entirely diverted. While barely eight, "he distinctly remembered having speculated on points of philosophy, and especially on the idea of duty, which presented itself to him in this way—If I could save my papa and mamma from being killed, I know I should at once do it. Now, why? To be killed would be very painful, and yet I should give my own consent to being killed." The solution presented itself as "a dim awe-stricken feeling of unknown obligation." When about nine, "he was much struck by his master's telling him that the word *sincere* was derived from the practice of filling up flaws in furniture with wax, whence *sine cera* came to mean *pure*, not vamped up." This explanation, he said, gave him great pleasure, and abode in his memory, as having first shown him that there is a reason in words as well as in other things. When a boy, he read through the whole "Edinburgh Review," of which his biographer says, "a diet than which hardly any could yield less wholesome food for a young mind, and which could scarcely fail to puff it up with the wind of self-conceit." We doubt the validity of this dictum. We conceive that, to a fresh elastic mind, the crossing of such varied territories of thought, the coming in contact with so many vigorous minds, the acquiring such stores of miscellaneous information, the mere reading of such a mass of masculine English, as the perusal of the entire "Edinburgh Review" implies, must have been beneficial, and tended to awaken curiosity, to kindle ambition, to stifle mannerism of style, and, as the likely result of the many severe criticisms in which the book abounds, to allay instead of fanning the feeling of self-conceit. Who but commends the industry of the boy who reads all the English essayists—a course of reading certainly much more dissipating; or the youth who reads all Bayle's "Dictionary"—a course of reading much more dangerous than the "Edinburgh Review?" Let the boy *read* at his pleasure—the youth will *study*, and the man *think* and *act*.

At Cambridge, Sterling did not greatly distinguish him self, nor did he bear any violent affection to his *alma mater*. For mathematics he had little taste; the classics he rather relished than thoroughly knew. He early commenced the study of philosophy, deeming it at once the key to a scientific theology and to a lofty literature, although latterly he all but left the cold and perilous crags of speculation for the flowery meadows of poetry and æsthetics. At the feet of Coleridge no one ever sat with a feeling of more entire and childlike submission; the house at Highgate was to him the shrine of a god, and his biographer regrets that he "did not preserve an account of Coleridge's conversations, for he was capable of representing their depth, their ever-varying hues their sparkling lights, their oceanic ebb and flow." He began soon to empty out his teeming mind, in the forms both of verse and prose. In the course of his short life we find him connected, more or less intimately, with the following periodicals, the "Athenæum," "Blackwood's Magazine," the "Quarterly," and the London and Westminster "Reviews." At a peculiarly dull period in the history of "Maga" he appeared, amid a flourish of trumpets, as a "new contributor," and did succeed in shooting a little new blood into her withered veins. In the "Quarterly" he wrote a paper on Tennyson, which was attributed at the time to Henry Nelson Coleridge. Differing as he did in many material points from the new school of Radicals who conducted the "Westminster," he seemed more at home in their company than in that of the knights of the Noctes; and his contributions to their journal are all characteristic. These articles have been reprinted by Dr. Hare, and, along with the poems, his tragedy of "Stafford," a few letters, and other remains, constitute all his written claims to consideration.

He has certainly in them raised no very great or compact basis for future fame; but we are entitled to adduce, in addition, the testimony of his friends, who all speak with rapture of the possibilities of his mind—of his talent as a debater—and of his ready, vivid, and brilliant talk. In him alone Thomas Carlyle met his conversational match; he alone ventured to face him in single combat, and nothing like their rencontres seems to have been witnessed since those of Johnson and Burke. Even in his "Remains" we may find faint yet distinct indications of all the principal features of his intellectual character. These, we think, may be classed under the three general characteristics of *sympathy*, *sincerity*, and *culture*. We do not mean that these sum up the whole of his idiosyncrasy, but simply that they are the qualities which have struck us most forcibly in the perusal of his works. He had, besides, as a writer, a fine inventiveness, a rich and varied stock of figures, a power of arresting and fixing in permanent shapes the thinnest gossamer abstractions, and the command of a diction remarkable more for its copiousness, flexibility, and strength, than for grace, clearness, or felicitous condensation. Perhaps his principal claim to reputation rests on his criticisms, and their power and charm lie in genial and self-forgetting *sympathy*. It is too customary to speak of this as a subordinate quality in a critic, as a veil over his eyes, and nearly inconsistent with the exercise of analytic sagacity. Those who talk in this manner are not so much guilty of a mistake as of a stupid blunder. Sympathy is closely connected with sight. It is a medium, which, like water poured into a bowl, enables you to see objects previously invisible. It, and it alone, opens a window into the breast and the brain of genius, and shows the marvellous processes which are going on within. It is not merely that the heart often sees farther than the intellect, but it is that sympathy cleanses and sharpens even the intellectual eye. Love, and you will understand. Besides, the possession of powerful sympathy with intellect and genius, implies a certain similitude of mind on the part of the sympathizer. The blind cannot sympathize with descriptions of scenery, and the lively motion and music of a mountain-stream sound like a satire to the lame who limp beside it. To feel *with*, you must always *find* yourself *in*, the subject or the person. Adam Smith doubtless was wrong when he explained every moral phenomenon by sympathy; it were a more probable paradox to maintain that a man's intellectual power entirely depends upon the depth, width, and warmth of his sympathies, and that Shakspeare was the greatest of men because he was the widest of sympathizers.

Waiving, at this stage of our paper, such speculations, we claim a high place for Sterling, as possessed of catholic and clear-headed sympathy. Merely to copy the names of a few of the characters whom he has analyzed with justice, and praised with generosity, is enough to prove this. He has painted Alexander the Great and Wickliffe, Joan of Arc and Gustavus Adolphus, Milton and Burns, Columbus and Coleridge, Simonides and Carlyle, Napier and Tennyson. We find him, too, on friendly terms at once with "Blackwood's Magazine" and the "Westminster Review;" writing in the "Quarterly," and calling Shelley a "generous heroic being;" and in his "Tales" and "Apologues" imitating the imaginative peculiarities, now of the Gothic, now of the Grecian, and now of the German school. We love this spirit much, not merely as proclaiming a warm heart, but as evincing a wide, keen, and open intellect. We contrast it favorably with a portion of the very class to whom Sterling belonged, whose fastidiousness is fast becoming frantic, who are loathing literature itself, although it is by it alone that themselves have risen, and whose hasty, splenetic, and contradictory judgments tend to exert a damping and discouraging influence upon youthful aspirants, who will ask, if such authorities tell us that nothing has yet been done, how can we expect ever to do any thing? Sterling, on the contrary, loved literature for its own sake, and had a true appreciation of its infinite worth and beauty. He was not like Byron, and one or two others we might name, who looked upon literature partly as a means for gratifying an ambition to which other avenues were closed, and partly as an outlet for the waste energy and superfluous fury of their natures, when their passions had not entirely exhausted them, and who, upon the first disappointment and chagrin were ready to rush into another field; nor did he resemble a class who have mistaken their profession, and expended powers, which might have led them to the highest distinction, in action, in travelling, parliament, or arms, on gaining a dubious literary success, which is despised by themselves; nor did he rank with the men whose love to literature is confined to an appreciation of those who resemble, or who follow their peculiar style. His circumstances saved him from the miserable condition of a hack author, and from all the heart-burnings, jealousies, and disgusts which degrade the noble pursuit of literature in his eyes, and turn its beautiful moon into the clouded lantern of a low, lurid, precarious life. Sterling, in his wide and trembling sympathies with literary excellence, and in his devoted enthusiasm for the varied expressions of the beautiful, as well as in the hectic heat and eagerness of his temperament, bore a striking likeness to Shelley, although possessing a healthier, happier, and better balanced nature.

While freely conceding him such qualities, we protest against some of his critical commissions as well as omissions. We are astonished at his silence in reference to John Foster, whose sturdy genius ought to have been known to him, and whose mind was moving more slowly and uneasily through the same process of speculative change with his own. We cannot at all understand his admiration for Montaigne, who appears to have been a very slight sublimation of sensual-indifference, and not more honest than the sensual-indifferent wealthy usually are. How grossly unjust he is to Rousseau and Hazlitt, when he calls them "declaimers and dealers in rhetorical falsehood! Grant that Rousseau was personally a poor scrannell, tortuous, and broken pipe, who can deny that a power, call it his genius or his demon, discoursed at times upon him sweet and powerful music, to which nations listened because they could not refrain, and which no term like rhetoric, or even oratory, nor any inferior to poetry, touching the verge of prophecy, can at all measure? No such utterances have come from Hazlitt; but if he resembled Rousseau in occasional bursts of vanity, he was certainly, on the whole, a sincerer man; he egotizes at his proper cost—his absurdities seem given in on oath. For downright honesty, and for masses of plain sense, and native acuteness, we are not afraid to compare and prefer many of his essays to those of the old Gascon, and, with all his faults and deficiencies, his match as a masculine and eloquent critic has yet to be made. What verbose affairs do even Jeffrey's criticisms, when collected, appear beside the lectures of Hazlitt, who often expresses the essence of an author by the scratch of his pen, and settles a literary controversy by an epithet.

Initiation into the mysteries of German philosophy and literature produced in Sterling a considerable degree of indifference towards the English classics. To Addison's essays—those cool, clear, whispering leaves of summer, so native and so refreshing—he never alludes, and we cannot conceive him, like Burke, hushing himself to his last slumber, by hearing read the papers in the "Spectator" on the immortality of the soul. And against Dr. Johnson he has committed himself in a set attack, of which we must speak more particularly. An author of celebrity maintains that no person can be a man of talent who does not admire "Dr. Johnson, and that all men of eminent ability do admire him." Without pressing the application of this assertion, we do think that those who, in the present age, find in him a hero, discover both candor and penetration—candor to admit and pass by his bulky faults as a writer, and penetration to see his bulky though disguised merits as a writer and a man. For one to call him a mere "prejudiced emphatic pedant," is simply to write down one's self an ass. For Coleridge to call him the "overrated man of his age" (how could the age avoid rating him highly, since he was, save Burke, the greatest man it had?) is for Coleridge to prove himself a privileged person, who said whatever he chose. Sterling's charges may be classified thus: Dr. Johnson's productions are "loud and swollen"—he could say nothing of poetry, and has said nothing of Shakspeare "worth listening to"—he had no "serene joy,"—and he wanted it because he had no "capacity for the higher kinds of thought." To the proof.

1*st*, His language was "loud and swollen." Granted. So is a torrent, or a river in flood. So are Thomson's "Seasons," Young's "Night Thoughts," Schiller's "Robbers," Coleridge's "Hymn to Mont Blanc," and "Religious Musings," Sterling's "Lycian Painter" and "Last of the Giants," all productions of genuine merit and meaning, and yet all stilted either in style or manner, or both. Johnson is often loud, but seldom *boss*—he can beat the drum, but he can shiver the castle-gate with his axe too. If his arm be sometimes "swollen" with indolence, it is as often swollen with heavy blows aimed, and not in vain, at the heads of his enemies. His very yawn is thunder—he swings in an easy chair, which many that mock him could not *move*. You may laugh at the elephant picking up the pin, but not ejaculating *you*, brained and battered, toward the skies.

2dly, He has said nothing of Shakspeare or poetry worth listening to. What! Is his dissertation in Waller on sacred poetry, be it true or false, not worth listening to? or his panegyric on the "Paradise Lost?" or his character of the "Night Thoughts?" or his comparison between Pope and Dryden? or his picture of a poet in "Rasselas?" or his unanswered overturn of the unities in his essay on Shakspeare? or several other portions of that "ponderous mass of futilities?" or his famous lines on Shakspeare? Mark, we are not asserting that all such passages are of the highest order of philosophical criticism, but we are asserting their intrinsic value, and their immeasurable superiority to the vague, empty, pointless, misty, and pseudo-German disquisitions which stuff many of our principal magazines and reviews in the present day. We are not prepared to sacrifice the poorest passages in the "Lives of the Poets"—nay, not even his notes on Shakspeare (which make Fanny Kemble swear—off the stage), for such a piece of elaborate and recondite nonsense, as recently was permitted to appear in a celebrated Scottish review, as a paper on Tennyson's "Princess," and was yet not the worst specimen of the kind of criticism referred to.

But Sterling accuses Johnson of wanting "serene joy;" an accusation, alas! too true. But, how could he have attained this, in the first place, under the pressure of that "vile body"—that huge mass of disease, bad humors, and semi-blindness, which he carried about with him, and under which he struggled and writhed like a giant below Etna?

In the victim of old, yoked consciously to a putrefying car cass, we may conceive stern submission, but hardly serene joy. We can account for a man like William Cobbett, high in health, clear in eye, and with a system answering, like the crystal mirror of a stream, to every feature of his intellectual faculties, reproaching Johnson with gloom, but must think it a sad mistake, if not an affectation, on the part of a philosophic valetudinarian like John Sterling. Besides, as it has been said that the laws of disease are as beautiful as those of health, the *intuitions of disease are as true as those of health.* In none of them is the whole truth found; but even as the jaundiced view is only a partial rendering of the creation and of man, so the view of one in perfect health and strength, with a sanguine temperament, and in circumstances of signal prosperity, is equally imperfect. The one may be called a black or yellow, the other a *white* lie. Surely the Cockney we have elsewhere commemorated as sitting with Carlyle in a railway carriage, rubbing his hands, and saying to the grim stranger—"Successful world this, isn't it, sir?" was as far astray as the author of Sartor glaring through the gloomy bile-spotted splendor of the atmosphere which usually surrounds his spirit. And whether are more trustworthy the feelings of the man standing before his fire watching the parturition of a pudding, and the simmering of a pot of mulled porter, and exclaiming "How comfortable!" or those of a traveller perishing among the midnight snows? There is truth, and equal truth, in all such angular aspects,—there is the whole truth in none of them, nor even in any conceivable mixture of them all. And it were difficult to imagine a man in temperament like Johnson forming essentially another view than what rushed in on him from every orifice of his distempered system.

There is a cant in the present day—a cant which Sterling was above—about health, healthy systems, healthy views, healthy regulation of body, as producing a healthy tone of mind, as if the soul and stomach were identical, as if good digestion were the same thing with happiness, as if all gloomy and distressing thoughts sprung from bile, as if one had only to lie down under the "wet sheet" to understand the origin of evil, to solve all the cognate, tremendous problems of the universe, and to obtain that "reconciliation" after which all earnest spirits aspire. Easy the process now for obtaining the "peace which passeth understanding!" Poor John Bunyan, why didst thou struggle, writhe, and madden, wade through hells of fire and seas of blood, to gain a result to which cold bathing and barks would have led thee in a month? Foolish Thomas Carlyle, why all that pother about everlasting noes and yeas, instead of anticipating Bulwer in the baptismal regeneration of the cold-water cure? This is a free translation of the doctrines propounded by our modern utilitarians, who hold that if they had had Dante and Byron in their hands, they would have made them happy men, and writers so sweet and so practical, and who can hardly credit you when you tell them that John Foster observed all the "natural laws," and was a gloomy "son of thunder," and that others break them daily, and are as merry as the day is long. It is vain to speak to them of temperament, of hereditary melancholy, of mental penetration so piercing as to amount to distemper, of visions of evil so vivid as to haunt every movement of the spirit, of hectic sensibility, of doubts so strong as to threaten to strangle piety and render devotion at times a torment—let the man but give up tobacco, and he will and must be happy? Foster evidently did not take enough of exercise, Carlyle smokes, and Cowper went to excess, it is well known, in the "cup that cheers but not inebriates." *Hinc illae lachrymae!*

Now, it is of course conceded that a well-regulated physical life will in some measure modify both mental views and mental happiness. But, in the first place, there are constitutions for whom a well-regulated means a generous mode of living. Such was that of Shelley, who, according to the testimony of his friends, was never so well or happy as when, at rare intervals, he departed from his usual fare of vegetables and water. Secondly, "Because thou art virtuous," is there no more vice in the world, no more misery—is every dark problem solved—are the old enigmas of death and sin made one whit plainer? nay, in proportion to the degree of personal purity, is not the feeling of sorrow and disgust at the follies and foulnesses of the world likely to gain strength? Ah! the utmost that the cleanest outward life can do is to produce in some minds a feeling that they have evaded, although not met, the grand difficulty, to produce in others a selfish self-complacency and forgetfulness, springing from a state of health so unnaturally constant as to be in reality a disease, and on minds of the higher order to produce little *permanent* effect at all. From another source must help come. From above, from the regions of spiritual truth, must descend that baptism of fire which confers ardent hope, if not happiness—that blessedness which is higher and better, even in its imperfection and chequered light, than the unthinking calm or mechanical gladness of the best regulated animalism. But Johnson, according to Sterling, wanted serene joy, not merely from the peculiarity of his temperament, nor merely from the state of his age and the degree of his culture, as affecting his impressions, but from his incapacity for the higher kinds of thought—as if all possessed of this capacity, as if Coleridge, for instance, or Schiller, or Carlyle, whom Sterling always ranks in the first class, have been serene, and as if this explanation of Johnson's want of peace, were not disproved by a hundred instances of men who, less entitled than he to the praise of the highest original or inventive genius—for example, Hall, Southey, Chalmers, and the lately deceased Hamilton of Leeds—have been distinguished by buoyant and child-like felicity. No; we are persuaded that from no defect in Johnson's intellect, but from constitutional causes, sprung his morbid melancholy; nay, that the strength of his intellect was proved by the control which it exercised over his temperament. A giant maniac required and obtained a giant keeper. Had he possessed the culture and shared in the progress of our age, we are not sure, if more than three or four of its literary heroes would have equalled him. Peace to his massive shade! He was one of the best, greatest, wisest, and most sincere of men.

While we are engaged in finding fault, we may notice our author's opinions on the connection between intellect and heart. Carlyle had maintained that a truly great intellect must always be accompanied by a noble moral nature; he had not asserted the converse, that a noble moral nature implies a great intellect. Sterling, in his reply, commits, we think, two mistakes. First, imagining that Carlyle had asserted this untenable converse, he presses him with the names of Newton of Olney, Thomas Scott, Calamy, Swartz, and Jeanie Deans, and asks if these were people of high intellect? But although the day includes the hour, the hour does not include the day. Carlyle's idea is, that while the moral nature has been found high and the intellect small, the intellect has never come to its true elevation without the correspondence of the heart. It is a question of facts. In the second place, Sterling and Carlyle attach different meanings to the word intellect. With the one it signifies the understanding, and he shows triumphantly how it has wedded wickedness or heartlessness in Tiberius, the Duke of Guise, Lord Bolingbroke, Voltaire, and Talleyrand. With Carlyle it means the higher power of intuition, genius, or reason, which, according to him, while often attended by a train of error-imps, or even big, burly vices, never exhibits profound and radical depravity, and is never unattended by a sense of the good, the true, the generous, and the just. It is obviously impossible to settle a controversy where there is a preliminary misunderstanding as to the terms, but we certainly incline to Carlyle's opinion —holding it, however, only as a general rule, and noting two distinct species of exceptions which we may call the mad and the monstrous case. There is first the *mad*, in which, as with Rousseau, and perhaps Mirabeau and Byron, a diseased organization has divided those principles of head and heart which are usually joined in the marriage chamber of the brain of genius. There is secondly, the *monstrous* case, where, as in Bacon, the moral sense, if not omitted entirely, seems to exist in an inverse proportion to the intellectual power—where an intellect vast, varied, and weighty as the globe, is balanced by a heart, hard and small as a pin-point. Ought we to add Napoleon as another instance of this second most rare and appalling formation?

We mentioned as the second general quality of Sterling his sincerity. Those much abused and desecrated terms, truth-seeker and beauty-lover, assumed too often by the selfish and the vain to distinguish them from the common crowd, came of their own accord and rested on his head. And if he did seem toward the close to relax somewhat in his devotion to truth, and to be smit with a fonder affection for the beautiful, it was because, while the latter melted into his embrace, the former fled ever before him into her awful shades. He turned from the haughty Rosalind of truth to the fair young Juliet of beauty. But his love, in both instances, was as pure as it was ardent. You do not see in him the death-wrestle of Arnold, who like Jacob at Peniel, appears panting as he cries to the mysterious form, "I will not let thee go except thou bless me; rather crush me by thy weight than tell me nothing." For such painful and protracted struggle Sterling was unfitted by temperament and by illness; but if not a rugged athlete, he was a swift runner in this great chase. His mind wrought less than Arnold's by research—more by rapid intuition. With less learning and perseverance, he had incomparably more imagination and more philosophic sagacity. Health and circumstances prevented him from effecting so much as Arnold, or leaving on the age the same impression of fearlessness, truthfulness, and moral power. More than even Arnold was he caught in the meshes of uncertainty, and to both death seemed the dawning of a light which they had yearned after, but never reached on earth. Both died too early for the world, but in time for their own happiness. It is clear that Arnold could not have remained much longer connected with the English Church, nor probably with any. Whither the restless progress of Sterling's mind would have led him we cannot tell, but it had conducted him to quaking and dangerous ground. Both, while in deep doubt upon many important questions, exhibited on the verge of death a child-like Christianity of spirit and language which it is delightful to contemplate; and both, through their moral likeness to each other, through their position and the progress of their thought, will, notwithstanding many mental dissimilarities, be classed together by posterity as two of the most interesting specimens of the enlightened minds of our strange transition period.

Sterling's culture was of a peculiar kind. His mind was not ripened under the scorching sun of science, but under the softer and more genial warmth of philosophy and literature. We are not sure if he had ever thoroughly mastered the original works of the German philosophers, or if his metaphysical reading was of an extensive range; we incline to think that he had acquired much of his knowledge of Kant and his brethren from the extempore versions of Coleridge, and that it was with the poets and such moral and religious writers of Germany as Schleiermacher that he was familiar. His historical knowledge was rather wide than accurate, and from severe personal research he shrunk with all the reluctance of a sensitive and nervous nature. With the classics of all polite literature he was intimately conversant. His theological attainments were respectable—there is no evidence that they were more, and latterly, indeed, he became deeply prejudiced against the present pretensions, and forms, and modes of investigating that science. His culture, altogether, was rather elegant than strict, rather recherché than profound; and from this we think, in part proceeded the uncertainty of his theological views. His clerical profession and his early feelings created an intense interest in theological subjects, and a yearning for deeper insight into them, but his tastes and his powers adapted him for a different pursuit. Theology, if we would find aught new in it, requires digging. Sterling could not dig, he could only fly; his verdicts, therefore, are valuable principally for their sincerity; they are rapid first impressions, not slow, deliberate, last judgments. The very power which rendered him a consummate critic of the fine arts, and often an exquisite artist, disqualified him for those laborious and complicated processes which go to build up the great idea of God's relations to mankind. Here he is a tongueless orator, a blind painter, a dumb musician, his powerlessness of execution being proportionate to the strength of his desire.

A man of genius John Sterling has often been called, nor are we disposed to deny him the precious but indefinite term. His sympathies, his temperament, his mode of thinking, all the moods and tenses of his mind, were those of genius. If not a man of genius, he was a most startling likeness or bust of one. Nevertheless, we have our doubts as to the originality or greatness of his vein. We argue this not, as some would absurdly, from his wide and generous sympathies; great genius implies a great genial nature as necessarily as a great river a great channel for its waters, and a broad nature, like a broad river, must reflect many objects. We argue it not from finding no extensive or profound work in the list of his writings—this his short life and his long duel with death sufficiently explain; and still less from his non popularity (in the popular sense) as an author; as he never spoke to the empty echo of popular applause, he never expected to receive a reply. But we imagine that we notice in the various productions he has left a sort of *tentative* process as of a mind distracted by various models and attempting different styles. We observe this not merely in his earlier but in his later works. We never from the beginning to the end of his career, find him in a path so peculiar and lonely that we cry out, "Let him prosecute this if he can till death." He never gives the impression, amid all his individual brilliancies of thought, invention, and figure, of a new, and whole, and undivided thing, leaving such influence on us as is given by the sight of a new comet in the heavens, or of a Faust, a Festus, or a "Rime of the Anciente Marinere" upon the earth. His genius rather touches, dances on a brilliant and shapeless fire-mist, than constructs it into fine or terrible forms. He has all the variety, vividness, truth, and eloquence which constitute an artist who *has genius*, but not the possession, the self-abandonment, the gigantic monotony, slowly evolving itself out of the wide circle of early sympathies, and wielding them all to its purpose—the one great thing in nature to tell—the one great thing toward man to do, which distinguish a prophet whom *genius has.*

There are two lights in which to regard Sterling's writings—either as trials of strength or as triumphs of genius. It is in the former light that we are disposed to regard them. They are of almost every variety of style, subject, and merit. We have poems, apologues, allegories, a tragedy, criticisms, novels, and fragmentary relics. Seldom do we remember the steep of fame scaled on so many sides by one so young. He resembled a captain who waiting for the ultimate order of his general, keeps his troops moving hither and thither in what seems aimless and endless ubiquity. So Sterling hung around all the alleys and avenues of thought, tarrying for the word "march and secure this or that one"—a word which never came. Yet assuredly his talent, tactics, and earnestness were of no ordinary kind. How much mild pathos has he condensed into the "Sexton's Daughter!" What fine though dim condensations many of his poetical lines are! How tenderly and truly does he touch what we might deem the yet sensitive and shrinking corpse of Wentworth! Napoleon, too, he has resuscitated; and it is at the touch of no earthworm that he springs aloft, gigantic, if not triumphant, from the tomb. And throughout the tales and apologues, which principally compose the second volume of his "Remains," there are sprinkled beauties of thought, sentiment, and expression, for which forty volumes of modern novels might be searched in vain.

On his "Thoughts" and "Letters," as in some respects the most interesting of his writings, we propose to pause for a little. Always are such writings, if from a sincere man, the most direct and genuine issues of his spirit—they are just the mind turned inside out. The naked man that can bear inspection must be handsome; the naked thought which delights must be beautiful and true. A very good and very clever divine has written "Adam's Private Thoughts." We are thankful to him; but what would we give for the private thoughts of Shakspeare, Milton, and especially of Burke, since he, less than most men, "hung his heart upon his sleeve for daws to peck at." Were but some one wiser and greater than Rousseau to shrive himself as honestly as he! An honest account of his inmost sentiments and his entire history, held up in the hand of any intellectual man, not insane, would stop almost the motions of society till it had been read and pondered. Autobiographies being in general the falsest of books, the exception would be the more prized. And thus, too, we should find that one fearless man had uttered feelings and thoughts participated in by the whole human race, and was the mouth of a dumb humanity.

Sterling's "Thoughts" are evidently sincere, but as evidently a selection. They are the collected cream of his mind. He does not open his soul *ad aperturam libri.* He gives us elegant extracts, and some of them might have been better entitled "How I ought to have thought at such and such a time." The whole collection is not so much of "thoughts" as of "after-thoughts." They were published, let us remember, before his death, in "Blackwood's Magazine." Had they been thorough-going utterances and written in blood, no periodical would have printed them. As it is, many of them are very beautiful and profound. We quote a few:—

"There is no lie that many men will not believe; there is no man who does not believe many lies; and there is no man who believes only lies.

One dupe is as impossible as one twin.

To found an argument for the value of Christianity on external evidence, and not on the condition of man and the pure idea of God, is to hold up a candle before our eyes that we may better see the stars.

The religion of all Pagans indiscriminately has often been written of by zealous Christians in the worst spirit of Paine and Voltaire.

Lies are the ghosts of truths, the masks of faces.

The firm foot is that which finds firm footing. The weak falters although it be standing upon a rock.

Goethe sometimes reminds us of a Titan in a court dress.

The prose man knows nothing of poetry, but poetry knows much of him.

No man is so born a poet but that he needs to be regenerated into a poetic artist.

There are countenances far more indecent than the naked form of the Medicean Venus.

Those who deride the name of God are the most unhappy of men, except those who make a trade of honoring him.

An unproductive truth is none. But there are products which cannot be weighed even in patent scales, nor brought to market.

There is a tendency in modern education to cover the fingers with rings, and at the same time cut the sinews at the wrist.

Better a cut finger than no knife.

The worst education which teaches self-denial is better than the best which teaches every thing else, and not that."

Sterling's letters are plain, unexcited, and unpretending. Their style, so much simpler than that of his essays and tales, suggests the thought that he must have elaborated the latter. They interest more from their good sense and information than as discoveries of character. They are full of generous and quiet criticism. Thus, of Lamb, he says—"I have been looking over the two volumes of his letters, and I am disposed to consider them the pleasantest in the language, not excepting the best of Cowper's, nor Horace Walpole's. He was a man of true genius, though on a small scale, as a spangle may be gold as pure as a doubloon." Speaking of his own poems, he says—"When I think of Christabel, and Herman, and Dorothea, I feel a strong persuasion that I deserve the pillory for ever writing verses at all. The writings of Schelling, Fichte, and some others, give the same uneasy belief as to prose." Again—"Lately I have been reading some of Alfred Tennyson's second volume, and with profound admiration of his truly lyric and idyllic genius. There seems to me to have been more epic power in Keats, that fiery, beautiful meteor; but they are two most true and great poets. When one thinks of the amount of recognition they have received, one may well bless God that poetry is in itself strength and joy, whether it be crowned by all mankind or left alone in its own magic hermitage. It is true that what new poetry we have is little cared for; but also true that there is wonderfully little deserving any honor. Compare our present state with twenty years ago, when Wordsworth, Byron, Shelley, Keats, and Scott as a novelist, were all vigorously productive. Carlyle is the one great star that has arisen since, and he is far more prophet than singer." He gives a striking anecdote of Thorwaldsen: "Did you ever hear the story of his being at a party at Bunsen's, whose house was on the Capitolian Hill, on the site of the temple of Olympian Jove, and where the conversation, as often, under Bunsen's guidance took a very Christian turn, till Thorwaldsen remarked, through the window commanding a noble prospect of Rome, the modern city, the planet Jupiter in great glory, and, filling his glass, exclaimed, 'Well, here's in honor of the ancient gods!'"

We mentioned at the commencement that we conceived John Sterling's progress was typical of that of a large and interesting class of intellectual persons in the present day. We proceed now to explain what we mean. It is an extremely important and serious aspect of his history at which we must now look. It is at his *religion.*

So far as religion can be called constitutional, John Sterling was constitutionally religious. The union of ardent temperament, high intellect, and pure morals, generally in this country generates a strong religious appetency, which was manifest in him. Dr. Hare has not traced so minutely and clearly as had been desirable the entire progress of his thoughts and feelings on this momentous topic. Indeed, there is, throughout all his memoir a shrinking, skulking, and want of plain speaking on the subject, unworthy of such a man writing on such a man, and this, we know, some of Sterling's warmest friends feel; but we think we can map it out with considerable accuracy, and in very few and very plain words. From the early piety of genius, he seems to have passed into the early skepticism of genius. While sounding on his dim and perilous way in those troubled waters, the great beacon-light of Coleridge attracted and seemed to save him. He became in theory, as he had been in feeling, a Christian. Influenced by his marriage and other circumstances, disciplined by various grave events, and not, he trusts, unguided by the Holy Spirit, he entered the work of the Christian ministry, labored for six months with exemplary diligence, and was only prevented by illness from prosecuting the calling. Afterwards, a change began gradually to pass over his mind. Loosened from professional ties —burning with a hectic speculation—impatient of the cant, and common-places, and bigotry of ordinary theologians—sick of the senseless controversies of his church—and attracted ever more and more by the learning and genius of Germany, his orthodox belief in Christianity was shattered, though his childlike love for it remained the same. At last he died, it must be told, more than doubtful of the divine origin of Judaism, unsatisfied of the evidences of Christianity, and yet ravished with the unutterable beauty and moral grandeur, of the latter; and his almost last words were a request to his sister to hand him the old Bible he was wont to use in Herstmonceux (where he had been curate) among the cottages.

Such is the plain unvarnished tale of Sterling's religious career. It is a very painful, very interesting, and very instructive narrative. We must be permitted to methodize our impressions of it under the following remarks:—First, It is not, alas! a singular case. Secondly, Its causes are not very recondite. And, thirdly, It teaches some momentous lessons.

1st, The case is not uncommon. Without alluding to innumerable private instances, the process through which Sterling was passing is almost the same with that less fully undergone by Foster and Arnold, and which, in Newman and Parker, in Carlyle and Emerson, may be considered perfected. In Shelley, it was different. In the first place, he unfortunately never enjoyed, we fear, the opportunity of seeing real religion incarnated in living examples; with that noble moral poem, sublimer far than a "Paradise Lost," a meek and humble disciple of Jesus, he seems never to have come in contact. 2dly, He was early repelled from just views of the subject by the savage stupidity of university tests and treatment. And, 3dly, The motion of his mind was accelerated by that morbid heat and misery which made his life an arm of Styx, and rendered his entire character and history anomalous. Shelley is the *caricature* of the unsatisfied thinker of the times; and while, as a poet, admired by all for his *potential* achievements, his creed, which creed was none, unless a feverish flush on the brow be a fixed principle of the soul, has only influenced those who are weak and morbid through nature, or raw and incondite through youth. Sterling, on the other hand, was the express image of such a thinker, in its highest and purest form.

Ere inquiring into the causes of that strange new form of skepticism, which has seized so many of our higher minds, let us more distinctly enunciate what it is not, and does not spring from. It is not, as some imagine, a mere disguise which the skepticism of Hume and Voltaire has assumed, better accommodated to the tastes and the progress of the present age. It is not the same with it, even as Satan towering to the sky was the same with Satan lurking in the toad. It differs from it in many important respects. 1st, It admits much which the unbelief of Paine and Voltaire denied; it grants the beauty, the worth, and the utility of our religion —nay, contends that, in a sense, it is a divine emanation, the divinest ever given to man. It does not sheathe, but tosses away the old poisoned terms imposture, fraud, priestcraft, cunningly devised fable. 2dly, It approaches religion with a different feeling and motive. It desires to find its very highest claims true. It has no interest that they should be false. The life of such an one as we describe is modelled on the life of Christ; his language is steeped in the Bible vocabulary, as in burning gold. Prayer and its cognate duties he practises, and his heart is ever ready to rise to the swells of Christian oratory and feeling, as the war-horse to the sound of the trumpet. He teaches his children to prattle of Christ, and weeps at eventide as they repeat their little hymns. He gives to the cause of the Gospel, and his cheek glows at the recital of the deeds of a Williams or a Waddell. The skeptic of the eighteenth century first hated religion, because it scowled on his selfishness—then wished it untrue—and then, generally with the bungling haste of over-eagerness, tried to prove it untrue. Thus Paine felt the strong right hand, which, in the "Rights of Man" had coped worthily with the giant Burke, shivered to splinters when he stretched it forth, in the "Age of Reason," against the "ark of the Lord." The doubter of our day (we speak, of course, of one class) loves religion, wishes it true, reverences every pin and fringe of its tabernacle, tries to convince himself and others of its paramount and peculiar divinity, and if, at last, the shadow of a cloud continues to hang over his head, it fails to disguise the fast-flowing tears wrung from his disappointed spirit. 3dly, It approaches religion, not only with a different feeling, but from a different direction. The skeptic of the eighteenth century approached it from the platform of matter—a platform in itself mean, even when including the whole material universe; the doubter now looks at it from the lofty ground of the ideal and the spiritual. "It contradicts the laws of matter," said the one. "I cannot, in all its parts," says the other, "reconcile it with the principles of mental truth." "It is something greater than matter," said the one. "It is something less than mind," says the other. "I cannot grasp it," said the one. "I can but too easily account for much of it," says the other. "It surpasses my standard," said the one. "It does not come up to mine," says the other. "Its miracles to me seem monstrous things which I cannot swallow," said the one. "To me," says the other, "they appear petty tricks, not impossible to, but unworthy of, a God." "Its prophecies seem to me all written after the event," said the one. "To me," says the other, "the objection is that they tell so little that is really valuable. What comparison between the fate of a thousand empires and one burst of pure truth?" "The whole thing," said the one, "is too supernatural and unearthly for me." "To me," says the other, "it bears but too palpable marks of an earthly though unparalleled birth—God's highest, it may be, but not his only or ultimate voice." "I wish I could convince every body that it was an imposture," said the one. "I wish," says the other, "that I could convince myself that it is what the world professes to believe it. "It is strange," said the one, "that, superstition as it is, it won't die." "It is far stranger," says the other, "how, if it be *par excellence* true, it is dying, and has become little else than a *caput mortuum.*' "But, then, it must be confessed," said the one, "that its external evidences are imposing, though not irresistible." "To me," says the other, "these seem its weakness, not its strength; and as to its vitals—its internal evidences—is it not, like Cato, day after day, tearing them out with its own suicidal hands—is it not rapidly becoming a worldly and mechanical, if not a carnal, sensual, and devilish thing?"

Such is a fair statement of the difference between the two skepticisms. As we proceed, we shall have occasion to refute the conclusions of the second variety. We now come to its causes. 1st, We may name the over stress which was long laid by the defenders of Christianity upon its external evidences. The effects of this have been pernicious in various ways. It could not, in the first place, be disguised that many who defended with the most success the external evidences were, if not secret skeptics, strangers to the living influence, and disbelievers in the peculiar doctrines of the Gospel. Such were Lardner, Watson, Priestley, Wakefield, and Paley. They first threw away the kernel of Christianity, and then did desperate battle in defence of the empty shell. Never were walls and bulwarks, containing *nothing*, more heroically defended. The school of Warburton and Hurd, indeed, were of a more Christian class, but their polemical bitterness and personal arrogance were intolerable. 2dly, Even the successful defence of the evidences seemed a poor exploit, when it was confessedly considered inadequate to impress the vital principles of Christianity upon the mind—stopping, it might be, the mouths, but not opening the hearts of its adversaries, whom it drove away from, instead of drawing into, the city of God; and the loud cheers, which followed each victory over a desperate but unconvinced foe, sounded harsh and horrible, as were one to encore the plunge of a lost spirit into the abyss. 3dly, If external evidences were the principal, if not sole proof of Christianity, what became of the belief of the majority of Christians, to whom these evidences were unknown, or who, at least, were quite incapable of estimating the true nature and weight of the argument founded upon them? If their belief was worthless, must not their Christianity be baseless and worthless too? If it was not, what a slur on those elaborate evidences, which in no instance could reach a result which was daily attained by thousands without any external evidence at all! 4thly, What was the *utmost* value of external evidences? Not to produce demonstrative conviction of the truth of Christianity, but only a very high degree of probability. But is the soul, with all its eternal issues, to depend upon a question of degree, of less and more, of a few grains above or scruples below? Is there no straighter, higher, nobler road to conviction? May there not be a voice within us, corresponding with a voice in Christianity, changing a faltering "perhaps" into a loud, confident, and commanding "it is, it must be so?" Thus felt Pascal, and this is the true history of his faith. He did not, as Cousin pretends, in order to avoid the gulf of universal skepticism, to which his thoughts and researches were leading him, and where he knew perdition weltered at the bottom, turn back and throw himself into the arms of implicit faith, which, like a nurse a child, had followed him to the brink. No, but dissatisfied with the common evidences of Christianity, as *demonstrative*, he leaned down and listened to the hidden river of his own spirit, as echoing the voice of inspiration, and it became to him an oracle—a proof unutterable, an argument unstateable in human terms, only to be fully written out in soul-cypher, and to be fully read by the eye of the soul.

Pascal, we must observe, felt the utmost value of external evidence; he believed that it made the truth of Christianity highly probable—nay, probable in the *highest* degree, though the highest degree of probability is still, of course, remote from absolute mathematical certainty. But there are others who look upon the evidences *pro* and *con* as nearly balancing each other, and what for them is to turn the scale? Nay, there are some who conscientiously think that, after all Paley and Watson have written, the evidences *con* outweigh the evidences *pro;* and what can our boasted external argumentations do any more for them?

Thus has external evidence in a great measure failed of securing its object, and has by this felt failure produced in many of our present thinkers the form of skepticism we now describe and deplore. In our humble judgment, instead of miracles being the principal proof of Christianity, Christianity is a much stronger proof of miracles. A Book intrinsically so divine, so simple, so far superior to all others, and so adapted to the wants of human nature, cannot be imagined to be deceived or to deceive others in the relation of facts. The quantity and singularity of such facts is itself an additional circumstance in their favor. A wise imposture would have sprinkled them more sparingly and artistically, and brought down in no case save in that of necessity, its *Deus ex machina.* The great purpose of miracles at first was to compel attention to the new system by the glare of grandeur it threw around it—a finger of supernal light must touch the head of the bashful boy-God, and mark him out to the world; their main use now is to corroborate a belief which has been formed upon quite independent grounds. "Culture," cries Strauss, "cannot believe in miracles." Culture, however, can and has believed in Christianity, and will not recal its belief, because she wears on her breast and forehead those mysterious ornaments which speak, not more forcibly than her whole dress and bearing, of a foreign and unearthly origin. Miracles must not be considered as splendid tricks—as mere mighty bravados, which whoso could not equal or explain was compelled to believe, as well as to believe whatever was said in the lecture that should follow or accompany those experiments. They were rather, in Foster's grand thought, the simple tolling of the great bell of the universe, to announce the great sermon that was to follow; and as the sermon continues after the bell has rung out, and becomes of its sound a memorial and testimony, so the marvellous words have outlived and do testify of the marvellous works.

A second cause of our recent refined skepticism may be found in the narrow, bigoted, and unworthy notions of Christianity which prevail, in the obstinacy with which they are retained, in the fury with which they are defended, and in the contrast thus presented to the liberal and fluent motion of the general age. This is a large text, and opens up a field which we have not at present time to embrace. Religious authorship may be taken as a correct index of the general state of religious culture and progress. Now this has decidedly improved since John Foster wrote his first essays, where he so sternly characterizes a large proportion of its writings, where he speaks of "one writer who seems to value religion as an assassin his dagger, and for the same reason—of another, who in all his motions is clad with sheets of lead—of a third, from whose vulgar illuminations of religious themes you are excessively glad to escape into the solemn twilight of faith—and of a fourth, who represents the Deity as a dreadful king of furies, whose dominion is overshadowed by vengeance, whose music is the cries of victims, and whose glory requires to be illustrated by the ruin of his creation." For such, perhaps, we may now search our religious literature in vain; but we could point out some curious specimens still extant: here a writer who would sacrifice all the records of creation to the arbitrary interpretation of a Hebrew particle; there another, who, in order to prove Christianity the most excellent of the sciences, raves like a maniac against all science, and cares less for the sun, moon, and stars, than for a farthing candle glimmering in the corner of a conventicle; a third, propounding the horrible doctrine, that if you are not immersed in water you must be immersed in everlasting fire; a fourth, turning the Bible into a padlock on the chains of the slave; a fifth, seeking to excommunicate from fire and water here, and from water hereafter, one of the most gifted and amiable, albeit misled men of the age, who came an invited and unassuming stranger to our shores; a sixth, hanging around the majestic form of Christianity a dirty finery, picked up from the cast-off clothes of second-rate poets, and sinking the mother-tongue of heaven into the sickly whine of a mendicant, as though Isaiah had become an old Jewish clothesman; a seventh, indulging, while defending religion, in the worst of human passions and language, as if rancor, and want of charity, and spleen, could be baptized and consecrated to Christ's service—as if the raven perched in Noah's ark were not a raven, a bird of foul feeding and bad omen still; an eighth, peppering bad poems with religion to make them sell; and a ninth, talking of the fearful secrets of future punishment as coolly as if he were not also in danger of the judgment, and who perhaps goes smacking his lips from the side of the great universe-darkening sacrifice to the Lord Mayor's feast! Add to this the deluges of commonplace, issuing in the form of religious pamphlets and periodicals of the day, and the thousand narrow and fierce controversial productions which each month spawns, and conceive of the three-piled disgust, which in so many of the refined and intellectual darkens into a deeper feeling, and provokes the cry, "If this be religion, better skepticism, pantheism, atheism itself."

This, indeed, thank God, is *not* religion. But it must bear the reproach of having turned away many who otherwise would have come near and seen this great sight, and found how vast the difference between those crackling, whizzing, empty, and transient fireworks, and the low light of the wilderness, uneclipsed by the noonday ardors, clear, innocuous, but piercing as the eye of the Inspired, kindled from, and pointing above—the bush ever burning and never consumed.

Thirdly, The divided and unhappy state of the Church must bear its full share in accounting for the evil, and this the more especially when at present both letters and science are approaching closely the ideal of a commonwealth—when associations of the scientific and literary are the order of the day—when rancorous personalities and jealousies are dying out—when an appeal made in behalf of the family of a deceased poet is responded to with such promptitude by men of all politics and creeds, as to show that an electric cord of communication is fast binding the literary world into one. And yet alas! alas! for the divisions of Reuben, and the rents in the seamless garment of Christ. Where any real love between various parties? Where aught but hasty and ill-considered armistices? Where any broad comprehensive plan of union? Where a genuine *esprit de corps* among Christian churches? Where any actual unions consummated, except in cases where the parties had come so near before, that their union lost much of its romance—where it seemed more a shaking of hands in the marketplace, than a marriage, and where, as at the peace of Amiens, every body on both sides was *glad*, but nobody proud? What philosophical examination of principles, conducted by wise and impartial men, such as should precede a great scheme of permanent union, has ever been even talked of; and are even the meanest and basest of old arts of polemical depreciation and abuse altogether obsolete? It were long to trace the causes of this sad spectacle, which just amounts to—the church inferior to the world, in culture and gentlemanly feeling, in Christian charity; but such is the fact, and prodigious the mischief which is springing from it. There are other causes which might have been illustrated, such as the contempt and prejudice entertained by many Christians for science and letters—the piece of well or ill adjusted mechanism to which the office of the ministry has been reduced—the superiority which the press has acquired over the pulpit—the political spirit which our churches of all kinds have been led to cherish—and the infection of German, and, in general of Continental modes of thought and speech. But, prominent above all, stands the enemy within the camp—the ghastly fact that Christianity has not the vital hold over men which it formerly possessed—that we are now rather haunted by its ghost than warmed by its presence—that formality, mechanism, and a thousand other evil influences have crushed and choked it—and that its extension, however wide and rapid, will in all probability extend its evils at even a greater ratio than its advantages—propagate more tares than wheat. We unite our feeble voice with that of Chalmers, and James, and Thomas Binney, in proclaiming this alarming state of matters. It cannot now be concealed that a great proportion of the mind of the country—of those who make our laws, who distribute our justice, whose eloquence fills our courts, whose talent informs our press, whose energy inspirits our business, whose genius animates our higher literature, whose benevolence supports our charities, and whose *beauty*, *taste*, and *accomplishments* decorate and refine our society, have travelled away from churches, and resigned faith in creeds, and that this they have done principally because the charm and the power which were wont to detain them there have departed. Were a dance of the living suddenly turned into a dance of the dead, though there remained the same splendor in the decorations, and the same lustre in the lamps, and even the same grace in the movements, would there remain the same delight in the spectators? Would not they rush forth in confusion and shrieking dismay at the sight of this ghastly mimicry of life, enacted where its pulse was beating highest, and where its stream most richly and tumultuously ran? Thus feel many to our deserted churches—deserted not of the dead but of the living, not of worshippers but of God. Pathetic the unseen Ichabod inscribed on the fallen cathedral—more pensive still the "Here God once dwelt," visible through the moonlight of meditation on the chambers of the soul in ruins; but, most sorrowful of all, the sight of a large assembly of professing Christians, where all the elegance, splendor, light, decency of deportment, eloquence of speaker—where sympathetic thrill, awful shadow, heaving breasts, and bursting tears themselves, will not disguise the fact that one is absent, and that this place is no more "dreadful" with his presence, nor glorious with his grace.

The statements thus made must be somewhat qualified. In the first place, we must not be understood to hold that all our modern skeptics are actuated by such motives, or influenced by such causes. Many, we fear, like their brethren in times past, just "hate the light because their deeds are evil," while others are stimulated to skepticism by vanity, pride, or ignorance. There is another class still, very intelligent but very inconsistent, of whom Miss Martineau may stand as a specimen, who, not merely doubting, but absolutely denying all the supernaturalism of Scripture, express their respect and reverence for the writers, although, on their own showing, those writers were either fools or rogues. But the class whom Sterling typified, while sorely perplexed about the supernatural part, and even the genuineness and authenticity of many of the documents, are smit to a passion with the grandeur and heavenliness of the system, even to its peculiarities of atonement, spiritual influences, &c.

Secondly, We must not be understood to homologate the train of thought which we have ventured to put into the mouth of the Sterling-skeptic, except so far as that relates to the insufficiency of external evidence, nor to insinuate that the causes we have mentioned excuse his skepticism. Prophecy, as well as miracles, we look on as powerfully corroborative of the divinity of religion, and the fate of nations, besides, not being the sole subject of prediction, is very important when taken in connection with that system which they opposed, and which proclaimed their destruction, as well as in itself. The internal evidence of Christianity seems complete, notwithstanding the fact of a partial decline; and the genius of our religion seems absolutely to forbid its contentedly taking its place at the head of other faiths; it must be all or nothing—a devil's lie or divine. And if it does not answer to the skeptic's idea of a unique and solitary emanation from heaven, may not the blame lie not with it, but with the nature of his idea—with himself?

Thirdly, We do not wish, from these giddy heights, to "waft a lesson of despair" to any one. We are sorry for the position of such men as Sterling, but it were to be weaker than old Eli, on their account to tremble for the ark of God. The lessons we do mean to draw are as follows: 1stly, of charity; 2dly, of warning; 3dly, of shame; and, 4thly, of courage.

1st, We have need of much charity at the present crisis. It will not do now to skulk from the field under a flight of nicknames. It will not do to call our opponents miscreants and monsters. There never were many in the world really deserving these names; fools only can believe that there are many now. Here, at least, in Sterling, Arnold, Foster, we have to do with mist-severed brethren upon one great common march, with sincere lovers of mankind, with practisers of the Christian virtues, with men who diligently discharged the duties of the Christian ministry, and whose latest deathbed murmur was of Christ. While we state their doubts, let us pity the pain and sorrow, amounting almost to distraction and despair, which attended them, and let us inquire, if we have no difficulties, may it not be because we have never thought at all? and let us envy them the resolution of their doubts, to which they have now attained, we trust, in that land where the strength of light is not measured by the intensity of shade—where, amid all the constellations which may garnish that upper firmament, that of the "Balance" vibrates no more—where the inhabitants bask in spotless love, and see in perfect vision. No such charity, however, can we or dare we extend to those half-fledged children of impudence and conceit, or else of pride and profligacy, in whom this age abounds, who, at the finding of each new difficulty (one, perhaps, resolved for centuries), raise a noisy Eureka, as they rush out with their filthy treasure—for those who cull from such writers as Shelley the blood-red stones of his blasphemy, that they may wreathe them into a necklace of ruin for themselves—nor even for those miniatures of Giant Despair, who seat themselves in we know not what " churches of doubters " or Doubting Castles, to confirm those misconceptions which they cannot or seek not to cure. The charity which would extend to such must verily be of that sort which covers a multitude of sins, and of sinners too.

2dly, We must take up anew a voice of warning—the voice of him who saw the Apocalypse. There is coming up the church a current of doubt, deeper far and darker than ever swelled against her before—a current strong in learning, crested with genius, strenuous yet calm in progress. It seems the last grand trial of the truth of our faith. Against the battlements of Zion a motley throng have gathered themselves together. Unitarians, atheists, pantheists, doubters, open foes, secret foes, and bewildered friends of Christianity, are all in the field, although no trumpet has openly been blown, and no charge publicly sounded. There are the old desperadoes of infidelity—the last followers of Paine and Voltaire; there is the soberer and stolider Owen and his now scanty and sleepy troop there follow the Communists of France—a fierce but disorderly crew; the commentators of Germany come, too, with pickaxes in their hands, crying, " Raze, raze it to its foundations !" Then you see the *garde mobile*—the vicious and the vain youth of Europe; and on the outskirsts of the fight hangs, cloudy and uncertain, a small but select band, whose wavering surge is surmounted by the dark and lofty crests of Carlyle and Emerson. "Their swords are a thousand"—their purposes are various; in this, however, all agree, that historical Christianity ought to go down before advancing civilization. Sterling and some of his co-mates the merciful cloud of death has removed from the fields, while others stand in deep uncertainty, looking in agony and in prayer above.

3dly, Of shame. While thus the foeman is advancing, what is Zion about? Shame and alas! her towers are well nigh unguarded; her watchmen have deserted their stations, and are either squabbling in her streets with each other, or have fallen fast asleep. Many are singing psalms few are standing to their arms. Some are railing at the enemy from the safest towers. The watchman who first perceived the danger and gave the alarm, almost instantly fell back in death.

4thly, Of confidence. Shall, then, these old and glorious battlements be trodden down? Between the activity of their foes and the supineness of their friends must they perish? No; vain is perhaps the help of man, but we too, will look above. We will turn our eyes to the hills, whence our aid is expected. Our grand hope as to the prospects of the world and the church has long lain in the unchanged and unchangeable love of Christ. As long as his great, tremulous, unsetting eye continues, like a star, to watch her struggles as the eye of love the tossings of disease, we shall not fear. And whenever the time arrives for that "Bright and Morning Star" starting from his sphere to save his church, he will no longer delay his coming, whether in power or in presence. To save a city like Zion, there might fall the curtain of universal darkness. That curtain shall not fall, but there may, in lieu of it, burst the blaze of celestial light; and who can abide the day of that appearing?

THE END.

NEW PUBLICATIONS

OF

D. APPLETON AND COMPANY,

346 and 348 BROADWAY.

Any of our Publications will be sent by mail, free of postage, to any part of the United States, on receipt of price.

The Eighteen Christian Centuries. By the Rev. James White, author of a "History of France." With a Copious Index. From the second Edinburgh Edition. 1 vol. 12mo. 538 pages. $1 25.

This is a striking and peculiar contribution to historical literature. It is the historical spirit of each one of the Eighteen Christian Centuries seen through the medium of a master mind. The history of each century, from the first of our era, is reviewed and generalized, grasped as a whole: its prevailing purpose or idea individualized, and its result, as a century, given to the reader. The work is singularly original, comprehensive, clear, and masterly. It will give the general reader a clearer idea of the general history of Christendom than can be obtained in many months of study, and will prove beyond question a welcome and valuable remembrancer to many especial students of history. It has been the general complaint against history itself, that it is too much a collection of mere dates, and such a complaint is the highest eulogy of this book, which dispensing with any but the largest divisions of time, except, indeed, when a date may serve to explain or illuminate some act or event, eliminates by its spirit entirely the prevailing lesson of history.

Fiji and the Fijians. By THOMAS WILLIAMS and JAMES CALVERT, late Missionaries in Fiji. Edited by GEORGE STRINGER ROWE. Illustrated with numerous colored Drawings and Wood Engravings. 1 vol. 8vo. Cloth, $2 50.

"*The story of their missionary labors and results possesses the deepest interest to all who believe in the redemption of the human race.*"—PORTLAND TRANSCRIPT.

"*This is a book of great interest and value. Its 550 pages contain such a fund of information, with regard to the Fijians and their island country, as has perhaps never before been placed between the lids of any English book.*"—HOME JOURNAL.

On the Origin of Species by Means of Natural Selection; or, THE PRESERVATION OF FAVORED RACES in the STRUGGLE FOR LIFE. By CHARLES DARWIN, M. A. 1 vol. 12mo. 432 pages. $1 25.

"*Readers of his delightful book, 'Voyage of a Naturalist,' will recognize in this new work his power as a writer, whatever may be the scientific verdict on his theories.*"—N. Y. OBSERVER.

"*The conclusions at which he aims are so startling, that they cannot fail to meet with considerable opposition. Mr. Darwin himself is far from anticipating that they will be generally received. But he has certainly a right to demand that they shall be opposed only in the same spirit of candor and moderation by which his advocacy of them is so eminently distinguished.*"—LONDON LITERARY GAZETTE.

The Path which Led a Protestant Lawyer to the CATHOLIC CHURCH. By PETER H. BURNETT. 1 vol. 8vo 741 pages. $2 50.

"*I was once a Protestant, and I became a Catholic. The main reasons which led to the change will be found substantially stated in the work.*

* * * * * * *

"*In the prosecution of this design, I procured all the works, on both sides, within my reach, and examined them alternately side by side. The investigation occupied all my spare time for about eighteen months. I examined carefully, prayerfully, and earnestly, until I was satisfied, beyond a doubt, that the old Church was the true, and the only true Church.*"—EXTRACT FROM PREFACE.

Reynard the Fox, after the Version of Goethe. By THOS. J. ARNOLD. With 60 Illustrations from the Designs of Wilhelm Von Kaulbach. 1 vol. 8vo. Cloth, gilt, $3 50; Mor., $5.

"*This excellent translation of the well-known German Poem is presented in a beautiful form, with illustrations on every page, which tell the tale as plainly as the verse does.*"—BOSTON ADVERTISER.

Great Facts; a Popular History and Description of the MOST REMARKABLE INVENTIONS during the Present Century. By FREDERICK C. BAKEWELL. 1 vol. 12mo. Illustrated. $1.

CONTENTS:—PROGRESS OF INVENTION; STEAM NAVIGATION; STEAM CARRIAGES AND RAILWAYS; THE AIR ENGINE; PHOTOGRAPHY; DISSOLVING VIEWS; THE KALEIDESCOPE; THE MAGIC DISC; THE DIORAMA; THE STEREOSCOPE; THE ELECTRIC TELEGRAPH; ELECTRO-MAGNETIC CLOCKS: ELECTRO-METALLURGY; GAS LIGHTING; THE ELECTRIC LIGHT; INSTANTANEOUS LIGHT; PAPER-MAKING MACHINERY; PRINTING MACHINES; LITHOGRAPHY; AERATED WATERS; REVOLVERS AND MINNIE RIFLES; CENTRIFUGAL PUMPS; TUBULAR BRIDGES; SELF-ACTING ENGINES.

Evenings at the Microscope; or, Researches among the MINUTER ORGANS and FORMS of ANIMAL LIFE. By PHILLIP HENRY GOSSE, F. R. S. 1 vol. 12mo. 480 pages. $1 50.

"*The object of this volume is to open the path to the myriad wonders of creation that are hidden from the unassisted human eye, and most successfully does it accomplish the purpose.*"—PRES. BANNER.

Leaves from an Actor's Note Book, with Reminis-cences and Chit-Chat of the Green Room and the Stage, in England and America. By GEORGE VANDENHOFF. 1 vol. 12mo. $1 00.

"*There are no reminiscences more entertaining than those of actors, and Mr. Vandenhoff, who is a fine scholar as well as a fine actor, has succeeded in presenting his in a peculiarly agreeable and attractive form.*"—NEW ORLEANS DELTA.

The History of Herodotus. A new English Version, edited with COPIOUS NOTES and APPENDICES, illustrating the History and Geography of Herodotus, from the most recent sources of information; and embodying the chief results, historical and ethnographical, which have been obtained in the progress of Cuneiform and Hieroglyphical Discovery. By GEORGE RAWLINSON, M. A., late Fellow and Tutor of Exeter College, Oxford, assisted by Col. Sir HENRY RAWLINSON, K. C. B., and Sir J. G. WILKINSON, F. R. S. 4 vols. 8vo. $10.

"*The delightful old story-teller, who has been reverently styled the father of history, has never been presented to the readers of the English language in so satisfactory a manner as in the present valuable edition. Though commenced only about seven years since, great portions of the work have been re-written, in order to incorporate, in a proper manner, the remarkable Assyrian discoveries which have shed light upon the obscurity of the past.*"—N. W. CHRIS. ADVOCATE.

Parties and their Principles: a MANUAL of POLITICAL INTELLIGENCE, Exhibiting the growth and character of National Parties, with an Appendix containing valuable, general, and statistical information. By ARTHUR HOLMES. 1 vol. 12mo. Cloth, $1.

"*No book yet published, relating to the subject, contains so much valuable information in brief space, so convenient for reference.*"—EV'ING POST.

"*The work was one greatly needed, especially to writers and politicians, and we think the author has succeeded admirably in his undertaking.*"—LYNCHBURG VIRGINIAN.

"*As a hand-book it will doubtless be found useful by all interested in National politics, and that includes all good citizens.*"—ALBANY ARGUS.

Loss and Gain; or, Margaret's Home. By ALICE B. HAVEN. 1 vol. 12mo. Cloth, 75 cents.

"'*Margaret' is just such a character as Alice Haven can create—no unnatural heroine is she, but an humble girl, striving amidst poverty, and discouragement and toil, to do right and meet the smile of Heaven.*"—GAZETTE, CHILICOTHE.

"*This story has all the grace and freshness of the earlier writings of Alice Neal, refined and purified by a pure morality and Christian sentiment.*"—MILWAUKEE SENTINEL.

Re-Statements of Christian Doctrine, in Twenty-five SERMONS. By HENRY W. BELLOWS. 1 vol. 12mo. 434 pages. $1 25.

"*His exposition of his faith is manly, eloquent, and full of earnest sincerity; and those who differ from him in sentiment will at least agree that he speaks out honestly what seems to him to be the doctrine of the Bible.*"—PROVIDENCE JOURNAL.

"*The volume will naturally be sought for by even many out of Dr. Bellows' denomination, who are curious to know more of the opinions of a man who has been accused of tendencies in the most widely diverse directions in his the logy.*"—SPRINGFIELD REPUBLICAN.

Here and There; or, Earth and Heaven Contrasted 1 vol. 12mo. 25 cents.

"*The idea of this little* brochure *is to set in contrast texts of Scripture on the same page, the first relating to 'Here,' and portraying the sorrows of our earthly pilgrimage; and the second, 'There,' telling the joys of Heaven.*" —BUFFALO COMMERCIAL.

Poems. By Anne Whitney. 1 vol. 12mo. 75 cents.

"*Anne Whitney's Poems are refreshing. Who is Anne Whitney?—What right has she, unknown, unheralded, to give to American literature the best volume of Poems published by any American woman in the last ten years.*"—Springfield Republican.

A Manual of Naval Tactics; together with a brief CRITICAL ANALYSIS of the PRINCIPAL MODERN NAVAL BATTLES. By James H. Ward, Commander U. S. N. With an Appendix, being an extract from Sir Howard Douglas's Naval Warfare with Steam. 1 vol. 8vo. Cloth, $2 50.

"*Captain Ward's Manual possesses not only a professional but an historical value.*"—N. Y. Herald.

The Manufacture of Photogenic or Hydro-Carbon OILS, from COAL and other Bituminous Substances capable of supplying Burning Fluids. By Thomas Antisell, M. D. 1 vol. 8vo. $1 75.

"*The author is connected with the U. S. Patent Office, and his position there has enabled him to present to the public the record of the origin of the infant art.*"—Boston Advertiser.

A History of the Four Georges, Kings of England, containing Personal Incidents of their Lives, Public Events of their Reigns, and Biographical Notices of their Chief Ministers, Courtiers, and Favorites. By Samuel Smucker. 1 vol. 12mo. $1 25.

"*Dr. Smucker has here made a valuable contribution to historical literature, and the student of history cannot obtain a better idea of the Augustan era, properly so called, than by a perusal of the 'History of the Four Georges.'*"—Augusta Chronicle.

Tent and Harem. Notes of an Oriental Trip. By Caroline Paine. 1 vol. 12mo. $1 00.

"*This is one of the most entertaining and instructive books of travel that has fallen under our eye for many a day. The style is clear and unaffected, and much which would have escaped the notice of a man, has been put within our reach by woman's cleverness.*"—Boston Monthly Magazine.

History of France, from the Earliest Times to 1858.

By the Rev. JAMES WHITE. 1 vol. 8vo. Cloth, $2.

"*A good, clear, concise History of France has long been needed, and such is the present volume.*"—COURIER AND ENQUIRER.

"*Its 600 pages contain every leading incident worth the telling, and abound in word-painting.*"—ATHENÆUM.

"*We can honestly recommend the book as being what it professes to be, an attractive popular History of France and the French people.*"—SPRINGFIELD REPUBLICAN.

"*The style is clear and sparkling, and carries one along so gracefully from fact to fact that the reader can hardly find a place where he can part company, even for a short time, with the author.*"—CHARLESTON CHRISTIAN ADVOCATE."

Morphy's Games: A selection of the Best Games

played by the distinguished champion, in Europe and America, with Analytical and Critical Notes. By J. LOWENTHAL. 1 vol 12mo. Cloth. 473 pages. $1 25.

"*Many friends, both in Europe and America, have frequently urged me to arrange a collection of my games, which they assured me would meet with kindly reception from chess-players generally. But continued contests during the past twelve months would have precluded my concurring with so flattering a request, had it not been for the assistance rendered me by my friend Herr Lowenthal. The Copious Notes with which this volume is enriched are mainly due to his well-earned reputation, and assiduity as an analyst, and will amply repay perusal from every lover of our noble game.*" —PAUL MORPHY.

Breakfast, Dinner, and Tea.

Viewed CLASSICALLY, POETICALLY, and PRACTICALLY. Containing numerous Dishes and Feasts of all Times and Countries, besides three hundred Modern Receipts. 1 vol. small 4to., gilt top. $1 50.

"*It is altogether the best book for a genteel housekeeper that we ever met.*"—NEW YORK OBSERVER.

"*The beau ideal of a Cook-Book.*"—PORTLAND TRANSCRIPT.

"*A more acceptable book to a young housekeeper it would be difficult to find.*"—CHICAGO RECORD.

"*We commend this book to literary cooks and persons in search of food for mind and body—particularly the body.*"—ST. LOUIS NEWS.

"*Every housekeeper who would deserve the best compliments of her guests, should own a copy.*"—CITY ITEM.

"*The receipts, which comprise Fish, Flesh, Fowl, and Fruit, are none the less practicable from the abundance of anecdotes with which they are garnished.*"—CINCINNATI GAZETTE.

www.ingramcontent.com/pod-product-compliance
Lightning Source LLC
LaVergne TN
LVHW020127110826
845151LV00001B/298